AF605845

ESSAYS IN THE HISTORY OF CANADIAN LAW

Volume XII

PATRONS OF THE SOCIETY

Professor Constance Backhouse

Chernos, Flaherty, Svonkin, LLP

Gowling WLG

Hull & Hull LLP

Mr. Wayne Kerr

The Law Foundation of Ontario

McCarthy Tetrault

Osler, Hoskin & Harcourt LLP

Pape Chaudhury

Paliare Roland Rosenberg Rothstein LLP

Professor Richard Risk and Gail Morrison

The Hon. Robert Sharpe

Torys LLP

WeirFoulds LLP

The Osgoode Society is supported by a grant from
The Law Foundation of Ontario

The Society also thanks The Law Society of Upper Canada
for its continuing support

ESSAYS IN THE HISTORY OF CANADIAN LAW

Volume XII

New Essays in Women's History

EDITED BY
LORI CHAMBERS AND JOAN SANGSTER

Published for the Osgoode Society for Canadian Legal History by
University of Toronto Press
Toronto Buffalo London

Toronto Buffalo London
utorontopress.com
Printed in Canada

ISBN 978-1-4875-5390-6 (cloth)
ISBN 978-1-4875-5391-3 (EPUB)
ISBN 978-1-4875-5392-0 (PDF)

Library and Archives Canada Cataloguing in Publication

Title: Essays in the history of Canadian law. Volume XII : new essays in women's history / edited by Lori Chambers and Joan Sangster.
Names: Chambers, Lori, 1965– editor. | Sangster, Joan, 1952– editor.
Description: Includes bibliographical references and index.
Identifiers: Canadiana (print) 20230488501 | Canadiana (ebook) 20230488617 | ISBN 9781487553906 (hardcover) | ISBN 9781487553920 (PDF) | ISBN 9781487553913 (EPUB)
Subjects: LCSH: Law – Canada – History. | LCSH: Women – Legal status, laws, etc. – Canada – History.
Classification: LCC KE394.E8812 2023 | LCC KF345.E8812 2023 kfmod | DDC 349.71–dc23

Cover design: Alexa Love
Cover image: Library and Archives Canada, Acc. No. 1982-100-2

We wish to acknowledge the land on which the University of Toronto Press operates. This land is the traditional territory of the Wendat, the Anishnaabeg, the Haudenosaunee, the Métis, and the Mississaugas of the Credit First Nation.

University of Toronto Press acknowledges the financial support of the Government of Canada, the Canada Council for the Arts, and the Ontario Arts Council, an agency of the Government of Ontario, for its publishing activities.

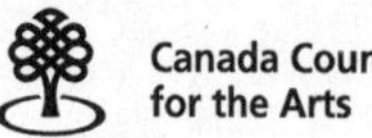

Funded by the Government of Canada
Financé par le gouvernement du Canada

Contents

Foreword

THE OSGOODE SOCIETY

This is the twelfth volume of the Osgoode Society for Canadian Legal History's series of *Essays in the History of Canadian Law*, which began in 1981. The series includes essays that marked the origins of the Osgoode Society's leading role in publishing work in all areas of Canadian legal history (Volumes I and II), explorations of the legal profession (Volumes IV and VII), a volume devoted to crime and criminal justice (Volume V), books honouring the contributions of leading scholars in the field (Volumes VIII and X), and books devoted to a single province or region (Volumes III, VI, IX, and XI). Perhaps surprisingly, this is the *first Essays in the History of Canadian Law* devoted to women, gender, and the law, although the Society has published numerous studies on aspects of the history of women and the law. We are therefore very grateful to Professors Lori Chambers and Joan Sangster, two of Canada's leading historians of Canadian social and socio-legal history, for the imagination and hard work that envisaged this volume and saw it through to fruition. The original essays in this volume use individual cases of women's interaction with the legal system to explore the power dynamics at the heart of that system. The essays deal with criminal, labour, matrimonial, electoral, and human rights law, with the common law and the civil law, from the mid-eighteenth to the late twentieth centuries. They analyse largely not what lawyers think of as leading cases, but "ordinary" cases that illustrate women's status rather than define it. While women often encountered laws and legal institutions that were constraining and oppressive, many challenged and resisted the assumptions and rules that stood in their way.

The purpose of the Osgoode Society for Canadian Legal History is to encourage research and writing in the history of Canadian law. The Society, which was incorporated in 1979 and is registered as a charity, was founded at the initiative of the Honourable R. Roy McMurtry, formerly attorney general for Ontario and chief justice of the province, and officials of the Law Society of Upper Canada. The Society seeks to stimulate the study of legal history in Canada by supporting researchers, collecting oral histories, and publishing volumes that contribute to legal-historical scholarship in Canada. This year's books bring the total published since 1981 to 118, in all fields of Canadian legal history – the courts, the judiciary, and the legal profession, as well as the history of crime and punishment, women and law, law and economy, the legal treatment of Indigenous peoples and ethnic minorities, and famous cases and significant trials in all areas of the law.

Current directors of the Osgoode Society for Canadian Legal History are Constance Backhouse, Heidi Bohaker, Brendan Brammall, Bevan Brooksbank, Shantona Chaudhury, Paul Davis, Linda Silver Dranoff, Timothy Hill, Jacqueline Horvat, Ian Hull, Mahmud Jamal, Rachel McMillan, R. Roy McMurtry, Waleed Malik, Dana Peebles, Linda Plumpton, Paul Schabas, Robert Sharpe, Jonathan Silver, Alex Smith, Lorne Sossin, Michael Tulloch, and John Wilkinson.

Robert J. Sharpe
President

Professor Jim Phillips
Editor-in-Chief

Acknowledgments

Creating an edited collection means relying on the goodwill of others. We were fortunate to be able to draw on the dedication and labour of all those involved in this collaborative effort, including editors, authors, reviewers, and copyeditors. We were blessed with a group of authors who were exceptionally committed to a feminist project of excellent research; they were supportive and encouraging, even when we found the project held up by the realities of a pandemic. Their cutting-edge work inspired us, as editors, to bring the project to completion.

We relied, throughout the project, on the advice and input of excellent supervising editors from the Osgoode Society for Canadian Legal History, Jim Phillips and Philip Girard. Their guidance was critical to the creation of volume and completion of the project. Jim Phillips has participated at all stages of the project and provided exceptional support. Anonymous reviewers for the press provided useful input on the papers. Many people associated with University of Toronto Press were also important to the completion of the book: thanks to Barbara Tessman, Christine Robertson, and Len Husband, and to Anna Jarvis for her just-in-time work on the index.

The Osgoode Society for Canadian Legal History has played a crucial role in the development and preservation of legal history in Canada, and we thank them for their academic leadership in general and support for this volume in particular. This book of essays began, pre-pandemic, with a workshop to discuss papers, supported by research funds from Trent University, the University of Toronto Faculty of Law, and the Osgoode Society. Funding for the book was also made available by the Osgoode Society.

Colleagues and family often provided much-needed background sustenance, both intellectual and personal, for our academic work. Joan would like to thank feminist colleagues at Trent and beyond with whom she discussed this research; her adult children, Kate, Beth, Laura, and Rob, spread from Canada to the United Kingdom; and especially her partner, Bryan Palmer, who listened to long discussions about her research on labour, arbitrations, and the law. Lori would like to thank feminist colleagues at Lakehead and the Canadian Law and Society Association; her adult children and their spouses, Geoff and Cassie, Catherine and Mark; and her partner, Michel Bédard. She would also like to thank Joan – it was truly a pleasure working together.

Contributors

Constance Backhouse is a professor of law and Distinguished University Professor at the University of Ottawa. She has published a number of prize-winning books: *Petticoats and Prejudice: Women and Law in Nineteenth-Century Canada*; *Colour-Coded: A Legal History of Racism in Canada, 1900–1950*; *Carnal Crimes: Sexual Assault Law in Canada, 1900–1975*; *Claire L'Heureux-Dubé: A Life*; and *Two Firsts: Bertha Wilson and Claire L'Heureux-Dubé at the Supreme Court of Canada*. Her most recent book is *Reckoning with Racism: Police, Judges, and the RDS Case* (2022). She was made a Fellow of the Royal Society of Canada in 2004 and named to the Order of Canada in 2008.

Michel S. Beaulieu, PhD, FRHistS, is the Associate Vice-Provost (Academic) and a professor of history at Lakehead University. He is also a docent of Social Science History at the University of Helsinki, a docent of Modern North American History at the University of Oulu, and an associate at the Wilson Institute for Canadian History, McMaster University. The past-president of the Ontario Historical Society and Champlain Society, he serves as the Honorary Colonel of the Lake Superior Scottish Regiment.

Lyndsay Campbell is a professor of law and history at the University of Calgary. She is the author of *Truth and Privilege: Libel Law in Massachusetts and Nova Scotia, 1820–1840* (2022) and a co-editor of *Canada's Legal*

Pasts: Looking Forward, Looking Back (2020) and *Freedom's Conditions in the U.S.-Canadian Borderlands in the Age of Emancipation* (2011). She co-organized "Beyond the Pale," a Legal Histories of Empire Conference in Ireland in 2022. Her current research mainly concerns the history of parliamentary privilege and privilege defences in libel law.

Sarah Carter is a professor and Henry Marshall Tory Chair Emerita in the Department of History, Classics and Religion, and Faculty of Native Studies of the University of Alberta. Her books include *Imperial Plots: Women, Land, and the Spadework of British Colonialism on the Canadian Prairies* (2016) and *Ours by Every Law of Right and Justice: Women and the Vote in the Prairie Provinces* (2020). She has served as editor of the *Canadian Historical Review* and is co-editor (with John Borrows and A.J. Ray) of the McGill-Queen's University Press Indigenous and Northern Series. She is a Fellow of the Royal Society of Canada.

Lori Chambers is a professor of Gender and Women's Studies at Lakehead University, Thunder Bay. She is the author of *Married Women and Property Law in Victorian Ontario* (1997), *Misconceptions: Unmarried Motherhood and the Ontario Children of Unmarried Parents Act, 1921–1969* (2007), *A Legal History of Adoption in Ontario, 1921–2015* (2016), and, with Nadia Verrelli, *No Legal Way Out: R. v Ryan, Domestic Abuse, and the Defence of Duress* (2021), as well as multiple articles in legal and historical journals. *Married Women* and *Misconceptions* received the Alison Prentice Award for the best book in Canadian women's history. She is a Fellow of the Royal Society of Canada, Class of 2021.

Donald Fyson is a professor of history at Université Laval (Quebec City). He specializes in the history of eighteenth-, nineteenth, and twentieth-century Quebec, notably its social, socio-legal, and socio-political aspects. He is particularly interested in the relationship between law, state, and society, notably as seen through the everyday operation of the criminal and civil justice systems. His current research projects include capital punishment and imprisonment in Quebec, 1760–1960, and homicides and violence in Quebec, 1760–1920.

Mélanie Méthot is a professor at the University of Alberta, Augustana Campus and the recipient of a SSHRC Grant for her research on bigamy in Canada and for her project dealing with bigamy in Australia. Méthot has a special interest in SoTL and is the founder of the Augustana Conference on Undergraduate Research and Innovative Teaching.

Laura Nigro is a teacher at St. Ignatius High School and chairperson of the Social Sciences Department. She holds a master's degree in history from Lakehead University, and focused her studies on Italian immigration and gender roles within the Italian-Canadian community. Her previous work includes co-authoring "A Century of Sport in the Finnish Community of Thunder Bay," which won the International Sports Heritage Association Communication Award and Best in Show (2014).

Jim Phillips is a professor of law, history, and criminology at the University of Toronto, and editor-in-chief of the Osgoode Society for Canadian Legal History. He was formerly law clerk to Madam Justice Bertha Wilson of the Supreme Court of Canada, and in 2013 won the Mundell Medal awarded by the attorney-general for Ontario for "a distinguished contribution to law and letters." He is the co-author of *A History of Law in Canada*, volume 1, *Beginnings to 1866* (2018) and *A History of Law in Canada*, volume 2, *Law for the New Dominion, 1867–1914* (2022). He has co-edited four volumes of the Osgoode Society for Canadian Legal History/University of Toronto Press's Essays in the History of Canadian Law and two other books.

Eric H. Reiter is a professor of history at Concordia University, where he teaches legal history and law and society. He is a member of the Centre interuniversitaire d'études québécoises and a retired member of the Barreau du Québec. His research focuses on the social history of nineteenth- and twentieth-century Quebec civil law. His book *Wounded Feelings: Litigating Emotions in Quebec, 1870–1950* (2019) was awarded the Canadian Historical Association's Best Scholarly Book in Canadian History Prize for 2020.

Joan Sangster, Vanier Professor Emeritus (Trent University), is a Fellow of the Royal Society of Canada and past president of the Canadian Historical Association/Société historique du Canada. She has written monographs, book chapters, and articles dealing with the history of feminism; women, work, and the labour movement; law and criminalization; and setter-Indigenous relations in Canada. Her most recent books include *Transforming Labour: Women and Work in Postwar Canada* (2010), *The Iconic North: Cultural Constructions of Aboriginal Life in*

Postwar Canada (2016), and *Demanding Equality: One Hundred Years of Canadian Feminism* (2021), which won the Hilda Neatby prize for the best book in women's and gender history.

Julia Smith is an assistant professor in the Labour Studies Program at the University of Manitoba. She studies the history of labour relations and women's labour activism in Canada. Julia has published articles on feminist union organizing and labour relations in the airline and banking industries. She is also a member of the Graphic History Collective and a co-author/co-editor of several graphic books, including *1919: A Graphic History of the Winnipeg General Strike.*

Taylor D. Starr is a PhD candidate in history at York University. Her research interests lie within the fields of institutional, cultural, intellectual, and legal history. She is working on her doctoral dissertation, "Invisible Barriers: Gendered Problems in Canadian Law Faculties, 1961–1994," which has received a Social Sciences and Humanities Research Council of Canada (SSHRC) Fellowship, an R. Roy McMurtry Fellowship in Canadian Legal History, a Feminist Historical Research Scholarship, and an Avie Bennett Historica Canada Scholarship in Canadian History.

ESSAYS IN THE HISTORY OF CANADIAN LAW

Volume XII

Introduction

JOAN SANGSTER AND LORI CHAMBERS

Feminists have long trained their critical eyes on the law. From the nineteenth through to the twenty-first century, those intent on altering women's subordination and oppression often saw challenges to the legal order as an avenue to equality, dignity, and autonomy. Nineteenth-century reformers tackled marriage and property laws that rendered women mere subordinate extensions of their husbands, legislation that denied them the vote, and a criminal code that offered women scant protection from violence. As these examples indicate, both an emphasis on women's right to the same, or equal, treatment with men, and a view that women's physical, psychological, or maternal "difference" from men should be recognized, coexisted, sometimes uneasily, in feminist legal strategies.

Even at a time when women did not practise (or certainly teach) law, and were barred from doing so in some provinces, feminists nonetheless became self-taught legal experts in order to mobilize for social change. In 1912, suffragist Helen Gregory MacGill (later a juvenile court judge) self-published *Daughters, Wives, and Mothers in British Columbia: Some Laws Affecting Them*, which became an influential blueprint for legal reform. Marie Lacoste Gérin-Lajoie made Quebec's *Civil Code* her focus of research in interwar Quebec, using her knowledge to press for family law reform before the provincial Dorion Commission on "des droits civils de la femme." These feminist projects reflect one of the most enduring themes in studies of women, gender, and the law: women's agency, expressed through their efforts to use, alter, or negotiate with the law, even when it was not constructed in their favour.

Many of these campaigners embraced western, Enlightenment-inspired notions of individual and social legal rights and had implicit faith in altering law through legislative change within the boundaries of parliamentary democracy. They were unaware of, or even dismissed, Indigenous law and jurisprudence, with its notions of rights and reciprocities that were different from those in British and French legal systems. Reform feminists understood that the law, in defining femininity and proper womanly social roles, was simultaneously defining acceptable masculine behaviour and character. In the time periods covered in this volume, reformers generally took the category of "woman" as a given. Feminists' hopes that changes to legislation, social policy, or the carceral system – whether it guaranteed the vote, age of consent laws, equal pay, widows' pensions, or humane treatment for juvenile offenders – would lead to better lives for all women may seem narrow and overly optimistic to us.

However, early feminists were not entirely naive or uncritical about the law; the notion that, before the 1960s, they were not cognizant of legal contradictions and complexities overstates the historical homogeneity of the women's movement. Feminists with a socialist or class analysis critiqued labour laws that were full of loopholes and structured fundamentally to support the owning class. Other critics of patriarchal power exposed the double sexual standard that characterized even reformist versions of divorce, child custody, and family law. High-profile cases of women incarcerated for merely defending themselves physically from violent partners sometimes mobilized feminists of very different political persuasions who called for justice and mercy rather than penal punishment.[1] Women whose commitment to equality focused on racial discrimination combined legal challenges with social mobilization to challenge racism in Canadian society – as African-Canadian women did with the Viola Desmond case.[2]

Scholarship that interrogated gender relations and the law expanded and diversified after the 1970s, encouraged both by a reinvigorated women's movement and the admission of a somewhat greater number of women to law schools and the profession. The latter was not a smooth, welcoming process, unimpeded by barriers of sexism and racism; as some pioneers remember, they endured university lectures that ridiculed violence against women and prejudice in the job market. They encountered continuing resistance to feminist, anti-racist, or anti-colonial legal theories, which were dismissed as mere subjective, political bias. However, encouraged by a feminist movement questioning the entirety of law as a set of institutions, ideologies, and social processes, and by new theoretical writing with a range of radical, Marxist, critical race, and liberal inflections, feminists cast more discerning eyes on the history and current manifestations of law. The androcentric nature of legal institutions, long portrayed as neutral, the class and race assumptions of legal practice and penal institutions, the artificiality of a public/private separation, the imprint of dominant ideologies on the law, settler assumptions embedded in law, the creation of new legal categories such as sexual harassment – and far more – were all part of this conversation. So too were efforts to connect feminism with analyses of race/ethnicity, class, and sexuality. If these legal scholars saw the law as a hegemonic set of assumptions that needed disruption, they also understood its two-sided nature: as both enabling and constraining, as a point of contention as well as inertia.

Examining law not simply as legislation and institutions but, more broadly, as discourse, practice, symbols, rhetoric, and language, and how they are articulated culturally, materially, and politically, these scholars faced some of the same frustrating contradictions of legal reform that earlier feminists had encountered: the unintended consequences, unexpected events, and resilient structures of inequality characterizing the law. In the process, feminist writing doubled down on analysis of these seemingly intractable problems and redefined and expanded the very definition of equality and feminism.

Canadian research was part of a national and international phenomenon that was also increasingly interdisciplinary, taking in humanities, social science, and law faculties, as well as a continuing custom of amateur and activist writing. Canadian legal historians participated in a transnational conversation, especially with American, British/Antipode, and French writers, but their writing also assumed its own character, shaped by history, politics, and culture, rendered distinct in part due to two founding western settler legal traditions – common and civil law – with those increasingly challenged by, and more recently recognizing, Indigenous legal traditions.

This volume is a tribute to decades of feminist historical research, a small slice of the path-breaking, sophisticated, and influential writing that has broken new ground in our study of the history of the law. The evolutionary, contextual emphasis that history offers provides invaluable insight into the developmental roots of law, an understanding of the present as well as the past, and some hint of how difficult creating a more egalitarian future will be. The essays represented here cross many thematic areas, from criminal to labour, civil, administrative, and human rights law; the articles span English and French Canada and range from the mid- eighteenth to the late twentieth century.

At the same time, the essays are more than a retrospective of Canadian legal history: they represent new approaches and concerns, as well as retilling of existing themes with new evidence and modes of storytelling. Some use established archival methods and sources to expand on, and reinterpret, legal events, such as Lyndsay Campbell's analysis of the *War-time Election Act*. Other essays, such as Sarah Carter's examination of Métis scrip, contribute both to the expansion of legal knowledge and to a re-telling of Canadian history – in this case questioning the economic origins of settler economic power in Alberta. Essays that plumb quasi-judicial tribunals as sources, such as those by Sangster and Smith, and Nigro, Chambers, and Beaulieu, remind us how important it is to move beyond the courtroom as such tribunals also defined women's legal protections and rights – or lack thereof. The popular press has long been an important source for historians; Mélanie Méthot and Donald Fyson put such sources to good use, either to reinterpret events that have been downplayed by historians, such as Delpit affair, or to provide new insights into the intersection of ethnicity, gender, and class, as in the case of Tommasina Teolis. In short, the collection is a marriage of established and new methods, sources, and approaches, all with this purpose of offering fresh insights into the gendered operation and experience of the law.

The diversity of methodologies and theoretical assumptions underpinning these essays also reflects the history and current character of women's and gender legal scholarship. In an earlier reflection on Canadian feminist scholarship as it emerged in the 1980s, Susan Boyd and Elizabeth Sheehy suggested that, despite theoretical differences, such scholarship defied easy categorization, as dialogue and borrowing of concepts were evident, with different theories, or hybrid ones, used according to the subject, audience, and academic goals at issue.[3] Subsequent reflections suggest the persistence of this process of productive borrowing and engagement, but also changing political and theoretical debates in scholarly writing as feminists variously stressed instrumental or social constructionist views, or equality liberalism or integrated feminism, and as they debated the veracity of conceptual frameworks from critical race theory to discourse analysis, Marxism, radical feminism, Indigenous knowledge, and intersectionality.[4]

Difference and debate, if sometimes difficult, have led to useful reflection, correction, and critique. Patricia Monture's classic essay on violence, for instance, pushed feminists to consider their failure to take into account dispossession and colonialism in their definitions of violence.[5] Writing on LGBTQ rights has challenged heteronormative assumptions embedded even in feminist writing, while Marxist dissections of law and the economy have led to rethinking about how the state operates – indeed, the influence of legal history extends beyond legal faculties to other academic disciplines, interdisciplines, the courts, and feminist advocacy groups. Like the essays here, legal histories are written at the interface of legal history and multiple other histories, of women and gender, the family, labour, violence, criminalization, settler colonialism, "race," and ethnicity.

Holding individual cases, or particular laws, up to scholarly scrutiny is an effective means of exploring the historical, gendering process of law; putting these cases in context also exposes the relationship between women's oppression and patriarchy, colonialism, racism, and class conflict. This method has facilitated a useful rethinking of the efficacy of various theoretical frameworks, as evidence and theory are interrogated in a dialectical, reciprocal manner. Toni Williams's discussion of the highly influential concept of intersectionality, for instance, asks whether this concept has proven useful in reducing Indigenous women's over-incarceration in light of the *Gladue* decision (1999), answering with a critical, insightful "no."[6] As writing on specific *Charter of Rights and Freedoms* cases has shown, scholarly scepticism, even about seeming advancements, is a healthy practice: scholars have traced both the potential and very real limitations of *Charter* challenges, including the pitfalls of individualist human rights thinking in pursuit of social, substantive equality.[7]

Probing specific historical cases, as this collection does, provides a similar micro and macro view of the legal process, in which a "thick description of a microscopic event allows a fuller dissection of how the law interacts with the wider social, political, economic, and cultural surroundings."[8] The use of a narrative, case study approach was pioneered in Canada by Constance Backhouse, who opened up the field of Canadian women's legal history with her path-breaking work *Petticoats and Prejudice* (1991), one of the first substantive monographs in this area.[9] This method of employing a more intimate, case-based approach to legal storytelling became one of the most evocative and revealing means of exposing the gender, class, and race-based inequities structuring the law, while never losing sight of "ordinary" women's experiences, struggles, and agency.[10] Elizabeth Sheehy's research on violence, Judy Fudge's on labour, and Sherene Razack's on race and colonialism (to name a few other feminist historians) have also used this method to advance our understanding of the law, as has another Osgoode collection of historical essays, *Work on Trial*.[11] As part of this tradition, this book is explicitly and unapologetically feminist, starting from the premise that women deserve material security, safety, and dignity in their lives, and have the right to equal protection of the law.

The historical case study method, as James Muir recounts, has both analytic and humanistic dimensions; in the latter case, narrative method humanizes the law and "permits the pinpointing of the concrete impact of the legal rules upon real people at specific times."[12] While for lawyers "the story behind the case is almost always irrelevant – what matters are the facts and reasoning" – for legal historians, both the story and the legal dispute are important.[13] Legal history is not presented as a series of cases in which wrongs are righted (and, in fact, often they were not) but rather as stories of "tenacious litigants."[14] Similarly, Judy Fudge and Eric Tucker argue in their introduction to *Work on Trial* that legal storytelling expands on, and adds texture to, case law analyses. "Legal reports of cases," they point out, "may beg as many questions as they answer," as legal disputes are examined in isolation from the "the social processes in which they are embedded."[15] A more fulsome historical narrative takes the reader from the specific case story to the broader context and back again: this not only gives us a better understanding of the case, but also offers "a lens through which we can better understand the context."[16] As a consequence, both the social relations shaping law and its precise articulation in specific circumstances are divulged.

The stories recounted in this volume vary from precedent-setting cases to lesser-known ones, from those driven by a plaintiff's unrelenting quest for personal justice to others in which state actors dominate. They employ multiple sources, from case law to media reports, trial transcripts, judges' notes, government and administrative documents, personal papers, and interviews. However different the time period or theme, the authors share a commitment to providing a rich historical and social context, to unravelling the process of legal decision-making, and to explaining the biographies of the people involved, whether they were unknown defendants or prestigious judges. In legal storytelling, as Fudge and Tucker stress, "character matters."[17] These cases also illustrate the normative pluralism of law: women were invariably agents attempting to advance their own interests through a legal system that constrained or oppressed them, in the process revealing the historical dialectic of power and resistance.

While arranged chronologically, these case studies also converge around particular themes. Patriarchy, class, and colonialism are the central themes explored in the chapters by Eric Reiter, Mélanie Méthot, Jim Phillips, and Sarah Carter, dealing with the nineteenth and early twentieth centuries. Violence – against women, by individuals and the state, and by women themselves – is the primary focus of the chapters by Constance Backhouse and Donald Fyson. These chapters cover cases spanning the period from the 1920s to the early twenty-first century. Lyndsay Campbell's essay provides a transition between the nineteenth and twentieth century as it documents the culmination of efforts by nineteenth-century suffragists to secure the vote, examining the federal state's highly contentious, partial extension of the franchise to only some "deserving" women during the First World War. In the last three chapters of the book, Joan Sangster and Julia Smith, Laura Nigro, Lori Chambers, and Michel Beaulieu, and Taylor Starr explore women's encounters with the law and various legal administrative tribunals in the latter part of the twentieth century. They also address the politics of legal confrontation and change: what are the strategies, pitfalls, and possibilities of efforts to use the law in a quest for gender, racial, and economic equality?

In chapter 1, Eric Reiter uses the case of Caroline Ferguson, a Quebec woman, to explore both the agency that women exerted in the legal arena and the constraints on that agency in a highly paternalistic, patriarchal society that was simultaneously structured by class relations. In the mid-nineteenth century, Ferguson undertook a number of public campaigns and litigations against powerful men whom she believed had wronged her name. The five actions that she launched – including for breach of promise, paternity, and libel – against three different men showed the extraordinary lengths to which she went to recoup her honour. This case study is not only the story of an exceptional woman: it also reveals how important moral reputation was to all women, how it could affect their marriage prospects and livelihood, and make the difference between social acceptance and ostracism. Women's role in the legal system is also a consideration. In Quebec, unmarried women had some ability to pursue cases in the courts, but Ferguson was never a completely independent legal actor: she was highly dependent on the support of men in these cases. Combining legal documentation with media commentary, Reiter shows how important the social commodity of "reputation" was to women, in contrast to men, and the immense power of gender ideologies in defining hegemonic notions of women's sexual purity and feminine respectability. Yet the courts were not an ideal or straightforward means of securing, or resecuring, respectability. Ferguson's valiant efforts to repair her reputation through legal channels had mixed results and came at a cost. Eventually, her rehabilitation was achieved more fully outside, rather than inside, the legal system.

In Mélanie Méthot's case study in chapter 2, a young Quebec wife, Jeanne Côté Delpit, desperately sought to sustain the legality of her marriage to Édouard Delpit, as she fought his efforts to secure an annulment through an ecclesiastical tribunal of the Catholic Church. Again, the case shows women's agency, despite the legal and social disadvantages they faced. Jeanne lost her case, despite considerable public sympathy for her. Tragically, she also lost her three children, as they were spirited away by Édouard's family into the United States and were permanently cut off from her after he relocated there and remarried. Jeanne Delpit did not want to stay in a toxic marriage, but she sought to use Quebec's civil law to have a "a separation from bed and board," with her husband providing some support to her as his estranged wife. Because Édouard wanted to remarry, he pursued an annulment instead. The legal issue and ensuing public debate centred on the place of religion in civil society: Did the Montreal Superior Court or the ecclesiastical tribunal have the ultimate power to rule on the marriage's legality? Was Jeanne a practising or lapsed Catholic when she married – an important question, as the latter finding would put her fate in the hands of the civil court. What ensued was a major legal battle and heated public controversy about civil and religious marriage law, the power of the Catholic Church, and the nature of men's and women's family obligations. Like the Ferguson case, the Delpit one prompted widespread media debate about proper gender roles and marriage. As Méthot points out, the Delpit case is often bypassed in historical accounts of controversies about the Catholic Church in Quebec in favour of the more famous Guibord affair. However, the Delpit marriage controversy was just as intense, widespread, and revealing. Méthot's chapter not only relays the social and political impact of this legal battle, but also suggests something about the character and personal intentions of Jeanne and Édouard, reminding us that legal battles are ultimately also human ones, often with tragic consequences.

While Jim Phillips's chapter on the Elizabeth (Eliza) and Robert Campbell case, debated by the Senate from 1876 to 1879, also documents the legal furore over a marriage breakdown, the issues involved were different. The case, as Phillips points out, was unique: it involved the longest Senate debate over a divorce; it was the only one that began as a request for a divorce but later became one of separation from bed and board; it generated other civil suits; and it sparked constitutional questions. Still, both Méthot's and Phillips's chapters remind us how central the law was to the regulation, if not outright control, of women's lives through the legal regimes determining marriage, separation, divorce, and family support. At a time when married women were defined and limited by their financial dependence, lack of property rights, and rigid social mores, a failed marriage could, for a woman, mean poverty, loss of custody of her children, and unimaginable social shaming. The long, intense, passionate, and often vitriolic debate in the Senate about the Campbell case indicates how much was at stake and speaks to the courage of Eliza Campbell. Phillips's chapter also highlights the role that the Senate played in dissolving marriages before Canadians had court access to divorce; section 91(26) of the *British North America Act* (*BNA Act*) gave Parliament jurisdiction over divorce. As a result, access to divorce was extremely limited, its availability further narrowed by considerations of wealth and social class. The fact that cases were discussed in the Senate, and recorded in its proceedings, involved a public airing of personal lives. This seems, on its face, to contradict our image of the Victorian penchant for privacy on sexual and familial matters. But it was not just contentious questions of marital fidelity that preoccupied senators in the Campbell case: constitutional conundrums were also involved. It raised two questions: What was the relationship between the Senate's control over divorce and the provincial jurisdiction over property and civil rights (section 92(13) of the *BNA Act*)? And, should Parliament pass legislation (which each divorce proceeding was) that effectively became a judgment in appeal from the Ontario Court of Chancery, which had earlier ruled on this case?

In chapter 4, Sarah Carter deals with a very different kind of controversy, but one that was also a tragedy: the violence of colonial dispossession. The case of Marie Rose Majeau Meunier indicates how dispossession commonly worked in the case of Métis scrip in the Canadian West. White settlers who secured Métis scrip – and used it to acquire

Métis land – often did so by fraud, subterfuge, trickery, and misrepresentation, knowing the courts would work in their favour if Métis people protested. White settlers used a myriad of intricate tactics and rationales, but, in the last resort, they were engaged in land theft. In Meunier's case, intimidation played a key role, as she was told by the men who came to her home representing wealthy owners and speculators that her parents could go to jail, and they would lose everything, if she did not sign away her rights. Meunier's example indicates how tenaciously Indigenous women fought back: knowing the importance of securing land title, they engaged with the law in order to try to secure their rightful entitlements. Not only was settler dispossession ongoing, but, when Indigenous protests were registered, the settler state responded with a remarkable amendment to the *Criminal Code* in 1921, which decriminalized scrip fraud and protected those who stole scrip. This change was designed to put a stop to cases like Meunier's but, arguably, protests over dispossession and Métis rights continue to this day. Certainly, Meunier, a Métis woman, directly confronted white, masculine settler privilege. Although she lost her case, it and other ones detailed by Carter point to a long history of Indigenous resistance: litigating Métis oppression has been an ongoing theme in Canadian history. Carter's chapter also uses legal history to make an important statement about how Canadian history has been narrated and memorialized: the white settler businessmen and developers who swindled Meunier and amassed part of their fortune through obtaining Métis scrip are celebrated as great builders of the West, a perspective that ignores both how they came to acquire land and the history of Métis resistance.

Constance Backhouse's chapter on the *Hubin* case, litigated in the 1920s, also deals with themes of violence and patriarchy, touching as well on ethnicity in the Canadian West. This important case, as well as others that Backhouse uses to contextualize it, reveals the ongoing development of the idea of "consent" in prosecutions for sexual assault. *Hubin* was significant, as it contributed to the historical foundation upon which the ideological understanding of rape was constructed, particularly the notion that women and children were routinely unreliable witnesses when it came to their accusations of sexual assault. As a consequence, proof beyond their testimony – that is, third-party corroboration – was required. While the cultural construction of rape in a way that protected masculine interests was already established, and the notion that accusations needed third-party evidence existed before *Hubin*, such ideas were extended and rigidified with the Supreme Court ruling that third-party corroboration was needed in sexual assault trials – a virtual impossibility in most cases. Despite the fact that Hubin had raped an underage girl (which should automatically have been a crime), and despite ample evidence provided by the girl and the investigators, he was ultimately acquitted by the Supreme Court of Canada. *Hubin* established a precedent that continues to plague women to this day as they attempt to recount their experiences of sexual assault in court. After *Hubin*, juries routinely concluded that it was dangerous to convict based on uncorroborated testimony, and Canadian legislators made this mandatory under the *Criminal Code*, precisely because they had more concerns about the "risks" male accused faced than about the violence women experienced. Feminist reformers in the early twentieth century were not overly concerned with sexual assault laws, focusing instead on other social and political issues. It was "second-wave" feminists who lobbied for overhaul of the *Criminal Code*: not until 1982 did Parliament pass a prohibition on judges' issuing warnings to juries about the need for corroboration. The idea that women and children are not just unreliable, but that they also fabricate stories, was deeply embedded in a patriarchal mindset. The myth that women lie about rape was difficult to dislodge, even after feminists in the 1970s challenged it – to some extent successfully. One could argue that residues of this idea remain, with police still reluctant to lay sexual assault charges and prosecutors reluctant to take such cases to trial.

Although those on the receiving end of violence have often been women, legal historians have not essentialized all violence as intrinsically "male" and passivity as "female": violence is explained with reference to ideological constructions of gender, "race," heteronormativity, and prevailing social and economic relations. Women were sometimes prosecuted for violence, although they were often judged by different standards than men, depending on the nature of the crime. In chapter 6, Donald Fyson explores the case of Tommasina Teolis, a forty-six-year-old Italian-Canadian woman in Montreal, who was hanged on 29 March 1935 for conspiring to have her much older husband, Nicola Sarao, murdered by two young Italian men. The apparent motive was insurance fraud. This case attracted the voyeuristic attention of contemporary journalists and, later, popular historians, largely because Teolis was decapitated during the hanging. In serious academic work about the death penalty in Canada, however, the Teolis case is barely mentioned. She was the only woman executed in post-Conquest Quebec who was of neither French nor English descent. In one sense an exceptional case,

Teolis's experience in the justice system and with the death penalty tells us a great deal about the relationship of both women and immigrants to capital punishment in public discourse in the first half of the twentieth century. Fyson analyses the construction of the execution, and of Teolis herself, in the contemporary press, in later debates, and in popular historiography, questioning the gendered arguments used by capital punishment abolition activists in search of commutations, as well as the voice and agency of women convicted of murder and sentenced to die.

Gender, Indigeneity, "race," and ethnicity are all salient to the issue of the vote in Lyndsay Campbell's chapter on the *War-time Elections Act* (*WTEA*) and *Military Voters Act* (*MVA*). Feminists' efforts to secure civil, educational, and political rights through campaigns for legislative and social change from the nineteenth century onward have been a constant theme in women's history. While historians have referred to the *WTEA*, Campbell provides us with the first in-depth analysis of the way in which politics, power, and law collided during the First World War to produce these two acts of Parliament. Having passed conscription in 1917 and faced with the fear of losing the election later that year, Conservative prime minister Robert Borden (along with some Liberal deserters to his cause) passed the *WTEA* to secure his re-election by enfranchising only some women and disenfranchising some men, primarily those who had immigrated from countries within "enemy empires" and who had become naturalized Canadians after 1902. At the time, provincial voter lists (some of which included women by 1917) determined federal ones. The Union government's desire to manipulate the federal franchise required extensive discussion about how to deal with the issue of voters lists in the upcoming federal election. Its solution was the *WTEA* (as well as the *MVA*, which enfranchised nurses as well as more soldiers overseas), which "sliced and diced" the electorate, based on language, race, ethnicity, gender, military service of relatives, and Indigeneity. Likely the most egregious and outrageous gerrymander in Canadian history (certainly twentieth-century Canadian history), the *WTEA* was most especially a western Canadian issue, due to recent immigration patterns and local politics: the men who were disenfranchised were often western settlers who had been naturalized after 1902 and came from "enemy" nations in Europe. Moreover, the western provinces (and Ontario) had all, by that point, enfranchised (most) women. Campbell documents and critiques the process of creating and implementing the *WTEA* and *MVA*, showing how political power and different notions of political rights shaped this history, in terms of not only gender, but also race and ethnicity. She shows that those arguing for and against the *WTEA* had different perspectives on the vote, with some positing that it was a universal right and others seeing it as a "privilege" or as legitimately circumscribed, with some citizens portrayed as more deserving than others of that privilege. Campbell, too, reminds us how fractured feminism could be: it was never a monolithic ideology (in the past or present), as feminists have proposed, and continue to propose, profoundly different understandings of the most basic of political rights.

In many of these essays, women's agency is a central theme, even where the protagonists are clearly disadvantaged by the law and constrained by the ideological suppositions underpinning it. This is true, too, for the chapter by Sangster and Smith, which also deals with questions of power and the state – in this case, with the quasi-judicial legal machinery regulating labour/employer relations. They examine a case taken to the Canadian Labour Relations Board (CLRB) concerning Wardair's disciplining of a flight attendant, Senka Dukovich, who dared to speak up about sexism in the airline industry in the 1980s. Dukovich was a union activist and a lawyer who used her flight attendant job to help put herself through law school. As a member of the CUPE Airline Women's Committee, she prepared a complaint on behalf of the union to be presented to the Canadian Human Rights Commission on sexism in airline policy. However, her comments to the press about this complaint resulted in her employer, Wardair, disciplining her for publicly tarnishing its reputation. Her temporary suspension was contested by her union before the CLRB, but, in a two-to-one decision, CUPE and Dukovich lost. Other cases often provided significant leeway to union leaders and activists criticizing their employers, so the authors ask why Dukovich's case was different and why her activism was such an anathema both to her employer and to a majority on the CLRB tribunal. Drawing on materialist and feminist approaches to legal and labour history, Sangster and Smith circle back to questions of power and ideology. Taking into account the political economy of the airline industry at the time (including employer offensives, anti-unionism, and deregulation) and also the dominant ideological suppositions about women service workers, they offer an explanation for Wardair's victory. Employers and boards of arbitration did not grant feminist activism the same respect as other union politics, and tended to construct feminists as irrational and vindictive: ideology was a powerful force in defining both "proper" femininity and "acceptable" forms of feminism. Yet, using the law to discipline feminists can backfire for employers: rather than discrediting Dukovich and the cause she represented, the very public CLRB hearings resulted in more attention to and sympathy for flight attendants' battle for workplace dignity, even if the board did not rule in Dukovich's favour.

Questions about women's human rights and state regulatory bodies are also explored in chapter 9, by Laura Nigro, Lori Chambers, and Michel Beaulieu, which provides the first academic discussion of the important human rights decision *Martinie v. The Italian Society of Port Arthur*. Giovannina (Joanne) Ruberto, a young Italian-Canadian woman living in Thunder Bay, decided to submit a membership application to the all-male fraternal Italian Mutual Benefit Society of Port Arthur (presently the Italian Society of Port Arthur). When the group denied her membership, she filed a complaint with the Ontario Human Rights Commission. She claimed she had experienced discrimination in clear violation of section 1 of the *Human Rights Code* of Ontario, which states that every person has the right to equal treatment with respect to services, goods, and facilities without discrimination due to one's sex. In June 1995, a human rights tribunal handed down its decision in favour of the society. Under section 18 of the *Human Rights Code*, as a "special interest organization" protecting Italian culture, the society was permitted to discriminate against Ruberto based on her sex. In order to protect the rights of a group, in this case Italian men, Ruberto's rights as an individual Italian woman had been violated. Little has been written about this important case, and it was not discussed in the Supreme Court of Canada decision that confirmed this interpretation of human rights codes, *Gould v. Yukon Order of Pioneers*. But *Martinie* is important, not only because of the specifics of the challenge and the fact that the Italian Society of Port Arthur continues to exclude women, but also because of the insight it provides about gender-based struggles within immigrant communities, and the limitations – and contradictions – of human rights regimes.

Taylor Starr's chapter is an appropriate closing essay for this volume, since it addresses perennial questions for feminists: How do we change the law in ways that actually matter for most women's day-to-day lives? Can law reform produce substantive social change, or are we always limited by its liberal, individualist assumptions, and the law's tendency to lag behind economic and social change? Starr explores repeated efforts to alter Ontario family law with respect to marriage breakdown and economic support after the resurgence of feminism in the 1960s. One of her key arguments is that reform efforts must be examined in the context of the women's movement, its changing ideas, feminist initiatives like the Royal Commission on the Status of Women, and court judgments that provoked public debate. Divorce, division of property, and spousal support were highly contested issues across Canada, especially after the much-publicized *Murdoch* Supreme Court decision in 1973 illustrated how undervalued women's unpaid familial labour was in the eyes of the court. Even though Irene Murdoch's circumstances were not the norm for most wives, the case became a symbol of the structural inequalities embedded in family law. Starr begins with a discussion of the Ontario Law Reform Commission, which began its investigation into the need for law reform in the province in 1967; examines the changes, both positive and negative, of the 1978 *Ontario Family Law Reform Act*; and concludes with struggles that led to the *Ontario Family Law Act* of 1987. In this time period, she examines legislative debates, lobbying efforts – particularly by feminist advocate Linda Silver Dranoff – and key legal judgments, including one by pragmatic feminist judge Bertha Wilson. One hard lesson reformers learned was that of unintended consequences: new legislation did not always fulfil their hopes; instead, it might create new problems, which then needed to be addressed with further reform. Starr traces this complex process of incremental amendment of the law, arguing that it took both "internal" and "external" lobbying to effect change. Lawyer practitioners worked from inside the legal system, and women's and legal reform lobby groups laboured from the outside to change public attitudes and ultimately secure legislation that better recognized women's needs on marriage breakdown. Their diligent efforts produced positive change, but the law was, ultimately, only one element sustaining women's inequality. Reform tended to aid middle-class women, and could not address lingering patriarchal attitudes and especially class disparities that sustained women's economic and social inequality.

This volume is a collection of case studies, not a comprehensive study of the history of women and the law (a project far too large for a single volume); as a result, there are significant gaps in coverage, geographically (the Far North and Atlantic provinces), thematically (sexuality, the carceral state), with regard to Indigenous jurisprudence, and also relating to "race" and racialization. All of these essays are also situated in the past, when the category of "woman" was largely taken for granted. Clearly, a second volume of essays on gender and the law, exploring all of these issues – and more – would be a welcome project.

Nonetheless, the essays here offer a glimpse of the strides made in feminist historical research, particularly scholars' efforts to understand women's agency in contesting the unequal relations of law, as well as the complex, unfolding drama of power and resistance, encompassing social relations of gender, class, "race," colonialism, and ethnicity. It is certainly time for the Osgoode Essays in the History of Canadian Law series to have a volume dedicated to women. We hope this book offers both celebration of the achievements of feminist legal historians and encouragement for further research and innovation.

NOTES

1 Karen Dubinsky and Franca Iacovetta, "Murder, Womanly Virtue, and Motherhood: The Case of Angelina Napolitano, 1911–1922," *Canadian Historical Review* 72 (December 1991): 505–31; Joan Sangster, "The Meanings of Mercy: Wife Assault and Spousal Murder in Post–Second World War Canada," *Canadian Historical Review* 97 (December 2016): 513–45.

2 Constance Backhouse, *Colour Coded: A Legal History of Racism in Canada, 1900–1950* (Toronto: University of Toronto Press, 1999), 243.

3 Susan Boyd and Elizabeth Sheehy, "Feminist Perspectives on Law: Canadian Theory and Practice," *Canadian Journal of Women and the Law* 2 (1986): 1–52.

4 Dorothy Chunn and Dany Lacombe, "Introduction," in *Law as Gendering Practice*, ed. Dorothy Chunn and Dany Lacombe (Toronto: Oxford University Press), 2–18.

5 Patricia Monture-Okanee, "The Violence We Do: A First Nations View," in *Challenging Times: The Women's Movement in Canada and the United States*, ed. Constance Backhouse and David Flaherty (Kingston and Montreal: McGill-Queen's University Press, 1992), 193–204.

6 Toni Williams, "Intersectionality Analysis in the Sentencing of Aboriginal Women in Canada: What Difference Does It Make?" in *Intersectionality and Beyond: Law, Power and the Politics of Location*, ed. Emily Grabham, Davina Cooper, Jane Krishnadas, and Didi Herman (London: Routledge-Cavenish, 2008), 79–104.

7 Judy Fudge, "The Canadian Charter of Rights: Recognition, Redistribution, and the Imperialism of the Courts," in *Sceptical Essays on Human Rights*, ed. Tom Campbell, Keith Ewing, and Adam Tomkins (Oxford: Oxford University Press, 2001), 335–8; D. Herman, "The Good,

the Bad, and the Smugly: Sexual Orientation and Perspectives on the Charter," in *Charting the Consequences: The Impact of Charter Rights in Canadian Law and Politics*, ed. David Schneiderman and Kate Sutherland (Toronto: University of Toronto Press, 1997), 200–17.

8 Backhouse, *Colour Coded*, 15–16.

9 Constance Backhouse, *Petticoats and Prejudice: Women and Law in Nineteenth-Century Canada* (Toronto: Women's Press, 1991).

10 For a fulsome description of narrative method, see Brian Foley and Ruth Ann Robbins, "A Primer for Lawyers on How to Use Fiction Writing Techniques to Write Persuasive Fact Sections," *Rutgers Law Journal* 32 (2001): 459–484, and Brian Foley, "Applied Legal Storytelling, Politics, and Factual Realism," *Legal Writing* 14 (2008): 17–52.

11 Elizabeth Sheehy, *Defending Battered Women on Trial: Lessons from the Transcripts* (Vancouver: UBC Press, 2014); Judy Fudge and Eric Tucker, *Work on Trial: Canadian Labour Law Struggles* (Toronto: Osgoode Society for Legal History, 2010); Judy Fudge, "The Supreme Court of Canada and the Right to Bargain Collectively: The Implications of the *Health Services and Support* Case in Canada and Beyond," *Industrial Law Journal* 37 (March 2008): 25–48; Sherene Razack, "Gendered Racial Violence and Spatialized Justice: The Murder of Pamela George," *Canadian Journal of Law and Society* 15 (2000): 91–130.

12 James Muir, "Introduction," in *Property on Trial: Canadian Cases in Context*, ed. Eric Tucker, James Muir, and Bruce Ziff (Toronto: Osgoode Society for Legal History, 2002), 2. See also, Kathryn Abrams, "Hearing the Call of Stories," *California Law Review* 79 (1991): 971–1052, and Patricia Monture-Okanee, "The Violence We Do."

13 James Muir, "Introduction," 2.

14 Ibid., 4.

15 Fudge and Tucker, "Introduction," in *Work on Trial*, 1.

16 Ibid., 4.

17 Ibid., 2.

1

The Trials of Caroline Ferguson: Reputation and Litigation in Quebec City, 1852–1857

ERIC H. REITER

[A woman's] principal merit is her virtue: it is often her only possession for which one esteems her and seeks her out. Should someone succeed in discrediting her in the hearts and minds of men, all is lost for her.

– François Dareau, *Traité des injures dans l'ordre judiciaire* (1775)[1]

... we may draw from it this useful lesson: that loss of virtue in a female is irretrievable – that one false step involves her in endless ruin – that her reputation is no less brittle than it is beautiful – and that she cannot be too much guarded in her behaviour towards the undeserving of the other sex.

– Mary Bennet on the elopement of one of her sisters, in Jane Austen, *Pride and Prejudice* (1813)

The words of French jurist François Dareau and English novelist Jane Austen reflect the common trope that a woman's good reputation, once lost, was difficult or impossible to restore. She had to be irreproachable in her own conduct, of course, but she also had to foresee and guard against all manner of attacks from others (roguish men especially) that, even if unjust, were damaging. All this did not mean that she should give up trying to repair her good name, if lost, but that the attempt was inevitably difficult, stressful, expensive, and uncertain of success. In Quebec City in the mid-1850s, a young woman named Caroline Jane Ferguson undertook an extensive, protracted, and highly public campaign of litigation, targeting three powerful men whom she accused of having wronged her in various ways. Though it was not unprecedented for women to seek legal remedies for injuries – suits for libel, seduction, paternity, and the like were common enough – the scope of Ferguson's attempts to redress her injuries was extraordinary.[2] She launched five major actions against the three men, and pursued all three up through the court system. Her story sheds light on the question of women's role within the legal system, and on the precariousness of their reputational capital in a society that was quick to give the benefit of the doubt and forgiveness to men, while holding women to strict standards of purity and passivity.

In this chapter, I present the story of Caroline Ferguson's litigation both for its own sake and as an illustration of the scope of women's legal agency and of the complex social politics of reputation in mid-nineteenth-century Quebec. I should note at the outset that Ferguson was an English-speaking Anglican from a privileged background, and so her story reflects a particular slice of Quebec (and Quebec City) society and should be understood within that specific context. My reconstruction of her experience is based on two complementary batches of sources. Most central are the archival files of her various legal actions, with newspaper coverage to fill some gaps.[3] Alongside that is a rich trove of personal correspondence, a source seldom available for legal historians. While the bulk of this dates from long after the litigation of the 1850s, it nonetheless offers fascinating insight into Ferguson's personality, rare for anyone in the period and especially so for women. It turns her from a one-dimensional litigant into a complex individual.

Alongside what her litigation tells us, however, is what it does not reveal: the stubborn shadows surrounding the legal process that remain despite the relatively abundant sources. Litigation produces copious documentation, but, since it is shaped to particular procedural or strategic purposes, it seldom delves deeply into the minds of the principals.[4] This limitation of the evidence, always an issue in legal historical writing, is compounded in cases like Ferguson's, in which highly subjective moral or emotional damage is being litigated.[5] The civil courts tended (and still tend) to deal with subjectivity by objectivizing it, stripping away the individual in favour of the reasonable, the comparable, the demonstrable. We will have occasion to establish some of her motivations and speculate on others, but in the end Caroline Ferguson's litigation retains many of its secrets.

The People and the Situation

The events we are concerned with began with a simple newspaper advertisement. In September 1851, Caroline Ferguson put an ad in the *Quebec Gazette*, seeking a position as a teacher in a school or family (figure 1.1). Wealthy timber merchant Duncan Patton spotted the ad and, after conferring with his wife, Mary, and following up with Ferguson's previous employer, he hired her to instruct the Pattons' numerous younger children in Indian Cove, St-Joseph-de-la-Pointe-Lévy, across the river from Quebec City and around the point. The Pattons' home would have been a welcome change from the boarding houses where Ferguson had been living.

Ferguson was of the proper class and background for a private teacher in a wealthy home: she was educated, came from a respectable family, and had been raised in some comfort (though she was no longer comfortable herself, hence the need to work). She was born on 15 December 1828.[6] Her father, merchant Daniel Ferguson, died young sometime around 1839, leaving his wife and two daughters in difficult straits. Caroline's mother, Maria Ann Ferguson, née Pozer, was the granddaughter of George Pozer, who had been Quebec City's wealthiest merchant.[7] Following an acrimonious and well-litigated inheritance battle in 1848–49, Pozer's fortune passed in its entirety to his grandson George Alford. Shut out of the succession, Maria Ann and her children were left to a precarious existence, reliant mostly on the munificence of Alford, whom they flattered, cajoled, and browbeat over the following decades. Caroline's letters to Alford, beginning in the early 1850s, show her skilfully cultivating her cousin, who over the years served as friend, psychotherapist, and, most importantly, financial benefactor.[8]

Before taking the position with the Pattons, Ferguson was in a state of off-and-on conflict with her mother, a difficult personality. She was raised mostly by her father's brother Alexander Ferguson until his death, and then, from about age eighteen, was forced into a succession of boarding houses.[9] Despite her difficult situation, she seems to have been exceptionally charming, and men were entranced by her. Her later letters reveal a quick wit and general vivaciousness, still evident despite the hard times she had to endure, particularly beginning in her thirties. No photographs of her are known to survive, but, at the start of her first trial, a newspaper described her as "a young lady of good family, highly educated, and possessed of considerable personal attractions."[10]

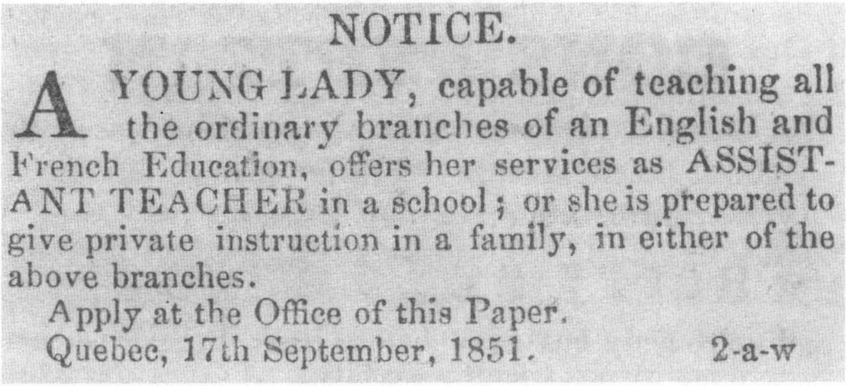

NOTICE.

A YOUNG LADY, capable of teaching all the ordinary branches of an English and French Education, offers her services as ASSIST-ANT TEACHER in a school; or she is prepared to give private instruction in a family, in either of the above branches.

Apply at the Office of this Paper.

Quebec, 17th September, 1851. 2-a-w

Figure 1.1. Caroline Ferguson's advertisement, which ran in the *Quebec Gazette* from 17 to 29 September 1851. *Quebec Gazette*, 19 September 1851, 3. Bibliothèque et Archives nationales du Québec, reproduced by permission.

In 1850, in her early twenties, Ferguson was courted by a merchant named Herbert Bell, but the engagement was called off, likely by mutual agreement.[11] Soon afterwards, she met at a boarding house Frederic Newton Gisbourne, an English immigrant at the start of a successful career promoting and installing telegraph systems.[12] The pair's behaviour caused rumours to circulate. One fellow boarder later testified that "they were in the habit of loud laughing & romping through the room, we could hear them although we could not see them. There was also squeeling [sic] occasionally with the loud laughing, they appeared to be chasing one another about with the sofa cushions."[13] Such stories certainly did not help her position in court later on.

Once established in the Patton household, Ferguson attracted the notice of the eldest son, James, six months younger than she was. James was soon to become a clerk with Allan Gilmour and Company, a Glasgow firm whose timber and other operations in Quebec were run by John Gilmour.[14] Duncan Patton had been a partner of the Gilmours and had continuing business relations with them; the wharves of the two firms were side by side at Pointe-Lévy on the south shore of the St. Lawrence River.

The only information about the earliest days of the relationship between James and Caroline comes from James's reluctant and hostile testimony during the litigation.[15] Soon after Caroline's arrival, relations between her and James, initially frosty, turned decidedly warmer, and James admitted that, after a few months, he had become "more intimate with her than common friendship" and "had an improper connection with the Plaintiff."[16] At Christmas, he presented her with a ring; perhaps indicative of her personality, a few days later she took it to the jeweller and exchanged it for a brooch.

Witnesses testified that, at the Pattons' house, the clandestine couple flirted more or less openly. One saw Ferguson "lying on a sofa in the [dining] room in what I conceived an immodest and improper position; her clothes were, whether through design or otherwise, a little above her ankles. When we came into the room the Plaintiff neither rose nor pulled down her clothes." On another occasion soon after, the same witness saw her upstairs overlooking the dining room "lying her full length on her body as I supposed and she was looking down into the dining room … and making amorous faces at the defendant: that is she was winking and nodding at the defendant."[17]

The "secret connection" between the lovers continued, "perfectly unknown" to the Patton parents, even after Ferguson became pregnant sometime in February 1852.[18] She was forced to leave the Patton household in May, when her initial engagement ended and Mary Patton declined to extend it – whether because she had discovered the pregnancy or for other reasons is unclear.[19] She lived with various friends and relatives, and the relationship with James continued.[20] The child, a boy, was born at the beginning of November 1852. His private baptism was recorded on 24 June 1853 (the reason for the long delay after the birth is unknown) under the name James Ninian, with the note "alleged Father, James Patton." A year later, in April 1854, he was received into the Anglican Church under the name James Ninian Conroy Patton (and noted as "illegitimate").[21] At the time of the birth, the elder James was still in the picture, and seems to have made vague promises about taking care of mother and child. His letters to Ferguson, which she kept (she told him to burn her letters to him, which he dutifully did, believing she had done likewise), indicate an ardent infatuation, described in highly emotional language. In one, he wrote that when he saw her walking towards the ferry, "I actually trembled as if I had taken a fit of ague. When I recovered from my surprise I ran down to the long wharf and watched you as far as my eyes could reach, and my heart filled when you were borne from my sight." He signed the letter "From one who loves thee ... Enclosed you will find a kiss, be careful you do not let it escape."[22]

Alarmed that James remained entranced by Caroline, his protectors tried to save the young man from what they saw as a disadvantageous match. In January 1853, the Pattons sent James off into the bush north of Berthier ("a most miserable place," he said) for a long timber scouting trip, complete with "two Indian guides." His (white) companions were charged with surveillance, but James found ways to write to Caroline anyway.[23]

More ominously, Patton's employer, John Gilmour, weighed in as well. In April 1853, Patton had accepted a position with the Gilmour firm on condition that he not continue to keep Ferguson as his "mistress or paramour," since "no mercantile house would employ a young man of that kind."[24] Despite those restrictions, he proved to be a troublesome hire, frequently absenting himself to visit his lover. One day, when Patton was away from the office, Gilmour was in a private room speaking with George Railton, his bookkeeper and confidential clerk, when the conversation turned to the absent young man. Details were contested in the subsequent litigation, but Patton's relationship with Ferguson came up.[25] Gilmour said that "it was an unfortunate transaction." Railton said something along the lines of "if he likes the girl, let him marry her." Gilmour disagreed, asserting "that it would not do, that she was a person of loose character and was kept by a person in Montreal." Railton remembered the word "whore" being used. Later, Gilmour confronted Patton, saying, according to Patton, "that I was not to be carrying on as I done, that Miss Ferguson had been boarding a long time at Mrs. Penn [Payne] and was often seen in the company of a Mr. Gisbon [sic] and he also said not to marry the girl unless I had a strong affection for her and if I had, then to marry her." Gilmour qualified that recommendation, however, adding that "no young man would marry a woman who would allow a young man to have illicit intercourse with her after a fortnight's acquaintance."[26] Exactly how word of those conversations got to Ferguson is unclear, but the relationship, and Gilmour's reactions to it, were being discussed soon after in a shop in Quebec City's Lower Town owned by Gilmour's brother-in-law, who may have been the source.[27]

The relationship continued into the summer of 1853. It ended only when, despite Ferguson's insistence, it became clear that Patton had no intention of marrying her. She began litigation soon afterwards.

Women as Litigants

Ferguson's gender constrained her experience in the legal system, though the particulars of her situation put her in a special category among female litigants. In Quebec civil law in this period (and indeed for long afterward), women were subject to various legal disabilities, incapacities, and double standards that limited their ability to act independently of men, though without ever completely excluding them from legal action.[28] Such constraints applied most strictly to married women, most of whose legal rights were exercised only through the authorization of their husband or a judge.[29] Widows and unmarried women of full age (like Ferguson) were free of most legal incapacities (they could, for example, undertake legal actions in their own name), but their scope for independent action was still heavily circumscribed extralegally, in ways that related both to their individual situations and to society's attitudes and assumptions about women. In Ferguson's case, her precarious financial state both limited her capacity for action and greatly increased the stakes of the actions she was undertaking. As a result, although formally she was an independent legal actor, practically she was dependent on the support of others – specifically, various men, as we will see.

Attitudes about women also affected what Ferguson could hope to achieve in seeking redress through the courts. Much rested on public perceptions of female virtue, and those opinions in turn depended strongly on the shelter of respectability that family or other supporters provided. Without a father or, indeed, any close male relative, Ferguson lacked an obvious protector at a time when English society in Quebec City seems to have been especially hostile towards young women. In September 1853, a few months before the litigation started, an anonymous scandal sheet called *The Scourge* circulated among the city's anglophone men, "attack[ing] in the language of the brothel even females of the highest respectability."[30] Ferguson herself had already attracted rumours, beginning in her late teenage years. When the Pattons were considering hiring her in 1851, they had heard things, but they "ascribed it to the general way in which young ladies' characters are generally attacked in this city."[31] A lawyer who testified on Ferguson's behalf about her character made the point still more clearly: "I allude to such remarks as are frequently made respecting a young lady who resides apart from her relations, without any protector, by persons who otherwise may know nothing against her."[32]

Going to court was a last resort, and one not always looked upon favourably. It depended on the action and the circumstances. Breach-of-promise actions tended to evoke sympathy for the fiancée, though only within certain parameters. Juries, judges, and the public all knew perfectly well that the marriage prospects of jilted women were materially worse than those of jilting men, and holding to account men who casually cast aside young women was seen as a chivalric duty. Seduction complicated the picture, however, in ways harder to predict. For some, it confirmed rumours about a plaintiff's lack of virtue; for others, it greatly increased the force of the narrative of a helpless young woman ill-used by a rogue.[33] Libel actions were more difficult to predict, and were harder on women trying to recover their virtue, since court proceedings amplified any defamation and even a successful action could only with difficulty overcome the tendency of the public to believe the slander.[34] The *Quebec Gazette*, hostile to Ferguson during the litigation, used her case to voice an opinion about libel actions generally: "The fact is, these libel suits have come to be looked upon as poor shifts, either to mend a doubtful character or to obtain a good one … In most instances the motive is palpably vindictive."[35] Ferguson would have known some of this as she weighed her options; her lawyers would have filled her in on the rest. That she went forward despite the odds is an indication of her character, certainly, but also of her motives. The desire to punish those who had wronged her may have overridden a more coldly rational assessment of her chances.

The Actions

The situation in which Ferguson found herself at the end of 1853 – unsupported and unemployed, at odds with her mother, her engagement broken off, and with a small child – demanded action, and her response was both vigorous and comprehensive. Over the next several years, she pursued five main legal actions against three powerful men, designed to punish the perceived wrongs against her, to reclaim her good name, and to provide recompense in the form of damages. The actions against all three defendants intertwined as they made their separate ways through the court system. They were, moreover, covered in the press in Quebec City and beyond, side by side with news of hostilities in the Crimea, the trials of the Gavazzi rioters in Montreal, and the search for the lost ships of the Franklin Expedition.[36]

Ferguson brought her complaints to lawyer Charles Gates Holt, a family friend who would go on to a prominent career but who in 1853 had been in practice only nine years.[37] As in most cases, the archive is silent on the behind-the-scenes discussions and strategizing that turned Ferguson's feelings into legal actions. A letter to George Alford, however, written soon after the litigation began, hints at how she must have narrated her story: she was "determined to struggle through the trouble & misery brought on me by a heartless villain"; her case would allow Alford and others to judge "of the cruel manner in which I was deceived"; and, once the case was over, "I will leave Quebec forever – I have brought disgrace upon my family but they will never again be troubled by me."[38] Disgrace, heartlessness, cruelty, misery: this emotional language was characteristic of her correspondence with Alford and echoed mid-nineteenth-century sentimental conventions.[39] Her initial meetings with Holt would have begun with her narrating her experience in a similar tone, which the lawyer then had to translate into legally cognizable injuries and actions.

Ferguson launched her actions into a fluid legal environment in those years before the codification of Quebec private law in 1866 and civil procedure in 1867.[40] With few home-grown legal treatises and with case reporting in its infancy, lawyers had to work from their own experience and knowledge, supplemented by principles and precedents drawn mostly from French and English sources.[41] The nature of Ferguson's actions presented other challenges as well. The law of slander and libel in Quebec was an unsettled and unpredictable amalgam of ideas of moral injury and corroboration drawn from French civil law mingled with English ideas of malice and privilege. Breach of promise too was fluid and controversial, tied up as it was with both seduction (where certain presumptions applied) and contractual issues (themselves muddied by theological ideas about free consent to matrimony). I will treat the different actions together, since, for Ferguson, they were part of a coordinated campaign and overlapped in time.[42]

Ferguson first targeted the "gallant gay Lothario" James Patton, filing an action in breach of promise in Superior Court on 13 August 1853.[43] A few weeks later, on 7 September, she sued John Gilmour in defamation for his remarks that had provoked the breach. Then, on 23 September, she followed up with paternity proceedings against Patton. The broken promise was a logical place to start, since the other complaints flowed from that source. Once launched, however, the actions assumed their own varied momentums.

In the breach-of-promise case, Ferguson alleged in her declaration instituting the case that, on New Year's Day 1852, Patton had promised to marry her, and that though she remained ready to marry him and had indeed demanded on 1 November 1852 (around the time the child was born) that he follow through on his promise, he refused.[44] The pregnancy and the child were left aside in this action. Paternity had to be proved separately, but leaving out the paternity claim would also have ensured that Patton's behaviour would be aired in court, since the birth of a child led to a presumption that a promise of marriage had been breached (for a woman of irreproachable sexual reputation, at least).[45]

Patton responded through his lawyer, Charles Alleyn, at first with a blanket denial, but two weeks later he refined his position with a motion to dismiss the action.[46] He acknowledged the New Year's Day promise but claimed that he had subsequently learned that Ferguson was "a person of a loose, immoral & lewd character." Such claims were a recognized defence to an action in breach of promise, though condonation, by continuing to see the other party, would negate it.[47] In support, James alleged that, in 1849, Caroline been forced to leave a boarding house for dubious conduct; that before James knew her she had lived in Ste-Marie-de-Beauce and "was in the habit of driving about at night unattended by any other females with different young men, ... & that she hath publicly declared that she never saw the man yet that she could not seduce"; and that he had been unaware of an eight-year age difference between them (in fact, she was only six months older).[48] The motion was dismissed and the case set for trial. At some point, James made "a very liberal offer" to settle the case, but Caroline refused.[49]

In the meantime, Ferguson launched the other two actions. Both stood on their own merits, but were also closely related to the breach-of-promise action, and much of the evidence overlapped.

Details of the paternity action are few, since the case file is missing and the action was not covered in the newspapers. Caroline's allegation was that James had failed to fulfil his promise to care for her and the child, leaving her "destitute and without means." She sued for £327 10s. (£300 for future maintenance and support, the rest her lying-in expenses). She also sought writs of *capias ad respondendum* in this and the breach action, claiming that Patton was planning to leave Canada and should be detained pending trial.[50] Interestingly, he was jailed on the two writs the day the paternity action was launched and held overnight before being bailed out by his father.[51]

In the case against John Gilmour, key documents are missing, and so we must turn to newspaper coverage of the trial for the initial framing of the action. Ferguson alleged that, around 1 May 1852, "Mr. Gilmour had said, in the presence of third parties, that 'she was a w----, and that she had been kept by a gentleman in Montreal'; that in consequence of this statement by Mr. Gilmour, one Mr. James Patton to whom she was engaged, refused to marry her, and that she was otherwise greatly injured in her reputation."[52] She demanded the massive sum of £10,000 in damages for slander. For his defence, Gilmour retained George Okill Stuart, a suitably eminent counsel, who had been attorney general and would later be chief justice of Lower Canada.[53] Gilmour opted to deny everything, in order to avail himself of the English rule that a general denial allowed the defence to put the plaintiff's general character in play, in order to mitigate damages.[54] At trial, his lawyers would add other defences: that the private conversations were privileged, that the required (in French law) corroboration of a second witness to the slander was missing, that there had been no malice, and that the action had been initiated some fifteen months after the alleged conversation and so was prescribed.[55]

The paternity and slander actions proceeded quickly, while the breach-of-promise case got hung up on interlocutory questions over Ferguson's choice of a jury trial.[56] In November 1853, Ferguson's witnesses in the paternity case were deposed via *enquête* (in which testimony was taken down in writing in advance of trial, supervised by a presiding judge).[57] For reasons that are unclear, Patton failed to bring his own witnesses forward within the required month, so he was foreclosed and, on 8 April 1854, judgment was rendered against him. He was declared the child's father and ordered to pay Ferguson £27 10s. for her birth expenses and her maintenance of the boy up to the initiation of the case, and to pay £20 per year support until the child reached age fifteen, so long as he was in Ferguson's custody.[58] Patton filed an appeal immediately, an odd step, given his initial failure to pursue his case.

The main event in late 1853 was the slander trial. Once again Ferguson opted for a jury trial. Gilmour opposed her request for an all-English jury, a nuisance objection, since only one witness testified in French. The court allowed his opposition, but soon after the parties agreed to an English-only jury, and twelve anglophones were duly impanelled. The trial began on 30 November before Justice René-Édouard Caron. Public interest was intense, and spectators packed the courtroom throughout the three days.[59] Ferguson's lawyer, Charles Holt, stressed the severity of the allegations: defamation was "one of the meanest social vices" and, quoting the French author François Dareau, a poison for which no antidote is known. Ferguson, he said, was well aware of the difficulties in taking on so powerful a man, but she "was driven to it by the consciousness that her reputation was wholly lost unless she unhesitatingly afforded the man who had slandered her an opportunity of making good his charges before a Court of Justice."[60]

Ferguson's star witness was James Patton himself. He had been excluded from testifying in the breach of promise and paternity cases since he was a party, but, in the libel trial, Ferguson could get him on the record. He was forced to sit stony-faced while his love letters to Ferguson (which filled more than four long columns in the newspaper) were read in court, which "caused great laughter in which Judge, jury, Counsel and audience joined." His testimony culminated in the self-serving conclusion that "it was because she volunteered to become my Mistress that I refused to marry her." Gilmour himself appeared last, limited to answering yes or no to a list of twenty-three pre-established questions, all of which he denied.

For the defence, George Okill Stuart opened by declaring the entire proceeding a vexatious attempt to extort money from a wealthy man, asserting that "there never was a case more harassing or oppressive, more disreputable or unwarranted." His long line of witnesses began with James's father, Duncan Patton, whose testy performance was frequently interrupted by applause from the public at every perceived point scored by Ferguson's lawyer. He was followed by a number of witnesses testifying to Ferguson's "lightness" of character (in the language of the time). Since the defence had opened the character issue, Holt was able to rebut with character witnesses of his own.

On the final day, the two lawyers hammered home their points. Stuart stressed "at considerable length … the great danger and injustice of permitting persons of this character to come before a Court and claim the same regard and consideration as those who have no blemish upon their reputation." Holt followed, pointing to the power the defendant held over most of his witnesses, and how Duncan Patton had hunted up evidence for Gilmour (to which Patton shouted out a denial, prompting one of the jurors to ask the judge to silence him). Holt concluded with a stark picture for the jury of just what Ferguson had suffered: "But for the defendant, she might now have been an honored wife, her child legitimated, and her husband an industrious and useful member of society. The one grave error would have been repaired, and years of happiness might have been in store for her." Instead, "Her lover had deserted her and cared not if with her child she perished in the streets. Her friends would not come near her, there was hardly a soul with whom she could exchange the good offices of friendship, the peopled streets were a desert to her." In determining the amount of damages, he said, the jury should award enough to deter the wealthy from thinking they could slander with impunity.

After deliberating an hour and a quarter, the jury found that Ferguson was of generally good character and had lost her promised marriage as a result of Gilmour's malicious slander. They awarded her £600 damages, which was met with general applause. Because of the "extraordinary interest" the case had generated, the pro-Ferguson *Morning Chronicle* published a full trial transcript on 30 December, and reprinted it in pamphlet form a few days later – likely an attempt to neutralize the earlier anti-Ferguson transcript that had already appeared in the *Quebec Gazette*.[61]

Ferguson's relief was short-lived, since, on 16 January 1854, the Superior Court granted Gilmour's motion to set aside the jury verdict and ordered a new trial, on the grounds that the jurors had not established with sufficient certainty that the defendant had spoken the words alleged.[62] Once again, Ferguson opted for a jury trial and an English-only jury; once again Gilmour opposed the latter. When the second trial went ahead in October, the jury would be mixed French and English, which would have added to the costs, as was no doubt Gilmour's intention.

Meanwhile, in February 1854, the breach-of-promise trial began, with Justice Jean-François-Joseph Duval presiding over an English-only jury.[63] Aside from the circumstances of the promise and breach, the jury was also asked to assess the truth of the allegations of Ferguson's earlier "loose, immoral and lewd character."[64]

Ferguson focused during the trial on establishing the promise, using James Patton's letters and witnesses who had known of the relationship, including one who claimed that James had told him he could not marry Caroline because "he had got his eye on another lady."[65] Justice Duval disallowed any evidence about the birth of the child, however. Patton's lawyers probed Ferguson's reputation and relationships before the time of the promise, to establish grounds for his breaking off the engagement.

Charles Holt summed up for the jury by stressing that Ferguson was not trying "to ruin or oppress the Defendant, for now she had no other feeling left for him but contempt."[66] Rather, she was trying to make it clear to the public that "these calumnies were totally without foundation." Exemplary damages, Holt argued, would allow the jurors to "shew the light in which they viewed the base and heartless attempt made by the Defendant to blast the reputation of her whom he had deserted." Justice Duval helped Ferguson's cause by explicitly directing the jury that "not one of the witnesses produced by the defendant testified to anything approaching to the charge of lewdness and immorality attributed to the plaintiff." Taking the hint, the jury rejected the allegations of immorality, affirmed that a promise had been made and broken, and found that Ferguson had suffered damage to the tune of £1000. The foreman reported to the court the jury's regret that they could not award more, "which remark created considerable clapping and applause which lasted until suppressed by the order of the Court."

James Patton moved unsuccessfully to overturn the jury verdict, then appealed both his losses on 11 May. The paternity appeal was dismissed on 3 October 1854, and he requested permission to take the case to the Judicial Committee of the Privy Council. That seems to have been a mostly symbolic expression of his outrage, since the application was eventually discharged for lack of proper service.[67] The breach-of-promise appeal moved more slowly, but the Court of Queen's Bench dismissed it, too, in March 1855.[68]

If we return to the busy autumn of 1854, the second Gilmour slander trial began on 9 October before the mixed jury and Justice Duval, who knew the case well after having presided at the breach-of-promise trial the previous winter. Ferguson's team was augmented by Jean-Thomas Taschereau, who provided French pleadings for the French jurymen; for the defence, George Okill Stuart handled both languages himself.[69] While the issues and testimony were mostly the same as at the first trial, Justice Duval's charge, in contrast to Justice Caron's in round one, strongly favoured Gilmour, at least according to the pro-Ferguson *Morning Chronicle*.[70] Despite this, the jury took an hour and a half to find once again that Gilmour had spoken the words maliciously and that Ferguson's general reputation had been good. Unlike its predecessor, however, this jury denied that Ferguson had lost her marriage as a result. Still, they awarded her £500 damages for the injury to her reputation.[71]

Once again, Gilmour sought to overturn the verdict, and his expensive lawyer earned his fee by filing a detailed list of thirty-two grounds. In April 1855, the majority of the Superior Court agreed with him and dismissed Ferguson's action, citing absence of malice in a confidential conversation and lack of corroboration.[72] Ferguson appealed, and the case continued.

By this time, as the cases descended into repetition and procedural wrangling, the affair had "seemingly ... lost all interest with the public."[73] Ironically, however, newspaper coverage of this latter phase led to the opening of the third front in the war over Ferguson's virtue.

On 12 October 1854, the day after the second slander trial ended and fourteen months after Caroline began her first proceedings, a new paper, the *Quebec Observer*, weighed in on the case. Its founder, owner, and editor, Charles Roger, was a familiar and controversial face on the English-language news scene, having previously worked for both the *Morning Chronicle* and, at the time of the earlier phases of the litigation, the *Quebec Gazette*.[74] Roger decided to stir the pot. In his local edition of 12 October 1854, and again two days later in his weekly edition (intended for circulation beyond Quebec City, as far as the United States and the United Kingdom), he published a highly unflattering editorial about Ferguson and the Gilmour case, entitled "Love, Slander, Sentiment, Cupidity and Stupidity." His effort to drum up sales failed, and his paper folded a few months later. Not a single copy of any issue of the *Observer* seems to have survived, but the relevant passages from the article were reproduced in Ferguson's subsequent legal action:

> She is so pretty, so young, so intelligent, so accomplished, and so good-natured and the agent of her ruin is so cruel & unfeeling to the last degree for refusing to ally himself for life with one who has the reputation of allying herself with anybody and at any time, that the thinking people of Quebec are influenced by this second "Cleopatra" who is dying of an injury to her character, that injured character being her sole wealth ... She lived at various places and in various ways not only as a concubine but as something worse, if report speaks truly ... Inconstancy is considered a good reason for getting rid of a wife, and is it to be no reason for getting rid of a miss? ... Her intimacy with Patton was not the result of one false step ... The woman who loves is much to be pitied when injured, but she who merely gratifies a carnal appetite for profit is unworthy of it ... A common woman cannot love everybody but there are women who can be extravagantly amiable to many people.[75]

Even accounting for the pugilistic tone of nineteenth-century journalism, this was clearly libellous. It had the desired effect of reanimating the debates surrounding the cases, as competitors bemoaned the sorry state of journalism, at least as practised by Roger, but it also provoked Ferguson's legal team into immediate action.[76] She had Charles Holt launch two substantially identical libel suits against Roger, the first on 14 October for £500, the second two days later for £1000 (the higher amount presumably because of the broader reach of the weekly edition).[77]

Roger's fellow editors quickly distanced themselves from their "eccentric" *confrère*, who "pants for notoriety, and considers it cheap at any price."[78] The *Morning Chronicle*, in a long editorial, insinuated base motives: "the doughty Editor of the 'Observer' would not have exhibited such *chivalrous manliness* had this slandered lady had a father, brother, or other male relative to protect her; while on the other hand, he knows and we know whence his mercenary pen derives its support."[79] The last remark picks up earlier suggestions the *Chronicle* had made about links between Gilmour and Roger during the first slander trial, when Roger was reporting for the *Quebec Gazette*: though they "would not venture to insinuate that there is a *quid pro quo* … there is something 'passing strange' … in the earnestness with which Mr. Gilmour is defended."[80] The *Chronicle* was most clearly on Ferguson's side, but other papers too used the cases to comment on the state of general morality. Earlier in 1854, for example, the *Toronto Colonist* had praised the large damages award in the breach-of-promise case as making "fast young gentlemen very careful not to deceive 'confiding innocence' by promising that which they never mean to perform."[81]

Ferguson's witnesses in the two libel cases were deposed promptly over two days in late November 1854, while Roger's appeared on twelve days scattered from November 1854 to April 1855. Roger's strategy, through his lawyer, Thornton Rudolph Smith, was to go straight at Ferguson's reputation to ground a truth defence.[82] The defendant's witnesses testified mostly to hearsay about Ferguson's reputation: Justice William Collis Meredith reserved the objections of Ferguson's lawyers about testimony of "rumors and reports."[83] The defence also filed questions for Ferguson to answer (since she could not testify) that were so obviously prejudicial that the court ordered them withdrawn as having "a tendency to degrade the plaintiff."[84]

In April 1855, the same day as it overturned the jury verdict in the second Gilmour trial, the Superior Court dismissed Ferguson's first action against Charles Roger for insufficient evidence.[85] Ferguson appealed, and in May 1856 the Court of Queen's Bench substituted a judgment awarding her £250 damages.[86] The second *Roger* case wrapped up in July 1856 (why it took longer is unclear from the record). The Superior Court awarded Ferguson £20 damages plus costs (which were taxed at £21 5d.).[87]

Finally, in 1857, the last acts of the long saga played themselves out. On 10 March, the Court of Queen's Bench dismissed Ferguson's appeal seeking to reinstate the jury verdict in the second Gilmour trial.[88] Though Chief Justice Louis-Hippolyte Lafontaine dissented, the majority found the conversation in question to be self-evidently privileged, despite the questionable link with the business of the office. Justice Thomas Aylwin, writing for the majority, made it clear that what mattered were the norms and requirements of commerce, not Ferguson's feelings: "To hold the contrary, would be to put an end to all confidence between master and servant, to repeal the obligation of keeping his master's secrets incumbent upon every servant, and to abrogate the duty of making known all things which tend to the prejudice of the master and which it imports him to know. If this were permitted, universal distrust must prevail and commercial intercourse cease."[89] The majority professed themselves shocked, but what outraged the male judges was not Patton's seducing and then abandoning a young woman, nor even his continuing to visit her when he should have been in the office, but rather how Ferguson's attempt to engage his responsibility would affect the functioning of the male workplace. Justice Aylwin again:

> Such a verdict, if sustained, would be to punish the master for the misbehaviour of his clerk; to stifle the just complaints of an injured employer, even in his own private office, in order to listen to the application of a female, who having lost her virtue, yet presumes to come into Court to claim damages properly due to outraged innocence alone. It would encourage profligacy and debauchery among clerks and their lemans, by forbidding, under a penalty, the very mention of it to be made even in the most private recesses, however publicly practised. Such a verdict is immoral in its tendency and subverts the domestic relations; it rewards immodesty and incontinency, and hands over to female frailty the honest gains of labour and enterprise. It allows the servant to run riot, while it mulcts his employer for the vicious indulgence.[90]

The majority here silently set aside the jury's factual finding that Ferguson's reputation was good: to the male justices, "innocence" was required, and it mattered little whether she had lost her virtue or, as the jury found, it had been taken from her. They set out a clear hierarchy: (male) employer over (male) employee, and both over "female frailty." Commerce required honest remuneration for honest work: the courts could not allow women to pick the pockets of hard-working men.

The same day that the Court of Queen's Bench ruled, Ferguson lodged a request for permission to take the case to the Privy Council, but she never pursued that prohibitively expensive step.[91] Her final acts were a motion (denied) for coercive imprisonment against Charles Roger, who was slow to pay his damages,[92] and a request for *certiorari* (granted) to have the second *Roger* case file sent to the Court of Queen's Bench. The latter indicated that she was contemplating some further action, but details are lacking.[93]

And, with that, the case files go silent.

Results and Motivations

Ferguson showed notable persistence in this long campaign, given her relatively disadvantageous position compared to the powerful men she was pursuing. In the end, after early successes, she had mixed results legally, a reflection of the difficulties for litigants generally, and for women particularly. Overall, she had been awarded £1,297 10s., plus child support (excluding court costs). That was a fraction of her initial demand of £12,827 10s., but that total had been greatly inflated by the huge sum she had sought from Gilmour for the slander and was unlikely to be awarded in full.

A damages award had to be enforced, which could be challenging. We already saw that Ferguson had trouble getting Charles Roger to pay: whether, in the end, he did is unrecorded. Collecting the £1000 James Patton owed was even more involved. Even before the trial, she had sought to garnish whatever of Patton's property was in the hands of the Gilmour Company, but, because he no longer worked there, there was nothing to garnish.[94] In May 1855, after Patton's appeal had been dismissed and the £1000 damages award became final, Ferguson sought court ratification for a payment to Patton of £600 from the judgment; since no money had likely yet changed hands, this was effectively an offer to forgo that amount and settle for £400.[95] While the court considered this, negotiations continued. Patton seems to have countered with an undisclosed offer, which Ferguson accepted only when Patton's friend, merchant Henry Scarth Dalkin, agreed to chip in a further £30. Dalkin failed to pay, and she sued him in debt on 30 August.[96] In one of

Dalkin's filings, he made the revealing statement that he had promised "that if Duncan Patton did not pay her I would see her paid." James certainly did not have £1000 to satisfy the court judgment, but his father probably did, so it is not surprising to find that Duncan was behind the negotiations. Two days after Caroline filed the debt action, the Superior Court ratified a settlement between Caroline and James, its terms, as usual, undisclosed.[97]

While that final amount was not recorded, if Ferguson was willing at the start to give up £600, it must have been considerably less than the £1000 the court had awarded her. What might explain her willingness to agree to reduce a final judgment? She certainly needed the money: she was, after all, still liable for the court costs from the *Gilmour* action, which would have been considerable, as well as whatever she owed her own lawyer. Indeed, how she paid for all this remains a mystery: her lawyer hinted cryptically during the first Gilmour trial that she would have been "utterly ruined ... had she not in the hour of her distress, received the aid of one or two generous but unknown friends."[98] Various factors may have made settlement appealing: an unwillingness to spend further time and money trying to extract more from James; a strategic desire to close one front in the war to focus on the ongoing *Gilmour* and *Roger* cases; or relative satisfaction with the public exposure in the trial of James's perfidy.

A more compelling reason is suggested by a single document Ferguson filed in the Gilmour slander suit. On 13 June 1854, just after Patton had launched his appeals, Ferguson had gone to notary Louis Prévost in Quebec City to give her lawyer, Charles Holt, full power of attorney to act on her behalf. In one of the terms of the notarial act, she committed to assign to her son, James Ninian Conroy Patton, then aged about twenty months, any monies coming to her "by virtue of any judgment or judgments or otherwise howsoever."[99] Why she filed a copy of the act in the Gilmour trial is unclear, though it would have served to neutralize the defence's argument that her case was a simple shakedown of a wealthy man. But if we take it at face value, it suggests that her legal actions were about more than just reclaiming her own reputation.

The welfare of young James preoccupied her during this period. A letter from her aunt Mary Pozer, written in July 1854, indicates that Ferguson was shopping the boy around to relatives, trying to find him a suitable home.[100] When she was unsuccessful in placing the boy with her own relatives, she resorted to the other side of his lineage. Turning to the Pattons would mean giving up her child (and forgoing the child support James had been condemned to pay) but would open to him privileges of wealth she could not herself provide. Class standing was important to Ferguson: her later letters show her to be acutely conscious of arresting her family's downward slide by carefully policing how her younger children dressed and with whom they associated. In young James's case, Ferguson had pointedly emphasized his links to the Pattons by opting for "Ninian" – a Patton family name – as the boy's middle name.[101] The child's future was likely part of the negotiations surrounding James Patton's damages, and, in the end, an informal adoption is precisely what happened.[102] In the 1861 census, the boy is listed as a family member in Duncan Patton's household at St-Joseph-de-la-Pointe-Lévy, nine years old and attending school. With the boy well placed, Ferguson could focus on getting her own life back on track.

The question remains of Ferguson's reputation following her mixed legal success. Her experience is harder to assess than that of the male defendants she had pursued, who, unsurprisingly, were able to put the matter behind them and move forward with more or less successful lives and careers.

For James Patton, breaking his promise of marriage and leaving Ferguson with a child caused him few, if any, apparent problems. He married Margaret Ann Hamilton in 1856, had a large family, and went on to a long career in the timber industry. When he died in 1903 of septic blood poisoning, a hagiographic obituary described his military service and charitable work, but of course passed over in silence the sensational trials of the 1850s and his first-born son.[103] John Gilmour too continued to flourish, though twenty-five years after parrying Ferguson's action he met an unhappy end when he either fell or jumped into the St. Lawrence River near Montreal after a trusted associate ran off with a large sum of the firm's money.[104] Charles Roger's last years were rockier, but due more to his questionable ethics and the vagaries of the publishing industry than to his role in the Ferguson affair. After his *Quebec Observer* folded in 1855, he edited a few other short-lived papers, published historical and travel books, and ended up a civil servant in Ottawa before he died in 1889.[105]

As for Ferguson, the experience continued to affect her in ways typical of women forced to defend themselves against reputational attacks. Her letters are filled with evidence of striving for respectability in the face of the downward trajectory of her life that had begun even before she moved to the Pattons', as her options became fewer and she was forced into situations she otherwise might not have had to endure.

Indeed, that was the real effect of the slanders of the 1850s: her reputation, and her welfare generally, depended in large measure on men, not least the three defendants in the litigation.

In the end, she seems to have succeeded in reclaiming at least something of her respectability, though at a cost. Whether by choice or because her notoriety had made staying untenable, she left Quebec City, a place she loved. By 1861, she had been accredited as a school teacher and was living as a governess in the home of a Montreal newspaper publisher, whose wife was a friend or relation.[106] She married in 1863 at age thirty-five, something not all breach-of-promise plaintiffs were able to do. But after the promising courtships of her youth, she settled for Quebec City bookseller and stationer Peter Sinclair, a much older widower with two grown children. The marriage proved difficult and often unhappy: she twice brought assault charges against Sinclair's adult son, suffered some abuse at the hands of her husband, raised four children in Ottawa (which she hated) and Montreal, endured various health problems, and barely made ends meet running a boarding house (with regular support from George Alford) after Peter's business failed.[107] The contrast between her children is telling. While James entered a professional career (engineer and surveyor), she struggled to educate (and even at times to clothe) her younger children, who all ended up moving to the United States. Ferguson died of pneumonia in Montreal in 1902, and her body was transported back to Quebec City to be buried beside her husband.[108] Her obituary in the *Montreal Daily Star* noted that she was the "granddaughter of the late Mr. George Pozen, sr.," misspelled, but her family was making sure to publicize her well-to-do roots.[109]

Conclusion

Who was Caroline Jane Ferguson? Her court actions were, in a sense, a public attempt for her to regain control of her biography from the men who had sought to define her – James Patton, John Gilmour, and Charles Roger, most notoriously, but also the judges, lawyers, and jurors who had to assess and judge her. Her opponents depicted her as a calculating scarlet woman by floating stories of previous pregnancies, assignations alone with men behind closed doors or on evening rides in the country, and insinuations of being kept by shadowy wealthy men. Against that was an image of someone who was, in the language of the time, "light" or "free" in her behaviour, but generally respectable. Her lawyer, Charles Holt, painted an intriguing picture of her in his summing up at the first Gilmour trial, an attempt to win the jury with a frank depiction of a self-confidently assertive young woman. He acknowledged her "giddiness of character," but laid it partly at the feet of her parents: an absent father, a mother whose "harsh treatment" forced Caroline to look out for herself. While certainly not "a paragon of perfection," he said, "she was nothing more than a young, refined and educated woman, perhaps impetuous and headstrong, frank and affable in her manners, with no *mauvaise honte*, but speaking her mind freely; not one of those young misses who sat with their hands crossed and answered with 'Yes, Sir' or 'No, Sir,' but one who always meant what she said and was but too ready to believe that every body else did so too."[110]

The politics of reputation were complex in 1850s Quebec City, as indeed they always are. While women could be held to an almost unattainably high standard, Ferguson's experience shows that even a woman who did not fit the demure stereotype of the helpless female could garner public sympathy.[111] And Ferguson was far too resourceful to be helpless. While it is hard to separate her own input from her lawyer's strategizing, she seems to have been savvy enough to keep her interests soberly in view in an emotionally charged situation – her carefully saving James Patton's love letters while getting him to destroy hers is a good example. For all her contradictions, and despite the rumours and innuendos, she clearly won over the public in the jurors' box, in the courtroom, and in the press (Charles Roger excepted).

The courts, however, were an uncertain way to reclaim or repair a reputation. Those with a clean name had much to lose by amplifying the slander. For those with a questionable, doubtful, or otherwise problematic reputation – a spectrum along which Ferguson certainly fit – a trip to court could underscore the injustice of an attack by publicly exposing and, if successful, punishing the defendant, but it could just as easily backfire and confirm suspicions about the plaintiff. Ferguson's letters and later life reveal the strength of character that had helped her pursue the vigorous legal campaigns of her youth. That she regained a degree of respectability is affirmed by the life-long support she received from the eminently respectable George Alford. She got that rehabilitation outside the legal system, however, and the lingering effects of the slander on the course of her life show how women's virtue could be protected through the courts, but only up to a point.

In 1923, long after Ferguson and everyone else involved in the 1850s litigation was gone, an anonymous columnist for *La Patrie* resurrected the story for a causes-célèbres column, under the title "The Poison of Calumny."[112] The account favoured her side and modestly suppressed (almost) all mention of her pregnancy, but its very appearance so long after the fact made the author's point that, unlike chemical poisons, slander had no antidote.

NOTES

I am grateful for the helpful comments and suggestions of the participants at the pre-publication workshop, as well as those from Peter Gossage and Shannon McSheffrey.

1 Author's translation.

2 For later examples, see Constance Backhouse and Nancy L. Backhouse, *The Heiress vs the Establishment: Mrs. Campbell's Campaign for Legal Justice* (Vancouver: UBC Press for the Osgoode Society for Canadian Legal History, 2004); Bettina Bradbury, *Caroline's Dilemma: A Colonial Inheritance Saga* (Vancouver: UBC Press, 2020).

3 The Superior Court case files are: *Ferguson v. Gilmour* (no. 1554), Archives nationales à Québec (ANQ), TP11, S1, SS2, SSS1, cont. 1960-01-353/950; *Ferguson v. Patton* (no. 1172), ANQ, TP11, S1, SS2, SSS1, cont. 1960-01-353/769; *Ferguson v. Roger* (no. 1499), ANQ, TP11, S1, SS2, SSS1, cont. 1960-01-353/924; *Ferguson v. Roger* (no. 1509), ANQ, TP11, S1, SS2, SSS1, cont. 1960-01-353/929. The case file for *Ferguson v. Patton* (no. 1624) appears to be missing.

4 Franca Iacovetta and Wendy Mitchinson, eds., *On the Case: Explorations in Social History* (Toronto: University of Toronto Press, 1998); Mariana Valverde, J.R. Miller, Doug Owram, Shirley Tillotson, Bryan D. Palmer, Franca Iacovetta, and Wendy Mitchinson, "*On the Case: Explorations in Social History*: A Roundtable Discussion," *Canadian Historical Review* 81 (2000): 266–92. See also Natalie Zemon Davis, *Fiction in the Archives: Pardon Tales and Their Tellers in Sixteenth-Century France* (Stanford, CA: Stanford University Press, 1987).

5 See Eric H. Reiter, *Wounded Feelings: Litigating Emotions in Quebec, 1870–1950* (Toronto: University of Toronto Press for the Osgoode Society for Canadian Legal History, 2019).

6 Unless otherwise indicated, all biographical information comes from documents available on Ancestry.ca.

7 On the Pozers, see Louise Dechêne, "Pozer, George," *Dictionary of Canadian Biography* (*DCB*), vol. 7, http://www.biographi.ca/en.

8 Pozer Papers, Saint-Joseph-de-Beauce, Société du patrimoine des Beaucerons (cataloguing in progress), formerly McCord Museum, Montreal, especially P016-B2, folders 19–20. I learned of the letters through Nancy Christie, "A 'Painful Dependence': Female Begging Letters and the Familial Economy of Obligation," in *Mapping the Margins: The Family and Social Discipline in Canada, 1700–1975*, ed. Nancy Christie and Michael Gauvreau (Montreal and Kingston: McGill-Queen's University Press, 2004), 69–102. Christie discusses how Caroline and her mother cultivated Alford, but does not connect Caroline to the litigation that is my subject here.

9 Robert Campbell, *A History of the Scotch Presbyterian Church St. Gabriel Street, Montreal* (Montreal, 1887), 504–5.

10 "Law Intelligence," *Quebec City Morning Chronicle*, 5 December 1853, 2.

11 Several letters refer to the engagement – see, for example, Pozer Papers, Herbert Bell to George Alford, 19 June 1850.

12 Gwynneth C.D. Jones, "Gisborne, Frederic Newton," *DCB*, vol. 12, http://www.biographi.ca/en/bio/gisborne_frederic_newton_12E.html.

13 *Ferguson v. Patton* (no. 1172), case file, deposition of Donald Fraser for defendant, 17 February 1854, 1.

14 Courtney C.J. Bond, "Gilmour, John," *DCB*, vol. 10; John Rankin, *A History of Our Firm: Being Some Account of the Firm of Pollok, Gilmour and Co. and Its Offshoots and Connections 1804–1920*, 2nd ed. (Liverpool: Henry Young & Sons, 1921), 95–105. Two paintings of the Gilmour wharves at Indian Cove, commissioned in 1840 from artist Robert C. Todd, are on display at the National Gallery of Canada, Ottawa.

15 James Patton testified in *Ferguson v. Gilmour*. At the time, parties were barred from testifying on their own behalf, so he could not testify in his own cases, and Ferguson never directly gave her side of the story in any of the actions.

16 *Ferguson v. Gilmour*, case file, deposition of James Patton for plaintiff, 30 November 1853, 4.

17 *Ferguson v. Patton* (no. 1172), case file, deposition of James Walsh for defendant, 17 February 1854, 1–2.

18 Ibid., case file, deposition of James Patton for plaintiff, 30 November 1853, 4.

19 Ibid., deposition of Duncan Patton for defendant, 1 December 1853, 2.

20 Ibid., deposition of James Patton for plaintiff, 30 November 1853, 4.

21 The baptism record gives his birth as 7 November 1852; the church reception and later his military records from the First World War give 4 November.

22 *Supplement to the Quebec Morning Chronicle, Dec. 30th, 1853* (the transcript ends on page 4 of the regular paper of that day), p. 1, col. 3.

23 *Ferguson v. Patton* (no. 1172), case file, plaintiff's exhibit no. 1, copy of letter, James Patton to Caroline J. Ferguson (Berthier, 8 January 1853).

24 *Ferguson v. Gilmour*, case file, deposition of James Patton for plaintiff, 30 November 1853, 2.

25 What follows is based on *Ferguson v. Gilmour*, case file, deposition of George Railton for plaintiff, 30 November 1853, 1–2.

26 Ibid., deposition of James Patton for plaintiff, 30 November 1853, 2–3.

27 Ferguson's lawyers identified the shop owner, William Hamilton, as the source, but he denied it. "The Gilmour Slander Case," *Quebec City Morning Chronicle*, 19 December 1853, 2; "Ferguson vs. Gilmour," *Quebec Gazette*, 20 December 1853, 2.

28 Jacques Boucher, "L'histoire de la condition juridique et sociale de la femme au Canada français," in *Le droit dans la vie familiale: Livre centenaire du Code civil (I)*, ed. Jacques Boucher and André Morel (Montreal: Presses de l'Université de Montréal, 1970), 155–67; Bettina Bradbury, *Wife to Widow: Lives, Laws, and Politics in Nineteenth-Century Montreal* (Vancouver: UBC Press, 2011); Brian Young, *The Politics of Codification: The Lower Canadian Civil Code of 1866* (Montreal and Kingston: McGill-Queen's University Press for the Osgoode Society for Canadian Legal History, 1994), 141–56.

29 Henry Des Rivières Beaubien, *Traité sur les lois civiles du Bas-Canada*, 3 vols. (Montreal, 1832–33), 1:14, 1:46–55.

30 No copies are known to survive. See "The Scourge," *Quebec City Morning Chronicle*, 1 September 1853, 2 (quotation); letter to the editor, *Quebec Mercury*, 15 November 1856, 2; letter to the editor, *Quebec Mercury*, 18 November 1856, 23.

31 *Ferguson v. Gilmour*, case file, deposition of Duncan Patton for defendant, 1 December 1853, 2.

32 *Supplement*, p. 2, col. 5, testimony of Robert Chambers for plaintiff in rebuttal, during the first Gilmour trial.

33 Compare Ginger S. Frost, *Promises Broken: Courtship, Class, and Gender in Victorian England* (Charlottesville: University Press of Virginia, 1995); Alecia Simmonds, "'Promises and Pie-Crusts Were Made to Be Broke': Breach of Promise of Marriage and the Regulation of Courtship in Early Colonial Australia," *Australian Feminist Law Journal* 23 (2005): 99–120; and Saskia Lettmaier, *Broken Engagements: The Action for Breach of Promise of Marriage and the Feminine Ideal, 1800–1940* (Oxford: Oxford University Press, 2010).

34 For women and defamation actions in Massachusetts and Nova Scotia in a slightly earlier period, see Lyndsay M. Campbell, *Truth and Privilege: Libel Law in Massachusetts and Nova Scotia, 1820–1840* (Cambridge: Cambridge University Press for the Osgoode Society for Canadian Legal History, 2022), ch. 6.

35 "Libel Suits Dismissed," *Quebec Gazette*, 10 April 1855, 2.

36 I have found a hundred articles on the various cases (including some reprints). The bulk of the coverage was in Quebec City's English papers: the *Quebec City Morning Chronicle* (thirty-one articles), the *Quebec Mercury* (eighteen), and the *Quebec Gazette* (eighteen). (As we will see below, the *Quebec Observer* extensively covered the case during its short run, but no copies are known to survive.) French-language coverage was minimal, in the *Journal de Québec* (three), the Montreal paper *Le Pays* (two), and a reprint article in *L'ère nouvelle* of Trois-Rivières. Other Montreal papers occasionally picked up the story (nine articles in the *Montreal Herald*; two in the *Montreal Gazette*), as did papers in Toronto, the United States, and as far away as Belfast, Ireland.

37 Holt was called to the bar in 1844, became Queen's counsel in 1863, was *bâtonnier* of the Quebec City bar in 1864, and became a judge of the Court of Sessions of the Peace in 1879, though he died nine months after his elevation: Pierre-Georges Roy, *Les avocats de la region de Québec* (Lévis: Le Quotidien, 1936), 219. His partner, George Irvine, played little direct role in these cases: Roy, *Les avocats*, 225; Jean Hamelin and Michel Paquin, "Irvine, George," *DCB*, vol. 12.

38 Pozer papers, letter, Caroline Jane Ferguson to George Alford, n.d. [soon after 8 November 1853], 1. The letter refers specifically to the breach-of-promise action.

39 On a slightly later period, see Sophie Doucet, "Sur le chemin du paradis: Les joies d'aimer, de croire et de s'accomplir de Marie-Louise Globensky (1849–1919)," *Revue d'histoire de l'Amérique française* 70 (2017): 5–29.

40 Young, *Politics of Codification*; Jean-Maurice Brisson, *La formation d'un droit mixte: L'évolution de la procédure civile de 1774–1867* (Montreal: Thémis, 1986).

41 Sylvio Normand, "Les débuts de la littérature juridique québécoise, 1767–1840," in *Essays in the History of Canadian Law*, vol. 11, *Quebec and the Canadas*, ed. G. Blaine Baker and Donald Fyson (Toronto: University of Toronto Press for the Osgoode Society for Canadian Legal History, 2013), 96–130; Sylvio Normand, "Legal Publishing in Quebec," in *History of the Book in Canada*, vol. 2, *1840–1918*, ed. Yvan Lamonde, Patricia Lockhart-Fleming and Fiona A. Black (Toronto: University of Toronto Press, 2005), 414–17; Raymonde Crête, Sylvio Normand, and Thomas Copeland, "Law Reporting in Nineteenth-Century Quebec," *Journal of Legal History* 16 (1995): 147–71.

42 Gaps in the surviving sources limit some of the detail. Most of the records of the second Gilmour slander trial and the paternity case are missing, for example, as seems to be the case too for all the appellate case files.

Reported judgments and the *plumitif* (the register of court proceedings) help somewhat, but still leave significant gaps.

43 "Breach of Promise of Marriage," *Quebec City Morning Chronicle*, 20 February 1854, 2.

44 *Ferguson v. Patton* (no. 1172), case file, declaration, filed 1 September 1853.

45 The law in this area was unclear at the time: see Philip Girard, Jim Phillips, and R. Blake Brown, *A History of Law in Canada*, vol. 1, *Beginnings to 1866* (Toronto: University of Toronto Press for the Osgoode Society for Canadian Legal History, 2018), 699–701.

46 *Ferguson v. Patton* (no. 1172), case file, defense *au fonds en fait*, filed 19 September 1853, and perpetual exception *péremptoire en droit*, filed 3 October 1853. Alleyn served as mayor of Quebec City in 1854, in the midst of the litigation, and went on to various provincial cabinet posts: Marcel Plouffe, "Alleyn, Charles Joseph," *DCB*, vol. 11.

47 Des Rivières Beaubien, *Traité*, 1:26–27.

48 *Ferguson v. Patton* (no. 1172), case file, defense *au fonds en fait*, filed 19 September 1853); ibid., perpetual exception *péremptoire en droit*, filed 3 October 1853).

49 Ibid., deposition of David Melrose for plaintiff, 17 February 1854, 1.

50 *Ferguson v. Patton* (no. 1624), declaration, filed as defendant's exhibit B in *Ferguson v. Patton* (no. 1172), case file.

51 Quebec Prison Register, Admissions, ANQ, E17, S1, P5, vol. 5, fol. 224, 23–24 September 1853. I thank Donald Fyson for this reference. See also *Ferguson v. Patton* (no. 1172), case file, notice of special bail, filed 20 October 1853.

52 *Supplement*, p. 1, col. 1.

53 Kenneth S. Mackenzie, "Stuart, George Okill," *DCB*, vol. 11, http://www.biographi.ca/en/bio/stuart_george_okill_1807_84_11E.html.

54 Cited by Justice Caron in his charge to the jury: *Supplement*, p. 4, col. 2. See Thomas Starkie, *A Treatise on the Law of Slander and Libel*, 2nd ed., 2 vols. (London, 1830), 2:87–9.

55 *Supplement*, p. 2, cols. 2–3.

56 *Ferguson v. Patton* (1853), 4 L.C. Rep. 383 (Sup. Ct.).

57 A copy of the depositions was filed in *Ferguson v. Patton* (no. 1172).

58 The judgment (unreported) is entered in *Ferguson v. Patton* (no. 1624), *plumitif*, ANQ, TP11, S1, SS2, SSS7, cont. 1980-09-026/2945 (1854, vol. 6).

59 "Law Intelligence," *Quebec City Morning Chronicle*, 5 December 1853, 2.

60 This and the quotations in the following three paragraphs come from *Supplement*, p. 1 cols. 1–2 and 7, p. 2 cols 1–2 and 6, and p. 4 col. 1.

61 "Law Intelligence," *Quebec Gazette*, 17 December 1853, 2; "Ferguson vs Gilmour," *Quebec City Morning Chronicle*, 30 December 1853, 2 (quotation); *Supplement*, reprinted as *A Full and Accurate Report of the Celebrated Slander Case of Ferguson vs. Gilmour* (Quebec City: Morning Chronicle, 1854). The *Gazette*'s report omitted the love letters and Duncan Patton's outbursts, and ended with a lengthy discussion of Gilmour's motion to overturn the jury verdict, which the *Chronicle* did not include. (The 1853 issues of the *Gazette* are available only at the National Archives, Kew, UK, CO 47/40. These are copies that were sent to the Colonial Office.)

62 *Ferguson v. Gilmour* (1854), 4 L.C. Rep. 57, 4 R.J.R.Q. 64 (Sup. Ct.).

63 "Law Intelligence," *Quebec City Morning Chronicle*, 24 February 1854, 1.

64 *Ferguson v. Patton* (no. 1172), case file, notes of trial proceedings and verdict of the jury, filed 18 February 1854, 2.

65 Ibid., certified copy of notes of evidence taken before the jury, filed 18 February 1854), and deposition of John Harvey for plaintiff, 17 February 1854, 1.

66 The following quotations are from "Law Intelligence," *Quebec City Morning Chronicle*, 24 February 1854, 1.

67 Court of Queen's Bench, Register of Judgments, vol. 11, pp. 677 and 681, Archives nationales à Montréal, TP9, S2, SS5, SSS11, cont. 2009-06-001/326 (QB Register).

68 "Law Intelligence," *Montreal Herald*, 26 March 1855, 2. Justice Thomas Cushing Aylwin dissented.

69 "Ferguson vs. Gilmour," *Quebec City Morning Chronicle*, 12 October 1854, 2. This is the only mention of Taschereau's participation in the case. At the time, he was the only lawyer in that prominent family who was not (yet) on the bench: Roy, *Les avocats*, 423–4.

70 "Ferguson vs. Gilmour," *Quebec City Morning Chronicle*, 12 October 1854, 2.

71 Ibid.

72 *Ferguson v. Gilmour* (1855), 5 L.C. Rep. 145; 4 R.J.R.Q. 74 (Sup. Ct.). Justice William Collis Meredith dissented.

73 *Quebec City Morning Chronicle*, 11 October 1854, 2.

74 Frederick H. Armstrong, "Roger, Charles," *DCB*, vol. 12. The *Observer* began publishing in April 1854.

75 Quoted in *Ferguson v. Roger* (no. 1509), case file, writ and declaration, 16 October 1854, 2–4 (parenthetical comments relating to the litigation omitted).

76 "Miss Caroline J. Ferguson and 'The Quebec Observer'," *Quebec City Morning Chronicle*, 17 October 1854, 2; "Miss Caroline Ferguson vs. Charles Roger, Editor of the Quebec Observer," *Quebec Gazette*, 17 October 1854, 2;

"Miss Ferguson and the *Observer*," *Quebec City Morning Chronicle*, 19 October 1854, 2 (reprinted 21 October in the *Quebec Gazette*); Anti-Haynau, letter to the editor, *Quebec City Morning Chronicle*, 25 October 1854, 2.

77 The first action was *Ferguson v. Roger* (no. 1499); the second was *Ferguson v. Roger* (no. 1509).

78 "Miss Caroline Ferguson vs. Charles Roger, Editor of the Quebec Observer," *Quebec Gazette*, 17 October 1854, 2.

79 "Miss Ferguson and the *Observer*," *Quebec City Morning Chronicle*, 19 October 1854, 2.

80 "The Gilmour Slander Case," *Quebec City Morning Chronicle*, 19 December 1853, 2. Roger is mentioned as reporting from the courtroom in "Ferguson vs. Gilmour," *Quebec Gazette*, 20 December 1853, 2.

81 Reprinted in *Quebec Morning Chronicle*, 8 March 1854, 2. See also (among others) "Breach of Promise of Marriage – Heavy Damages," *Ottawa Citizen*, 25 February 1854, 2; "Heavy Damages for Breach of Marriage Promise!" *Pittsfield (MA) Sun*, 2 March 1854, 2; untitled, *Kenosha (WI) Telegraph*, 24 March 1854, 1; untitled, *Belfast (Ireland) News Letter*, 3 April 1854, 4.

82 Roy, *Les avocats*, 409. He was assisted by Charles Secretan Jr. (403).

83 *Ferguson v. Roger* (no. 1509), case file, depositions of defence witnesses.

84 *Ferguson v. Roger* (no. 1499), case file, transcript on first appeal (1857), 5.

85 Ibid., 7–8; *Quebec City Morning Chronicle*, 10 April 1855, 2 (reprinted 12 April 1855 in the *Quebec Mercury* and 16 April 1855 in the *Montreal Herald*).

86 QB Register, 11: 169.

87 *Ferguson v. Roger* (no. 1509), case file, judgment (8 July 1856, Bowen CJ, Meredith and Morin JJ); Bill of Costs (Exhibit 2), filed 24 November 1856.

88 *Ferguson v. Gilmour* (1857), 1 L.C.J. 131, 4 R.J.R.Q. 79 (QB). "Court of Appeals," *Quebec City Morning Chronicle*, 11 March 1857, 2; "Court of Appeals," *Quebec Gazette*, 12 March 1857, 2.

89 *Ferguson v. Gilmour* (1857), 1 L.C.J. 131 at 136 (QB).

90 Ibid., 137. "Leman," already archaic at the time, means paramour or mistress: *Oxford English Dictionary*, s.v.

91 QB Register, 11: 314.

92 "Libel Suit," *Quebec City Morning Chronicle*, 19 March 1857, 2 (reprinted 19 March in the *Quebec Mercury*, 23 March in the *Montreal Herald*, and 24 March in the *Montreal Gazette*).

93 QB Register, 11: 388, 392, referring to *Ferguson v. Roger* (no. 1509); the case file contains nothing after 1856.

94 *Ferguson v. Patton* (no. 1172), case file, *præcipe* for writ of *saisi arrêt*, issued 13 January 1854, and declaration of John Gilmour garnishee, filed 24 January 1854.

95 Ibid., motion for *acte* (filed 4 May 1855).

96 *Ferguson v. Dalkin*, case file, ANQ, TP11, S1, SS2, SSS1, cont. 1960-01-353/1208 (no. 2230), and *plumitif*, ANQ, TP11, S1, SS2, SSS7, cont. 1980-09-026/2955 (1855, vol. 8).

97 *Ferguson v. Patton* (no. 1172), *plumitif*, ANQ, TP11, S1, SS2, SSS7, cont. 1980-09-026/2951 (1855, vol. 4). *Ferguson v. Dalkin* was withdrawn by mutual consent on 4 December.

98 *Supplement*, p. 4, col. 1. No hint of their identity survives. Though the crime of maintenance barred the funding of litigation for others, an exception was recognized for charitable assistance: John Henry Willan, *A Manual of the Criminal Law of Canada* (Quebec City, 1861), 44.

99 *Ferguson v. Gilmour*, case file, procuration and letter of attorney, 13 June 1854, no. 4962, notary Louis Prévost. The *plumitif* does not record when the copy was filed in the case.

100 Pozer papers, letter, Mary Pozer to Caroline Jane Ferguson, 5 July 1854.

101 By his other middle name (Conroy), Ferguson similarly sought to connect him to a potential supporter: his godfather Robert Conroy, timber merchant and future mayor of Aylmer, Quebec. Advantageous associations like this were common, and reciprocity was expected: Sherry Olson and Patricia Thornton, *Peopling the North American City: Montreal 1840–1900* (Montreal and Kingston: McGill-Queen's University Press, 2011), 88.

102 Before Quebec allowed formal adoptions in 1924, informal placements were common: Dominique Goubau and Claire O'Neill, "L'adoption, l'église et l'état: Les origines tumultueuses d'une institution légale," in *L'évolution de la protection de l'enfance au Québec: Entre surveillance et compassion*, ed. Renée Joyal (Sainte-Foy: Presses de l'Université du Québec, 2000), 97–130, esp. 100–4. Beyond Quebec, see Veronica Strong-Boag, *Finding Families, Finding Ourselves: English Canada Encounters Adoption from the Nineteenth Century to the 1990s* (Don Mills, ON: Oxford University Press, 2006), 9–16.

103 "The Late Major James Patton J.P.," *Quebec Chronicle*, 22 August 1903, 5.

104 Rankin, *A History*, 109–10; "A Most Mysterious Affair," *Montreal Daily Witness*, 27 February 1877, 3; "The Search for Mr. Gilmour," *Montreal Daily Witness*, 3 March 1877, 3; "A Mystery Solved," *Montreal Daily Witness*, 26 June 1877, 8; "Inquest on the Body of the Late John Gilmour, Esq.," *Montreal Daily Witness*, 27 June 1877, 8.

105 Armstrong, "Roger, Charles"; "An Old Citizen Gone," *Ottawa Evening Journal*, 27 July 1889, 1. Ironically, among his books was *The Rise of Canada, from Barbarism to Wealth and Civilisation*, published in 1856 during Ferguson's libel action by her future husband, Peter Sinclair.

106 *Journal de l'instruction publique* 5, no. 6 (June 1861): 99; 1861 census, Montreal, district 32, household of Donald McDonald. Both of these sources refer to "Jessie C. Ferguson," a name Caroline used from time to time.

107 Her letters detail this period of her life. The assault charges are in ANQ, TL31, S1, SS1, nos. 147271–72 (15 November 1864) and nos. 62842–43 (21 November 1866); I thank Donald Fyson for these references. Resorting to running a boarding house was typical of women of her social position: Bettina Bradbury, "Pigs, Cows, and Boarders: Non-Wage Forms of Survival Among Montreal Families, 1861–91," *Labour/Le travail* 14 (1984): 32–41.

108 "Mrs. Peter Sinclair," *Montreal Gazette*, 8 December 1902, 9; Gordon A. Morley and William J. Park, *Mount Hermon Cemetery Quebec City Tombstone Inscriptions*, 2nd ed. (Quebec City: Société de généologie de Québec, 2007), Q-30.

109 "The Late Mrs. Sinclair," *Montreal Daily Star*, 8 December 1902, 7.

110 *Supplement*, p. 4, col. 1.

111 Ginger Frost emphasizes women's dual aspect in breach-of-promise cases, combining elements of helplessness and initiative: Frost, *Promises Broken*, 27.

112 "Le poison de la calomnie," *La Patrie (Montreal)*, 17 February 1923, 15 (author's translation).

2

A Cause Célèbre: Marriage, Quebec Law, and the Delpit Affair of 1901

MÉLANIE MÉTHOT

Attracting the attention of newspapers around the world, the 1901 Delpit case gained the status of cause célèbre. An analysis of the social, legal, religious, and personal discourses surrounding this case reveals many of the tensions and debates within Quebec and Canadian society concerning religion, marriage, and the law, as well as the way power relations worked themselves out when a marriage came apart. The Delpit case left a mark on Quebec's jurisprudence, although, for many years, judges in the *belle province* didn't follow its precedent.

Legal cases, whether they were won or lost, publicized or forgotten, can shine light on both the historical context framing the case and its human dimensions, as Constance Backhouse has shown.[1] Told as stories, case studies draw readers in and simultaneously illuminate important aspects of society. The Delpit case reveals multiple stories, all interconnected: first, the personal and familial experience of marital breakdown, especially for those with less power in the marriage; second, prevailing social views of marriage that lauded paternalistic protection yet aided patriarchal control; and third, how debates about religion and marriage prompted social and political conflict that spoke to English-French tensions in Canada, as well as religious ones.

Divorce, Annulment, and Separation from Bed and Board: Ending a Marriage in Quebec

On 17 March 1900, Édouard Delpit wrote to the Quebec ecclesiastical tribunal requesting an annulment on the grounds that he and his spouse, both Catholics, had been married by a Protestant minister.[2] Although his young wife, Jeanne Côté, had no desire to continue living with him, she did not want their marriage voided. She responded by petitioning Montreal Superior Court for a separation from bed and board.[3] Upon agreement between Côté and Delpit, those proceedings were halted until the ecclesiastical tribunal reached a verdict on the status of the marriage.[4] In December 1900, the Vatican declared the 1893 union void and null, with each party free to remarry. In January 1901, Édouard then asked the Superior Court to rescind the civil effects of the void marriage. Superior Court judge John Sprott Archibald wrote a lengthy decision explaining why he went against the ecclesiastical tribunal and declared the Delpit-Côté marriage valid. Archibald's decision exhaustively discussed the history of marriage law in the British Empire and, more specifically, in Canada, both before and after Confederation. The *Montreal Weekly Witness* enumerated fifteen points of the judgment, including the fact that there was no established church in Canada, that the law relating to marriage had been enacted without reference to religious beliefs, and that the Quebec *Civil Code* did not require a religious ceremony to validate a marriage. Archibald articulated a concept that infuriated ultramontanes: "Marriage is a civil contract."[5]

Defeated, Édouard moved to the United States, determined to obtain a divorce from Jeanne and secure the custody of their three children. Jeanne and her counsel applied for custody, but in vain, as her children had already been removed from Canada. According to newspapers, Jeanne restarted the proceedings for a separation from bed and board in August 1901.[6] Despite all the moral support from the press and the financial backing of the Protestant Ministerial Association, Jeanne never saw her children again. She died poor in 1926 as the widow Delpit; she never accepted Rome's verdict.

The Delpit case is situated within the complicated legal context of marriage and divorce in Quebec. If contemporaries understood or accepted that the Delpit spouses wanted to put an end to their cohabitation, they often confused the options available to the young couple. According to the 1866 *Civil Code of Lower Canada*, the dissolution of a marriage could happen only when one of the spouses died. At Confederation, the federal Parliament received jurisdiction over marriage and divorce, but the *Civil Code* continued to regulate marriage in Quebec. Ill-suited couples could petition Ottawa for the dissolution of their union through a private act of Parliament.[7] Constance Backhouse notes that Catholic legislators representing Quebec silently voted against some divorce petitions, but when they came across Catholic couples seeking to break their matrimonial bonds, they voiced their opposition loudly.[8] Divorces were thus off limits for Catholics living in Quebec. Because a Unitarian minister had performed the marriage service for Édouard and Jeanne, the young man could have tried his luck at the federal level. It appears he had the means to pay the prohibitive costs,[9] but he could not accuse his wife of adultery, which was, in effect, the only grounds for dissolution of marriage.[10] If Édouard had the means but no grounds, subsequent events reveal that Jeanne had grounds but no means.

While divorces were unattainable for Catholic spouses, couples could ask the ecclesiastical tribunal for an annulment. Social historian Serge Gagnon stresses that separations were exceptional in Ireland and in Quebec, both Catholic nations.[11] In *La dissolution du lien matrimonial en droit canonique et en droit civil canadien*, Mgr. Lucien Beaudoin explained that "divorce is the breaking of the bond of a validly contracted and consummated marriage between Christians." In the case of an annulment, "the marriage could not exist because the substantive and formal conditions necessary for the validity of the marriage were not met by both spouses, or at least by one of the spouses."[12] Some of the religious conditions corresponded to those included in the *Civil Code*, such as age, consent of the parents, and consent of the parties given in front of two witnesses, but, at the time, canon law also required that the marriage be celebrated by one of the spouses' parish priests.[13] Édouard took the annulment route because it was the only one available to him. Refusing to accept that the ecclesiastical tribunal could nullify her marriage, Jeanne turned to Montreal Superior Court and asked for a separation from bed and board. Fewer than 250 Montreal couples chose that path between 1795 and 1879, but Quebec historian Marie-Aimée Cliche found that the number increased substantially between 1900 and 1939. She attributes the growth to the increased financial autonomy of working wives.[14]

Divorce, annulment, and separation from bed and board involved very different processes and resulted in distinct situations. In Quebec, married couples had the obligation to live together. To put an end to a difficult situation, especially in cases of repeated violence or adultery, individuals (mostly women) asked the Superior Court for the right to live separately and to split the *communauté de biens*.[15] Obtaining a separation from bed and board did not dissolve the union – hence, individuals could not embark on another matrimonial adventure. The only way Catholics living in Quebec could remarry before the death of a spouse was to obtain an annulment. Montreal's judicial district saw eighty-three annulments between 1900 and 1939.[16]

The Slender Historiography of the Delpit Case

A decade after the Delpit case sparked the passions of Canadians, E.M. Sait, professor of politics at Columbia University, emphasized its significance for Quebec and Canadian politics and society: "[It is] through the force of its argument and its reliance on broad principles of law that *Delpit v Côté* will leave its impress upon the jurisprudence of the future. The slowly developing spirit of anti-clericalism has begun to make itself felt upon the bench."[17] If students of Canadian history are familiar with the Guibord affair – which also involved a conflict between the church and secularism – few have heard of the Delpit case, despite jurists having discussed its impact.[18] While some scholars saw the case as a turning point, others refused to recognize its importance. Thirty years after Judge Archibald legally recognized the validity of the Delpit marriage, despite the ecclesiastical tribunal's having declared it null, Judge C.E. Dorion professed, "Civil marriage does not exist, and these words have never been pronounced in our courts; but some recent judgments, by an abusive interpretation, have introduced it without naming it." Dorion concluded: "Marriage remains a religious marriage, subject to the articles of the Civil Code, and, by virtue of these articles, also subject to the discipline of each church."[19]

In 1940, French-Canadian historian Robert Rumilly devoted eight pages to the court case, justifying its inclusion in his opus *Histoire de la Province de Québec* because "the case lay the groundwork for a series of similar trials, which will resound throughout the country." Rumilly argued that the Vatican devised the decree *Ne Temere* (1907), which reinforced the Council of Trent's prescriptions on the sacramental nature of marriage, in part because of the Delpit affair. He briefly mentioned the spouses but quickly turned his attention to the skilled lawyers who argued the case, the intelligent judge who ruled in favour of civil marriage, and the sentiments of the governing elite, who sided with the shocked Montreal archbishop. According to Rumilly, Quebec politicians sensed that the Delpit case threatened provincial jurisdiction almost as much as it did ecclesiastical jurisdiction.[20] Other historians concentrate on the church's attitude in the case. Jean Hamelin and Nicole Gagnon describe the clergy's intransigence, explaining how the Quebec clergy held that civil law was limited to sanctioning marriages performed according to the rules of the confession to which the spouses belonged. They argue that the Delpit-Côté case contested nineteenth-century jurisprudence, which had endorsed the church's interpretation, emphasizing how Protestant ministers refused to accept that Rome had power to invalidate a marriage celebrated by one of their own.[21]

More recently, in the conclusion of his monograph on nineteenth-century marriage in Quebec, Serge Gagnon briefly mentions the case but fails to explain its relevance.[22] Also failing to consider the wider context, philosophers Jocelyn Maclure and Charles Taylor refer to the Catholic Church's efforts to exercise temporal power in Quebec and cite the decisions in both the Guibord and Delpit affairs to show how the state succeeded in opposing religious powers. They misuse the cases to contend that the *British North America Act* affirms the independence of state and church.[23]

In his excellent review article on marital status and impediments in Quebec, Michel Morin demonstrates that, despite three distinct judgments on the right of a Protestant minister to marry two Catholics, a 1912 legal clarification by the Supreme Court of Canada, and the 1921 Privy Council decision in *Malvina Despatie v. Napoléon Tremblay*, the Catholic Church continued to exercise great power in Quebec in relation to marriage.[24] Although the Judicial Committee of the Privy Council cited the Delpit affair in its judgments, the Quebec judiciary continued to ignore it for a long time. Nevertheless, the marital woes of Édouard and Jeanne shed light on social, religious, and legal understandings of marriage at the beginning of the twentieth century in Quebec.

In this chapter, I shine the spotlight on Édouard and Jeanne and their family, analysing media coverage of their marital troubles in over 500 news items, editorials, letters to the editor, and commentaries.[25] By focusing on the elites or the law, scholars miss the opportunity to explore what marriage meant to individuals. Examining extensive textual sources, I dissect social attitudes and uncover some of the more personal consequences of marriage dissolution. The Delpit affair tells us much about Catholic-Protestant and French-English relations, as well as debates about who qualified as Catholic in terms of marriage law, but it also reveals strongly felt emotions and views about marriage, divorce, and annulment at the time.

In 1901, Montreal printer Charles Hébert published two pamphlets about the Delpit case, one in French, the other in English, both containing "the narration of facts, a dissertation on marriage laws of the Province of Quebec, all the documents of the civil and ecclesiastical courts, the original text of ecclesiastical sentence of Quebec and Rome, ecclesiastical enquête, judgement in extenso of Judge Archibald."[26] In addition to the newspaper coverage and the pamphlets, my analysis centres on two pastoral letters, Jeanne's and Édouard's letters published in newspapers, as well as the Delpit annulment case file held at the Vatican, the description of the content of an annulment file held at the Propaganda Fide Historical Archives, and the case files of Jeanne's request for a separation from bed and board and of Édouard's divorce, which was secured in Nebraska.

The plot unfolds in five acts. In Act 1, after hearing from the spouses and multiple witnesses, Mgr. Marois declared the Delpit-Côté marriage null on the ground of "clandestinity." Jeanne appealed to Rome, but the Vatican confirmed the decision, revealing how the Catholic Church exercised considerable control over its flock, but at the same time, how some individuals followed canonical rules out of convenience rather than as an act of faith. In Act 2, the *Montreal Weekly Witness* led a campaign against Édouard and the Catholic Church. The press coverage highlights the patriarchal nature of society, with husbands having a responsibility to take care of their wives, who in turn expected respect, companionship, and some authority over their children. More than anything else, the press stories indicated that Jeanne wanted to fulfil her motherly role and yearned to receive her children's love and respect. Notions of "race" seep through the press discourse, highlighting French-Canadian and British nationalisms. Archbishop Paul Bruchési took centre stage in Act 3, first threatening two newspapers with censorship for having made statements he deemed anti-religious, and then issuing two pastoral letters on the sanctity of marriage. It is clear that the church had great influence over its brethren, but it also faced resistance, both from within and from an increasing mixed-religious population. While other scholars focus on the intransigence of a Catholic Church that was always intent on imposing its own doctrine, I present a more nuanced portrait of Archbishop Bruchési. The cleric proclaimed that, although the ecclesiastical tribunal had the right and duty to define and regulate marriage, individuals alone were responsible for following the canonical rules. He also pointed out that the church could not regulate the civil aspects linked to the annulment of marriage, such as alimony. The archbishop acknowledged that the civil courts had the power to deal with such issues. In Act 4, I turn the investigative light on Jeanne and Édouard, who both published letters in the local press about their marital woes.[27] The final act deals with the Archibald decision and its aftermath. English newspapers celebrated the judgment; among the French press, a few ultramontane pundits criticized the Protestant judge for refusing to bow to the ecclesiastical tribunal, yet others remained neutral or even endorsed the judgment.

The Ecclesiastical Tribunal: *Baptisé Catholique, Catholique Toujours*

Before analysing documents related to the ecclesiastical trial, it is worth establishing what we know about the main protagonists. The Delpit affair revolves around Édouard Delpit, his wife, Jeanne Côté, and their three children, Joseph (six, at the time of the tribunal), Louise (four) and Marie (two). Grandson of a rich Louisiana tobacco dealer, son and nephew of successful French novelists, older brother to five siblings, among them Louise Delpit, the future professor of French at Smith, the elite women's college in Massachusetts, Édouard Delpit arrived in New York from France in 1888 and made his way to Manitoba.[28] The following year, aged eighteen, he successfully passed the qualifying examination for the Canadian civil service.[29]

In Montreal, Édouard ran the short-lived *L'Opinion Publique*. Within a few weeks of its birth, the paper charged *L'Étendard*, one of Quebec's ultramontane dailies, with "great disservice," stating that the newspaper was falsely accusing Delpit's weekly of being an enemy of the church. The young journalist felt the need to affirm his newspaper's Catholicism with a libel threat.[30] Although Édouard asserted his newspaper's Catholic orientation, he married as a Protestant. With the blessing of the parents of the bride, Minister Barnes joined in matrimony the twenty-three-year-old journalist and sixteen-year-old Jeanne Berthe Côté. Montreal dailies announced the happy event.[31] Despite marrying in a Protestant church, the young couple had their first child baptized at Nôtre-Dame Basilica in Montreal.

From 1896 to 1901, Édouard advertised himself in the Quebec City directory as the private secretary to Quebec lieutenant governor Joseph-Adolphe Chapleau, which suggests that the family moved to Quebec

City, although the young man purchased an empty lot on Chemin des Ormes in Montreal for six hundred dollars.[32] When Chapleau died, Delpit was by his side.[33] He then became private secretary to Louis-Amable Jetté, Quebec's next lieutenant governor. Édouard accompanied his employer on trips and attended state dinners, cultural events, and funerals of dignitaries. Meanwhile, Jeanne gave birth to Louise in 1896, and to Marie in 1897.[34]

Preparing the way for the arrival of his extended family, Édouard leased a sumptuous three-storey brick house in uptown Quebec City.[35] The Delpit clan immigrated in May 1898, joining their prodigal son and his young family. Édouard Delpit Sr. and his wife, Joséphine, arrived from France with their four adult daughters and their three-year-old grandson, Édouard. Passenger lists confirm that the members of the Delpit family (although not Jeanne) crossed the Atlantic on a regular basis, spending most summers in France.

When Édouard Delpit Sr. died in February 1900, dailies published long articles about his life. The notices emphasized the novelist's piety and concluded with the observation that "his unshakable faith allowed him to pass through the cruelest trials."[36] After the death of her husband, Joséphine and her four daughters moved to New York, taking Jeanne's three children with them. The 1901 census is the last time before her death in 1926 (not counting the coverage of the Delpit affair) that we find Jeanne in the public record; she lived with her father, her stepmother, Victoria Laflèche, and two half siblings in Montreal. While Jeanne remained conspicuously absent from the public record, newspapers often mentioned members of the Delpit clan. The timeline paints the Delpits as a tight-knit family with substantial financial means and a certain standing in society.[37] Besides the death of her mother only a few months after she married Édouard, the profession of her father (civil servant), and his marriage in 1894 to eighteen-year-old Victoria, the mother of Jeanne's five half-siblings, we know much less about Jeanne Côté and her family. The coverage of the Delpit affair fills many gaps and gives us a glimpse of their marital life.

The saga took a tragic turn a few weeks after the death of Jeanne's father-in-law. It might have been brewing before, but, officially, it is only in March 1900 that her husband wrote to the ecclesiastical tribunal to ask for an annulment.[38] Édouard argued that, as two Catholics who had married in front of a Protestant minister, his union to Jeanne was invalid. While, as noted above, Jeanne did not wish to continue living with the Delpit clan, she did not want her marriage to be annulled. She requested instead a separation from bed and board, an application that was delayed until the ecclesiastical tribunal rendered its judgment.

In the two months following Édouard's application, the tribunal heard from ten witnesses, in addition to the testimony of the couple themselves. Jeanne and her father appeared first. They had to prove that Jeanne, although baptized and duly confirmed as a child, had renounced Catholicism before she married Édouard, since the Catholic Church accepted that a mixed marriage could be celebrated by a Protestant minister.[39] The young mother contended that, prior to her marriage, she had not been a Catholic for about five years. She claimed that she had returned to the fold only a year and half before the annulment application, and went on to explain how her parents practised Spiritualism. She highlighted the fact that her parents removed her from the convent and enrolled her in a Methodist school. When they transferred her to another Catholic school, she was not to follow Catholic rituals. Jeanne offered her mother's burial in a Protestant cemetery as proof that the family had renounced their faith.[40] Her father corroborated her testimony. While Jeanne presented herself as a repentant Catholic, Mr. Côté boasted that he had no religion. The matrimonial judge might have questioned his sincerity, since the widower had married his second wife, Victoria, in a Catholic church and the couple had had their children baptized, but Côté seemed authentic in claiming his second wife was the practising Catholic in the couple.[41]

Jeanne and her father delivered solid, consistent, and logical testimonies, refraining from slandering Édouard and his family. In contrast, Mrs. Caron, the wife of a friend of Édouard's whom the couple had visited as newlyweds, stated, "I have less confidence in Mrs. Delpit. We found her childish. I would not believe her even under oath." Married at sixteen, Jeanne was indeed still a child when she had visited Mrs. Caron.[42]

Like Mrs. Caron, Édouard's mother displayed a keen dislike of Jeanne. She described her daughter-in-law as "very hypocritical and very selfish. She lies with so much pluck that I think she is unconscious of the fact. I do not think I could believe her even under oath." Mrs. Delpit added that Jeanne never spoke a word to make her believe she was a Protestant. Her testimony reveals that the matriarch was unable to conceive that her treasured son would have turned his back on the family's faith. To explain why he married in front of a Protestant minister, Mrs. Delpit reasoned that "I would rather think, and such was my late husband's conviction, that in all that matrimonial affair, my son Édouard was under the influence of hypnotism, and that he would have never thought of this marriage had he enjoyed his free will." For the rational observer, it is harder to conceive of a sixteen-year-old schoolgirl hypnotizing a twenty-three-year-old gentleman than to imagine a young man, having left France at seventeen to start a new life across the ocean, rejecting his parent's faith.[43]

On the stand, Édouard attempted to validate his mother's strange interpretation, giving Jeanne inordinate agency when he affirmed that he was engaged to another woman, but Jeanne hurried him into marriage. Since their first child was born a solid fourteen months after the union, if Jeanne indeed pressured him into marriage, it was not to legitimize the birth and save her honour.[44]

While Jeanne did not deviate from her claims, Édouard contradicted himself in words and deeds, nor did he receive support for his assertions. Trying to prove his wife's Catholic devotion, he testified that Jeanne's family had protested about the fact that his mother-in-law was to be buried in a Protestant cemetery, but those interrogated on this point denied that the family had made a fuss.[45] He tried to attribute Jeanne's lack of religious zeal to the fact that she was concentrating on caring for her children, but, a few months later, Édouard accused Jeanne of cruelty and of not taking care of their children.[46] His discourse changed according to what he had to prove.

In his ecclesiastical sentence, Mgr. Marois referred only to those witnesses whom he believed had confirmed that Jeanne had never abandoned Catholicism. He did not take note of the witnesses who stressed Édouard's questionable claims to Catholicism. Marois's interpretation of the testimony of Jeanne's aunt divulges his reluctance to consider the young mother as anything other than Catholic. The aunt affirmed that her niece "was practicing no religion at all." When the judge insinuated Jeanne was claiming to be an apostate in order to secure the validity of her marriage, the aunt seemed incredulous, excited, if not plainly insulted: "I beg your pardon ... When they started that club of spiritualists, they were all excommunicated from the pulpit, all those participating in the proceedings, even those who witnessed the proceedings were excommunicated. Even, when my sister died, my mother had to ask leave to go and see her." The aunt ended her testimony with a shocking revelation about the Côtés, one that pointed once more to their Protestant leanings: "They did not believe in confession made to the priest: they confessed to God."[47] Aunt Margaret exposed the tribunal's hypocrisy, highlighting that the Côtés did not have to abjure since they had, in effect, been excommunicated.

In the end, the ecclesiastical tribunal followed the motto Catholic today, Catholic always. Afterall, Jeanne had presented herself as a repentant Catholic. The tribunal annulled the marriage on the ground that, in canon law, a Protestant minister could not celebrate the union of two Catholics. Of the ten witnesses, only Mr. Côté freely admitted he had no religion at all. The other testimony points to the influence the Catholic Church held over its brethren. The episode shows that the church was carefully shoring up its own power with the tribunal's judgment.

Jeanne's request for a separation from bed and board confirms that she did not want to continue to share her life with her husband. For a practicing Catholic, the annulment should have been an acceptable exit strategy, since it opened the door to a new marriage. Was it out of religious fervour, an unshakable belief in the sacramental nature of marriage, that Jeanne refused to consider her union with Édouard null and void? I suspect that Jeanne was primarily afraid of losing her children. In separations, mothers in Quebec usually received the charge of their young children.[48] Jeanne might have thought that the church would not entrust the education of her children to someone it perceived as a heretic. Fearing the influence the clergy exercised in Quebec society, she preferred to pose as a Catholic. Moreover, as historian Thierry Nootens notes, "very rare but scandalous procedures, the applications for annulment of marriage led to a close examination of the good faith of the wife who had believed herself legally married: this good faith could give civil, financial effects to the aborted union."[49]

In the Delpit file in the Vatican, we find a few newspaper articles, Bruchési's pastoral letter, and a letter from Jeanne to the pope. Trying to reverse Marois's verdict, Jeanne portrayed Édouard as an insincere Catholic, and her father as the one who insisted on keeping her away from the church's influence, confiding that her own mother "wanting to follow the traditions of the country, had my marriage blessed by a Catholic priest without my father's knowledge." Jeanne accused Marois of not knowing ecclesiastical law. She quoted the words of St. Paul to the Corinthians: "If any brother has a wife who is not of the faithful and agrees to remain with him, let him not leave her." Blaming her father for the Protestant marriage, she ended her letter reiterating her faith: "Not only am I willing to stay with my husband, but I also formally declare that outside the Catholic Church there is no salvation." Her letter to the pope confirmed that she was desirous of being considered a fervent Catholic.[50]

The Press Gets Involved, and Jeanne Emerges Victorious

The media reaction to the ecclesiastical judgment centres on the civil status of Jeanne and her children. As can be seen in figure 2.1, of the five main actors discussed in the press, "the children" appears most often. The *Vancouver Daily Province*'s statement that Jeanne "could not think of separating permanently from her little ones," encapsulates the tone of many of the articles.[51] One Ottawa paper articulated plainly what many others thought: "There is too much daylight in the Dominion to permit the majority of the people believing the three children of Madame Delpit are illegitimate because a Quebec ecclesiastical court has decreed that the marriage of a husband and wife was illegal because being nominal Catholic (which fact is disputed and established we think) the ceremony performed by a Protestant minister was invalid."[52]

When Rome confirmed the ecclesiastical tribunal's judgment, the public continued to see Jeanne first and foremost as a caring mother deserving of the church's assistance.[53] Reporters painted her as a victim when they stressed that, at the time of the marriage, "she was a girl of sixteen, just out of school.[54] The journalists who mentioned her Protestantism, never specifying that she claimed to have returned to her Catholic roots, were also garnering sympathy for the victim.

In contrast to the massive support for Jeanne, none of the hundreds of articles had anything positive to say about Édouard. In a letter published in the anti-Catholic *Montreal Weekly Witness*, Reverend Massicotte echoed what many other commentators denounced: Édouard was avoiding his manly duty by refusing to take care of his wife.[55] *La Presse*, a politically independent Montreal daily identifying as the voice of the working class, described annulments as "usually very advantageous for one of the spouses, especially the husband, who thus evades the charges of marriage."[56]

Not only did Édouard, with his action to annul, not conform to the masculine discourse of the time, but, to some, his origins mattered greatly. Signing "Manhattan," a special correspondent for the *Cincinnati Commercial Tribune* stressed the relevance of his origins: "Though born in the Roman Catholic Church, and baptized according to its rites, [Édouard] became, in time, like thousands of other Frenchmen,

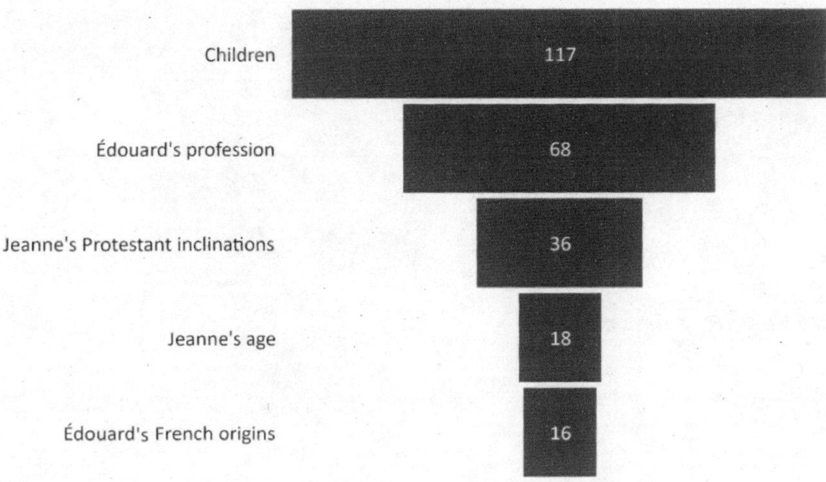

Figure 2.1. Media coverage: The actors

Source: "Delpit" search conducted in BAnQ newspapers, Proquest Historical Newspaper, Newspaperarchive.com, Gallica.bnf.fr, Trove.nla.gov.au, Paperspast.natlib.govt

a practical and avowed infidel."[57] People also recognized that Édouard was using a legal subtlety that did not exist in his native country, as the revolution had made religious marriage secondary to civil marriage.

More often than his origins, papers mentioned his employment as private secretary to a government official. Although Édouard had not committed any legal offence, social pressure forced him to resign. Thomas Chapais reported that "some ministers are anxious to have an opportunity to get rid of Mr. Delpit."[58] Throughout his fifteen years at the head of *Le Courrier du Canada*, Chapais campaigned for the maintenance of traditional Catholic values and opposed democracy, socialism, and atheism.[59] *La Vérité*, Jules-Paul Tardivel's ultramontane weekly, observed that Édouard's resignation "must have brought real relief to the entire French-Canadian public."[60] If the Catholic papers recognized that the church alone had the authority to regulate marriage, they did not appreciate Édouard forcing its hand and jeopardizing its power. Figure 2.2 illustrates how the press framed the question around the right of the ecclesiastical tribunal and, ultimately, Rome to decide on the validity of marriages. Thus, the Delpit affair has parallels to the

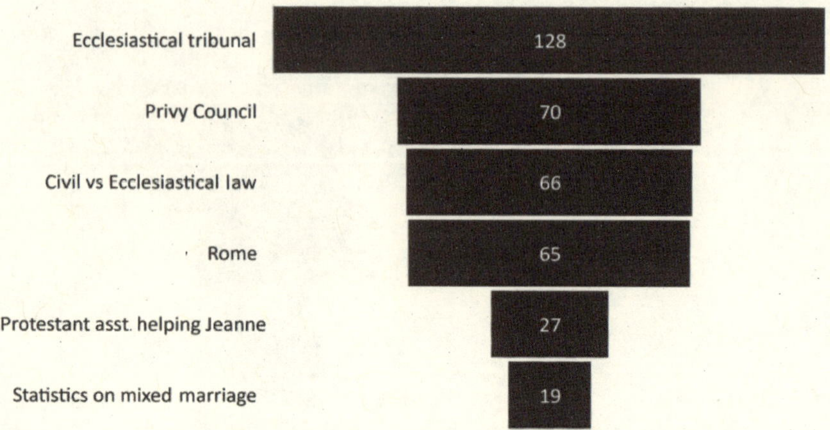

Figure 2.2. Media coverage: The institutions

Source: "Delpit" search conducted in BAnQ newspapers, Proquest Historical Newspaper, Newspaperarchive.com, Gallica.bnf.fr, Trove.nla.gov.au, Paperspast.natlib.govt.

Guibord affair, but also to the more recent Manitoba School Question, which had inflamed the passions of Canadians in the 1896 election.[61]

Many observers mentioned the possibility of the Privy Council limiting the authority of the Catholic Church once and for all. Commenting on the case in the *Canadian Law Times*, L. Maxwell Lyon stated: "The Delpit case may be the means of obtaining an authoritative and definite statement regarding the limits of the respective jurisdiction of the ecclesiastical and temporal courts in the Province of Quebec."[62] While the majority complained about the church's power, Chapais gloated that "it is the Church who has defended in the world, and sometimes against the world, the holiness, dignity and perpetuity of marriage. In vain the human passions have grumbled, in vain the human powers have threatened, in vain the flesh and blood have rebelled and have pushed the clamour of covetousness and rage: the church has remained the unshakeable guardian of Christian marriage." He concluded that the happiness of the country and the future of the French-Canadian "race" depend on the church.[63]

Far from believing that Quebeckers were stuck in the dark ages, as the *New York Times* and other papers argued, Catholic papers felt that French Canadians had superior morals because of their unique understanding of the sanctity of marriage.[64]

Once Édouard asked the Superior Court to ratify the ecclesiastical decision and annul the civil effects of his marriage, reporters reduced the case to a confrontation between civil and ecclesiastical law. Catholic papers insisted that marriage was a sacrament. As Chapais extolled, "For Catholics, marriage being essentially a sacrament, if there is no sacrament, there is no marriage. So the door is wide open to civil marriage, which the codifiers in their wisdom wanted to exclude from our law."[65] Tardivel attacked controversial anti-Catholic writer and journalist Goldwin Smith, who advocated for the modernization of the law of marriage and divorce. Tardivel accused Smith of wanting to adopt civil marriage as "some revolutionary governments in Europe have done" and wondered if the province was "already ripe for this extreme application of the dissolving doctrines of liberalism."[66] Both Chapais and Tardivel exposed their Catholic conservatism and their faith in the supreme authority of the church.

Non-Catholic papers rejected the notion that the church had sole jurisdiction over marriage, making it clear that Rome should not have the power to wield its religious sword over British subjects. Some insisted that it did not matter if Jeanne was a Protestant at the time of her marriage: "The important question is whether marriage as civil status in the Province of Quebec is to be governed by the Church or by the State."[67] If the church really had the legal authority, then, argued Reverend MacVicar in an opinion piece, "it should be decided whether the Privy Council in England or the Court of Rome was paramount in this country."[68] Gallus, from the Protestant weekly *L'Aurore*, put it simply: "If it is the law, the law is arbitrary, unjust, revolting, inhuman, and it must be changed."[69]

Many believed that the Privy Council would finally impose civil marriage in the province. A decade after the Delpit case, an Australian paper offered its take on the affair, questioning why the archbishop did not ask Édouard to appeal the Archibald judgment that the marriage was valid. The author proclaimed:

> There can only be one answer. Should the matter come before the Privy Council, Roman priests know too well the decision which would be handed out would be contrary to her [the church's] erroneous interpretations of

> the laws of Quebec. Rome's prelates prefer that the law be left undefined and indefinite, for to have the faithful in Quebec and elsewhere believe that their marriage would be valid performed by a Protestant minister, would mean a great loss of prestige and tremendous loss to the coffers of the Church and the pockets of the priests.[70]

Beyond the wrong assumptions about marriage generating revenues either for the church or for priests, the commentator did not understand that the archbishop had no hold on Édouard, who only wanted to free himself from Jeanne so he could marry another woman. Why would he subject himself to an excessively long judicial process?

Media mentions of the Privy Council had serious implications for the institutions and the individuals involved in the saga. They reminded the Delpit clan that, even if they won an appeal, the highest court would not look favourably at the ecclesiastical decision. Édouard even had reason to believe he would win if he dragged Jeanne to the Court of Review. Shortly after Archibald declared the Delpit union valid, three Court of Review judges refused to follow his precedent in the Durocher case.[71] In *Durocher*, Judge Lynch of the Quebec Superior Court had disagreed with the ecclesiastical court, which had granted an annulment. Although Lynch had declared the marriage between the two Catholics who married in the United States valid, Judges Lemieux, Curran, and Mathieu quashed his initial judgment, arguing that the parties could not marry in the United States and without the consent of the father of the underage bride.[72] The three Catholic judges validated the ecclesiastical tribunal's decision.

The Delpit clan might have assumed that they would win at the Supreme Court of Canada, since Jeanne did not have the funds to pay for proper counsel. But Édouard could no longer count on his privileged, moneyed position, as Jeanne had received the moral and financial support of those Protestant associations motivated to take the case all the way to the Privy Council. The consensus was that the London tribunal would not judge in his favour. Observers pointed out that invalidating the marriage because it was celebrated by a Protestant minister would complicate the status of many Canadians. Perhaps exaggerating the number of couples affected, a British Columbia weekly claimed:

> The anguish in the minds of many thousands [of] superstitious couples, on being told that they are not married and that their children are illegitimate is deplorable. Marriage is a simple business contract and should

> never be in the hands of any church. The mummery and mockery of a church ceremony is simply a relic of barbarism more fitting to the age of the Druids than to the twentieth century. The system which gives the Church of Quebec or anywhere else, the opportunity to terrorize credulous and unsophisticated folks into a reverence for their formalities is simply abhorrent to liberal minds.[73]

If French Canadians felt superior because of their respect for the sanctity of marriage, English Protestants looked down on them for their apparent backwardness and obsequiousness with regard to the church.

The *Montreal Weekly Witness* led the campaign against Édouard, publishing more than fifty news items, editorials, commentaries, and letters, but no other papers criticized the church so openly and vigorously as the radical Montreal weeklies *Les Débats* and *L'Avenir*.[74] Louvigny de Montigny, who had recently become editor of *L'Avenir*, denounced with eloquent verve the ecclesiastical decision in Delpit and called on both Protestants and Catholics to protect Jeanne and her children.[75] *Les Débats* also condemned Mgr. Marois, who had accepted Delpit's claims as "truthful and sincere." It implicitly criticized the ecclesiastical court through its attacks on Édouard:

> Mr. Delpit asks the newspapers not to forget that he and his wife have always been Catholic. Mr. Delpit should have started by not forgetting [this] himself when he got married by a Protestant minister. Sir, either you were Catholic when you got married or you weren't. If you were not, your marriage is valid, and no authority can override it other than the Senate for a good reason. Or you were, and then, perfectly knowing the laws of the Province of Quebec, you deliberately deceived a young woman who had faith in you, you knew that it was only a comedy that you played with her. And it is today your own turpitude that you invoke to repudiate the mother of your children! Fi sir! Fi![76]

Archbishop Bruchési Reacts: The All-Powerful Catholic Church?

The intensely critical tone of the two radical papers attracted the ire of Montreal archbishop Paul Bruchési, who threatened to ban them for undermining the authority of the church.[77] The *Globe*, a key paper in English Canada, noted the significance of the threat: "It is needless to say that if the papers are put under the ban of the Church they will be ruined."[78] The press believed that the church held tremendous power over its faithful and that the clergy would successfully convince citizens to cancel their subscriptions to any papers condemned by the church.

While *Le Courrier du Canada*, *Le Journal des Campagnes*, and *La Vérité* supported the archbishop wholeheartedly, other papers carefully navigated this minefield. *Le Trifluvien* questioned how journalists could publish such irreverent words about a sacrament, and its journalists encouraged radical colleagues to retract their more controversial statements. Nevertheless, even this Catholic paper concluded that "this incident incites reflection."[79] The proprietor of *Le Réveil*, Aristide Filliatreault, reacted with his usual anti-clerical stance.[80] Eventually, *Les Débats* and *L'Avenir* printed retractions, which, even if insincere, proved that the archbishop had considerable influence.[81]

Although Quebec newspaper proprietors could not afford to displease the church, they did not back down completely. After *La Presse* published Édouard's letter, *Les Débats* commented, "and now in our country, the depositary of the old traditions of the French galantine, *La Presse* forgetting its priestly vocation, its providential mission to elevate and ennoble the moral convictions of the masses, becomes the voice of insults thrown in the face of a Canadian by a foreigner to obey an unhealthy need to claim and flatter the vulgar emotion of greed."[82] By using the word "foreigner" to describe Delpit and "Canadian" to refer to Jeanne, the paper displayed its French-Canadian nationalism more than an anti-Catholic stance. *Les Débats*, a liberal and anti-imperialist paper, which published the writing of journalist Eva Circé-Côté, assumed a feminist tone in its defence of Jeanne, titling its article "Respect for the Woman."[83]

Bruchési's threat attracted the attention of papers as far afield as New Zealand. The *Otago Daily Times* noted that "it is quite a number of years since a Roman Catholic Bishop in Canada attempted to interfere with the liberty of the press and to place newspapers which did not express views in accordance with the church under the ban."[84] The Delpit affair was indeed becoming an international cause célèbre.

The local, national, and international press also picked up Bruchési's pastoral letter on the sanctity of marriage. Bruchési justified the decision of the ecclesiastical tribunal by reminding his brethren of the supreme authority of the church when it came to marriage, but he recognized that the civil authorities had to deal with temporal matters such as financial details. He asserted that, "in Christian marriage the natural contract and the sacrament are one and the same thing." He affirmed the indissolubility of marriage and reiterated the right of the church to place conditions on people who wanted to marry. Next, he reluctantly acknowledged that a mixed marriage celebrated by a Protestant minister was valid, "but to judge if one of the parties is really heretical, or to declare when a Catholic denying practically his faith becomes a heretic, especially in that which concerns the sacrament of marriage, this belongs to the ecclesiastical tribunal alone." He explained that, if a marriage was contracted in good faith but proved to be invalid, "there is no dishonor to the parents, neither to the children of the marriage." The church accepted going through a proper ceremony to render the union valid. He also specified that, in case of separation, the civil authorities had the power to grant an allowance for the children and the wife, admitting that papal authority had no "efficacious jurisdiction" in such matters. He concluded by remonstrating against the journalists who treated the difficult and complex question too lightly.[85]

The pastoral letter focused on the authority of the church to define and regulate marriages, not on the specifics of the case at hand. Bruchési only touched on Édouard and Jeanne, when he specified that the couple could revalidate their marriage. It was probably what he hoped for. Since Jeanne was not trying to annul the marriage, he was aiming his comments at Édouard, who clearly was only too happy to free himself from his responsibilities.

After Archibald rejected the ecclesiastical decision, Bruchési reaffirmed his belief that the church had received from its divine founder the power and the right to regulate all that concerned Christian marriage. Until that point, the archbishop had believed that provincial legislation recognized the impediment of clandestinity. He specified he did not want to enter any criticism of the judgment from a legal standpoint, which, he said, concerned the civil tribunals of the country and the empire, but he felt it was his "duty to declare that for a Catholic, a clandestine marriage is always null and void." He warned that "the Church pronounces the sentence of excommunication against any of its members who presume to contract marriage before a heretical minister, be it a question of two Catholics or a Catholic and a Protestant." For true believers, such a sentence was a serious punishment. He ended on an encouraging note, stating that the church could absolve those who were guilty of such a fault,[86] as it clearly did in the Delpit case. Interestingly, Jeanne declared that she had not officially asked for absolution, something the ecclesiastical tribunal used against her, even if she declared that she dealt with her faults in the confessional.

As the *Sydney Watchman* perceptively pointed out, although the church lost the Delpit case, its authority went unchallenged, as the question never reached the Privy Council. The church's position was even confirmed a mere week later in the *Durocher* appeal. Still, media coverage of the affair proves that the church faced considerable opposition: indeed, no papers supported the "brethren" whom the ecclesiastical tribunal had freed from matrimonial responsibility. Many questioned why the church granted Édouard his annulment, and they were not convinced that the young French man was a Catholic at heart.[87]

Édouard's and Jeanne's Letters: The Scoundrel and the Loving Mother

As we have seen, the press sided with Jeanne. Under the weight of public opinion, Édouard felt the need to clarify the situation.[88] In a recognition that his French origins bothered many of his critics, he started his public letter specifying that he had been born in France but was a British subject. He argued that the law in Quebec stated that "a Roman Catholic priest cannot legally solemnize marriage between two Protestants, and conversely, that a Protestant minister cannot legally solemnize marriage between two Roman Catholics." In this, he revealed his misunderstanding of his own faith, since canon law, not civil law, forbade priests from uniting two non-Catholics. Protestant denominations saw marriage as a rite and did not prohibit ministers from celebrating the marriage of non-Protestants. Édouard explained that, if some found the law tyrannical, he himself had no opinion as to whether it needed to be changed, adding with disarming logic, "I do not see how I can be blamed for invoking it as long as it exists."[89] Far from buying his explanation, papers continued to criticize him for avoiding his marital responsibilities.

Despite the negative reactions in the press to Édouard's letter, reading it retrospectively, one sees that he presented himself as a gentleman, even a knight in shining armour who refused to go to battle for himself but felt he had to do so when "my adversaries are now trying to inculpate my mother and sisters." He assured readers that he would have preferred not to expose his marital troubles. He charged Jeanne with posing as a Protestant, accused her of not caring about the children, and reminded readers that she too wanted a separation. He pointed out that the annulment worked perfectly to liberate both. He affirmed that he was aware of the obligations imposed by a putative marriage and asserted that he was paying her an allowance according to his means.[90] Yet, in his civil suit, he was de facto asking to put an end to the putative effects of the marriage and, thus, to end his support. He admitted that he wanted out, and was using the law to accomplish this end: "I would like to see the man who, in my place, would display such magnanimity, who would commit such a foolish act [marrying Jeanne again]. After seven years of most miserable life, after having put up with every kind of outrage to avoid scandal, I am forced to a separation."[91] People could sense that Édouard was exaggerating – after all, the couple had had three children. Since he had declared in the annulment proceedings that Jeanne could not practise her faith as she was taking care of the children, it was harder to believe him when he stated that, to her, "the children hardly existed." Some observed that it was only when the Delpit clan arrived in Quebec that the young couple's relationship soured. And, contrary to her husband's fluctuating discourse, Jeanne's legal fight to be reunited with her three children corresponded with the maternal discourse to which she held fast throughout the saga.

A week after Édouard published his letter, the *Witness* printed Jeanne's reply. Like her husband, she started with a comment on the proper way a wife should behave, which did not involve her talking about their private business in newspapers. Yet, she stressed, she had no choice but to reply to her husband's false accusations. Jeanne chose the most damning testimony at the ecclesiastical tribunal to share with readers, including the detail that a witness affirmed that Édouard had named their dog Pius the Ninth. In her letter to the pope, she even stated that he used a rosary as a leash. She was hoping to show that Édouard was no Catholic at heart. She pointed out that the public was against him because he was "a man who uses his own hypocritical demeanor to benefit thereby." She mocked him for wanting to convey "cruelty of a wife to a husband," stressing that she was an innocent sixteen-year-old girl when she married him, while he had already been engaged to a woman and had started a business in Manitoba and in Montreal before he met her. She lashed out: "I was the slave and tool of that man." Her letter reveals that, not content to stay home in his shadow, she expected to share his public life.[92]

Jeanne also spoke the language of motherly virtue: "One would require to know little of the feelings existing between a mother and her offspring to place any faith in the imaginary statement of Mr. Delpit on my conduct towards the children." She might have been exaggerating when she affirmed that her husband encouraged the children to insult her, as it is hard to imagine such young children showing a lack of respect towards their mother, but one sees that she took her role seriously. Commentators agreed that she should be part of any decision making about the children. The *Daily Whig*, Kingston's liberal and reform-minded paper, related that "in October last, while the case was pending in Rome, Mr. Delpit sent his mother and four sisters and his three children to New York, where the latter now are, in care of the former. They were sent from Quebec without their mother's consent and without her wishes having been consulted."[93] The same newspaper later commented that "it is unheard of to say that a mother shall be deprived of her children and still more unheard of to think the courts would sanction such a thing."[94] Paternal authority, if solid in law, had its limits in terms of public opinion.

Jeanne also accused Édouard of physical violence. He slapped her in the face in the presence of his family and friends. A writer using the pseudonym Vieux Rouge did not comment on the "slapping,"[95] but he did play down Édouard's claims of violence perpetrated towards him:

> His wife threw a casserole or a pot at his head. It really was not worth noting this trivial incident, and I must say that the former secretary of His Excellency is not an observer, for he would know that out of a hundred well-matched unions, and consecrated by the Catholic authorities, in Canada, or elsewhere, there are at least ninety couples who fight and curse each other from morning to night and from evening to morning until the time when the roughness of the corners has worn out by rubbing and then they live in a relative armed peace, while looking at each other like pottery dogs.

Vieux Rouge noted that "two spouses who don't fight have no affection for each other."[96] Other papers were not as blunt, but they noted that Édouard had nothing serious with which to reproach his wife.[97]

Jeanne's letter reveals an intelligent and articulate young woman. Édouard included in his own letter the affidavit of his maid and the family doctor, but Jeanne astutely recognized, perhaps under the guidance of her skilled attorney, Eugène Lafleur, that their testimony was coloured by loyalty to their employer.[98] Jeanne encouraged readers to dismiss the views of a chambermaid and a hired man. Knowing that doctors' statements carried more prestige, she questioned why Dr. Grondin had said such things about her. She defended herself by clarifying that she had to leave her children daily, the doctor having prescribed treatments in the hospital to take care of her broken health. Despite her compelling claim, Jeanne regretted that, as a result, she allowed the Delpit clan to take care of the children. "From that moment," she lamented, "I could not get control or care of my children." She reported that her mother-in-law told her to abandon her children if she wanted to be maintained by her husband. The young mother appealed to the public by pointing out that Delpit was cruelly concealing in a foreign country the three children born of their marriage. She ended on a powerful note: "I, their mother abandoned penniless in Montreal, have not even the privilege of seeing my dear little ones, estranged from me by the treacherous action of their father."[99]

The press reacted strongly to these new revelations. Far from enhancing his image, Delpit's explanations resulted in papers berating him even more soundly as the heartless husband. Jeanne had been much more convincing by appealing effectively to the maternal sensibilities of all mothers, and invoking the duty of fathers to protect mothers. Moreover, she had remained consistent throughout every proceeding while Édouard's shifting claims gave his detractors reason to distrust him.

By granting the annulment, the ecclesiastical court opened the door to a new Catholic marriage for Édouard. But he had to wait for the civil court to cancel the civil effects of his marriage, and Judge Archibald refused to invalidate the marriage.

Archibald's Judgement: *Plus Ça Change ...*

If Édouard's skilled attorney and counsel, Mr. Bisaillon and Gustave Lamothe, had their way, Archibald would not have presided over the case.[100] They were trying to get Catholic judge Michel Mathieu, who had already, according to Jeanne's counsel, pronounced himself against her case.[101] Archibald reassured the parties involved that he would judge on the law, not from a religious standpoint.[102] A Presbyterian born in Nova Scotia, admitted to the Montreal bar in 1871, and appointed to the Superior Court in 1893, John Sprott Archibald often represented the federal government in court cases.[103] When he announced his retirement in 1922, *La Presse* reported that the judge "always stood out for his uprightness and his love of work." The paper mentioned his important judgment in *Delpit v. Côté*, which it characterized as having upheld the validity of a marriage between two Roman Catholics that had been solemnized under licence by a Protestant minister, adding that Archibald had supported the same opinion in *Dépatie v. Tremblay*, "which the Privy council subsequently maintained, and which now establishes jurisprudence in such cases in our province." The same information resurfaced when the judge died in 1932.[104] Archibald's contemporaries incontestably associated him with the Delpit affair – I identified more than one hundred news items that discussed his decision. It was seen as a judgment that would set a legal precedent.[105]

In February 1901, the *Canada Law Journal* asserted that, with respect to the Delpit question,

> any Provincial Court will not conceive itself bound to adopt the view of the ecclesiastical tribunal as to the invalidity of the marriage. It may well be that even if the ecclesiastical tribunal has correctly interpreted the laws of their Church (as to which we refrain from offering any opinion), the marriage, though void according to the ecclesiastical law, is perfectly valid and binding upon the parties according to the law of the land. And while the parties, if Roman Catholics, may have subjected themselves to the spiritual censure of the Church, yet so far as the legal obligations and status both of themselves and children are concerned, the marriage may be absolutely valid and binding on all concerned.[106]

Not surprisingly, all English newspapers celebrated Archibald's decision, seeing it as a victory over Rome. They reduced the lengthy judgment to a basic statement: "Marriage is a civil contract, and … religious differences cannot affect it." Some French newspapers remained neutral,[107] while others highlighted the positive aspects of Archibald's judgment. The *Journal de Waterloo* stated that "Judge Archibald declares that the state has no right to intervene in the internal laws of any church, but that parties belonging to any church have the perfect right to turn to the civil authority to marry."[108] *Le Réveil*'s reaction, though completely in favour of the civil judgment, confirmed the place that the Catholic Church occupied in Quebec: "A Canadian judge rose to the occasion and rendered a judgment which will probably attract public scorn, but his conscience will give him an adequate reward."[109] While Bruchési would not comment on Archibald's decision beyond the fact that he had thought that the marriage law in Quebec corresponded to canon law, the ultramontane Chapais decried the verdict: "This decision is too grave, too fatal, too erroneous, too contrary to law, too disastrous in its consequences, for Catholic opinion not to be moved by it. For our part, we refuse to bow to this ephemeral sentence."[110] Despite a string of jurists commenting favourably on the decision, both Chapais and Bruchési were subsequently proven right.[111] Michel Morin demonstrates that the Quebec judicial elite continued to recognize the right of the church to regulate marriages. Moreover, he argues that "Quebec has never known a separation between church and state, but rather a gradual dissociation, which has not yet been completed."[112]

Denouement and Conclusion

Nearly thirty when Archibald denied his request, Édouard could not imagine waiting for years before he could marry his new intended. He was determined to free himself from Jeanne, and thus moved to the United States to secure a divorce. Quebec papers mentioned that he was in New York discussing the possibility of a Maryland divorce. Jeanne's supporters reassured her that Édouard would not be able to get a divorce unless she agreed to it.[113]

Édouard and his New York attorney, a certain Carruthers, realized that making his intentions public would curtail any chance of securing his freedom. He therefore shrewdly petitioned for his divorce in Nebraska. Jeanne had no real opportunity to contest Édouard's claims. Just as he had taken the annulment route because it was offered to him, Édouard chose the Nebraska jurisdiction because it allowed him to seek the divorce without having to contact Jeanne. The law required him only to publish a notice in the local paper. He petitioned "on the ground of extreme and repeated cruelty and [asked] that the custody of the minor children of plaintiff and defendant be awarded to plaintiff."[114] Jeanne had about a month to find out about the new scheme and to oppose the action. Advertising in the local newspapers of a far-away little town was an ingenious, if nasty, tactic: none of Jeanne's allies saw the notice.

The affidavit filed by Delpit seems to have been full of lies or, at the very least, exaggerations. Édouard falsely claimed that he had been a resident of Nebraska since April 1901. He alleged that, from 1 August 1894 – before the birth of their first child – Jeanne, "regardless of her duties as a wife, has been guilty of extreme violence and repeated cruelty and has treated plaintiff in a cruel and inhuman manner, and since the date last aforesaid has at various times used vile and opprobrious language to and respecting plaintiff and had called him vile and abusive names." No one could suspect from the affidavit that Jeanne was only seventeen at the time. Édouard specified that his wife, on 28 May 1899, and at various other times, called him "a damned liar," "whoremaster," "dirty pig," and "thief." He accused her of having struck their three-year-old son with a ruler on his hand, arm, and body. According to him, she had also struck the little boy with her fist "with such violence it caused severe pain and bruises." He painted her as "possessed of high ungovernable and vicious temper, and wholly unfit to be entrusted with the care, custody and education of said children."[115] Since Jeanne failed to answer the petition, Judge H.M. Grime granted the divorce and custody of the three children to Édouard.[116]

Before he received his divorce, Édouard eloped with Clotilde Jetté, the youngest daughter of his former employer, Lieutenant Governor Jetté. His actions showed total disregard for the young woman. He had pleaded ignorance of the existence of the "clandestine clause" when he asked to annul his marriage to Jeanne, but in 1901 he could no longer claim to be ignorant of the necessity for Catholic couples to marry in front of their own priest. Thus, with the elopement, Édouard had knowingly and willingly compromised the legitimacy of his second marriage. If Clotilde had not petitioned the ecclesiastical court for an annulment in 1905, we might have never known about this marriage.[117] Completely free to marry according to ecclesiastical law, Édouard had nevertheless committed bigamy according to criminal law, leaving Jeanne with grounds to seek a divorce.

Édouard's actions reveal his true character, as an opportunist who took advantage of legal loopholes to avoid his marital responsibility. Jeanne may have won at the Superior Court, but it was a hollow victory, since the Delpit clan had already kidnapped her children. Her in-laws did not have her consent to take them out of the country.[118] No Canadian court had granted custody of the children to their father. A Nebraska judge did, but only in 1902. Despite Édouard's vile attacks on her behaviour as a mother, both Jeanne's discourse and her persistent actions to gain custody of her children point to her desire to be reunited with them. Perhaps the young mother kept her married name all those years so her children could one day find her under their patronym.

If Jeanne had known about Édouard's marriage to Clotilde, she could have petitioned for a divorce. Her "friends," however, may not have supported her in that venture, since Protestant associations had their own political agenda. They were mostly interested in getting the case to the Privy Council and not to the Canadian Parliament. If she had pursued a divorce, we might have discovered that she had only posed as a Catholic during the ecclesiastic trial to get her children back. Her tragic history shows that, in the end, money made a difference. Her rich in-laws quickly moved her children out of the country, and she died without ever seeing them again.

When the Privy Council in *Dépatie v. Tremblay* ruled in favour of state rather than religious law, the basic principle of Archibald's decision was upheld, yet his judgment continued to inspire strong resistance within some quarters of the Quebec legal community. Archibald's decision was eventually confirmed as good law, but, perhaps even more significant, the Delpit affair shines light on the ever-present tensions between Catholics and Protestants that so defined Quebec and Canadian society in this period. It also reveals French-Canadian nationalism (defined in opposition to both France and English Canada) and Anglo-Canadian dislike and suspicion of supposedly backward, church-dominated Catholic Quebeckers. The case illustrates the power the church exercised in Quebec but also exposes the resistance it faced, not only in the anglophone press but also in the francophone. Moreover, Jeanne's own reactions, her father's attitudes, and Édouard's actions all point to their ambivalent relationship with church doctrine.

The case confirms that, in the discourse of the press, marriage as a civil institution was meant first and foremost to protect the most vulnerable, the wife and children. Both French and English commentators, Catholics and non-Catholics, believed Édouard had a responsibility to provide for his young wife and children. Marriage kept women in their homely place. Those who made and enforced the law were not happy about the men who broke the rules or threatened the status quo. Ultimately, though, the law did little to limit the power of an abusive and uncaring patriarch, despite social and political claims of concern about the abuse of paternal power. Most, if not all, observers felt sympathy for poor Jeanne, who was robbed of her motherly role. Even twenty-first-century readers may feel the pain of the young mother who never again held her three little ones in her arms.

NOTES

1 See, for example, one of my favourite of Backhouse's case studies, *The Heiress vs the Establishment: Mrs. Campbell's Campaign for Legal Justice* (Vancouver: UBC Press, 2004).

2 Charles Hébert, *The Delpit Case* (pamphlet) (Montreal, 1901).

3 Separation of Bed and Board, n.d., *Côté v. Delpit*, Bibliothèque et Archives nationales du Québec-Montréal (BAnQ-M), TP11, S2, SS2, SSS1, (no. 2737).

4 *Globe* (Toronto), 19 February 1901.
5 *Montreal Weekly Witness*, 2 April 1901.
6 *Montreal Weekly Witness*, 13 August 1901. The archive file does not reveal a particular date for the uptake of the proceedings, but it contains documents pertaining to Édouard's civil action.
7 Only in Quebec and Ontario, since the other provinces had their own divorce courts.
8 Constance Backhouse, "Pure Patriarchy: Nineteenth-Century Canadian Marriage," *McGill Law Journal* 31 (1986): 281. Interestingly, a New Zealand daily reported that "Roman Catholic senators of Quebec have always refused to concur in divorce bills granted by the State in cases of Roman Catholics, contending that the Church of Rome alone has jurisdiction." *New Zealand Mail*, 7 March 1901.
9 His lifestyle points to financial ease. I found, however, a seizure against him, a civil suit, and two notices of protest. *La Minerve* (Montreal), 25 February 1895. On 31 May 1902, Delpit accepted responsibility for a friend's debt for $572.22, but when Lammar failed to reimburse Clémentine Bélanger, Édouard did not honour his engagement. *Clémentine Bélanger v. Édouard Delpit and Walter L. Lammar*, BAnQ, TP11, S1, SS2, SSS1 (no. 1975); Protest, 3 December 1903, *John Buckworth Parkins*, BAnQ, CN301, S383 (4531); Protest, 19 May 1904, *Joseph Allaire*, BAnQ, CN301, S377 (11132).
10 James Snell, *In the Shadow of the Law* (Toronto: University of Toronto Press, 1991), 50. A Massachusetts paper reported the difficulty for Quebeckers to obtain a divorce, stating that, although applications had been made to the Canadian Parliament for divorces on a variety of grounds, only those based on adultery were granted. *North Adams Transcript*, 13 March 1901.
11 Serge Gagnon, *Mariage et famille au temps de Papineau* (Quebec City: Presses de l'Université Laval, 2020), x.
12 I translated all the French quotations. Lucien Beaudoin, *La dissolution du lien matrimonial en droit canonique et en droit civil canadien* (Hull: Ateliers de l'imprimerie Leclerc, 1948), 217.
13 Ibid., 254.
14 Marie-Aimée Cliche, "Les procès en séparation de corps dans la région de Montréal 1795–1879," *Revue d'histoire de l'Amérique française* 49, no. 2 (1995): 3–33; "Les procès en séparation de corps dans la région de Montréal 1900–1930," *Canadian Journal of Law and Society* 12, no. 1 (1997): 74, 96.
15 The matrimonial regime in Quebec was inherited from old French Laws.
16 Cliche, "Les procès en séparation de corps," 76.
17 E.M. Sait, "Theocratic Quebec," *Annals of the American Academy of Political and Social Science* (1913): 81.

18 *Brown v. Les Curés et Marguilliers de l'Œuvre et de la Fabrique de la Paroisse de Montréal* (1874), LR 6 PC 157, [1874] UKPC 70 (PC). Historians use the story of the humble printer's remains, encased in several feet of reinforced cement, to highlight the battle between ultramontanes and Quebec's *libres penseurs* taking place in the last decades of the nineteenth century. Alvin Finkel and Margaret Conrad, *History of the Canadian Peoples*, vol. 2, *1867 to the Present* (Toronto: Copp Clark, 1998), 165.

19 C.E. Dorion, "La Loi du Mariage dans la Province de Québec," in *Le droit civil français* (Montreal: Barreau de Montréal, 1936), 132.

20 Rumilly based his claims on archival sources, newspaper clippings, and even oral history, but the lack of footnotes prevents readers from properly assessing his interpretation. Robert Rumilly, *Histoire de la Province de Québec*, vol. 10, *Israël Tarte* (Montreal: Édition Bernard Valiquette, 1940), 32–9.

21 Jean Hamelin and Nicole Gagnon, *L'histoire du catholicisme québécois: Le XXe siècle*, vol 1, *1898–1940* (Montreal: Boréal Express, 1984), 322.

22 Gagnon, *Mariage et famille*, 273.

23 Jocelyn Maclure and Charles Taylor, *Secularism and Freedom of Conscience* (Cambridge, MA: Harvard University Press, 2011), 55–6.

24 Michel Morin, "De la reconnaissance officielle à la tolérance des religions: L'état civil et les empêchements de mariage de 1628 à nos jours," in *Le droit, la religion et le "raisonnable": le fait religieux entre monisme étatique et pluralisme juridique*, ed. Jean-François Gaudreault-Desbiens (Montreal: Éditions Thémis, 2009), 54–92; Professor of law and canon law, Ernest Caparros also notes that the jurisprudence in Quebec applied articles 127 and 129 of the Civil Code by giving full force to canon law. "La 'Civilization' du droit canonique: Une problématique du droit québécois," *Cahiers de droit* 18, no. 3 (1977): 717.

25 Online databases of historical newspapers allowed me to collect the impressive corpus. It seems like every town's paper picked up the story. Newspapers from as far away as Australia and New Zealand shared their take on the Delpit affair.

26 The subtitle of this Hébert pamphlet was *The Delpit Case*.

27 A "layman" in his account of the case highlighted that no spouses accused the other of adultery; instead, he pointed to "deep-rooted incompatibility of temper, character, and education on both sides." Hébert, *The Delpit Case*, 4.

28 On Louise Delpit, see John William Leonard, ed., *Woman's Who's Who of America, 1914–15* (New York: American Commonwealth Co., 1914),

https://ia800500.us.archive.org/24/items/womanswhoswhoofaooleon/womanswhoswhoofaooleon.pdf. On Édouard Delpit's arrival in North America, see *Le Courrier du Canada*, 16 May 1888.

29 *Sessional Papers of the Dominion of Canada*, vol. 7, *Fourth Session of the Sixth Parliament, Session 1890*, 7b-63.

30 *L'Étendard* (Montreal), 20 January 1893. Édouard might have been reacting to another item *L'Étendard* reported. The paper stated that his uncle Albert Delpit had died of an overdose of chloral, a drug he had been abusing for the past ten years. *L'Étendard* (Montreal), 16 January 1893.

31 *La Patrie* (Montreal), 8 May 1893; *Le Quotidien* (Chicoutimi), 9 May 1893.

32 *Le Prix Courant* (Montreal), 21 August 1896. Delpit also entered a business partnership with his wife's uncle and aunt, investing $500. Société between Édouard Delpit, Emilie Campbell and Elzéar Derome, 3 May 1897.

33 The bond uniting the two men must have been strong. Chapleau included a clause in his will stating "I give my former secretary Édouard Delpit money he may owe me." Ministère des Affaires Culturelles, *Rapport des Archives du Québec*, vol. 41 (Roch Lefebvre, Imprimeur de Sa Majesté la Reine, 1963), 164, https://numerique.banq.qc.ca/patrimoine/details/52327/2276325?docsearchtext=%C3%89douard%20Delpit.

34 Many efforts to locate baptismal records were unfruitful. More than likely, the two girls were never baptized in the Catholic faith.

35 Lease, 26 March 1898, *Cyprien Labrecque*, BAnQ-Q, CN301, S351 (no. 7660).

36 *Le Soleil* (Quebec), 16 February 1900.

37 Inventory of A.A.E. Delpit, 4 January 1901, *Joseph Allaire*, BAnQ-Q, CN301, S377, (no. 9285). The notarial act explains that the Delpit spouse had opted for a judicially separated property in 1878, and that the novelist owed his wife, Joséphine, a considerable amount of money.

38 Hébert, *The Delpit Case*, 88.

39 Rumilly argues that it is because of the Delpit affair that *Ne Temere* took a harsher line and ruled that even mixed marriages had to be celebrated by Catholic priests.

40 Hébert, *The Delpit Case*, 50, 66–72.

41 Ibid., 49, 73–6.

42 Ibid., 70, 84–7.

43 Ibid., 38–42.

44 *Kingston Daily Whig*, 16 January 1901; *Le Réveil* (Montreal), 27 January 1901.

45 Hébert, *The Delpit Case*, 34–7.

46 Édouard Delpit, "Au Rédacteur de la Presse," *La Presse* (Montreal), 26 January 1901.

47 Hébert, *The Delpit Case*, 48, 57, 58, 61, 54, 83.
48 Cynthia Fish, "La puissance paternelle et les cas de garde d'enfants au Québec, 1866–1928," *Revue d'histoire de l'Amérique française* 57, no. 4 (2004): 509–33.
49 Thierry Nootens, *Genre, patrimoine et droit civil: Les femmes mariées de la bourgeoisie au début du 20e siècle, 1900–1930* (Montreal: McGill-Queen's University Press, 2019), 102.
50 Jeanne Delpit to the Pope, 1900, Caso matrimoniale di Edward Delpit, Vatican Archives, DAC 50/1 fascicule 10.
51 *Vancouver Daily Province*, 25 January 1901.
52 *Ottawa Evening Citizen*, 20 July 1900.
53 Ibid., 19 December 1900.
54 *Indianapolis Journal*, 4 April 1901.
55 *Montreal Weekly Witness*, 8 January 1901. Analysing the 1920 Stevenson affair, Nootens notes how husbands had to provide for their wives. Nootens, *Genre, patrimoine et droit civil*, 166.
56 *La Presse* (Montreal), 22 May 1900.
57 *Cincinnati Commercial Tribune*, 2 April 1901.
58 "L'affaire Delpit," *Le Courrier du Canada* (Quebec City), 11 January 1901.
59 Elzéar Lavoie, "Les crises du Courrier du Canada: Affaires et rédactions," in *Les Ultramontains canadiens-français*, ed. Nive Voisine (Montreal: Boréal Express, 1985).
60 *La Vérité* (Quebec), 26 January 1901.
61 Kenneth McLaughlin, "'Riding the Protestant Horse': The Manitoba School Question and Canadian Politics, 1890–1896," *Canadian Catholic Historical Association Historical Studies* 53 (1986): 39–52.
62 *Canadian Law Times*, 21 March 1901.
63 *Le Courrier du Canada* (Quebec City), 19 January 1901.
64 *New York Times*, 27 January 1901.
65 *Le Courrier du Canada* (Quebec City), 2 April 1901. Journalist, lawyer, law professor, and Canadian parliamentarian Rodolphe Lemieux expressed the same idea in a letter published in the *Montreal Weekly Witness*. He insisted that civil marriage did not exist in Quebec. *Montreal Weekly Witness*, 31 July 1900.
66 *La Vérité* (Quebec City), 2 March 1901.
67 *Globe*, 24 December 1900.
68 *Globe*, 12 December 1900.
69 *L'Aurore* (Montreal), 7 February 1901.
70 *Sydney Watchman*, 24 August 1911.
71 *La Presse* (Montreal), 18 May 1901.

72 *Durocher v. Degré* (1901), 20 Que SC 456. Prominent Buffalo attorney Lewis Skelton rightly noted in 1912 that the question in the *Durocher* case was "quite different," explaining that the young couple married in front of a "Minister of the Gospel" in the United States, and that person was not competent to record items in the civil registry in the province. Despite what the popular press published on the *Durocher* case making it a question of civil and ecclesiastical courts, the *Revue Légale* clarified that the young couple secretly went to the United States (fraude de loi), and they were not married by their own priest. The editor quickly added that a marriage of two Roman Catholics by a Protestant minister is not illegal. "Des décisions judiciaires rapportées durant ce mois dans la puissance du Canada," *Revue légale* 8 (1912): 215–16.

73 *Sandon (BC) Paystreak*, 2 February 1901.

74 The radical paper *Les Débats*, published between 1899 and 1903, adopted the motto "Ni vendu ni à vendre à aucune faction politique."

75 *L'Avenir* (Montreal), 30 December 1900.

76 *Les Débats* (Montreal), 6 January 1901.

77 *Sherbrooke Tribune*, 7 January 1901.

78 *Globe*, 7 January 1901.

79 *Le Trifluvien* (Trois-Rivières), 8 January 1901.

80 *Le Réveil* (Montreal), 15 January 1901.

81 *La Vérité* (Quebec), 19 January 1901.

82 *Les Débats* (Montreal), 3 February 1901.

83 Andrée Lévesque, *Freethinker: The Life and Works of Eva Circé-Côté*, trans. Lazer Lederrendler (Toronto: Between the Lines, 2017), 13.

84 *Otago (NZ) Daily Times*, 23 February 1901.

85 *Montreal Weekly Witness*, 15 January 1901.

86 *Montreal Weekly Witness*, 9 April 1901.

87 The *New York Times*, 27 January 1901, repeats several times that Édouard is a "scoffer and an infidel."

88 *La Presse* (Montreal), 27 September 1900.

89 *Montreal Weekly Witness*, 2 January 1901.

90 He stopped paying this allowance as soon as he moved to the United States.

91 *Montreal Weekly Witness*, 29 January 1901.

92 *Montreal Weekly Witness*, 5 February 1901.

93 *Kingston Daily Whig*, 16 January 1901.

94 *Kingston Daily Whig*, 12 August 1901.

95 Analysing assault and battery cases, Kathryn Harvey argues that violence in late nineteenth-century Montreal resulted from "unequal distribution of economic and legal power between men and women, as well as in

men's almost unrestricted right to chastise their wives. In part husbands beat their wives because they thought they could get away with it." Slapping one's wife would not have surprised many and, thus, it might have been overlooked by the courts. Kathryn Harvey, "To Love, Honour and Obey: Wife Battering in Working-Class Montreal, 1869–1879," *Urban History Review* 19, no. 2 (1990): 139.

96 *Le Réveil* (Montreal), 27 January 1901.

97 *L'Avenir du Nord* (Saint-Jérôme), 10 January 1901; *Washington (DC) Evening News*, 7 January 1901; *Les Débats* (Montreal), 6 January 1901.

98 Lafleur's biographer does not make much of his Protestant background. Raised a Baptist, Lafleur joined the Anglican church as an adult. David Ricardo Williams mentions the gap between Roman Catholics and Protestants but ends the biographical notice with: "Lafleur was an anomaly, Protestant of foreign background, yet a member of both the French Canadian and the English Canadian establishments. In fact, he was truly bilingual, bilegal and bicultural, but single-mindedly Canadian." David Ricardo Williams, "Lafleur, Eugene," *DCB*, vol. 15, http://www.biographi.ca/en/bio/lafleur_eugene_15E.html.

99 *Montreal Weekly Witness*, 5 February 1901.

100 Admitted to the bar in 1880, Lamothe was called to sit on the Superior Court in 1915 and was appointed Chief Justice of Quebec three years later. Justice Greenshields, "The Late Chief Justice Gustave Lamothe," *Canadian Bar Review* (1923): 62–7.

101 "The Delpit Case," *Montreal Weekly Witness* and *La Presse*, 12 February 1901.

102 *Montreal Gazette*, 13 February 1901.

103 I am grateful to Jim Phillips for sharing his research notes on Archibald.

104 *La Presse* (Montreal), 26 August 1922 and 18 January 1932. Papers also brought up Archibald's judgment in *Johnson v. Sparrow* (1899), 15 S.C. 104, which established that a Black man had as much right as another to occupy an orchestra chair in a theatre. Archibald maintained that the fact of purchasing a ticket was already a contract that bound the seller.

105 *L'écho des bois francs* (Arthabascaville), 27 April 1901.

106 "Marriage Laws in Quebec," *Canada Law Journal* 37 (1901): 91.

107 *La Patrie* (Montreal), 30 March 1901; *Les Débats* (Montreal), 31 March 1901; *Le Soleil* (Quebec City), 1 April 1901; *Le Canada français* (Saint-Jean-sur-Richelieu), 5 April 1901.

108 *Journal de Waterloo*, 4 April 1901; *La Gazette de Berthier*, 5 April 1901; *Le Trifluvien* (Trois-Rivières), 5 April 1901.

109 *Le Réveil* (Montreal), 30 March 1901.

110 *Le Courrier du Canada* (Quebec City), 2 April 1901.

111 George S. Holmested, "The Marriage Laws of Canada," *Canadian Law Review* 2, no. 9 (1903): 529; "Courts Christian," *Canadian Law Times* 23, no. 10 (1911): 369–81; "The Marriage Laws and the Council of Trent," *Canada Law Journal* 47, no. 15 (1911): 481–91; Lewis Stockton, *Marriage Considered from Legal and Ecclesiastical Viewpoints in Connection with the Recent Ne Temere Decree of the Roman Catholic Church* (Buffalo: Huebner-Bleistein Patents Co., 1912), 87; J. Charbonneau, "Eugene Hebert vs Dame Emma Clouâtre," *La revue légale* 18 (1912): 134; J.H. Blumenstein, "Matrimonial Jurisdiction in Canada," *Canadian Bar Review* 6, no. 8 (1928): 583.

112 Morin, "De la reconnaissance officielle," 91.

113 *La Presse* (Montreal), 6 June 1901; *Baltimore Sun*, 5 June 1901.

114 *Sidney (NE) Telegraph*, 28 September 1901. The paper had not covered the initial story.

115 Cheyenne (NE) County District Court, "Delpit v. Delpit," 28 September 1901.

116 *Sidney (NE) Telegraph*, 1 March 1902. To get a glimpse of Canadians seeking American divorces, see James Snell, "The International Border as a Factor in Marital Behaviour: A Historical Case Study," *Ontario History* 81, no. 4 (1989): 289–302, and Philip Girard and Jim Phillips, "Rethinking the 'Nation' in Legal History: A Canadian Perspective," *Law and History Review* 29, no. 2 (2011): 607–26.

117 Without fanfare, Clotilde demanded the annulment on the ground that the marriage was never consummated and that Édouard was living in Saigon. Giovanni Pizzorusso, "Jetté v Delpit," *L'inventaire des documents d'intérêt Canadian dans les archives de la Congrégation "De propaganda Fide," 1904–1914* (Rome, 1992).

118 *New York Times*, 6 August 1901.

3

The Trials and Travails of Eliza Maria Campbell: Gender and the Law in Ontario in the 1870s

JIM PHILLIPS

In 1879 the Parliament of Canada legislated by private act a separation from bed and board of Elizabeth (Eliza) Maria Campbell (née Byrne) from her husband, Robert, an apparent exercise of its jurisdiction over "marriage and divorce" conferred by section 91(26) of the *British North America Act* (*BNA Act*).[1] It was only the tenth divorce act passed by Parliament since Confederation, and it was the only divorce act among the 266 passed between 1868 and 1914 that was not for a divorce *a vinculo matrimonii* (divorce from the bonds of matrimony, which allowed the parties to marry again) but for a divorce *a mensa et thoro* (separation from bed and board, which did not). Eliza Campbell's act was the longest of those 266, and the only one that began, in 1876, as a bill to grant her husband a divorce from her and was transformed along the way into a bill to grant her a separation from him.[2] It was also the only act passed at the behest of a woman whose husband had won a suit for criminal conversation, an action taken by a man against another man for having had sex with his wife. The Campbell matrimonial dispute was a part of parliamentary proceedings each year between 1876 and 1879, taking up around one hundred pages in the Senate Hansard and twenty-eight in the Commons Hansard. It also involved twenty-two days of hearings before a Senate divorce committee in 1876 and 1877, and a further three days before a differently constituted committee in 1879. Before and after 1876 the breakdown of the Campbell marriage also generated seven civil suits in the Ontario courts.

Within the confines of Parliament, the Campbell divorce case produced passionate and at times vituperative debate, accusations of conspiracies, and denunciations of members of Parliament and senators as either hoodwinked by a beguiling and shameless harlot or heartless accomplices to a husband's cruelty. The case was extensively reported in the *Globe* and the local newspapers in the Campbells' home town of Whitby, Ontario, with the same dominant themes as those debated in Parliament. It consumed Whitby throughout. Local residents, inhabitants of Toronto and Ottawa, and senators and MPs all had opinions about the case that reflected both their views of the individuals concerned and their attitudes towards marriage, especially the appropriateness of Robert Campbell's conduct as a Victorian husband.

In Parliament, the case also raised a number of legal and constitutional questions. The most important of these was the meaning of section 91(26) of the *BNA Act*, which gave Parliament jurisdiction over "marriage and divorce." Did the word "divorce" include both kinds mentioned above, or only divorce *a vinculo matrimonii*? A related question was whether Parliament was precluded from passing a statute for a separation from bed and board because, in doing so, it legislated in respect of custody and support (alimony), both subjects that normally came under the provincial property and civil rights power, section 92(13) of the *BNA Act*. A third major point of contention was that the Ontario Court of Chancery had previously decided that Eliza Campbell had been guilty of adultery and had denied her alimony on that ground. In contrast, the Campbell divorce act stated that she had not committed adultery, and awarded her support, a synonym for alimony. Thus for some Parliament passed legislation that was effectively a successful appeal judgment from the Ontario Court of Chancery.

Although at one level this chapter is a legal history of the events following the breakdown of the Campbell marriage, the social and legal aspects of this story were inextricably interlinked. The content and operation of the law can never be properly understood if it is divorced (excuse the pun) from its personal, social, and ideological context, and the Campbell case serves as a vivid reminder of that fact. The context in this case was how the parties in a marriage should conduct themselves. Gender relations were a central concern of all Canadians before, during, and after the 1870s. The marriage bond was seen as the cornerstone of society, and marriage entailed reciprocal rights and duties.[3] A husband had a duty to support and care for his wife, through thick and thin, and the wife had concomitant duties of obedience and fidelity in matters sexual and non-sexual. These beliefs were shared by Protestants and Catholics alike, and while the former were accepting of divorce in exceptional cases, it was always frowned upon.[4] I am not suggesting that marriages invariably, or indeed generally, reflected the ideal in practice, or that many people did not deal with their marital disputes outside the law. "Self-divorce" was endemic, although it is an immeasurable phenomenon precisely because it took place outside the legal system and generally involved people from the less affluent social classes.

The Campbell case centrally involved the law, but it was also ultimately determined by parliamentarians' views of the conduct of the parties in exercising their marital rights and duties. Although, as I explain below, opponents of the bill were "right" in law that Eliza Campbell's separation act should not have been passed, because it was unconstitutional, it did succeed. It succeeded because enough elite men were persuaded that she had been treated unfairly by both her husband and the law, and it was the manly duty of senators and MPs to defend and protect her, whatever the law said. It thus reveals that married women, while they were far from equal under the law in almost all respects, could, in some circumstances, prevail in legal disputes with their husbands. It similarly reveals that they could do so only if they were seen by men as suitable candidates for what, in a different context, has been termed "chivalric justice."[5]

This chapter begins with a brief account of the Campbell and Byrne families, their hometown of Whitby, and the Campbell marriage. The second section deals with the denouement of that marriage on the evening of 26 August 1873 and the immediate aftermath. The third section, covering the period from October 1873 until 1876, deals, necessarily briefly, with the three pre-1876 court cases involving, directly or indirectly, Eliza Campbell on one side and Robert Campbell on the other. These first three sections, which are set in Toronto and Whitby, provide the necessary background for when the story shifted to Ottawa and the long-drawn-out parliamentary divorce proceedings that culminated in May 1879, when Governor General Lord Dufferin gave Eliza Campbell's divorce act royal assent, the first Canadian divorce act not to be reserved for London's approval.

The Campbell and Byrne Families and Marriage

Robert Campbell and Eliza Byrne were both residents of Whitby when they met in the early 1860s.[6] Robert had been born in Forres, Scotland, on 6 July 1833, and moved with his family to Canada West as a teenager. The Campbells settled in Whitby around 1860 and prospered. By mid-century, Whitby had grown to a town of some 7,000, mostly immigrants from the British Isles and their descendants. It had a thriving agricultural export trade: lumber and wheat were exported to the United States via the town's natural harbour, and, after the completion of the Grand Trunk railway in 1856, to Montreal and Toronto. Although its population declined slightly through the 1860s and 1870s, and the harbour trade shrank as the railway replaced water-borne transport, men like Robert Campbell and his brother and business partner James did well by transitioning from raw materials and craft production to mass-produced goods. Robert and James were among a "rising class of businessmen and entrepreneurs."[7] They were wholesalers and retailers of a wide variety of goods. In 1862, their department store sold men's and women's clothing of all kinds, as well as haberdashery, shoes, bedding, curtains, carpets, groceries, and seeds.[8] Much of their stock was imported from the United Kingdom, and both Campbells travelled there on business frequently in the later 1860s and early 1870s. In 1874, Robert was said by Samuel Hume Blake, vice-chancellor of the Ontario Court of Chancery, to have amassed "what, in this country, is looked upon as a considerable fortune."[9] James Campbell was married to Rebecca, and the Campbells had a sister living in Whitby along with her husband, John Anderson, a farmer until 1870, when he became a butcher.

Eliza Byrne was born at L'Orignal, Canada West, in 1844. Her parents, the Rev. James Thomas Byrne, a Congregationalist minister, and Henrietta Byrne, had resided in England until he was sent to L'Orignal by the London Missionary Society in 1838. His task was to show French-Canadian Catholics the folly of their ways. He later moved to Ottawa, then Brockville, and then, in the early 1850s, to Whitby. He and Henrietta had seven children, four girls and three boys, of whom Eliza was apparently the favourite. In the early 1870s, two of Eliza's siblings were in Whitby, including her married brother James Byrne, a druggist.[10]

Robert and Eliza were married by her father in his house on 6 April 1863, at the respective ages of twenty-nine and nineteen.[11] On the surface it must have seemed like a perfect match. Eliza was, by all accounts, very attractive, a good musician and singer, the life and soul of church socials and house parties. No doubt there were a number of young Whitby men disappointed by her decision to marry Robert Campbell, who believed he had made a catch. Eliza must have felt that she too had done well. She had married a mature man who was rising in the world, and who was somewhat captivated by her, even if he did not share her tastes and accomplishments. By 1873 the Campbells had three children, two boys, James (nine) and Robert (seven), and a six-year-old girl, Edith Holmes Campbell. In early 1873 Eliza became pregnant with their fourth child, John Francis, born in December 1873.

Although there is no evidence of serious difficulties with their marriage during its first decade, they were not a well-suited couple. Having heard testimony from them and others in the 1874 alimony case, Vice-Chancellor Blake provided a succinct account of their different personalities and the nature of their marriage. He described Eliza Campbell's fondness for music and the social life of the town, and contrasted this with the tastes of Robert Campbell, a man "of good business habits" who "took but little, if any, interest in that which pleased his wife." The marriage, said Blake, "was not ... a well assorted one," for "neither party sought to accommodate" their differences. Robert was absorbed by his business, "and he gave himself up to that to the exclusion, ... to some extent, of the attention which his wife might have reasonably asked of him." As he increasingly did so, "she looked for and obtained, in the society of others, the enjoyment and admiration which she vainly sought at the hands of her husband. Gradually that which amounted almost to estrangement grew up between them."[12] In January 1873, Eliza began to openly express her feelings, in words and actions. Robert perceived that she "was very much dissatisfied with the house, and her lot, and her children." She went out a good deal and "neglected the house." She took up with "frivolous people."[13] On one occasion she asked what Robert would be prepared to give to have her leave him. She could not have been very happy with the coldness of his reply. He would give her nothing, and if she wanted to leave him, she should do it honourably and not disgrace him. In these inauspicious circumstances, Robert nonetheless went to the United Kingdom at the end of June 1873.

Robert got back to Whitby at midnight on 18 August 1873, and slept the night with Eliza in their home. The following day he got his first intimation that she might have behaved inappropriately over the preceding months. He discovered a letter to Eliza from a man called Godfrey Parks, written from Concord, Ontario, on August 14th.[14] It alluded to his plans to visit her in September; asked whether, if he did so, he would be in time to avoid Robert, whom Eliza and Parks referred to as "the G-d-n" (guardian); and asked her to "tell me where you think the suspicion is." Parks had been briefly a resident of Whitby in the winter of 1872–73, during which time he had engaged in social visits at the

Campbell house. He had also applied for a job as bookkeeper with the Campbell firm in February 1873 but had not been hired.

Robert's reaction to reading the letter was, he consistently acknowledged, the conclusion that Eliza had been unfaithful. He showed the letter to his brother James, but said nothing to Eliza. The next day he took the opportunity of her absence from the home to search through the drawers of her secretaire, where he found various notes and a letter written by her to Parks.[15] It was not clear whether the letter was a copy or an original that she had written but not sent, but it showed that she had written to him more than once. It expressed a hope that Parks would visit Whitby soon, and that they could go for a carriage drive in the evening. She called the prospect of such a drive a "dream … too sweet to indulge in." It was written before Robert had gone to the United Kingdom, for she expressed uncertainty about when she would be able to go to Toronto to meet Parks because she did not know when Robert would be leaving. But she assured Parks that, if she got the chance, she would visit him in Toronto and would attend Holy Trinity Church with him, even though it was a little "high" for her – as one would expect of the daughter of a Congregationalist minister. Somewhat ironically, given that Eliza's correspondence with him had been what aroused Robert's suspicions, Godfrey Parks plays no further part in this story. He joined the newly formed North-West Mounted Police as a constable and died on 26 October 1874, soon after he reached the North-West Territories.[16]

Robert did not speak to Eliza about his discoveries or suspicions; indeed, he remained superficially cordial. He did show the letters to his brothers-in-law James Anderson and James Byrne, as well as to Rev. Byrne, and he questioned Martha and Jane Newsom, sisters who, at different times, were domestic servants to the Campbells. Nobody knew anything of Parks, but the Newsoms told him that thirty-one-year-old George Gordon had visited the house on a number of evenings in his absence, often as the only caller, and had frequently stayed late, still there when the servant went to bed. Robert knew Gordon because he had visited the Campbell home, with others, a number of times, on at least one occasion staying too late for Robert's liking. Gordon's family had immigrated to Upper Canada from Forfar, Scotland, in 1837 and had settled on Bayside Farm, about a mile outside Whitby. They were among the first white settlers in Ontario County. The Gordons and the Campbells had known each other since the mid-1840s, and the Gordons and the Byrnes were also well acquainted. George lived on the farm and ran it with his father, and was also an officer in the militia. The Gordon family was sufficiently well educated and financially well placed that George's older brother James had apprenticed at a law firm in Toronto, been admitted to Osgoode Hall Law School in 1859, and been called to the bar in 1864. The person who signed the $500 bond for him when he was admitted to the Law Society was Robert Campbell. James Gordon practised in Whitby until his retirement in 1899.[17]

In response to the information provided by the letters and his questioning of local residents, but without talking to Eliza, Robert decided to separate from her. She was, in his oft-repeated words, not a "fit guardian" for his children. He made arrangements to take the children to Southampton on the Huron shore on 25 August, the Monday following his return from the United Kingdom, ostensibly to visit relatives on his side of the family. When he left, he asked James Campbell and John Anderson to "watch" the house during his absence. He was convinced that Eliza had, at best, behaved highly inappropriately, and, at worst, had had an affair or affairs, and he thought she might use the opportunity of his absence from Whitby to transgress again. If she did, he wanted to "catch her in the act."

The Evening of 26 August and Its Aftermath

James Campbell dutifully did what he was asked on the evening of 26 August 1873. What exactly transpired that night was the key question over the ensuing years. George Gordon came to the Campbell house, stayed some hours, and left well after midnight. During the time he was there James Campbell was outside the house, sometimes in the yard, sometimes on the verandah leading to the front door, moving around in stockinged feet while he tried to find a vantage point from which he could see the couple inside. He never did see anything, for the curtains remain closed and the blinds fixed throughout the evening. At one point he was joined by John Anderson, who also crouched and hid and tried to listen and see. They heard nothing out of line until midnight but claimed to have heard things afterwards.

Nothing further can be said with certainty about that evening. In the court cases and proceedings before the Senate divorce committee, Campbell's and Anderson's accounts were contradicted in numerous ways by Eliza Campbell. Some of the disagreements were on relatively inconsequential points, such as when Gordon arrived at the house – closer to nine or ten – and how he got there – by walking Eliza home from a social evening at her parents or by turning up independently. There was a similar disagreement about when Gordon left, whether around 1 a.m. or closer to 3 a.m. More importantly, Campbell and Anderson claimed, from the noises they heard and the conversations they thought took place after midnight, that Eliza and Gordon had twice had sexual intercourse after midnight, which she consistently and vehemently denied. Campbell and Anderson never claimed to have seen this happen; they merely deduced it from the noises they heard and snippets of conversations they reported. All that is certain is that Gordon and Eliza were in the parlour together the entire time that he was at the Campbell home. They did not go upstairs, where the children were sleeping, nor were they seen performing any compromising acts by the other occupant of the house, Jane Newsom, who remained mostly in her room at the back of the kitchen on the main floor. We do not know the truth about the alleged sexual goings on, but, in my judgment, the evidence leads to a conclusion that sex did not occur.

The competing accounts of what happened that night were repeated in three fora over the next three years – the Courts of Common Pleas and Chancery and the Senate. There was no material disagreement on many issues, despite efforts by lawyers to challenge the witnesses on matters such as exactly where James Campbell stood or crouched as he strained to see and listen, or exactly where Gordon and Eliza sat on the couch. The principal differences between the accounts on each side involved what words were used in conversation and, more importantly, their meaning. James Campbell claimed, and Eliza Campbell flatly denied, to have heard sounds of kissing, Gordon telling Eliza that she had nice breasts, Eliza asking Gordon whether he best liked it "sideways, topways or bottomways" (bottomways was the answer), and Eliza telling Gordon that she was not happy with her husband and wanted to leave him and go to California. In contrast, Eliza said that such claims were all fabricated. She described instead an evening of general conversation, of her singing and reading to Gordon, and of them looking at images in a stereoscope and playing draughts (checkers).[18]

In some cases, the parties agreed on what words were used, with Eliza insisting that they had been misunderstood. James Campbell said, for example, that Gordon had asked Eliza about the location of her navel, the implication being that, in his fumblings with the clothing of the pregnant Eliza, he had mistaken it for her vagina. But Eliza said she had sung a number of songs that night, one of which was "The Pirate's Serenade." When the song ended, she asked Gordon if he would like to be a naval officer, and he said he preferred the army. Hence the word used was *naval*, not *navel*. James Campbell said he heard another conversation in which Eliza ask Gordon not to "push it in too far." Eliza said that that remark was a reference to the stereoscope, which was partially broken, and if a slide was pushed into the instrument too far it would come out at the bottom.

Another issue that also produced competing accounts, and that became important later, concerned a confrontation on Whitby's main street after Gordon, Campbell, and Anderson had left the Campbell residence. The parties disagreed about the time this occurred. Whenever it was, James Campbell and Anderson had gone to the Campbell store about half a mile down the street to warm themselves with whisky. After a few minutes they saw Gordon walking towards them and challenged him. James Campbell asserted that he accused Gordon of having "criminal connection with my brother's wife," and that Gordon admitted doing so, saying that he could not help it. Gordon told a different story. James had accused him of attempting to seduce Eliza, not of actually doing so, and Gordon had denied the attempt and, of course, its consummation.

James Campbell immediately summoned Robert back to Whitby and told him his version of the events that evening. Robert told his father-in-law the story and asked Rev. Byrne to take his daughter away from the Campbell home. The Byrnes refused to believe that sex had occurred and urged Robert to meet and reconcile with Eliza, but to no avail. Robert insisted that his wife was an "impure woman" and, now that he was confident he had confirmation, they must separate. He did not contact Eliza and did not sleep in their house again until after he threw Eliza out, an incident discussed below. He conveyed a message to her that he could not live with her anymore and that she should leave. Eliza quickly came to hear from her father and brother what had been said about her, denied the accusation of adultery, and demanded that Robert talk to her. She wrote to him on 28 August, the day Robert returned to Whitby, asking him to meet with her and listen to her explanation. She acknowledged that she had been "imprudent" but insisted that "I have not been guilty of the charge James has imputed to me, that of having criminal conversation with that man, or any approach to it." She must have suspected that he would not listen, for the same letter reminded him of his duty if he chose to desert her: "If you do not meet me, remember you have to make an allowance for me and your unborn child."[19]

Eliza denied the charge of adultery to all who would listen. As the *Whitby Chronicle* succinctly explained, she "demanded vehemently to be confronted with her accusers, and refused to leave the house, asserting that the stories ... were untrue, that she was an innocent and a faithful wife ..., and that the whole case against her was a vile conspiracy got up by the brother," who had never approved of his sister-in-law.[20] Robert Campbell was utterly unmoved, refusing to speak with Eliza and communicating with her through an intermediary, presumably James Byrne, that he wanted her out of the house. When that did not work, he had her forcibly removed on the evening of 24 September. He was able to persuade two Whitby constables to act outside their authority and assist him to carry his five months–pregnant wife downstairs, out the door, and down the front steps, with her protesting all the way. She was deposited on the ground, from where her brother James helped her up and took her to his house. Eliza had to recuperate in bed for a week, unable to attend a hearing before the Whitby magistrates consequent on her immediately laying an information for assault against Robert.

Eliza was taken to her parents' house, where she resided for some years. She gave birth there to her and Robert's fourth child, John Francis, in December. Throughout the next few years, Robert and Eliza Campbell both continued to live in Whitby, he in the family home and she with her parents. Eliza's father died in November 1874 on his way back from a trip to Albany, New York – according to his obituary from a broken heart and shame at the scandal.[21] These events were, not surprisingly, the talk of the town over the next two to three years. Initially locals were in two sharply opposed camps over the rights and wrongs of the business. The *Whitby Chronicle* at first studiously avoided taking sides, calling the whole affair "an unhappy and sad one" pitting "a refined, well-educated lady, very much admired for her beauty and accomplishments" who had "never before [had] the breath of scandal whispered ... against her good name" against "a highly respectable businessman," who must have thought himself "grievously wronged" to bring "such a charge against his wife" and thereby to "break up his household." Yet elsewhere, the newspaper evinced some support for Eliza, asking people not to prejudge the facts without clearer evidence. It also acknowledged that "people take sides and sympathize with one and the other," with, "as is usual on such occasions," the "greatest sympathy ... being given to the woman," whose reputation would suffer no matter what the result of the coming legal battles and who, "in her delicate condition, is reported as suffering torments of body and mind inconceivable."[22] Over a short period of time the balance of opinion shifted, and Robert was cast as the villain for his refusal to listen to Eliza's explanations and attempt a reconciliation, and he was joined in the rogues gallery by his brother when enough people became convinced that James had perjured himself at Robert's request. Whitby residents stopped taking their business to the Campbells as a result.[23]

The Campbells Go to Court

Three lawsuits involving the Campbells were all launched at about the same time, all of them before Eliza Campbell had been ejected from the house. The first two were played out in the Court of Common Pleas, and, while the causes of action were different, they involved the same factual question – had Eliza and Gordon had sex the night of 26 August.[24] They produced contrasting results, largely because Eliza Campbell and George Gordon were precluded from testifying in the first trial but were able to do so in the second.

An action for criminal conversation was launched by Robert Campbell against Gordon almost immediately after his return to Whitby, claiming $3,000 in damages.[25] This tort – not uncommon in nineteenth-century England and Canada but now defunct – was an action that a man could take against another man for having sex with his wife.[26] The trial took place in Toronto over two full days in mid-October, before Judge Thomas Galt and a jury.[27] Robert Campbell's principal counsel was Robert Harrison, one of Toronto's leading lawyers, who in 1875 was appointed Chief Justice of the Court of Queen's Bench. Gordon was represented by another pillar of the Toronto legal establishment, Malcom Crooks Cameron, and by his brother James Gordon.[28] Obtaining the services of Cameron, who at the time was also leader of the opposition Conservative Party in Ontario, and who would be appointed to Queen's Bench in 1878, demonstrated that the Gordon and Byrne families were not without means. For her part, Eliza's principal financial backers were her mother and her druggist brother James.[29] The courtroom was packed to the rafters, mainly by residents of Whitby, and reporters attended from the Whitby newspapers. On the second day interest was even greater than on the first, with "a great many people" unable to get in. "It was one dense closely packed mass of humanity," Robert's lawyer Robert Harrison confided to his diary.[30]

Robert Campbell won the case. Whether he would have won had Eliza and Gordon been able to testify cannot be known, but the fact is that they were precluded from doing so. The common law had long provided that spouses could not give evidence against each other, and that the parties to a lawsuit were similarly not competent witnesses because they were "interested" in the outcome and thus susceptible to committing perjury. The "party witness disqualification," as it was known, was removed in Ontario in 1869, and the bar on spouses testifying was repealed in 1873. However there was one caveat to both these evidence law reforms. Parties and spouses were neither competent nor compellable to give evidence "in any proceeding instituted in consequence of adultery."[31] Thus James Campbell's and John Anderson's evidence could not be refuted by the only two people in a position to do so. The inability to testify also meant that Eliza could say nothing of the events immediately before and after 26 August, which showed that her husband had already made up his mind to separate from her and thus had an incentive to have the two men watch the house to garner, or perhaps fabricate, additional evidence. The jury took an hour to find for Robert, and awarded him the full sum claimed of $3,000. Robert never collected on the debt, unable to satisfy writs of execution against Gordon's property.

The second case, which was initiated in late September 1873 by Eliza Campbell, accused James Campbell of defamation. Acting on behalf of his brother, James had told shopkeepers in Whitby to deny Eliza credit, informing them that Robert would not pay the bills because she had been adulterous with Gordon. Because married women still did not have the right to launch legal actions in their own right, the style of cause was *Robert Campbell et ux v. James Campbell, et ux* meaning "and wife." Thus Eliza's action against her brother-in-law was, ironically, conducted in the name of her husband. The defamation suit was heard in Toronto on 26 and 27 March 1874, before John Hawkins Hagarty, chief justice of Common Pleas, and a jury, Eliza claiming damages of $10,000 from her brother-in-law.[32] Eliza was represented by the lawyers who had defended Gordon in the criminal conversation action; James Campbell by those who had represented his brother in that case. The trial saw three witnesses testifying who had not been able to do so earlier – Robert and Eliza Campbell and George Gordon. Eliza and Gordon thus had their first opportunity to present a different version of what had happened on the fateful night. She insisted that "no improper familiarity took place between her and Gordon." Gordon also gave evidence, entirely consistent with Eliza's. He was the final witness on the first day of the trial.

When court opened the next day, "densely crowded" by a throng taking "the greatest interest … in the proceedings," the first witness was George Gross, a hardware merchant who lived above his store in Whitby's business district. Gross provided the first evidence that James Campbell had not told the truth, albeit on what might be thought a small issue. Gross testified to being woken up by a row in the street at about 1:30 a.m. on the night of the 26th, and claimed to have heard Gordon deny the adultery. Gross's testimony thus contradicted James Campbell's on two points – the time at which Gordon, Campbell, and Anderson had left the Campbell house, and the content of the conversation in the street, especially the fact that Gordon had supposedly admitted the adultery. Gross also recounted that he had been subjected to witness intimidation after he had told people in Whitby that James Campbell had not testified truthfully at the criminal conversation trial. Two other witnesses gave accounts of the late-night altercation on Whitby's main street that were inconsistent with James Campbell's. Cameron attacked the Campbell brothers for fabricating evidence in order to be rid of Eliza. About three-quarters of the way through, Cameron's "elegant and pathetic appeal," which asked the jury to decide between Eliza and "the two dastards, Campbell and Anderson," was warmly applauded by the spectators, and Hagarty had to issue a stern warning and threaten with jail anybody who disturbed the proceedings.

The jury took some hours to return a verdict for Eliza of $1,000; the length of their deliberations was the result of ten of the twelve jurors wanting to award her $10,000, a very large sum. There were celebrations outside the courtroom, but nothing like there were in Whitby when the news reached the town. People paraded through the streets in a torchlight procession led by the town band, and halted in front of James Byrne's house, where Eliza was staying. There, "hearty cheers" were given for Eliza Campbell, James Byrne, and Cameron, and a fireworks display followed. James Byrne was the local hero, for having stood by his sister emotionally and financially.[33] Local opinion was still very much on Eliza's side more than a year later. When the *Oshawa Reformer* raked up the case, publishing articles that were critical of Eliza, the *Whitby Chronicle* castigated its proprietor for doing so "in opposition to all the merchants, traders and business men – aye, and even the women – of the town of Whitby."[34] In the end Eliza never collected her money, the verdict being overturned and a new trial ordered by Justice John Wellington Gwynne of Common Pleas, who ruled that the jury's verdict had been "attributable to sympathy with the wife, rather than to an intelligent and impartial appreciation of the evidence."[35] Eliza never proceeded with the new trial.

In the third case Eliza applied for alimony as soon as she had been thrown out of the family home. Alimony was an equitable remedy for the failure of a husband to fulfil his common law duty to support his wife. It had been available in Ontario since the establishment of a Court of Chancery in 1837, and successive chancellors had consistently found for women who applied – women deserted by their husbands who had committed adultery or who had subjected them to violence and/or other treatment that, according to the court, entitled them to no longer live under the same roof. These chancellors were elite men who had no truck with any suggestion that the fundamental inequality of marriage should be changed, but they were nonetheless tough on men who did not carry out their side of the marital bargain. Women won most cases – provided they had not themselves committed adultery, which justified a husband refusing support – but were less successful in collecting their awards.[36] As it took time for the Campbell case to go to trial, Robert paid Eliza $50 a month interim alimony as the law required, although he tried to get out of that on an interlocutory motion.[37] When the case was heard, Vice-Chancellor Blake found James Campbell and John Anderson more credible than Eliza and George Gordon, whose evidence "bears marks of having been discussed between them, after they were aware of the statements of Campbell and Anderson, and that they then agreed to make up the story." Not only did Eliza not get a larger monthly award than the $50, she was no longer entitled to receive that amount, and Robert stopped paying it.

Robert Campbell Petitions Parliament for a Divorce

In 1874 Robert Campbell began proceedings to obtain a divorce. At this time the only way for residents in Canada except the Maritime provinces and British Columbia to get divorced was by a private act of Parliament.[38] A parliamentary divorce was available only on the ground of adultery, the ultimate "offence" against the sanctity of marriage, and the language used to describe claims of adultery was always more redolent of the criminal law than the civil. An accusation of adultery was invariably referred to as a "charge," the act itself as a "crime." Like any other act of Parliament, a divorce bill had to pass three readings in both houses. Unlike most acts of Parliament, divorce bills started in the Senate. Robert's application was only the sixth made to Parliament since Confederation; of those six, one had been rejected and another had succeeded only on the third attempt.[39]

Robert Campbell's petition, like all parliamentary petitions, had to be presented by a senator. The senator who did so was usually someone from the petitioner's area, not infrequently someone who knew the petitioner or their family. Robert asked David Reesor of Markham, whom he did not know but who lived reasonably close to Whitby, to present his petition, and, from then on, Reesor was the sponsor of the bill. Reesor claimed later that he was not optimistic about Robert's chances of success, telling him, "frankly and distinctly, that from what he had heard outside," he had doubts as to whether Robert could make his case.[40] He nonetheless agreed to present the petition. He then turned out to be Eliza Campbell's staunchest supporter.

The petition was accepted, and on 8 March 1876, the bill passed second reading by a vote of 33–14, all fourteen nays being Catholics.[41] Having passed second reading, the bill was referred to a select committee of nine – Reesor and eight other senators of his choosing. (Not until 1888 was there a standing committee on divorce.) The identity of these men is important to this story, for they made the decision to reject the claim of adultery and give Eliza Campbell her own unique remedy. Reesor chose four fellow Ontarians – James Cox Aikins, Elijah Leonard, Walter Dickson, and Benjamin Seymour, of whom only Dickson was a lawyer. In addition, two men were from Nova Scotia – Robert Dickey and Henry Kaulbach – both of whom were both lawyers. Prince Edward Islander Robert Haythorne and Clement Cornwall of British Columbia, another lawyer, completed the membership. Although the committee had four lawyers, it was relatively inexperienced at this work: Haythorne, Kaulbach, Leonard, Reesor, and Seymour had not previously served on a divorce committee, and Aikins and Cornwall had served on only one. Two of the lawyer members had more experience: Dickson had served on five committees and Dickey on six. Dickey was chosen as the chair.

The committee met for twelve days in March. A verbatim transcript of the proceedings was published as a 254-page appendix to the Senate *Journal* of 1876. All senators and MPs could vote on divorce bills, and thus the evidence was always made available to them. Both parties were represented by counsel, who took each of their witnesses through their direct examination and cross-examined the other side's witnesses. Robert's lawyer was thirty-seven-year-old William Henry Walker, who had been called to the bar in 1867 and practised in Ottawa. Although this was his first divorce case, he had a good reputation as a lawyer and was made a QC in 1889.[42] Eliza's lawyer was a man much better known to Canadian historians, William McDougall, the first governor of the North-West Territories, who was prevented from entering Red River in 1869 by the Métis under Louis Riel and was recalled to Ottawa in disgrace. Thereafter McDougall never again held significant political office, although at the time of the divorce proceedings in 1876 he was a member of the Ontario legislative assembly.[43] Eliza could afford McDougall in part because the Senate divorce committee ordered her husband to provide her with $500 for the conduct of her defence, a not uncommon practice.[44]

The key question before the committee was whether Robert Campbell could "prove the preamble" in his draft bill. The preamble of all divorce bills provided the names of the parties, the date and place of the marriage, and the allegation of adultery, with varying degrees of detail about with whom, where, and how often. If a male petitioner had been successful in an action for criminal conversation, that was also stated. The rest of the always short, one- or two-page, bill – the operative provisions – simply stated that the parties were divorced and could marry again.

At the committee proceedings, evidence was taken about all the issues discussed above – the Campbell marriage, the letters from Parks, the alleged events of 26 August 1873, and Robert Campbell's actions before the 26th and following James Campbell's report of that night. Robert Campbell testified for more than two days, James for three, Eliza for almost three, and John Anderson for the best part of one day. Some of the people who had given evidence in the court cases made cameo appearances, all called by McDougall. Gordon did not testify; by 1876 he had moved to Manitoba. Walker's strategy was to have the Campbell brothers and Anderson tell the story of the letters and the night of 26 August. In contrast McDougall not only had Eliza Campbell deny everything and recount in graphic detail her expulsion from the marital home, but he also cross-examined Robert Campbell extensively on his motivations and actions. Why did he jump so precipitously to the conclusion that Eliza was not a "fit" wife? Why did he not talk to her between the discovery of the letters and his departure for the Huron shore, or after his return to Whitby? McDougall also had some of the minor players testify that Eliza was well-respected and liked in the town and that her story was believed.

The taking of evidence wrapped up on 28 March, and a majority of the committee (seven of nine) quickly decided that the preamble "had not been proved" – that is, that Eliza Campbell had not committed adultery. Kaulbach and Cornwall dissented. The following day, MacDougall presented the committee with a petition on Eliza's behalf asking for "amendments" to the bill. The petition recounted Eliza's violent ejection from the family home and stated that she was "desirous of being divorced *a mensa et thoro*, or separated as to bed and board from Robert Campbell." She also wanted to retain custody of her youngest child and to be given custody of her daughter "at least, if not of her other children." A further requested "amendment" was that Robert Campbell should be ordered "to make adequate provision for her and the children."[45]

On 31 March, the committee made its report to the full Senate. The failure to "prove the preamble" would normally be the end of the matter, at least for 1876, because a petitioner could always try again with more and better evidence. But there was still Eliza Campbell's petition to deal with, and, by a 5–4 majority, the committee opted to request instructions from the full Senate as to what to do with it. When that request was debated in the Senate, the only members who spoke were those who had been on the committee. Reesor moved that the petition be referred back to the committee to investigate Eliza's allegations of mistreatment, and, if they were found true, to amend the bill in order to "secure to the Petitioner and Respondent respectively, the rights and privileges which would be secured to them under a decree for judicial separation in England." The reference to England was to the fact that it had long been possible to obtain a divorce *a mensa et thoro* there from the ecclesiastical courts, because it was merely a separation order, regularizing the parties living apart but not dissolving the marriage. The matrimonial jurisdiction of the ecclesiastical courts was abolished in 1857, when the Court of Divorce and Matrimonial Causes was established with jurisdiction over both forms of divorce.[46] Reesor argued that what prevented Eliza from getting a separation was the lack of a court in Ontario with jurisdiction to make such an order. By contrast the civil law of Quebec permitted the Superior Court in that province to grant judicial separations, a point I will return to later.[47]

On the other side, Kaulbach was vehemently against any consideration of the petition, principally on the ground that even discussing any kind of support for Eliza would involve the Senate effectively constituting itself as a court of appeal reversing Blake's decision in the Court of Chancery that had dismissed her claim for alimony. He also argued that Eliza could not be allowed to propose amendments to Robert's bill that would effectively make it her bill. If she wanted a divorce, she should present her own petition after giving due notice. Kaulbach had wanted to grant Robert his divorce; he thought Eliza guilty "beyond a reasonable doubt." Dickey was prepared to have Eliza's petition discussed on a deferred basis, in the next session. His motion to refer the matter back to the committee prevailed 30–14. Six of the committee members voted in favour, and two (Dickson and Kaulbach) against, while Cornwall was not present for the vote. Unusually for a vote on anything involving divorce, ten Quebec senators, seven of them Catholics, were among the majority, possibly because they were voting for the possibility of passing an act granting a separation, something not unlike what could be obtained in the Quebec Superior Court.[48]

After two further days of deliberation, the committee came back with another report. They found Eliza's allegations in her petition to be true, and presented what they termed an amended bill, with the amendments all having been proposed by McDougall. It was not an amended bill: it was an entirely different one. What had been *An Act for the Relief of Robert Campbell* had become *An Act for the Relief of Robert Campbell and Eliza Maria Campbell*. What had been a bill granting Robert a divorce *a vinculo matrimonii* became a bill granting Eliza a divorce *a mensa et thoro*. What had been a preamble asserting that Eliza had committed adultery with Gordon and stating that Robert had won the criminal conversation action became a preamble asserting that Robert had "treacherously deserted" Eliza, had taken her three children from her, had violently removed her from the marital home, and had repeatedly accused her of adultery and done his best to prove that fact. The operative provisions of the bill were not the usual few lines declaring the parties divorced and free to remarry, but ten clauses granting her a separation that had the same "force and consequence" as one granted by the English court, giving her custody of Edith Holmes and John Francis Campbell and requiring Robert to pay for the support and maintenance of Eliza and the two children. The amounts were left blank, to be filled in at a later stage in the parliamentary process. The committee report acknowledged that it was proposing "a new precedent in legislation" and recommended that discussion of the bill be postponed until the following session.[49]

Chivalry Triumphant: A Fractious Senate, 1877–1879

Before I analyze the debates that took place in the Senate in 1877 and 1879, a brief chronological summary may be useful.[50] The separation bill drawn up by McDougall in 1876 eventually passed the Senate, but not before two tied votes (31–31) on second reading. On a third, and decisive, vote, the bill passed second reading 34–28 after long debate in a slightly differently constituted Senate.[51] It then passed third reading in a much-reduced house, 25–16. As soon as it did so, nineteen senators entered a written protest in the *Journal*, a highly unusual event. Only a few days before the end of the parliamentary session, the bill was sent to the Commons, which refused to deal with it because Eliza Campbell had not given the requisite notice of her intention to petition for a divorce. Robert Campbell had given notice, but Eliza never had, and the Commons refused to allow her to rely on Robert's notice. Eliza's attempt to bring the bill back in the Senate in 1878 again failed for lack of notice, but she did better in 1879 because she put in the requisite notice. With her petition accepted, matters proceeded as usual. A new committee, again of Reesor's choosing, was struck, consisting of six members who had served on the 1876–77 committee (Dickey, Dickson, Haythorne, Leonard, Reesor, and Seymour) and three who had not (William Brouse of Ontario, who was appointed to the Senate only in 1878; James Ferrier, a Quebec Protestant; and Alexander Macfarlane of Nova Scotia). It therefore did not include the two men who had dissented in 1876, Cornwall and Kaulbach. Both Eliza and Robert were present for the two-day hearing, but only Eliza gave evidence. She briefly recounted the history of the marriage breakdown – mostly her ejection from the house when she was five months pregnant – and, less briefly, described Robert's recent settlement offers made once her petition was accepted by the Senate. Those offers were not what one would call reconciliatory: he would take her back as a "guilty woman" who, in the fullness of time, he might forgive. After Eliza rejected that, Robert then offered a derisory property settlement, which she also refused. The committee reported that they had found Eliza's preamble proved, setting the stage for the longest and most acrimonious debate yet.[52]

Opponents of the bill raised many procedural and substantive objections. Nonetheless the bill passed second reading 30–22 and third reading 34–26. Almost immediately all twenty-six of those who opposed the bill signed on to some or all of a twelve-point "dissentient."[53] After more lengthy debate, a version of the bill passed the Commons 56–38, with Prime Minister John A. Macdonald one of those opposed. The contentiousness of the Campbell bill in both 1877 and 1879 can be discerned from this bare recitation. It should be added that sixty-two senators participated in the votes on both 12 and 18 April 1877, and sixty on the third-reading vote in 1879 – over 80 per cent of the seventy-seven members. These numbers are exceptional, given that, on most days, fewer than fifty senators were present for votes. The bill was also much talked about outside the confines of the formal floor debates. Members buttonholed each other in and out of the Senate building, making their arguments and lobbying, just as they did with any contested piece of legislation. An exchange between two British Columbia senators, lawyer Clement Cornwall and Dr Robert Carrall, is illustrative of the many informal discussions that took place. As we will see below, Carrall voted for the bill while stating that he had not read the evidence. Cornwall criticized him for this, and Carrall insisted in response that it did not matter, because "he had obtained information on the subject from those who had heard both sides, and he considered his knowledge as full, accurate and extensive as that of any member of the committee."[54] Robert Campbell himself was also involved in the lobbying: he hung around the Senate, passing out a circular stating his case, and visited some members where they lived to press his view that the bill should not become law. The Senate debates were at times angry and impassioned in equal measure, becoming quite personal and certainly nonparliamentary. Cornwall described them as "unseemly proceedings," both "partial" and "rancorous." For him, they showed that the Senate was not the place to decide whether a couple should be divorced, a matter that needed a "calm judicial spirit."[55]

This partisanship and rancour occurred in part because the bill posed deep and difficult legal and constitutional questions. But the issues raised by the bill went beyond legal arguments. Central to the votes cast by many senators were their views of what was just and right about how both Robert and Eliza Campbell had behaved as a married couple. Was Eliza Campbell, as Nova Scotia senator and former Crown prosecutor Henry Kaulbach claimed, a woman of "licentious and depraved habits" who had been "totally reckless of the decencies of the married life" and who now "asked this House to whitewash her skirts"? Or was she, in Carrall's words, a "lady who had been wronged," who had "come to this Senate" and "asked for redress for her little ones and herself"? Was Robert Campbell, again in Carrall's words, "the man who had taken ... scandalous means of obtaining evidence to defame the character of an injured lady"? Or was he, again according to Kaulbach, a man who had been kind and considerate to his wife and children and was now falsely accused of cruelty and desertion? Kaulbach insisted that Robert Campbell had acted in a moral and manly way, for it would have been "inconsistent with the position of a just and honourable man, a husband and father, to live in the same house with ... an adultress."

On the surface the Senate debates of 1877 and 1879 were dominated by legal and constitutional issues, with lawyers over-represented among the speakers. Only two of those lawyers, Dickey and Thomas Heath Haviland of Prince Edward Island, made arguments in favour of the bill in the Senate, while ten spoke in opposition to it. The opponents of the bill "won" the legal arguments, yet those in favour of it prevailed. For a majority of senators the law mattered less than did their views of the Campbells as players on the matrimonial stage – that is, the extent to which Robert and Eliza had conformed to appropriate gender roles in their marital relations.

Opponents of the bill offered three principal legal arguments, with Alexander Campbell –an accomplished lawyer (later minister of justice) and a minister in all of John A. Macdonald's cabinets – the most prominent speaker. In 1877 he was the leader of the opposition Conservatives in the Senate; in 1879 he was government leader.[56] The first argument concerned the meaning of the word "divorce" in the phrase "marriage and divorce" in section 91(26) of the *BNA Act*. For those opposed to the Bill it meant only a divorce *a vinculo matrimonii*, and did not include a divorce *a mensa et thoro*. Separation was an entirely different matter from divorce. Separation did not dissolve a marriage; indeed separation made it possible for the parties to reconcile and live together again. Supporters of the meaning of divorce as limited to *a vinculo matrimonii* could point to multiple precedents. In the first place, in the pre-Confederation era, imperial instructions to colonial governors had always meant only divorce *a vinculo matrimonii* when the word was used. In addition, in the area of divorce, the Senate had inherited the powers of the House of Lords, which prior to 1857 was the only body empowered to grant a divorce in the United Kingdom and granted only divorces *a vinculo*. Finally, the *BNA Act* did not explicitly assign "separation" to either level of government. It did not do so because separations in the United Kingdom before 1857 were dealt with by the ecclesiastical courts, which Canada did not have. In Quebec, separations were dealt with by the civil law and, like all the civil law, were included in the compendious term "property and civil rights" in section 92(13) of the *BNA Act*. This argument was bolstered by reference to the question of why divorce had been included in section 91 at all, rather than seen as a part of property and civil rights. The apparent inconsistency in putting divorce into section 91 was explained as a measure to protect Quebec's Protestant minority. Were divorce to be under provincial jurisdiction, Quebec would never pass a divorce act, and Protestants in the province would be forever deprived of this remedy for marital failure. Making divorce a federal head of power meant that they would have the option of a parliamentary divorce.[57]

The second principal argument against the bill was related to, but distinct from, the first. As noted above, separation was not included in either section 91 or 92, but its two main incidents – alimony and custody – were in section 92, as part of property and civil rights. Parliament could not legislate in these areas as a general matter, and thus it could also not legislate in a particular case. This argument also engaged concerns related to the Confederation bargain between French and English Canada. Property and civil rights had been made a provincial power largely to protect Quebec's civil law from federal interference. In an appeal to Quebec nationalism, Alexander Campbell pointedly asked the Quebec senators "if they would sanction a departure from the ordinary course of jurisprudence, and adopt a bill which would reverse the decision of a court of competent jurisdiction upon a question of property and civil rights."[58] The link to the status of the civil law precipitated a rare intrusion into a divorce bill debate for a Quebec Catholic (other than stating that divorces were anathema to Catholic doctrine.) François-Xavier-Anselme Trudel, a lawyer and a leader of the ultramontane movement within the Catholic Church, was adamant that Parliament could deal only with divorce, not separation, because of the division of powers.[59] Another Quebec senator, Edward Penny, concurred. If Parliament could legislate separation for couples in Ontario, it could do so for people in Quebec – an unthinkable interference with the civil law. Some non-Quebec senators took the same line. Sarnia's Alexander Vidal, a land surveyor and banker, expressed sympathy for Eliza Campbell but thought Trudel's argument – that the only aspects of property and civil rights that were under federal jurisdiction were marriage and divorce, and the latter did not include separation – "unanswerable."[60]

The third principal argument against the bill was that it overturned, by legislation, a court decision – that is, the judgment of Vice-Chancellor Blake denying Eliza Campbell alimony. Although the term was not used, this was essentially an argument about the separation of powers between the legislature and the courts. As Alexander Campbell put it, "one of the most eminent judges in the country" had dealt with the alimony question in this case, and it was not for the Senate to reverse that decision. The Senate was not a court of appeal from a decision of one of the "ordinary tribunals of the country," a point also made by Penny, who emphatically rejected a suggestion that Parliament was in any sense the highest court in the land. It was not a court at all, and, although it acted judicially when it came to divorces, it was a hybrid, acting "legislatively though on judicial grounds." Lawrence Power of Nova Scotia considered it "exceedingly improper" of the Senate to "constitute itself a court of appeal." Alexander Campbell called the bill an extraordinary interference with the administration of justice, for Parliament had not been asked to pass an act overturning a court decision for 200 years, and had not actually done so since the reign of Henry VIII. Ottawa lawyer Richard Scott, a prominent Catholic, found the bill without precedent, and represented the Senate setting itself above the courts. He also argued that Parliament could not refuse other petitions for alimony if it allowed this one.[61]

In addition to these arguments, opponents of the bill offered other less significant but still sharply pointed critiques. The bill made a mockery of parliamentary procedure. The Senate divorce committee had not dealt with the bill presented to it; rather, it had written an entirely different one: "they must reverse each enacting clause of the original bill; they must reverse the preamble, they must reverse the title." Alexander Campbell could not accept, "by any sort of logic," that this was an amendment of the original bill. It was an exercise in "perverted ingenuity." In addition, opponents castigated the bill for being directed at one man, for legislating a "strange and novel and wholly unprecedented liability" on Robert Campbell, "an "extraordinary and unjust" measure that was like Parliament "passing an Act to declare that one man was in debt to another."[62]

Among opponents of the bill, Nova Scotia's Henry Kaulbach was the most consistent – his senatorial colleagues on all sides would likely have said persistent or something more pejorative – and he adverted to all these legal arguments. But his bull-in-a-china-shop style, and his dismissive conviction that his opponents simply were unable to understand what he knew to be right, could not have endeared him to his colleagues. His effectiveness was arguably further reduced by his continued insistence that Eliza Campbell had committed adultery and, thus, that the preamble of the original petition had been proved and a divorce should have been granted to Robert Campbell. Whether Kaulbach was right about that was beside the point, now that the Senate was debating a different bill. He made thinly veiled attacks on the integrity of the Senate divorce committee members in 1876–77 and an outright assault on Reesor for having packed the 1879 committee, an accusation that angered senators on both sides.[63] Kaulbach was asked more than once not to discuss the details of the evidence, but he ignored the requests. He constantly injected into those details attacks on Eliza's character. She had engaged in "lewd conduct," had "secret correspondence with a young man [Parks] ... of a grossly vile and sensual character," and was "a fit subject for any seducer" and "a woman of licentious and depraved habits." On a number of occasions when Kaulbach said such things in the Senate, he was met with cries of "shame."[64]

Supporters of the bill sought to counter the legal arguments, with lawyer Robert Dickey, the chair of the committee, taking the lead. A former member of the Nova Scotia Legislative Council who had attended the Charlottetown and Quebec Conferences, Dickey insisted that the word "divorce" in the *BNA Act* could mean both kinds of divorce. For this assertion, he relied on standard English works that used both the terms divorce *a vinculo* and divorce *a mensa et thoro*. On this point he was supported by Reesor, who, although not a lawyer, had obviously done some reading and consulted counsel. Reesor conceded that there was no precedent for the bill but argued that new circumstances called for new precedents, and he claimed that "eminent lawyers" in Ontario, whom he did not name, agreed that a divorce *a mensa et thoro* was a part of English law and within Parliament's jurisdiction. Lawyer Thomas Heath Haviland of Prince Edward Island cited English law books to the same effect – that both kinds of divorce were categorized under the umbrella term. Haviland was responding to Trudel's statement that neither in Roman nor French law did divorce mean anything but the dissolution of the marriage. Dickey also suggested that doubts about its constitutionality were not a reason not to pass the bill: all divorce bills were reserved for London's approval, and if this one was unconstitutional, London would say so.[65]

The bill's supporters countered the concern about interference with the property and civil rights power with an argument that Parliament often legislated in an area of section 91 jurisdiction in ways that impinged on section 92. They cited as examples federal powers over interest, trade and navigation, bankruptcy, and copyright. In this Dickey and Cornwall, who made these points, were correct as a general matter. They were also fortunate that they were not precluded from asserting this principle in broad terms, because all the complex jurisprudence about exactly where the section 91/92 divide was, especially the divide between property and civil rights and federal powers like trade and commerce, lay in the future. Cases on the division of powers were extremely limited in the 1870s, comprising a few from provincial courts, nothing from the Supreme Court of Canada because it did not start sitting until 1876, and nothing from the Judicial Committee of the Privy Council. Early discussions of federalism did not take place in the courts. They occurred in the context of disallowance disputes, or when some provinces struck statutory consolidation commissions in the 1870s. The Campbell separation bill was yet one more example.

The contention that Parliament could legislate widely in areas coming under section 92 so long as the legislation was linked to a section 91 power worried some Quebec senators, who in 1879, in the midst of debates over the bill, got the Senate to agree to an amendment of the private bill procedure whereby all such bills would be referred to a committee to report on their constitutionality. To similar effect, there were a number of attempts made to shelve the bill while it was referred to the Supreme Court of Canada. Finally, Reesor and others countered the argument about overturning the Chancery decision in two ways, neither of which addressed the separation of powers point but both of which made reversing Chancery not only acceptable but the right thing to do. One argument was that Parliament had new evidence in the form of testimony adduced before the Senate divorce committee. Another was that the issue was the broader one of separation, not the narrower one of alimony, and Parliament was not interfering with the Ontario courts because there was no court in Ontario with the power to grant a separation. Thus the Senate was merely filling a gap, not usurping the function of the courts. Dickey contrasted Ontario with Quebec: if a petitioner from Quebec asked Parliament for a separation he would oppose it, because the Quebec courts routinely granted separations.

Alexander Campbell et al. had the better of the legal arguments. The contention that divorce in the *BNA Act* meant both kinds of divorce was untenable. As noted above, when the act was formulated, divorce was made a federal power as a way of protecting minority rights in Quebec, where all residents could obtain the civil law equivalent of a divorce *a mensa et thoro*. Custody and alimony were both within the property and civil rights power, and while custody was an issue occasionally pronounced on in parliamentary divorce acts, alimony never was. Even dealing with custody, and thus legislating with respect to property and civil rights, occurred only when a divorce was granted, and the Campbell Bill was not one for divorce. The fact that there was no court in Ontario that could grant a separation did not mean that the Senate could deal with individual cases or individual provinces. Parliament had the power under section 101 of the *BNA Act* to establish additional courts "for the better administration of the laws of Canada" and could therefore have created a national divorce court, with jurisdiction over separation, but it had not done so. The contention that the bill was effectively an appeal from the Chancery decision was arguably the weakest of the opponents' legal arguments in an era of parliamentary supremacy constrained only by section 92 of the *BNA Act*. Yet at the same time, those who made that argument were invoking the general principle that Parliament made the law, the courts applied it, and Eliza Campbell's proper remedy was an appeal to a higher court.

Having said this, the legal arguments were largely beside the point. Opponents of the bill may have had the better of the legal debates, but they could not carry the day, either in 1877 in the Senate or in 1879 in both houses. The irascible Kaulbach believed that colleagues in the Senate had been beguiled by Eliza Campbell, had allowed sympathy for her to take control of them and "perverted the good judgment" of some. "There seemed to be some magic about her that prejudiced the minds" of senators, he complained. Others who opposed the bill were aware that their legal arguments had to contend with the fact that, as William Miller of Nova Scotia put it, "a majority of the House has hitherto shown a very strong desire to favour the petitioner." Lawrence Power, who had been appointed to the Senate at thirty-six, thought he knew why – the foolishness of old men. "Gentlemen of the mature years," he opined, noting that many senators fit the bill, "have as warm a sympathy as younger men are generally supposed to entertain." They had forgotten, or chose to ignore, the fact that "hard cases make bad law," and were inclined to let compassion blind them to the "weight of the arguments."[66]

Many senators saw Eliza Campbell as the innocent, if foolish, victim of an intractable husband who had treated his wife in a cruel and unmanly way. She needed rescuing, and senators could do that. A Carrall speech of 1877 exemplifies this point. He had not been on the committee nor, as noted above, had he read the evidence, but he had heard enough about the case to know that

> his sympathies were with the lady, and he would vote for her in the face and teeth of the lawyers who had shut the courts in her face ... She had then come to this Senate – who were looked upon as the fathers of the country – and asked for redress for her little ones and herself ... After being seven years a senator ... there was no vote he would give with more zeal and earnestness, not only in justice to the lady who had been

> wronged, but against the man who had taken such scandalous means of obtaining evidence to defame the character of an injured lady, and as a rebuke to the courts to which they had taken her.[67]

Two years later his ardour for the cause had not diminished. In responding to one of the suggestions that the bill be referred to the Supreme Court, he castigated the idea as just a delaying tactic and insisted that

> I shall oppose, with all of my character, any such reference, in the full conviction in the justice of this lady's demand, of her virtuous character, and of the complicity of her husband's friends in one of the most villainous, infernal, foul, low and cowardly conspiracies which it has ever been my lot to have cognizance of … I feel that every hon Senator, having the honest intention to act in a judicial spirit, when appealed to, will not reject the petition of the unfortunate victim of a vile, low bred conspiracy that has been entered into by a man who forcibly expelled his wife from his house without giving her anything to support her.[68]

Carrall's rhetorical flourishes were not based on any belief in the equality of women, but on the fact that their very inequality, natural and social, meant that they needed the protection of chivalrous men. He had a duty, as all men did, to stand up and defend a woman wronged, because she could not defend herself. In his view Robert Campbell was the worst of men. He had dismally failed in his duty to honour and protect the mother of his children: he had wrongly accused her of a lack of virtue and then fabricated evidence, in cahoots with his brother and brother-in-law, to prove her unworthiness and thereby deprive her of her children and financial security. The idea that "chivalric justice" on occasion underpinned the treatment of women has generally been used to refer to the criminal justice system, but it had purchase in other legal and social contexts. As in the criminal law, such "justice" was a double-edged sword. It benefited the very few women who were able to exploit it – one of whom was Eliza Campbell – but at the same time it reinforced female and male stereotypes and rested on class privilege.

Another knight in senatorial garb was Billa Flint, a Brockville businessman, temperance advocate, and ardent Methodist. He was described by Mackenzie Bowell as "a man of great energy, and strong feeling, no matter which side he took, whether in politics, social life or religious questions," and those characteristics come through strongly in his attitude towards Eliza Campbell. Responding to one of Kaulbach's tirades, he declared himself "pained" to hear such an attack on "an unfortunate and unprotected woman." Eliza had been "cruelly turned out of doors and deserted ... and ... persecuted ... by the man who sought for a divorce." It was "inhuman to persecute an unprotected female in the manner in which this lady had been persecuted by her husband." The Campbell brothers should be prosecuted for what they had done, "a dastardly attempt to ruin the character of a helpless woman." If they were in court, and he was on the jury, "he would sit there until he died before he would render a verdict against her." Flint thought the best evidence of her innocence was that all of Whitby, except those connected to the Campbell brothers, believed her "innocent." Kaulbach seized on that last statement and criticized Flint for it because he had referred to something that was not in the evidence taken before the committee. Flint's response to that was blunt: Kaulbach was a lawyer, and he was not, and what mattered was that he thought from all he had heard that Eliza was "a defenceless woman" who had been treated cruelly by a husband with an "unfeeling nature," a man he would never call a gentleman. Any coolness Eliza had shown her husband at any point was only to be expected, given Robert's cold and unfeeling treatment of her throughout the marriage. The Campbells were an "ill assorted pair," and "if they planted a rosebush alongside an iceberg could they expect it to bloom?"[69]

Carrall and Flint used dramatic language, but Reesor was Eliza Campbell's most dogged and persistent supporter, even though not so prone to rhetorical flourishes. He was the person responsible for shepherding the bill through the Senate, and he rarely spoke without referring to Eliza Campbell as a woman alone, bereft, and badly treated. When he moved in 1877 for the postponed committee report of 1876 to be brought forward, he said the question at issue was a simple one: "whether Robert Campbell should be compelled to do his duty and support his wife, or whether she should be left upon the world to sustain herself as best she could." The appropriate adage was "no wrong without a remedy." There was little about Reesor that predicted he would be an ardent defender of wounded womanhood. He was a successful businessman from Markham (originally called Reesorville), a justice of the peace, lieutenant-colonel in the militia, editor of the *Markham Economist*, and a reeve of Markham, and he had been elected as a Liberal to the Province of Canada Legislative Council in 1860. Thus, like many of the original seventy-two senators appointed in 1867, he was a moderately successful pre-Confederation businessman and politician. Yet he was also something of a social reformer and a committed evangelical. Perhaps most importantly, he likely had prior knowledge of the Campbell scandal that made him partial to Eliza's cause: his eldest daughter, Marion, was married to Dr. Colburn of Oshawa, where the scandal from the neighbouring town of Whitby was widely discussed.[70]

Whatever his motives, Reesor succeeded in getting Eliza Campbell what she wanted. Although we cannot know how much difference it made, he was responsible for exposing an action by Robert Campbell that reinforced the perception of him held by some that he was a devious and vengeful character. In 1877 the Ontario Assembly had enacted a provision that amended the province's dower law so as to do away with the long-standing need for a wife's consent if the husband wanted to "bar" her dower interest in his land, in certain circumstances. Those circumstances were that the wife had been living apart from her husband "under such circumstances as by law disentitle her to alimony." This provision was buried away in a seventy-eight-section omnibus act (it was section 35) and, according to Reesor, had been inserted very late into the bill by a friend of Robert Campbell, to enable him to enhance the value of his land after he had failed to get his divorce. Robert duly applied to Chancery for an order eliminating Eliza's dower interest, trying, unsuccessfully, to have the case heard *ex parte*, which the statute permitted but did not require. When the *ex parte* motion failed, McDougall defended the action and won. Chancellor Spragge refused to grant the requested order, in part because it was a summary proceeding and Robert Campbell relied on the formal record of the 1874 alimony case, which stated that alimony was denied but not why, and in part because McDougall drew to his attention the still unresolved divorce proceeding, in which the draft bill stated that she had not committed adultery. Spragge thought that, in the circumstances, "it would be unseemly, and I think improper, to make such an order as is prayed for in this petition." Spragge also adverted to the fact that, between the hearing of the case and his judgment, the provision had been repealed, the work of McDougall, at that time the MPP for Simcoe South.[71]

The Denouement: The House of Commons, 1879

In a turnaround from 1877, in 1879 the House of Commons also passed the Campbell Act. The mover of the bill was, interestingly, McDougall, who had won the seat of Halton for the Conservatives in 1878. In the Commons, he provided a largely accurate but occasionally misleading account of the events from 1876 on, and, in addition to reciting familiar arguments about Ontario courts not having jurisdiction and the federal Parliament possessing it under section 91(26), he made sure he discussed both the shenanigans over Eliza Campbell's dower right and Robert Campbell's circulation of a paper to MPs claiming that Parliament was making itself into a court of appeal.[72] Although constitutional expert and former member of Alexander Mackenzie's cabinet David Mills, Prime Minister Macdonald, and three other MPs made the familiar arguments against the bill – the meaning of section 91(26), interference with property and civil rights, and acting as an appeal court – they did not persuade enough MPs to vote against it, and the bill prevailed 56–38 on third reading. This was a smaller percentage of the House membership (45 per cent of 206 MPs) than had participated in the Senate votes. Forty-three of the fifty-six in favour were McDougall's colleagues from Ontario; Quebec senators voted 17– to 5 against, while those from other provinces were largely absent and the senators who did attend split 8–6 in favour of the bill.

The debates were much shorter and much less acrimonious than in the Senate, and one gets the sense that MPs simply wanted to see the end of the matter. Rather than occupy many days, debate took place on only three – 2, 9, and 13 May 1879 – and the one on 9 May was limited to the hour allowed for private bills. Prime Minister Macdonald cut off the debate after an hour, declaring that public business should not be held up longer over one case. The final debate on third reading did take up a whole evening until past midnight, but that was the only occasion when the discussion of the bill could be called extensive. The final bill granted Eliza separation from bed and board, custody of her youngest child, Francis William Campbell, $500 a year for herself, $200 a year for the support and education of Francis, and a stipulation that a failure to pay would be a contempt of court by Robert.

Postscript and Conclusion

Robert Campbell stayed in Whitby for more than a decade and then moved to Marshall, Missouri, in 1885. He died there on 23 February 1915. He must have still been well off when he left Canada, as he acquired a great deal of real estate, both town stores and farm land, in the vicinity of Marshall, and died a rich man. In 1883 he got married for a second time, presumably after getting an American divorce, to

Figure 3.1. Eliza Campbell's gravestone, Lot 3327, Mount Pleasant Cemetery, Toronto

Photograph taken by author.

Jane Laird, and after she died in 1913 he married again, a woman from Whitby called Clara Shier.[73]

I know less about Eliza Campbell's later life. She was presumably able to support herself on her alimony payments, at least until Robert left Canada and took himself out of the reach of Canadian law. In the 1880s she, her mother, Henrietta, and her sister Annie all moved to Toronto and shared a house. Eliza died there in 1910. She is buried in Mount Pleasant Cemetery, her gravestone a simple but powerful marker of the profound effect that the events surrounding the breakdown of her marriage had on her and of her conviction that she had been ill-treated. As figure 3.1 shows, beyond her name and the years of her birth and death, it contains one simple message: "I did not commit adultery."

Those few simple words capture both the triumphal end of her battle with her husband and the law in the 1870s, and the bitterness that it must have engendered. Although she won in the Senate, she did so because she was able to persuade a small group of elite men to support her cause, to take up the standard of justice for her according to their own lights. Although the evidence of the gravestone comes from a time more than thirty years after the events described here, it is compelling proof that the accusation of adultery must have scarred her for the rest of her life. She had denied committing adultery since 1873, and that denial was the one substantive statement that she wanted on her gravestone.

NOTES

1 *An Act for the Relief of Eliza Maria Campbell*, SC 1879, c. 79. All divorce acts were entitled "An Act for the Relief of ..."

2 For post-Confederation parliamentary divorce see Jim Phillips, Philip Girard, and R. Blake Brown, *A History of Law in Canada*, vol. 2, *Law for the New Dominion, 1867–1914* (Toronto: Osgoode Society for Canadian Legal History and University of Toronto Press, 2022), 544–52, figure at 547, slightly augmented by further research since the book was published.

3 The significance of marriage as the perceived bedrock social institution of this period has been the subject of many studies, too numerous to list here. Surveys may be found in Phillips et al., *History of Law in Canada*, vol. 2, ch. 15; James G. Snell, *In the Shadow of the Law: Divorce in Canada, 1900–1939* (Toronto: University of Toronto Press, 1991); Snell, "The White Life for Two: The Defence of Marriage and Sexual Morality in Canada, 1890–1914," *Social History/Histoire sociale* 26 (1983): 111–28; and Constance Backhouse, "Pure Patriarchy: Nineteenth-Century Canadian Marriage," *McGill Law Journal* 31 (1986): 264–312.

4 Catholic doctrine did not permit divorce at all, which was reflected in article 185 of the *Civil Code of Lower Canada*, which declared marriage to be dissolvable only by death. Anglicans had a largely similar view, not permitting the remarriage in church of divorced persons. The other Protestant denominations were more liberal but still highly disapproving of the practice, seen as an occasionally necessary evil.

5 For the use of this phrase, see Carolyn Strange, "Wounded Womanhood and Dead Men: Chivalry and the Trials of Clara Ford and Carrie Davies," in *Gender Conflicts: New Essays in Women's History*, ed. Franca Iacovetta and Mariana Valverde (Toronto: University of Toronto Press, 1992), 149–88.

6 This account of the family histories of the Byrnes and the Campbells, and those of the Campbell marriage and its breakdown that follow, is derived from a variety of sources, principally the 250-page *Report of the Select Committee of the Senate on the Bill Intituled An Act for the Relief of*

Robert Campbell together with the Minutes of Evidence, 31 March 1876, in *Senate Journals*, 1876, Appendix 1 (*Committee Report*). Other sources are newspaper reports and reported decisions of the three pre-1876 legal cases discussed in the later sections. There is also biographical information in the Whitby Archives. For the history of Whitby, see Leo Johnson, *History of the County of Ontario, 1615–1875* (Whitby: Corporation of the County of Ontario, 1973).

7 Johnson, *History of the County of Ontario*, 247.

8 *Whitby Chronicle*, May–August 1862.

9 *Campbell v. Campbell*, [1875] OJ No. 202, para. 22.

10 Information on the Byrne family is from *Committee Report* and from the Rev. Byrne's obituary in *Whitby Chronicle*, 26 November 1874.

11 *Whitby Chronicle*, 9 April 1863.

12 *Campbell v. Campbell*, [1875] OJ No. 202, para. 22.

13 Quotations are from *Committee Report*, 9.

14 The letter, an exhibit in the defamation and alimony cases, is reproduced in *Committee Report*, 27, Exhibit 3.

15 The letter is in *Committee Report*, 27–8, as Exhibit 5.

16 Ibid., 21. NWMP Personnel Records, Library and Archives Canada, RG 18, vol. 10037.

17 James Gordon, Past Member Database, Law Society of Ontario Archives (LSO Archives).

18 A stereoscope was a device for viewing a pair of separate images, left-eye and right-eye views of the same scene, as a single three-dimensional image. It was invented in the 1830s and became a popular form of home entertainment from the mid-nineteenth century. Sets of stereo-cards could be bought by those who owned a stereoscope. See, *inter alia*, Ray Zone, *Stereoscopic Cinema and the Origins of 3-D Film, 1838–1952* (Lexington: Kentucky University Press, 2007).

19 *Committee Report*, 182–3, Exhibit 20.

20 *Whitby Chronicle*, 2 October 1873.

21 *Whitby Chronicle*, 26 November 1874.

22 *Whitby Chronicle*, 2 October 1873.

23 *Whitby Chronicle*, 2 April 1874, speech of Malcolm Crooks Cameron to the jury referring to their failing business as a result of community disapprobation.

24 At this time there were two superior courts of common law in Ontario, Queen's Bench and Common Pleas, with identical jurisdiction. The third superior court was Chancery. For this arrangement, see John D. Blackwell, "William Hume Blake and the Judicature Acts of 1849: The Process of

Legal Reform at Mid-Century in Upper Canada," in *Essays in the History of Canadian Law*, vol. 1, ed. David Flaherty (Toronto: Osgoode Society and University of Toronto Press, 1981).

25 The case was not reported in the law reports but was extensively covered in the *Globe*. For the preliminary stages see the *Globe*, 23, 27, and 29 September 1873, and for the trial see the same paper, 16 and 17 October 1873.

26 For Britain see Miranda Wojciechowski, "Criminal Conversation, Predatory Reading: Consent and Critical Practice at the Crossways," *Nineteenth-Century Gender Studies* 16 (2020); Susan Staves, "Money for Honour: Damages for Criminal Conversation," *Studies in Eighteenth-Century Culture* 11 (1982) 279–97; and Lawrence Stone, "Honor, Morals, Religion and the Law: The Action for Criminal Conversation in England, 1670–1857," in *The Transmission of Culture in Early Modern Europe*, ed. Anthony Grafton and Ann Blair (Philadelphia: University of Pennsylvania Press, 1990), 276–316. There is no account of its use in Canada, but it likely was frequently employed. In the prior divorce cases of John Martin and Henry Peterson, for example, the male petitioners for divorce took such an action against their wives' lovers before applying for a divorce: see *Senate Journals*, 9 March 1870, 41, and 10 March 1875, 103.

27 Galt, a Tory and a pillar of the Church of England, was likely to disapprove strongly of any form of marital misconduct. See "Hon Thomas Galt," electricscotland.com/history/Canada/galt.

28 For Cameron, see Margaret Evans, "Cameron, Sir Matthew Crooks," *Dictionary of Canadian Biography* (*DCB*), vol. 11, http://www.biographi.ca/en/bio/cameron_matthew_crooks_11E.html. Cameron was an ineffective politician, too High Tory for the new age, but his social attitudes, including his belief in the need to defend "wronged" women, may have persuaded him to take this case. At the same time, he may simply have been neglecting politics for his profession, something he was accused of doing by members of his own party.

29 *Whitby Chronicle*, 26 November 1874.

30 *Globe*, 17 October 1873. For Harrison see Carole B. Stelmack, "Harrison, Robert Alexander," *DCB*, http://www.biographi.ca/en/bio/harrison_robert_alexander_10E.html, and Peter Oliver, ed., *The Conventional Man: The Diaries of Ontario Chief Justice Robert A. Harrison, 1856–1878* (Toronto: Osgoode Society for Canadian Legal History and University of Toronto Press, 2003), 486. Harrison was very well connected, having at one time worked under John A. Macdonald when he was attorney general of Canada West, and frequently conducted Crown prosecutions. In 1876 he

was appointed Chief Justice of the Court of Queen's Bench directly from the bar.

31 *An Act to Amend the Law of Evidence in Civil Cases*, SO 1869, c. 13, s. 5 (c), and *An Act to Amend the Law of Evidence*, SO 1873, c. 10, s. 3.

32 The trial was not reported in the law reports. What follows is largely from the *Whitby Chronicle*, 2 April 1874. See also *Globe*, 27 and 28 March 1874, and Benchbooks of Justice John Hagarty, Archives of Ontario.

33 *Whitby Chronicle*, 2 April 1874.

34 *Whitby Chronicle*, 15 July 1875

35 Gwynne's decision is at [1875] O.J. No. 136, quotations are from para. 31, (1875) 25 *Upper Canada Common Pleas Reports* 368.

36 For the operation of the Court of Chancery in alimony cases in nineteenth-century Upper Canada, see Lori Chambers, *Married Women and Property Law in Victorian Ontario* (Toronto: Osgoode Society and University of Toronto Press, 1997), ch. 2.

37 *Campbell v. Campbell*, [1873] O.J. No. 306, 6 Practice Reports 128, referee George Smith Holmested. For the principal proceedings see *Whitby Chronicle*, 7 January 1875; *Globe*, 16 September 1875; and *Campbell v. Campbell*, [1875] O.J. No. 202, 22 *Grants Chancery Reports* 322.

38 For Canadian divorce law in the 1870s see Phillips et al., *History of Law in Canada*, 2: 537–52, and John Alexander Gemmill, *The Practice of the Parliament of Canada upon Bills of Divorce* (Toronto: Carswell, 1888). The latter has an account of the Campbell case at 165–74.

39 For these figures, and for parliamentary divorce procedure in this period, see Gemmill, *The Practice of the Parliament of Canada*, ch. 4.

40 *Senate Debates*, 12 April 1877, 352.

41 This vote was typical of most votes on divorce bills. For the vote and subsequent committee appointment see *Senate Journals*, 8 March 1876, 61–3.

42 William Walker, Past Member Database, LSO Archives.

43 For McDougall, see Suzanne Zeller, "McDougall, William," *DCB*, vol. 13, http://www.biographi.ca/en/bio/mcdougall_william_13E.html. For his experience in Red River see Phillips et al., *A History of Law in Canada*, 2: ch. 7.

44 *Senate Journals*, 10 and 31 March 1876, 68–9 and 138.

45 *Senate Journals*, 29 March 1876, 131, and 23 April 1879, 166–7.

46 *Divorce and Matrimonial Causes Act*, UK Statutes 1857, c. 85.

47 See, *inter alia*, Phillips et al., *History of Law in Canada*, 2: 159–62; Marie Aimée Cliche, "Les séparations de corps dans le district judiciaire de Montréal de 1900 à 1930," *Canadian Journal of Law and Society* 12 (1997) 71–100; and Cliche, "Les procès en séparation de corps dans la région de

Montréal, 1795–1879," *Revue d'histoire de l'Amérique française* 49 (1995): 3–33.

48 For this and the preceding paragraph see *Senate Debates*, 3 and 5 April 1876, 282 and 293–5; *Senate Journals*, 5 April 1876, 160–1.

49 For this paragraph see *Senate Journals*, 8 and 10 April 1876, 178–81 and 200; *Senate Debates*, 10 April 1876, 323–4. Other provisions of the bill included making non-payment by Robert a contempt of court. This was included in the bill that was finally passed in 1879.

50 This summary is based on the *Journals* and *Debates* of the Senate and the House of Commons. Only quotations are specifically cited.

51 The two tied votes came about when Reesor moved to send the bill to committee of the whole, and Alexander Campbell moved an amendment that this be done in six months' time, effectively killing the bill. The tied vote meant that Campbell's amendment was defeated. Reesor's main motion was then voted on, with everybody voting the opposite way, producing another tied vote and another defeated motion.

52 Robert Campbell's offer was three of his stores/houses in Whitby, one for her to live in, the other two to provide rental income. They were "not in the business area of town," and she had them valued at producing $200–300 a year, out of which she would have to pay the taxes. Most importantly, Robert did not offer her the freeholds; he was willing only to convey them to trustees, with Eliza being an income beneficiary.

53 The "dissentient" was initially signed by twenty-seven senators, but one of them, Jean-Baptiste Guevremont, had not been present for the vote, and Rule 35 specified that only those who voted could enter a dissent. His name was removed.

54 *Senate Debates*, 19 April 1877, 438. For Carrall, see Dorothy Blakey Smith, "Carrall (Carroll), Robert William Weir," *DCB*, vol. 10, http://www.biographi.ca/en/bio.php?id=carrall_robert_william_weir_10E.html, which notes that his most notable achievement as a senator was to champion a bill to make July 1st Dominion Day.

55 *Senate Debates*, 19 April 1877, 438.

56 See Donald Swainson, "Campbell, Sir Alexander," *DCB*, vol. 12, http://www.biographi.ca/en/bio/campbell_alexander_12E.html.

57 This explanation was offered by Trudel (*Senate Debates*, 21 March 1879, 115–16) and is the standard explanation for the presence of divorce in section 91: see Jim Phillips and Tom Collins, "The Colonial Origins of the Division of Powers in the *British North America Act*," in *Law, Life and the Teaching of Legal History: Essays in Honour of G. Blaine Baker*, ed. Ian

Pilarcyk, Brian Young, and Angela Fernandez (Montreal and Kingston: McGill-Queen's University Press, 2022).

58 *Senate Debates*, 12 April 1877, 348.

59 See Nadia Eid, "Trudel, Francois Xavier Anselme," *DCB*, vol. 11, http://www.biographi.ca/en/bio/trudel_francois_xavier_anselme_11F.html.

60 *Senate Debates*, 25 April 1879, 378–9. For Vidal, see *The Canadian Biographical Dictionary and Portrait Gallery of Eminent and Self-made Men: Ontario Volume* (Toronto: American Biographical Publishing Company, 1880), 361–2.

61 Quotations in this paragraph are from *Senate Debates*, 12 April 1877, 347–9 and 354, and 21 March 1879, 115.

62 Quotations in this paragraph are from *Senate Debates*, 12 April 1877, 348 and 349.

63 Reesor left off the committee the two senators who had voted for Robert Campbell in 1876, Cornwall and Kaulbach: he did ask them to serve on the committee, but they declined. The gravamen of Kaulbach's complaint was that Reesor should not have included anybody who had previously voted in favour of the bill, a demand that was effectively impossible to meet.

64 *Senate Debates*, 18 April 1877, 423–4.

65 Quotation in this paragraph is from *Senate Debates*, 12 April 1877, 353.

66 Quotations in this paragraph are from *Senate Debates*, 18 April 1877, 422–3, and 18 April 1879, 279 and 299. Power, a lawyer, was appointed in 1877, when his father, Nova Scotia liberal Patrick Power, was an MP and Mackenzie was prime minister. The appointment was attacked in the Senate as unseemly. See David B. Fleming, "Power, Patrick," *DCB*, vol. 11, http://www.biographi.ca/en/bio/power_patrick_11E.html.

67 *Senate Debates*, 18 April 1877, 422.

68 *Senate Debates*, 18 April 1879, 286.

69 Quotations in this paragraph are from *Senate Debates*, 18 April 1877, 424–5, and Larry Turner, "Flint, Billa," *DCB*, vol. 12, http://www.biographi.ca/en/bio/flint_billa_12F.html.

70 Quotation in this paragraph from *Senate Debates*, 9 April 1877, 315. For Reesor, see George Maclean Rose, *A Cyclopedia of Canadian Biography, Being Chiefly Men of the Time* (Toronto: Rose, 1888), 704.

71 For this complicated business, see *An Act to Provide for certain amendments to the Law*, SO 1877, c. 8, s. 35; *An Act to Amend the Law of Dower*, SO 1879, c. 22, s. 3 (2); *Re Campbell*, [1877] O.J. No. 224 and [1878] O.J. No 187, 25 *Grant's Chancery Reports* 187 and 480; *Senate Debates*, 21 March 1879, 118–19; and *Commons Debates*, 2 May 1879, 1709.

72 McDougall's introductory speech is in *Commons Debates*, 2 May 1879, 1706–10. The other commons proceedings from which this section is compiled are *Commons Journals*, 2, 5, 9, and 13 May 1879, 350, 357, 410, and 431–2, and *Commons Debates*, 9 and 13 May 1879, 1878–83 and 2004–12.

73 Campbell Family File, Whitby Archives.

4

Meunier v. McDougall and Secord, 1911: A Métis Woman Takes on Land Speculators and Settler Privilege in Alberta

SARAH CARTER

"Sensational Case in Supreme Court" was the headline on the front page of the *Edmonton Capital* on 21 February 1911. Marie Rose Majeau Meunier, a Métis woman from Morinville, Alberta, had entered action in civil court against two of the city's most powerful and wealthy men, John A. McDougall and Richard Secord. They had both amassed fortunes through dealings in Métis scrip, and Meunier claimed that her scrip and, therefore, her valuable land had been taken from her through trickery and forgery.

Richard Secord and John A. McDougall are remembered and celebrated as founding settler fathers of Edmonton, with schools named after them and books written about them.[1] There is a Mount Secord in Alberta "to commemorate the contribution made by Richard Secord … a prominent Edmonton pioneer, to the development of Western Canada."[2] Marie Rose Majeau Meunier, however, is largely forgotten outside her own family and community. Bringing her story to light helps us understand how settler colonialism dispossessed Indigenous people, and divulges the intricacies of the shady tactics used in this dispossession. But the case also illustrates that Indigenous people could engage with the law. This example may allow us to see that "the site of settler law is also a creative space, one that offers significant opportunities for engagement by Indigenous people with settler power."[3] Meunier was not alone in legally challenging the fraud and deceit Métis scrip holders contended with; nor was she the only Métis woman to do so.

As Indigenous rights lawyer and author Jean Teillet has argued, the Métis have resisted the injustices of colonialism not only militarily, but also through the courts. She argues that "litigating Métis rights became a continuation of the Métis Nation's ongoing resistance ... The court was simply another forum to continue what is now a two-hundred year war" for recognition and land rights.[4] Only one of the many Métis who "for two hundred years ... have been caught in the currents and riptides of law," Meunier played a small but important role in this resistance.

Meunier v. McDougall and Secord also demonstrates how Indigenous dispossession was transformed into the heroic narratives of the successes and acumen of powerful and wealthy settler men. As Emma Battell Lowman and Adam J. Barker write, these "narratives are the means through which violent colonization is transformed into the story of heroic struggle and the inevitable establishment of an exceptionally successful, just and distinct society."[5] The heroes of this age in Edmonton and district were McDougall and Secord, renowned "builders" of the Northwest. The city and province were the creations of "strong men, dogged, persistent men," according to historian John MacGregor.[6] Forgotten is the story of how white masculine settler privilege was confronted by a disenfranchised Métis woman.

Although presented in the press reports as an illiterate "half-breed" woman who spoke little English, Marie Rose Majeau Meunier had a rich and deep history in territory that became the province of Alberta and belonged to an extensive network of Métis and Iroquoian kin, with parents who were prominent in that world. She was fluent in French (perhaps Michif). Marie Rose Majeau was born in 1883 at St. Albert, North-West Territories, just northwest of present-day Edmonton, the daughter of Octave and Émilie (L'Hirondelle) Majeau. She was descended on her mother's side from Jacques L'Hirondelle, a Mohawk trapper and voyageur who had worked for the North West Company in the Athabasca region in the early nineteenth century. L'Hirondelle, who was born in Kahnawake, Quebec, became a freeman (no longer under contract to a trade company) in 1818 and married a Métis woman, Josette Pilon.[7] One of their sons, Jean Baptiste L'Hirondelle, married another Métis woman, Catherine Loyer, at Lesser Slave Lake, and they made Lac Ste. Anne, about eighty kilometres west of present-day Edmonton, their home. Their daughter Émilie married Octave Majeau, born in Grand-Saint-Esprit, Quebec. The Mohawk, Québécois, and Métis people of Lac Ste. Anne and St. Albert were Roman Catholics, and the mission at Lac

Ste. Anne drew many to that settlement and later to the Michel First Nation Reserve west of St. Albert.

Marie Rose Meunier's parents were married at Lac Ste. Anne in 1868, and they then lived in St. Albert. According to a memoir written by Frank Oliver, a politician and editor of the *Edmonton Bulletin,* Octave Majeau was a prospector turned farmer and one of the first settlers in St. Albert. He was known as "Little Majeau."[8] Octave acquired a substantial piece of land at St. Albert (more than 1,200 acres).[9] In 1880, he became the first signator (and possibly prepared) a "Petition from the Residents of Edmonton" to Prime Minister John A. Macdonald expressing concern for their land rights as Métis people, and asking that a commission be appointed to issue Métis scrip in that district.[10]

Octave Majeau was involved in a land dispute in 1896 concerning his river lot F in St. Albert. After seasons of high water, the river had receded and a large tract of land appeared that had previously been under water. The land was claimed by settler Louis Como as his homestead, but Majeau contended that the land belonged to him. Majeau had lived on that river lot for twenty-three years, and had chosen the place because of its access to water. In August 1896, about sixty armed men tore down Como's house and threw it into the river with his furniture and ordered him off the land. The party included twelve men from Michel Reserve, about forty Métis, and a few white settlers. When brought to trial, they alleged that they were protecting their river lots and hoped that, if they put Como off, it would prevent others from claiming the land. Thus, the Majeau family had a history of fighting for its land rights. Majeau stated that the men who hurled Como's shack into the river had gathered together in order to render justice.[11] The Dominion Land Office backed down and cancelled Como's entry.[12]

Toward the end of the 1890s, the Majeau family, which by then had twelve children, moved to the Métis settlement of Lac La Nonne, about a hundred kilometres northwest of St. Albert. The Majeaus built a large house that overlooked the lake and that, according to a local history, "became a landmark, a haven of refuge, a source of advice and succor, a meeting place, for Mr. and Mrs. Majeau were skilled in many things, not the least of which was hospitality." Twenty or more people might be at their Sunday dinners, and guests might include "a priest, a Mountie, a cattle buyer, a horse trader, a peddler, an old buffalo hunter, a surveyor, a gold seeker, or a wanderer."[13] Émilie Majeau was a healer

Figure 4.1. The home of Marie Rose Majeau Meunier's parents, Octave and Émile (L'Hirondelle) Majeau, Lac La Nonne, Alberta, n.d. Marie Rose is the fourth adult from the left. Her husband Adélard is standing by the horses.

Courtesy of the Morinville Cultural and Historical Society

and midwife, drawing on local herbs for her natural medicine, applying knowledge handed down to her by her grandmother Josette Pilon. It is estimated that she brought over 200 babies into the world. In 1902, when she was nineteen, daughter Marie Rose married a Lac La Nonne settler from Quebec, Adélard Meunier, and they lived in that settlement until early 1910, when they moved to Morinville, about twenty kilometres north of St. Albert. Marie Rose's older sister Josephine had earlier married Telséphore Meunier, brother of Adélard, and they settled in Mosside, Alberta.[14] Another sister, Marie Caroline, married Belgian settler Camile Verstraete of Villeneuve.

As a Métis, Marie Rose Majeau received scrip from the Canadian government for 240 acres of land in November of 1900. The term "scrip" refers to a certificate that entitled the bearer to receive land or money. In Manitoba after 1871, adult Métis were granted money scrip that could be exchanged for dominion lands, while Métis children were granted individual patents to 240 acres. Scrip commissions, inaugurated in 1885, extended the process to the Métis of the Northwest. They offered money scrip, which was a coupon payable to the bearer and exchangeable at the Dominion Lands Office, or land scrip, which, once cashed in, entitled the grantee to land in the amount of 80, 160, or 240 acres. Those who accepted money scrip could sell it at any time, but land scrip was not transferable. The grantee of land scrip had to be present at a Dominion Lands Office to apply the scrip coupon to a legally defined parcel of land, for which a patent would then be issued. The "Rule of Location" meant that the grantee had to present the scrip coupons to a Dominion Lands agent and select the land. The terminology used was that the land was then "entered" or "located." The scrip could only then be transferred or conveyed, prior to the issue of the patent. No one under the age of twenty-one could transfer such right to the land.

Marie Rose Majeau (whose last name on her scrip certificate was incorrectly spelled "Mageau") applied for her scrip along with several of her brothers and sisters, and her mother, at St. Albert in October 1900.[15] This scrip commission was chaired by ex–North West Mounted Police officer James Walker and J.A.J. McKenna, a loyal Department of Indian Affairs employee. This commission, one of twelve that travelled the west from 1885 to 1921 to enumerate Métis and issue scrip, was appointed to settle the claims of Métis born in the Northwest between 15 July 1820 and 31 December 1885. Mother Émilie had received scrip for $160 in June of 1885, and in 1900 she applied for, and received, scrip for her deceased son, Joseph, who was born in 1870 and had died at the age of twelve days at Lac Ste. Anne. All family members but one signed with an "X." Vital Majeau, six years older than his sister Marie Rose, signed his name. In the case of Marie Rose and the other children, priests wrote letters testifying to their baptism and that they were the legitimate children of Octave and Émilie.

In settler societies where land was awarded to Indigenous people as individuals rather than as collectives, the result was inevitably that more lands transferred to the control of colonial powers/settlers.[16] Unscrupulous speculators obtained scrip certificates, sometimes through fraud and without the knowledge and consent of the original holders, and sold them for profit. Imposters were sometimes hired to pose as Métis certificate holders. "Widespread corruption, if not outright fraud," was the result of the individual and transferable rights awarded to the Métis.[17] William Street, a lawyer from Ontario who was a member of the 1885 scrip commission, described what happened to one Métis woman at Qu'Appelle who reluctantly agreed to receive money scrip, despite the disapproval of her community about participating in the process:

> I prepared, and handed to her, scrip for $160.00, explaining its nature to her, and she went out of the door and was received by a crowd of curious friends,

> to whom she exhibited her scrip. They were not pleased with her for having allowed herself to be persuaded to come before us, and had almost succeeded in satisfying her and themselves that her scrip was valueless, when Charles Alloway, the agent of a banker in Winnipeg who, with other speculators, had come after us to purchase the scrip from the half-breeds, stepped up and offered her $80 in cash for it. This she gladly accepted, and the money was handed to her in clean, crisp $10 bills. The news quickly spread that we were really giving something which could be turned into cash, and from that hour we were besieged from morning til night by applicants.[18]

Throughout the Prairies, frauds and abuses resulted in the Métis retaining little of their land. Speculators used a number of tactics, including forgery and impersonation, to acquire land due to scrip holders. Most Métis were illiterate and, like the majority of the Majeau family, signed their names with an "X." A speculator, pretending to be the agent of the Métis "vendor," would "pick out some local Indian or half-breed and take him to the Dominion Land Office and present him as the person named in the scrip," and have him or her sign a form of Quit Claim Deed. This mark would be "witnessed" by two persons, often other land dealers. One impersonator named Alex L'Espérance attested to securing fifty conveyance instruments and forty-eight land scrip coupons in eight locations.[19] The practice of impersonation was widespread. As Jean Teillet has written, "it was a system that could not have been implemented unless it was aided and abetted by land agents, lawyers, the Dominion Lands Office and perhaps the scrip commissioners themselves. Everybody knew about it."[20]

Profits were vast for speculators. As a columnist wrote in 1911, "there are today in Winnipeg and elsewhere in the West, men who are in the millionaire and near-millionaire classes, who laid the foundation of their fortunes, and made the bulk of them, by their dealings in scrip."[21] These included prominent men such as Donald A. Smith, Lord Strathcona, and Charles Alloway, the man alluded to above as "the agent of a banker in Winnipeg," who helped to establish the largest private bank in Canada, Winnipeg's Alloway and Champion Limited.[22] The bank made huge profits by dealing in Métis scrip, reselling lands to settlers who wanted to avoid the homestead requirements or who wanted more land than provided in the homestead grant. Charles Alloway, who was "at home in the bush and fluent in Indian languages, facilitated most of this business."[23]

Father Albert Lacombe, an Oblate missionary in Alberta, published a letter in the *Edmonton Bulletin* and Manitoba *Free Press* in 1896 criticizing the scrip process that permitted the "unscrupulous white man" to obtain scrip for a "mere song." Lacombe wrote that, "no sooner did it become known that the government of Canada contemplated issuing scrip to the half breeds, than the sharks set to work to devise safe means to rob them." He asked that it be "made impossible for these unprincipled wolves to rob the confiding and innocent half breeds of their property."[24] But the work of the unprincipled sharks and wolves continued well into the twentieth century.

John A. McDougall and Richard Secord also made fortunes through acquiring Métis scrip. The two Ontario-born men were teachers initially, but both became traders, speculators, and politicians. In his adulatory book *Edmonton Trader* (1963), J.G. MacGregor celebrated McDougall, from his first trek west in a snow storm in 1875. Although experiencing many hardships along the way, McDougall helped Edmonton grow from a trading post to a modern metropolis, according to MacGregor. The firm of McDougall & Secord was established in 1897, and land became its specialty. They described themselves as "general merchants, wholesale and retail: buyers and exporters of raw furs; dealers in land scrip and northwest lands; outfitters for survey parties, traders, trappers and miners."[25] Business was lucrative. As MacGregor wrote, "the first five years of the new century did well by McDougall and Secord, and before long … they were credited on the books as having a capital of a million dollars each. The long years of hardship, assiduous trading, and unbounding faith were paying off."[26] The Métis scrip business was particularly profitable. MacGregor noted that scrip could be purchased for a bottle of whisky and that "it was the thing to do." The partners made an ideal team, as McDougall "had lots of money and Secord knew lots of Metis."[27] Secord had traded for furs in northern Alberta, becoming Edmonton's premier fur dealer in the 1890s. The leading force behind the campaign promoting Edmonton as the gateway to the Klondike, McDougall & Secord made enormous profits.

In the summer of 1899, McDougall & Secord made Métis scrip a major area of investment, focusing on the new disbursements in the Athabasca District. Secord was familiar with this environment, where many Métis were already in debt to him. Astonishingly, Secord was appointed government scrip commissioner. He settled old debts with Métis clients by accepting scrip. Secord went on a buying frenzy, equipped with satchels of five- and ten-dollar bills to entice sales. By 1902, he was the largest scrip-buyer north of Edmonton; together, Second and McDougall owned 47,000 acres of scrip valued at $2.75 per acre.[28] The two men helped cement their power bases by entering politics. McDougall was the fourth mayor of Edmonton (1896–7) and a member of the Legislative Assembly of Alberta for Edmonton (1909–13). Secord was a member of the Legislative Assembly of the North-West Territories (1902–5).

In late 1909 or early 1910, Marie Rose Meunier learned, although it is not clear how, that her scrip had been obtained in 1904 without her knowledge or permission by McDougall & Secord. In 1905, they had located her scrip, without her presence at the land office as legally required, on valuable land in the townsite of Mannville, on the route of the new Canadian Northern Railway (CNR) just over one hundred miles east of Edmonton. In 1905, the CNR surveyed the townsite of Mannville, which was then located wholly on the north side of the track. Shortly after the survey, McDougall & Secord secured land on the south side of the track and tried to start a townsite there.[29] This started a "bitter feud" in Mannville between residents of the north and south side of the tracks. Secord and McDougall – like many prominent men of western Canada who made fortunes by anticipating where railway townsites might be established, acquiring that land, and enticing the railway company and businesses to locate to it – made tempting offers to businesses to locate in Mannville and succeeded in selling many town lots, and they offered a grant of land to the Anglican Church. Both the north and south sides of the townsite boomed.

Marie Rose Meunier consulted Edmonton lawyer E.B. Edwards about her stolen scrip. Born in Peterborough, Edwards was called to the Ontario Bar in 1873 and later appointed a King's counsel. He came to Edmonton in 1906. Edwards was a Liberal, a Baptist, and a military man, rising to the rank of lieutenant colonel and was organizer and commanding officer of Edmonton's 101st Regiment.[30] In June 1910, Edwards began a lengthy correspondence with Ottawa officials of the Department of the Interior.[31] In a letter of 4 June, he stated to the secretary of the department that scrip had been issued to Marie Rose before she reached the age of twenty-one, that her father, Octave, had "apparently" taken possession of it, and that "as far as can now be ascertained it was sold or pledged by him without her knowledge or permission."[32] According to Edwards, Marie Rose had never signed a document or transfer relating to her scrip.

Edwards was informed by L. Pereira of the Department of the Interior that Marie Rose Majeau's scrip certificate had been delivered to her on 3 November 1900, that the department had received this certificate in February 1902, and it had then been exchanged for two scrip notes for 140 acres and 80 acres, respectively, and that these had been sent to the Imperial Bank of Canada at Edmonton on 28 February 1902. The scrip notes were located on land (the legal description was the northeast quarter and the north half of the southeast quarter of Section 24, Township 50, Range 9, west of the Fourth Meridian) on 24 August 1903, assigned in the name of McDougall & Secord, and the patent to the land had been issued to them on 20 January 1905. All seemed correct, proper, and in order – but was it?

The documents in the file under the name Marie Rose Mageau have different dates than most of those claimed by Pereira. On 13 November 1904, the Dominion Lands Office at Battleford produced a certificate that stated there were no decrees or other instruments "which affect lands of Marie Rose Mageau." On 14 December 1904, McDougall & Secord sent the registrar's certificate together with the transfer from "Marie Rose Mageau" to them and the legal description of the land cited above. The transfer was approved on 29 December 1904, and the patent issued on 20 January 1905. An obvious question is whether the certificates were "doctored" or manufactured later to show that these transactions were conducted after Majeau had reached the age of twenty-one – that is, after November 1904.

Replying to Pereira in early July, Edwards asked, "By whom was the scrip certificate assigned or transferred?" He continued, "My instructions are that the holder did not assign it or transfer it, or authorize the sale of it to any other person."[33] P.G. Keyes answered that Marie Rose Majeau must have agreed because "such scrip must be located by the grantee personally," and "only then could the land upon which the scrip was located be transferred."[34] Edwards's replied later that month that Majeau did not make any entry personally, did not know anything about an entry being made, and had been underage at the time. He concluded his letter by stating that the "circumstances call for an investigation."[35] No such investigation was undertaken, but Edwards continued his fact finding and ultimately launched a court case.

Not receiving an answer to his letter of late July, Edwards wrote about a month later, asking when and by whom the right to Marie Rose Meunier's land had been transferred to McDougall & Secord. Six weeks later, Edwards was informed that his client had assigned the land to the two Edmonton men on 1 December 1904. After paying a fee of fifty cents, the lawyer received copies of the documents in October 1910. The transfer of land form was signed by Marie Rose "Mageau" with an "X." On this form, the witness(es) to her signature are obscured by a fold in the paper. It stated that she lived in St. Albert. There is no mention of her married name, Meunier. The document stated that $480 had been paid to her by McDougall & Secord. On the certificate, Albert Tate of Edmonton swore that he was personally present, that "Mageau" was personally known by him and known to be of the full age of twenty-one, and that the instrument was executed by her at "Lake St. Ann." This was sworn at Edmonton on 1 December 1904, but the signature of the official is illegible.[36] Moreover, Albert Tate clearly did not know Marie Rose that well, as he attested to a misspelling of her last name and did not seem to know her married name.

There are several irregularities associated with this document. First, Meunier denied knowledge of the document, telling Edwards that she had not been present in the offices, had not signed the document, and had not received the sum of $480. Second, her last name became Meunier in 1902, and she could not have legally signed/marked a document in 1904 with her unmarried name. Third, as indicated above, her unmarried name was misspelled. Finally, the transfer stated she was a resident of St. Albert in 1904, and the certificate stated that the instrument had been executed by her at "Lake St. Ann," when, in fact, she lived at Lac La Nonne from the later 1890s until the spring of 1910.

On 1 December 1910, Edwards drew up a statement of claim for his client. It stated that "Marie Rose Mageau" (Edwards had used "Majeau" in his correspondence with the Department of the Interior, but now used "Mageau"), married in 1902 to Adélard Meunier, had, in November 1900, received a scrip certificate entitling her to 240 acres of land, and that her mother had then taken possession of the certificate (earlier Edwards believed her father had possession of it). The statement continued that, years later, Marie Rose had learned that her certificate had come into the possession of McDougall & Secord and that the company had located her scrip without her knowledge or permission on land in Mannville. In her statement of claim, she denied having signed the transfer to McDougall & Secord or anyone else, or having received a $480 payment. The statement described her as "illiterate and wholly unaccustomed to business affairs."[37]

Meunier retained Edwards by early June 1910, and it was likely under his instructions that she registered a caveat in the Northern Alberta Land Registration District on 12 November 1910 claiming an interest as beneficial owner in the lands patented to McDougall & Secord. Edwards notified McDougall and Secord of her action in a letter dated November 12, writing that he had been instructed by Meunier "to take proceedings to have a transfer purporting to be made by her under her maiden name of Marie Rose Majeau to you [land description] set aside and to have the land reconveyed to her; it being claimed by her that this transfer was not executed by her or with her authority or knowledge – that it is, in fact, a forgery." Edwards noted the date of the registration of the document with the Department of the Interior at Ottawa on 27 December 1904 and that the patent was issued to McDougall & Secord. The letter concluded, "Before commencing action, I should be glad to know whether the claim will be recognized by you."[38]

Edwards was then visited by the lawyers for McDougall & Secord to obtain information about the claim. Just six days later, on 18 November, Richard Secord and two other men (Edward Chevigny and Henry Fraser) went to the Meunier home near Morninville when Marie Rose's husband was absent and "endeavoured to induce the Plaintiff to sign some papers, the contents of [which] were unknown to her."[39] They threatened that, if she did not sign, it would "cause trouble" for her parents. They told her that her father was in trouble, as he had illegally signed the transfer of her scrip. She refused to sign. On that day, McDougall and Secord registered in the Land Titles Office a transfer from themselves as individuals to their company McDougall & Secord Ltd. the north half of the southeast quarter of Section 24 at Mannville.

The men returned to the Menuier home on 23 November, while her husband was still absent, and "by threats and undue influence and by fraudulent misrepresentations, induced the Plaintiff to sign some papers" produced by Secord, who paid her $500 and left with the papers. She was told that, if she did not sign, her parents would go to jail and they would lose everything they had. According to her testimony reported in the *Edmonton Capital*, she was told by these men that "the transfer was forged by her father, and stated that her father would be sent to prison unless she signed the deed." It was further reported that "five hundred one dollar bills ... were piled by this agent before her and she was told that all this money would be paid to her if she attached her signature to the quit claim deed."[40]

The document Meunier was forced to sign is today in the City of Edmonton Archives.[41] It contains many spelling and typographical errors, which possibly indicates that it was cooked up quickly. This Quit Claim Deed legally transferred the property from her to McDougall & Secord. It granted, released, and quit unto McDougall & Secord any interest or claim to the land, and stated that Meunier withdrew her caveat. It began by setting out that Marie Rose Majeau was entitled to scrip number 2298 and that McDougall & Secord paid Octave Majeau for that scrip, although no date was given for that transaction. It acknowledged that Meunier claimed she was a minor at the time of the sale of her scrip, and that it was when she became twenty-one that the scrip was located upon the land at issue, that the location papers were filed in December 1904 "purporting to have been made" by her, and that she "alleges she did not execute the said transfer." The preamble ended with "whereas McDougall and Secord, Limited, are the equitable owners of the said lands,"

> NOW THIS INDENTURE WITNESSETH that the said party of the first part in consideration of $500.00 [the space left blank and the amount written in by hand] to her, now paid by the party of the second part (the receipt whereof is hereby her acnowledged [sic], DOTH HEREBY GRANT, release, and quit-claim unto the said party of the second part, its successors and assigns, all the right, title, interest claim and demand whatsoever, bot [sic] at law and in equity, or otherwise hosoever [sic] and whether in possession or expectancy of her, the said party of the first part, of int [sic] to or out of all that certain parcel of land [land description].

The document continued in very formal legal language that must have been mystifying to Menuier or any member of the public:

> TO HOLD the said lands and premises with alland [sic] singular the appurtenances thereto belonging or appertaining into and to the use of the said part of the second part, its successors and assigns forever, and the party of the first part hereby releases all or any caveat or caveats filed by her or on her behalf against the said land, and in particular a certain caveat filed against the said land on or about the 12th day of November, 1910, claiming an interest as beneficial owner therein.

There were three witnesses to the signature of "Mary-Rose Majeau": Samuel Majeau, E. Chevigny, and Henry Fraser.

In her statement of claim, Meunier declared that she "would not have signed ... but for the said false statements and representations and the undue influence." She had since learned that the statements and representations of Secord and his henchmen concerning the potential arrest and incarceration of her father were false and had been fraudulently used to induce her to sign. The papers she had been forced to sign had not been read to her or explained to her, and

Figure 4.2. Marie Rose Majeau Meunier, husband Adélard Meunier, and children (left to right) Emma, Florentine, Clara, and Odille, n.d.

Courtesy of the Morinville Cultural and Historical Society

"she would not have signed the same if she had known the meaning and effect of them."

It would have been intimidating and frightening in the extreme to have Secord and two other men show up twice at the Meunier home while Marie Rose was alone. (The statement of claim said that two men were with Secord. These men were presumably Chevigny and Fraser; the presence of the third witness of the 23 November document, Samuel Majeau, is a mystery.) Secord and McDougall were growing wealthier and more powerful; in 1909, they had formed a joint stock company, McDougall & Secord Ltd. Between 1908 and 1914, their listed assets doubled from $2 million to over $4 million.[42] In 1911, McDougall & Secord planned to build a "sky-scraper" of ten or twelve stories on Jasper Avenue at a cost of $500,000.[43]

Adélard Meunier returned home on the evening of 23 November, and the couple travelled to Edmonton the next morning to ask Secord to give up the papers that Marie Rose had been induced to sign. The Meuniers tried to return the money, but Secord refused to accept it or return the papers. On that day, McDougall & Secord registered the Quit Claim Deed of the lands that they purported had been executed by Marie Rose to them. This transaction included a release of the caveat registered against the lands by her. That day, they also registered transfers from themselves as individuals to their joint stock company the northeast quarter of Section 24, except the land they had already sold as town lots. The businessmen must have thought the matter would quietly end with the Quit Claim Deed registered and with Marie Rose paid $500, but she persisted.

The statement of claim concluded with the statement that Marie Rose Meunier, "by reason of her ignorance and illiteracy and her want of knowledge of business affairs was not on equal terms with the Defendant Secord and the said Defendant was in a position to exercise and did exercise undue influence over the Plaintiff in procuring the execution of the said papers." Her statement contended that the lands in question at Manville were worth $5000, "or thereabouts," and that the $500 "is a grossly inadequate consideration therefor for the said scrip." She therefore asked that the Quit Claim Deed and release be cancelled, arguing that she was entitled to the "beneficial ownership" of the land. She asked that the men be "ordered to account for the proceeds of the portions of the lands sold by them," and "in the alternative, and without waiving foregoing claim, that the Defendants may be ordered to account to the Plaintiff for the value of the said scrip," and that an injunction be issued to restrain McDougall & Secord from selling or disposing of any more of the land.

In their statement of defence, prepared by the Edmonton firm of Emery, Newell, Ford, Bolton and Mount, and dated 12 January 1911, McDougall & Secord admitted only to their various land registration actions. They admitted that they had obtained Marie Rose Meunier's scrip certificate in 1901 but denied that she had only recently learned of that or that it had been obtained without her knowledge and authority. They claimed she had signed the documents and sold and transferred the land. (This, of course, was in contradiction to what Secord had told Meunier – that her father had illegally signed the transfer.) They further claimed that they were not bound or liable to pay anything to her, but that they had paid the $500 to "settle any doubts which might exist." There had been no fraud, threats, or undue influence, as alleged by Meunier. They claimed that she had signed "with full knowledge, independent advice and after intelligent negotiations for the price to be paid ... and [the document] having been read over and interpreted and explained to her before the signing thereof."[44] They lied.

The case was heard before Justice Nicholas du Bois Dominic Beck on 20 February 1911. Beck was born in Coburg, Ontario, but had grown up and first practiced law in Peterborough. In the mid-1880s, he had settled in Winnipeg to invest in railways and real estate. He moved to Calgary in 1889, joining the law firm of James A. Lougheed (himself heavily involved in Métis scrip acquisition). Two years later, Beck headed north to Edmonton, where he joined the law firm of Emery et al. (who were representing McDougall and Secord in this case) and was appointed a judge in 1907.[45]

It does not appear that French translation was available in the Alberta Supreme Court at that time. Meunier was certainly at an extreme disadvantage in giving her testimony. According to one newspaper report, in court she told "in pantomime how the men who secured the quit claim from her came to her home during her husband's absence and representing that the transfer was forged by her father and that her father would be sent to the penitentiary unless she signed the quit claim, piled the $500 in one-dollar bills on the table and told her that they were all hers if she signed."[46]

On 28 February 1911, the action was dismissed "by consent of the parties" without costs, and with counsel for the plaintiff and defendants consenting. The document was signed by Judge Beck. The dismissal did not become public, it seems, until over a week later, and the details of the amount of the settlement were never revealed. The headline in the *Edmonton Capital* of 8 March 1911 was "Case Involving Mannville Townsite Has Been Settled." A good guess is that Meunier settled for much more than the $500 she had previously been paid by Secord, given that the statement of claim declared the lands were worth $5,000. Such settlements were reached when both sides had strong incentives, and they prevented either party from suing or continuing the claim. A settlement might specify that any information about the agreement be confidential.[47]

Secord and McDougall must have feared that they were going to lose. There were a great number of irregularities and strong evidence that Edwards could have raised. Witnesses could have been called, including the men who had accompanied Secord to the Meunier home. Marie Rose had been a minor at the time of her allegedly transferring the land. In addition, the speculators were confronting a well-established Métis family, and, according to a newspaper report, "the case is attracting an immense amount of interest among the halfbreed residents of the district, many of whom have gathered to watch the progress of the case."[48] (This is slightly reminiscent of the famous Pierre Guillaume Sayer trial at Red River Colony in 1849, when three hundred Métis, led by Louis Riel Sr., assembled outside the court. That trial was a victory for the Métis, establishing their right to free trade and ending the monopoly of the Hudson's Bay Company.)

Marie Rose Majeau Meunier was perhaps fortunate to have reached a settlement. Other Métis men and women around the same time tried to use the legal system to assert their rights with regard to scrip, but they were seldom successful, as their allegations of fraud failed to stick. The system was stacked against them. In 1905, a federal scrip inquiry was appointed under Judge R.H. Myers of Winnipeg, with hearings held that summer in Killarney, Manitoba. The issue had to do with the claims of Canadian-born Métis who were living in the United States. Their claims had been disallowed by the 1900 and 1901 scrip commissions chaired by James McKenna, but, in 1904, an Order-in-Council reversed this decision and allowed the claims, and a clause was later added to this Order-in-Council providing that the Métis grantee did not have to be present at the Dominion Lands Office to make a land entry. Scrip speculators very quickly rose to the occasion – suspiciously quickly, according to critics. They acquired scrip for as little as $100 for land that was worth $1,000. According to a report in the *Winnipeg Tribune*, one firm stood to make half a million in scrip deals. The author of the article suspected that "someone in Ottawa with a close knowledge of interior department affairs has been more than courteous in the matter of imparting information to a Winnipeg firm of scrip buyers."[49]

Canadian Métis living in North Dakota were indignant and besieged Minister of the Interior Frank Oliver with letters. They sent a petition to Ottawa in May 1905 stating that they had been induced by lawyer and speculator Ronald C. Macdonald of Winnipeg, posing as a Canadian government agent, to "sign releases of our rights to such scrip in his favor."[50] They had "thought we were signing a petition to get our scrip." The Métis stated that Macdonald had "taken advantage of our lack of education to obtain our signatures to these releases through fraud and false representations" and asked the department to order an inquest. Some settlers supported an inquest: they wanted the Métis to be given fair compensation, but they were also angry that a few speculators had reaped such profits. Macdonald, in particular, seemed to have insider information, and his activities became the focus of the inquiry.

Macdonald had worked hard to have McKenna's decision reversed so that the Métis resident in the United States could be granted scrip, from which he sought to profit.[51] Prime Minister Wilfrid Laurier refused an investigation in Parliament but approved an inquiry by a judge and appointed Myers. Macdonald was charged with fraud.

Among the over 100 complainants who gave evidence at the hearings in Killarney were Métis women. Minnie Poitras, born in Medicine Hat, was seventeen in 1901 when she applied for scrip at Birtle, Manitoba. At that time, she and her family had been living for nine years in North Dakota. Her application was disallowed in 1901, but her claim was reconsidered in 1904, and scrip of 240 acres was issued to her, according to her application file, but she never received it. At the inquiry, Poitras stated that she had been approached by Macdonald in southern Manitoba and in North Dakota.[52] He told her he was going to great expense fighting the Canadian government to get her scrip for her and he asked her to sign a paper, telling her that she would get $200 for her scrip and threatening that, if she did not agree to sell to him, he would not fight for her claim. In August 1904, she signed a paper that she thought authorized Macdonald to act for her. She later received notice from Ottawa that scrip had been issued on her account to Macdonald, which she had not expected as she had received no money for it from him.

Olivia Marcille and Angelia Davis both told the inquiry that Macdonald had asked her to sign a paper that she believed was a scrip application. Neither agreed to sell their scrip to Macdonald.[53] Theresa Boyer had applied for scrip in Swift Current in 1901 but was turned down as she was residing in North Dakota. Macdonald told her he would fight for her scrip, and she signed papers that were not read or explained to her, but she did not agree to sell her scrip. She received from Macdonald goods to the value of $5 at a local store.[54] Other women and men gave similar testimony.

Despite this wealth of testimony, Judge Myers's report exonerated Macdonald, although the recommendation was that several of the Métis be given back their scrip, because it was found that, in a few cases, the Métis might not have understood what they were signing. Myers found that Macdonald and his representatives were "not guilty of deceit, misrepresentation, or any wrong doing ... and that the charges were unfounded and should never have been brought."[55] Macdonald became an alderman in Winnipeg and a millionaire. The *Tribune* mocked him in 1912 when he proposed establishing an "exclusive social club of wealthy old timers. A few of the conditions requisite for membership are, first, that you must have more money than you know what to do with."[56]

The case of Annie Young Battley's scrip also demonstrated a Métis woman's determination to achieve justice and expose deceit (with the assistance and likely encouragement of her settler husband, W.J. Battley). Annie Young was born at Lac Seul, Ontario, the daughter of a Hudson's Bay Company man from Scotland and Magna "Muh-kwa" Thompson.[57] Annie married W.J. Battley in 1902. Both were lay preachers for the Salvation Army. She applied for scrip for 240 acres in Winnipeg in May 1902, signing her own name (in fact, there were two scrip notes, one for 160 acres and one for 80 acres). Barrister Lendrum McMeans and his partner W.J. Robinson, scrip buyers in Winnipeg, somehow acquired her scrip. McMeans alleged that he had purchased her scrip for $50 and that it was later sold first to a Robert Henderson for $300 and then to Andrew Wright for $1,000.[58] Yet Annie Battley believed she had not sold her scrip and was the only person entitled to it.[59] A letter in her scrip file, however, prepared and signed by W.J. Robinson and bearing (allegedly) her signature and that of her husband, dated 21 June 1902, asked that the secretary of the Department of the Interior forward her scrip to her, in care of McMeans. Secretary P.G. Keyes wrote commissioner McKenna on 29 July 1902, enclosing an order received through McMeans from Annie Battley "for the delivery to her, in care of Mr. McMeans of the scrip to which she is entitled." Regardless of these arrangements, it is apparent that Battley never intended that McMeans would keep and sell her scrip notes.

McMeans and Robinson had entered into a partnership for the purchase of scrip, but the two had a falling out in 1903, with Robinson taking McMeans to court, alleging that he was entitled to a share of the proceeds from scrip sold by McMeans.[60] Robinson actively sought the scrips of not only Annie Battley but the other Young siblings, travelling to Lac Seul in 1902.[61] There are letters from him in their scrip application files, and by early 1903, he was intervening to ensure that the Young scrips were sent to him, and not to McMeans.[62]

In 1904, Andrew Wright, the third purchaser of Annie Battley's scrip, asked the Battleys to go with him to Wolseley, Saskatchewan, where he had located land at Wapella, as the law required that the scrip recipient be present when the land was located. The Battleys agreed, but it soon became clear that they were not going to permit Wright to locate using Annie's scrip. When the scrip was produced by Wright at Wolseley, W.J. Battley asked to see it, and he then placed it in his pocket, saying "at last

I have got hold of it."[63] Wright immediately had W.J. Battley arrested on a charge of theft, and this case was heard at Moosomin in February 1904. The case was dismissed: Justice Wetmore found that the contract drawn up by McMeans for the purchase of Annie Battley's scrip was not binding, and that the accused was charged of stealing scrip certificates whereas the documents produced in court were scrip notes.[64] The Battleys were briefly victorious, and Annie had her scrip.

This was followed by an "action for replevin" launched by Wright in 1905. Replevin is "an ancient common law action that allowed a person to bring a summary action to recover personal property unlawfully taken. It is now a form of summary action that allows the plaintiff to take custody of personal property in which the ownership is disputed."[65] The action was first heard before Justice Perdu, of the King's Bench, Manitoba, who decided in favour of Wright.[66] The Battleys appealed this decision, and the case was heard on 14 July 1905. Wright asked that the two scrips be returned to him. The Battleys argued that the plaintiffs had no legal or beneficial interest in the scrip. Justice Dubuc upheld the decision of Judge Perdu, finding that Annie Battley had deliberately assigned her scrip to McMeans, and that the transaction was legal and valid. The scrip had been wrongfully taken from Wright, and he was entitled to recover it.[67] The Battleys, shouldered with costs in these cases, would have paid a heavy price for these unsuccessful legal battles. Sadly, within four years, Annie had died at the age of twenty-eight, leaving her husband and three small children.

Other efforts of Métis women seeking justice were also unsuccessful. One of Marie Rose Meunier's sisters, Marie Mélina Majeau, contacted two firms of Edmonton lawyers early in 1911 to find out what had happened to her scrip, which had been issued in October 1901.[68] The Department of the Interior informed her that her scrip was located by a settler in Bentley, Alberta, in March 1902. She clearly knew nothing of this. A follow-up letter was written to the department by the firm of Cormack & Mackie, asking "by whom the transfer was signed, who was witness, and in what Land Office the land was located," but there is no reply on file or further correspondence on the matter.

The *Meunier* case was not the only time McDougall & Secord were accused of using impersonation to gain access to scrip. Antoine and Joseph L'Hirondelle (brothers of Marie Rose Majeau's mother, Émilie) sued the Crown in 1916 for the return of scrip coupons that had wound up in the possession of McDougall & Secord.[69] The L'Hirondelle brothers too retained lawyer E.B. Edwards, who wrote to Minister of Justice C.J. Doherty that this was a case of "fraud and forgery and impersonation." The legal representative of the Department of Justice advised that, if this case were successful before the Supreme Court, "there would be not only hundreds, but thousands of cases of a similar nature ... as there is no doubt that there were more forgeries and impersonations in scrip cases in Western Canada than you can even realize."[70] The court ruled in favour of McDougall & Secord.

In 1921, Secord once again faced charges of fraud and forgery. In the case of Elizabeth Hyslop (née Houle) of Fort Resolution, it was alleged that, in 1903, Secord had bribed a Métis woman to go to the Edmonton land titles office and claim she was Hyslop, who had been issued scrip for 240 acres.[71] Secord was the witness to the "X" of the impersonator of Hyslop. The matter was first brought to the attention of the Department of the Interior by an Edmonton law firm in 1914, then dropped, emerging again in 1920. According to legal scholar Don Purich, it was Métis political activist John Graham of Wabasca, Alberta, who laid the charge of forgery against Secord in this case.[72] The formal charge was "subornation of perjury." One Alberta newspaper reported that the charge was an outcome of a dispute and fist fight between Secord and a Calgary hotel man on whose property Secord held a mortgage. "The hotel man vowed vengeance and is now prepared to reap it." It was also reported that the chief witness was a "halfbreed woman who has sworn that she impersonated many halfbreed women throughout the country in the name of the accused."[73] At the preliminary hearing, in police court in Edmonton, a woman named Flora Taylor gave evidence that she had impersonated Hyslop, receiving ten dollars and a shawl from Secord.[74] Conveniently, before Secord could be brought to trial, the case was dropped. An astonishing amendment to the *Criminal Code* of June 1921 provided that "prosecution shall not be taken after three years from offence in connection with any offence relating to or arising out of the location of land which was paid for in whole or in part by scrip or was granted upon certificates issued to halfbreeds in connection with the extinguishment of Indian title." This change "effectively decriminalized scrip fraud."[75]

This remarkable amendment, Secord's success at evading charges, and his "friends in high places" willing to even amend the *Criminal Code* to save him from jail by decriminalizing scrip fraud became a campaign issue in Alberta in the federal election in the fall of 1921. One critic, Mary McCallum, a journalist from western Canada and assistant secretary of the Canadian Council of Agriculture, made a direct reference to the case when she spoke at a rally for a Farmer-Labour candidate in Toronto. Criticizing the attachment of Prime Minister Arthur Meighen's Conservative government to "big interests," McCallum "accused the Government of deliberately amending the Criminal Code of Canada in order to rescue from legal action and certain punishment one of his friends in Alberta. 'There was the man, held in jail awaiting trial, and as certain of conviction as he could possibly be,' she stated. 'Yet that man, who happens to be an Edmonton millionaire, had to be released because of one tiny amendment to the Criminal Code.'"[76]

Although the story of the hotel keeper in Calgary was the catalyst for the 1921 Secord case may have been true, it was also the case that the Métis of Alberta and its supporters were behind the Hyslop action. The sudden *Criminal Code* amendment was devised not only to save Secord from jail but also to try to put an end to calls for an investigation into many other such cases. In early November 1920, H.C. Macdonald, an Edmonton lawyer, wrote to N.O. Coté, the controller at the Lands Patent Branch of the Department of the Interior, to make inquiries into the land location of the scrip of sixteen individuals, all from northern Alberta, who had, according to their scrip documents, travelled to distant land offices, including Battleford, Moose Jaw, and Regina, to appear in person to locate land for third parties. As Frank Tough and his colleagues at the Métis Archival Project have shown, the land was located by fraudulent imposters in the vast majority of cases.[77]

Macdonald stated to Coté that he had been retained by the attorney general of Alberta to investigate the circumstances under which lands were located, and he informed Coté that complaints had been made about fraud.[78] At the same time, a former Edmonton alderman and hotel owner, J.C. Calhoun, was "delegated by a number of persons of white and Indian blood" in Alberta's north to "seek redress in connection with the location of halfbreed land scrip" during 1900–3. A petition from Alexis Lafferty, an advocate for his people, the Métis, and friend of Calhoun, was forwarded to the prime minister in November 1920. Seventeen cases were singled out in this petition, including the Hyslop (spelled Heaslip) case. Their request for an investigation was turned down: in his reply, Meighen observed that scrip was granted to individuals, that the government had no control over what people did with their scrip, and that individuals could take their cases to the courts.[79]

The *Criminal Code* amendment of 1921 was designed to put a stop to these petitions for investigation and redress. Coté informed Calhoun in December 1920 that there would be no investigation, that their agents had "always been most careful in dealing with Halfbreed locations," and that agents were "not to accept such locations unless they were satisfied that the person desiring to locate was the actual grantee of the scrip."[80] Coté further insisted that "many of the original grantees and witnesses are dead and it would be impossible, at this date, to locate many of the others or obtain satisfactory or reliable evidence relating to those transactions which took place so many years ago." Calhoun and his associates kept up the pressure, requesting that the *Criminal Code* amendment be nullified. The Alberta Métis Association, formed in 1928, was successful in the 1930s in pressuring the United Farmers of Alberta government to create the Ewing Commission to look into economic and social issues, including land rights.[81]

Marie Rose Majeau Meunier's battle with John A. McDougall and Richard Secord was one of a staggering number of Métis Nation court cases over a host of issues including land and resources, hunting and fishing rights, and the abuse and injustices faced by Métis women – indeed, these cases continue to this day. Meunier contributed to the two-hundred-year-long legal fight for Métis rights. Métis women have played an important but, as yet, little recognized, role in this ceaseless determination to use the legal system for redress. Settled out of court, this case did not break new legal ground, but it underscored the formidable obstacles that Métis plaintiffs faced when wealthy land speculators had influential, powerful allies in legal and government circles. While some settler Albertans, such as E.B. Edwards, saw the justness of the cause, settler supporters were few. Edmontonians such as Emily Murphy, devoted to the cause of votes for (some) women and reforming the legal system with respect to women and property, was silent on the issue of fraud and Métis scrip and the plight of women such as Meunier.

Historian Sherry Farrell Racette has written that Métis women were particularly focused on land rights. She quoted a Métis woman of southeastern Saskatchewan who said that "the women never stopped talking about the lost lands. They were more bitter than the men who were told there was more land and they believed that."[82] There is ample evidence that Métis women sought and fought for land rights, and this would be a fascinating topic to pursue further. Several widows of the Batoche settlement secured homesteads after 1885, for example.[83] But federal authorities threw roadblocks in the way of Métis women acquiring homestead land as deserted wives or widows, including questioning the validity of their marriages and the legitimacy of their children.[84] Other obstacles to Métis women obtaining land far into the twentieth century included that they were not permitted to own land on the Alberta Métis settlements.[85]

John McDougall and Richard Secord never were "caught." As Secord's biographers wrote, the two "were never convicted of wrong doing, and as the years passed the prestige of the partnership increased with its prosperity."[86] As for Marie Rose Majeau Meunier, her husband, Adélard, with whom she had five children, died in 1918. She later became Mme Hermel Potvin, and she died in 1969 in Edmonton, after living most of her life in Morinville. She left three sons and seven daughters, as well as numerous grandchildren and great-grandchildren. She was celebrated as a "pionnière de Morinville."[87] The family is remembered through Majeau Lake, a bird sanctuary in the Lac Ste. Anne district. The site is not as tall, cold, and magisterial as Mount Secord, but is a tranquil setting with an abundance of hiking trails and wildlife.

NOTES

1 David Leonard et al., *A Builder of the Northwest: The Life and Times of Richard Secord, 1860–1935* (self-published by Richard Y. Secord, 1981); J.G. MacGregor, *Edmonton Trader: The Story of John A. McDougall* (Toronto: McClelland and Stewart, 1963). Secord was a grand-nephew of Laura Secord, of the War of 1812 fame.

2 Leonard et al., *A Builder of the Northwest*, 178.

3 Miranda Johnson, "Writing Indigenous Histories Now," *Australian Historical Studies* 45 (2014): 324.

4 Jean Teillet, *The North-West Is Our Mother: The Story of Louis Riel's People, The Métis Nation* (Toronto: HarperCollins, 2019), 459–61.

5 Emma Battell Lowman and Adam J. Barker, *Settler Identity and Colonialism in 21st Century Canada* (Halifax: Fernwood Publishing, 2015), 33.

6 MacGregor, *Edmonton Trader*, 204.

7 The Majeau family tree has been deeply researched by genealogists. See, for example, "Octave Majeau," Geni, https://www.geni.com/people/Octave-Majeau/932073 and http://telusplanet.net/dgarneau/majeau.htm.

8 Frank Oliver, "The Founding of Edmonton" (unpublished paper prepared for the Historical Society of Alberta, 1921), 7, available on the website Peel's Prairie Provinces, http://peel.library.ualberta.ca/bibliography/2879.html.

9 See more Mageau/Majeau family history at "L'Hirondelle, Emilie + Octave Majeau" (blog), http://ouicbeau.blogspot.com/2015/02/lhiirondelle-emilie-no-11-eng-no-2-fr.html?m=1.

10 "Petition from the Residents of Edmonton Signed by Octave Majeau, Covering Letter Dated May 19th 1880," available at http://www.metismuseum.ca/media/document.php/14575.Petition%20from%20the%20Residents%20of%20Edmonton%20Signed%20by%20Octave%20Majeau.pdf. The original document is in *Epitome of Parliamentary Documents in Connection with the North-West Rebellion, 1885* (Ottawa: Department of the Secretary of State, 1886), 305–6.

11 "The St. Albert Affair," *Edmonton Bulletin*, 13 August 1896, 4.

12 "Local," *Edmonton Bulletin*, 10 August 1896. I could find no record of Louis Como's homestead entry and cancellation. He did receive patent to land in St. Albert in 1904 (entered in 1899), Provincial Archives of Alberta (PAA), Alberta Homestead Records, file 740037, film 2099.

13 Barrhead and District Historical Society, *The Trails Northwest: A History of the District of Barrhead Alberta, 1867–1967* (Edmonton: Commercial Printers, c. 1967), 32–3. The novel *Nipsya* by Georges Bugnet, translated from the French by Constance Davies Woodrow (New York: Louis Carrier, 1929) was based on the story of Octave and Émilie Majeau. The main character is a Métis woman. See George Melnyk, *The Literary History of Alberta* (Edmonton: University of Alberta Press, 1998), 142.

14 For Josephine Majeau Meunier, see Find a Grave, https://www.findagrave.com/memorial/148745165/josephine-meunier, and PAA, Homestead File 2153297, reel 2940.

15 Marie Rose Majeau's scrip application is at Library and Archives Canada (LAC), RG 15, D-II-8C, vol. 1357, form E, no. 2298, claim no. 3009. The scrip application of her mother (Émilie L'Hyrondelle) is D-II-8B, vol. 1329, claim 635, and her mother's application for her deceased son, Joseph Majeau, is D-II-8C, vol. 1357, form F, no. 1122, claim no. 3014.

16 Frank Tough and Kathleen Dimmer, "'Great Frauds and Abuses': Institutional Innovation at the Colonial Frontier of Private Property: Case Studies of the Individualization of Maori, Indian and Métis Lands," ch. 7 of Christopher Lloyd, Jacob Metzer, and Richart Sutch, *Settler Economies in World History* (Boston: Brill, 2013).

17 Ibid., 206.

18 Quoted in Camilla Augustus, "'Half-Breed Homestead': The North West Métis Scrip Policy, 1885–1887" (master's thesis, University of Calgary, 2004), 57.

19 Frank Tough and Erin McGregor, "'The Rights to the Land May Be Transferred': Archival Records as Colonial Text – A Narrative of Metis

Scrip," *Canadian Review of Comparative Literature / Revue canadienne de littérature comparée* 34 (2007): 52. See also Teillet, *The North-West Is Our Mother*, 385–6.

20 Teillet, *The North-West Is Our Mother*, 386.

21 Hay Stead, "The Story of Halfbreed Scrip," *Raymond Rustler*, 20 January 1911, 11.

22 Historical Buildings Committee, "67 Main Street: Alloway & Champion Building," 28 February 1986, http://www.winnipeg.ca/ppd/historic/pdf-consv/Main667-long.pdf.

23 Ibid., 2.

24 Father Albert Lacombe, "Half-Breed Scrip," *Edmonton Bulletin*, 12 October 1896, 2.

25 MacGregor, *Edmonton Trader*, 210.

26 Ibid., 239.

27 Ibid.

28 Leonard et al., *A Builder of the Northwest*, 79.

29 Mannville and District Old Timer's Association, *Trails to Mannville and Districts* (Mannville, AB: Mannville and Districts Old Timer's Association, 1983), 14.

30 C.W. Parker, *Who's Who in Canada* (Toronto: International Press, 1914), vols. 6/7: 844.

31 Homestead File, Provincial Archives of Alberta (PAA), reel 2739, file 966816.

32 E.B. Edwards to Secretary, Department of the Interior, 4 June 1910, PAA, reel 2739, file 966816.

33 Edwards to Pereira, 5 July 1910, PAA, reel 2739, file 966816.

34 P.G. Keyes to Edwards, 19 July, 1910, PAA, reel 2739, file 966816.

35 Edwards to Secretary, Department of the Interior, 30 July, 1910, PAA, reel 2739, file 966816.

36 Edwards to the Secretary of the Department of the Interior, 8 September 1910, P.G. Keyes to Edwards, 19 October 1910, and Transfer of Land Certificate, 1 December 1904, all PAA, reel 2739, file 966816.

37 Statement of Claim, 1 December 1910, Marie Rose Meunier and John A. McDougall and Richard Secord, Supreme Court of Alberta, Judicial District of Edmonton, PAA, available through the website Law and Original Order: Discovering Alberta's Court Records, at https://provincialarchives.alberta.ca/static/interesting-cases/civil-meunier-mcdougall-secord.html.

38 E.B. Edwards to Messrs. MacDougall [sic] & Secord, 12 November 1910, McDougall and Secord Ltd. Fonds, City of Edmonton Archives. MS-594.

Thanks to City of Edmonton Archivist Tim O'Grady for finding this and other documents in the midst of the pandemic, when I could not visit the archives reading room.

39 Statement of Claim, 1 December 1910.

40 "Case Involving Mannville Townsite Has Been Settled," *Edmonton Capital*, 8 March 1911, 1.

41 E.B. Edwards to Messers. MacDougall [sic] & Secord, 12 November 1910, City of Edmonton Archives. Edwards attached to this letter the document Meunier was forced to sign dated 23 November 1910. The quotes in the following paragraphs are from this document.

42 Leonard et al., *A Builder of the Northwest*, 126–9.

43 "Will Erect $500,000 Sky-Scraper on Jasper," *Edmonton Capital*, 5 January 1911, 1.

44 *Meunier v. McDougall & Secord*, 12 January 1911, PAA.

45 Richard A. Willie, "Beck, Nicholas Du Bois Dominic," *Dictionary of Canadian Biography*, vol. 15, http://www.biographi.ca/en/bio/beck_nicholas_du_bois_dominic_15E.html.

46 "Sensational Case in Supreme Court," *Edmonton Capital*, 21 February 1911, 1.

47 Thanks to James Phillips, University of Toronto Faculty of Law, who notes that "a settlement simply means that the parties to litigation agree to resolve their dispute without a trial/hearing." He was not sure why the phrase "consent of the parties" was used, but continued: "there is a difference between parties negotiating their own settlement and parties agreeing to have their dispute resolved by arbitration. Arbitration is still consent if both have consented to accept binding arbitration, but the precise terms of the settlement are the work of the arbitrator, not the parties." He further added that "judges would intervene in a variety of contexts once the judge was apprised of the issues and thought it made sense to settle not litigate." Jim Phillips to Lori Chambers, email, 8 September 2022.

48 "Sensational Case," *Edmonton Capital*, 21 February 1911, 1.

49 "Stand to Make Half a Million in Scrip Deals," *Winnipeg Tribune*, 17 May, 1905, 1.

50 "The Scrip Deal," *Winnipeg Tribune*, 18 May 1905, 5.

51 Michel Hogue, *Metis and the Medicine Line: Creating a Border and Dividing a People* (Chapel Hill: University of North Carolina Press, 2015), 200–1.

52 "Enquiry into Scrip Deals," *Winnipeg Tribune*, 26 July 1905, 1. The 1901 scrip application of Minnie Poitras is in LAC, RG 15-D-II-8-C MIKAN 1514040, vol. 1364, file ref. 947431, claim no. 160.

53 "Story of the Halfbreeds," *Winnipeg Tribune*, 29 July 1905, 1.

54 'Want More Evidence," *Winnipeg Tribune*, 5 August 1905, 1.
55 "That Scrip Commission," *Winnipeg Tribune*, 3 March 1906, 1.
56 "Ex-Ald R.C. Macdonald," *Winnipeg Tribune*, 3 February 1912, 2.
57 Logan Hayward, "Annie Young Battley," Scribd, https://www.scribd.com/document/176657801/Battley-Annie-nee-Young-b-1878.
58 "That Scrip Case," *Winnipeg Tribune*, 19 February 1904, 4.
59 "Full Court Judgements," *Winnipeg Tribune*, 14 July 1905, 5.
60 "Robinson vs. M'Meals [sic]," *Winnipeg Tribune*, 8 June 1903, 6.
61 W.J. Robinson to J.A.J. McKenna, 29 December 1902, LAC, MIKAN no. 1515986, RG 15, D-II-8-C, vol. 1371, form E, no. 3639, file ref. 754797, claim no. 1993, scrip application of John Young for his absent son, Thomas Young.
62 See, for example, Robert Young to J.A.J. McKenna, 17 January 1903, asking that the instructions to send the scrip of Robert Young to L. McMeans be revoked, cancelled, and made void, and that it be sent instead to W.J. Robinson. This letter was prepared for Robert Young's signature. LAC, MIKAN 1515933 vol. 1317, reel C-15010, http://data2.archives.ca/e/e455/e011361940.pdf.
63 "That Scrip Case," *Winnipeg Tribune*, 10 February 1904, 4.
64 Ibid.
65 "Replevin," Irwin Law Canadian Online Legal Dictionary, https://www.irwinlaw.com/cold/replevin.
66 *Wright & McMeans v. Battley*, reported in "Other Judgements by Mr. Justice Richards," *Winnipeg Telegram*, 2 June 1904, 10.
67 *Wright v. Battley*, 1905 Carswell Man 53, 15 Man. R 322, 1 WLR 563. More research should be undertaken into who exactly W.J. Battley was. A man by that name in Winnipeg sold real estate by auction through the firm Flaherty & Battley Auctioneers and Valuers. For example, W.J. Battley advertised to sell by auction $60,000 of real estate in July 1905, including over 1,000 lots in Fort William. See advertisement, *Morning Telegram*, 7 July 1905.
68 PAA, Homestead File 655893, reel 2078.
69 The L'Hirondelle family are listed in the scrip application of Antoine L'Hirondelle for his deceased brother Auguste. LAC, MIKAN 1512039, RG 15, D-II-8C, vol. 1356, form D, no. 2496.
70 Tough and Dimmer, "'Great Frauds and Abuses,'" 240.
71 PAA, Homestead File 681725, reel 2084.
72 Donald Purich, *The Metis* (Toronto: James Lorimer and Co., 1988), 124.
73 "Edmonton Millionaire Committed on Serious Charge," *Wetaskiwin Times*, 21 April 1921, 6.

74 Métis Archival Project, *Métis Scrip in Alberta* (Edmonton: Rupertsland Centre for Métis Research in Collaboration with the Métis Nation of Alberta, 2018), 24.

75 Ibid.

76 "Food Growers Going to Starve," *Globe*, 14 November 1921, 6.

77 Métis Archival Project, *Métis Scrip in Alberta*, 23.

78 H.C. Macdonald to N.O. Coté, 1 November 1920, PAA, Homestead file 681725, reel 2084.

79 Purich, *The Metis*, 124.

80 N.O. Coté to J.C. Calhoun, 17 December 1920, PAA, Homestead file 681725, reel 2084.

81 Métis Archival Project, *Métis Scrip in Alberta*, 25. Frank Tough is the founder and director of the Métis Archival Project.

82 Quoted in Sherry Farrell Racette, "Sewing for a Living," in *Contact Zones: Aboriginal and Settler Women in Canada's Colonial Past*, ed. Katie Pickles and Myra Rutherdale (Vancouver: UBC Press, 2005), 39.

83 Parks Canada, "Batoche National Historic Site" (pamphlet) (Ottawa: Parks Canada, 2005), 19–20. It is noted that Marguerite Dumas Caron and Josephte Paul Tourand took out second homesteads at Batoche.

84 See the case of Margaret Spence, described in Sarah Carter, *Imperial Plots: Women, Land the Spadework of British Imperialism on the Canadian Prairies* (Winnipeg: University of Manitoba Press, 2016), 170–1.

85 Constance Brissenden, ed., *Memories of a Metis Settlement: Eighty Years of East Prairie Metis Settlement with Firsthand Memoires, 1939 to Today* (Penticton, BC: Theyus Books with East Prairie Metis Settlement, 2018), 14–15.

86 Leonard et al., *A Builder of the Northwest*, 79.

87 "Morinville," *Le franco-albertain*, 13 August 1969, 6.

5

Credibility, Corroboration, and Legal Betrayal of Rape Victims

CONSTANCE BACKHOUSE

Under common law rules, testimony from a single witness can be sufficient to convict someone at a criminal trial if it meets the burden of proof "beyond a reasonable doubt." The criminal burden of proof sets a much higher threshold than in a civil trial, which uses the "balance of probability" test instead. Few have quarrelled with this, because the fear of wrongfully jailing anyone is always of legitimate concern. Much less defensible have been the historical efforts by Canadian legislators and judges to go further than requiring proof "beyond a reasonable doubt." Together they set about establishing an additional thicket of "corroboration rules" in cases of sexual assault.

In the 1927 case of *Hubin v. The King*, the Supreme Court of Canada defined the doctrine of corroboration to tar the testimony of women and girls as inherently suspect, cementing into law the notion that victims of sexual assault lacked credibility.[1] In doing so, it reinforced a practice that continues to have resonance legally and culturally: the ritual doubting of women's sexual assault testimony. A fuller examination of the precedent-setting ruling allows us to inquire into the historical rationales offered by criminal law authorities for betraying the ideals of fairness and gender parity.

Evidence from the Protagonists

On 1 December 1926, thirteen-year-old Sophie Oleksiuk took the witness stand and was duly sworn in before the County Court Judge's

Criminal Court in Winnipeg, Manitoba.[2] The presiding judge was fifty-eight-year-old Richard Alexander "Dick" Stacpoole, a British-born lawyer who had practised law for several decades in Winnipeg until his elevation to the bench two years earlier.[3] Sophie testified that she lived with her parents, two brothers, and three sisters on a farm "on the crossing road" east of Lockport, Manitoba. Her grandparents, aunt, and uncle lived nearby, all of them apparently part of a Ukrainian community that had taken up farming north of Winnipeg.

Sophie explained that she had left home around 9:00 a.m. on 20 September 1926 to walk to the Lockport post office to pick up the mail. A man she later identified as Leo Paul Hubin, a native of St. Boniface, Manitoba, drove by just after she had passed the Canadian Northern Railway track. He was driving a flashy four-passenger, two-door McLaughlin coupe, which he had purchased from a dealer that spring. Although he was travelling in the other direction, he turned his car around, returned to stop beside Sophie, and offered her a lift to town. Although she did not know the man, she was still about two miles shy of Lockport, so she accepted the ride. She became alarmed when Hubin turned north on the next crossroad. She told him she wanted to get out. He assured her that he was only going "a little way" and then would take her directly to the post office. Instead, he drove her four miles further out of her way.

Under questioning from the prosecutor Andrew Allison "Andy" Moffat,[4] Sophie described what happened next: "he asked me if I had been fucked, and I said 'no,' and he asked me if I would like it, and I said 'no.' Then he said 'Let me touch it,' and I said 'no,' and started to cry. I said I wanted to get out, and he said 'All right, jump out.' I jumped out and he jumped with me out, and he held my coat, and pushed me down. Then he pulled my pants off and stuck his private part into mine."[5] Sophie explained that she "hollered" when Hubin "put his private" into her, although when the defence lawyer, John (Jack) Myer Isaacs, asked her if she hollered "very much," she said "no."[6] When he asked if there was "any bleeding," she answered "yes." She testified that Hubin tore her bloomers in his haste to pull them down, and the prosecutor produced her ripped undergarment as "Exhibit No. 1." She told the court that she refused to get back into the car and Hubin drove off, abandoning the frightened, crying girl by the roadside. Sophie did not go straight home. Distraught and embarrassed, she continued on to the post office. A few wagons, a car, and several others on foot, including two schoolmates, passed her. One lady noticed her tears and asked her what was wrong. She told none of them what had happened, because she "didn't want them to know." She didn't tell her grandmother either when she passed her relatives' farm because, as she told the court, "I was ashamed to tell." The story came out only after she arrived home and her fifteen-year-old sister, Mary, questioned the tearful young girl. After Sophie divulged what had happened, her mother, Dora Oleksiuk, went to the police. Hubin was arrested four days later and held in custody in the Winnipeg Provincial Jail.[7]

By 1911, upwards of 30,000 Ukrainians had set up farms in rural Manitoba on the traditional lands of the Anishinaabeg, Cree, Dakota, Dene, and Métis Nations. They came at the invitation of Canadian interior minister Clifford Sifton, who wished to supplant the Indigenous inhabitants with "stalwart peasants in sheepskin coats."[8] Between 1911 and 1931, the Ukrainian share of the Manitoba population rose from 7 to 10 per cent.[9] Despite Sifton's welcome, the immigrants were not all met with open arms. Earlier settlers who defined themselves as white castigated the newcomers as "racialized" outsiders. The *Winnipeg Telegram* condemned "Slavonic" immigrants as "primitive" and "the scum of Europe."[10] Female immigrants were singled out for particular critique.

In 1918, Lendrum McMeans, a senator from Manitoba, asserted on the floor of Parliament that "foreigners" did not have "the same standard of morality as exists among the native-born or English-speaking classes,"[11] and his colleagues complained that it was unfair to set a uniform age of consent for sexual intercourse for all women.[12] PEI Senator Patrick Charles Murphy explained that, as a physician, he was "in possession of knowledge that in the West some young women of from twelve to fourteen years of age, especially those from eastern countries, are just as old and as fully matured as our women in eastern Canada are at twenty or twenty-five," adding, "so you can readily see the injustice that might be done."[13] Attitudes such as this might have complicated the prosecution of Leo Hubin at the outset, except that Parliament had ultimately decided to hold the age of consent constant, with no exception for "foreign" immigrant girls.[14]

The charge against Hubin was carnal knowledge of a girl under the age of fourteen, which sealed any further inquiry into Sophie Oleksiuk's "morality" as legally irrelevant. Mere proof that the accused man had sexual intercourse with twelve-year-old Sophie, with or without her consent, constituted a criminal act.[15] And, in the Winnipeg courtroom that morning, no one asked whether Sophie was Canadian-born, although Judge Stacpoole did note for the record that she was of "foreign extraction but speaks English well."[16]

The press described Hubin as a "St. Boniface man," marking him for readers as a man with francophone origins. His Franco-Manitoban heritage could also have had some bearing on the case. By the early twentieth century, the British had edged out the early Red River Métis colonists to dominate Manitoba in population as well as economic, social, and political power. Francophones were relegated to just 7 per cent of the Manitoba population, many of whom were congregated in the St. Boniface community that formed the French-Canadian cultural centre of western Canada.[17]

At the time of his arrest, Hubin was married and living with his wife in the Olafsson Block, a downtown apartment.[18] Although the city directory listed his occupation as "chauffeur," Hubin told the police that he spent most days in the pool room at the Seymour Hotel on Market Avenue.[19] The Seymour bustled with horsemen, cattle traders, contractors, and workmen who imbibed ten-cent whisky at a rollicking bar with brass rail, brass spittoons, and sawdust on the floor. The rotunda sported the proprietor's stuffed hunting trophies, and the poker room in the hotel's dome was a long-time local favourite until the yellow-brick edifice, built in 1882, was razed in the 1960s to make way for the new city hall.[20]

Hubin chose not to take the stand at the trial, and the only legal record of his version of the events is from the two statements he gave to the police. In the first, he said that on 20 September, he left home at 9:00 a.m. and "went straight to the Seymour Hotel." There he talked to "Mr. Lett, the pool marker," for ten to fifteen minutes. Next, he said he drove his car to the City Dray Garage, where he spoke with Karl, the mechanic, about fixing the tail light. Karl was busy working on another car, so Hubin claimed that he went back home, where he told the police he remained from 10:30 to about 12:30 p.m. Then he said he walked back to the Seymour Hotel where he played pool with Mr. Lett and Bert Davey all afternoon.[21]

No sooner had he signed the first statement than Hubin asked to revise it. In his second statement, he advised that he left home at 9:00 a.m. bound for the Seymour Hotel, talked with Mr. Lett, the pool-marker, until 9:30 a.m., and then drove his car to his mother's St. Boniface home on 368 Ritchot Street. He left there around 10:30 a.m. to pick up his sister, Mrs. Rougeau, from her home on Des Meurons Street. He drove her back to his mother's, and then returned to his own home, "arriving about noon." He completed this statement as follows: "I don't think I ever saw that little girl before, at least not to talk to. I might have seen her before, but I don't know."[22] Two different statements, two different alibis, two different sets of witnesses.

The trial judge, who actually saw and heard Sophie testify in court, and the appellate judges, who sifted through the transcripts, were uniformly positive about Sophie Oleksiuk's testimony. Collectively, they described her as a young girl whose narrative was "well-connected," a witness who was "convincing," unhesitating," and "absolutely truthful."[23] They branded Hubin's statements as "false," "weak," "quibbling," and "a tissue of lies."[24] In the ordinary course, this should have been an easy victory for the prosecution, even under the burden of proof "beyond a reasonable doubt." What happened?

The Complicated Common Law and Legislative Framework

The belief that women and children tended to lie about sexual assault had developed deep roots in English common law after the English judge Sir Matthew Hale enunciated an internally inconsistent, unsubstantiated statement in his early eighteenth-century legal treatise. In an adage that would be solemnly repeated by generations of judges, Hale claimed that rape "was an accusation easily to be made, and hard to be proved, and harder to be defended by the party accused, though never so innocent."[25]

Hale was clearly wrong about the ease with which victims disclosed sexual assault. Sophie Oleksiuk's was a case in point – shame and fear erected powerful impediments for many. Hale also contradicted himself in suggesting that such charges were both hard to prosecute and hard to defend. In fact, the former was accurate, but the latter demonstrably false, as perennially low conviction rates amply revealed.[26] Yet Hale's statement would serve as the historical foundation for a legal presumption that women and children were inherently untrustworthy when they testified about sexual assault. His only justification for fearing false complaints amounted to two cases of "malicious prosecution" that he said had "come within his own knowledge."[27] What could have prompted this non-empirical conjecturing? What could account for the rapidity and tenacity with which the presumption took hold in English and Canadian trials? At the heart of the problem may have been the belief that women who had sex outside of marriage were sullied in some way.[28] Women so besmirched – whether by consensual or coercive sexual acts – appear to have become somehow less believable, less credible in the eyes of the law.

Based upon Hale's common law dictum, English and Canadian judges concluded that they were obliged to warn juries that it was dangerous to convict upon the uncorroborated testimony of female rape complainants.[29] Then, moving well beyond the common law *preference* for corroboration, Canadian legislators expanded upon this rule to make it *mandatory* under the *Criminal Code*. Members of Parliament introduced the mandatory rules in waves – listing some sexual offences in 1892, others in 1920, and still more in 1925.[30] In the Hubin case, the charge was carnal knowledge of a girl under fourteen. In 1925, one year before Sophie's assault, the legislators had mandated corroboration for this too.[31]

Although the male legislators gave no rationale for the 1925 corroboration amendment, there had been fulsome debates regarding earlier legislation.[32] Ontario Liberal MP Byron Moffatt Britton was one parliamentarian who was flummoxed by the need for corroboration. In 1898, he asked his fellow legislators directly why any corroboration was required in sexual assault cases when there was "no such requirement with regard to nine-tenths of the criminal cases that come before the courts."[33] What explanation did the parliamentarians give for this?

There were persistent expressions of concern over the risks that might befall men falsely accused of sexual assault. Ontario Liberal MP Malcolm Colin Cameron wagered that "the chances [were] ten to one" that the female's "story is not true," while in "at least 50 per cent of the cases the man was not at fault." He abhorred the prospect of "incontinent" convictions against men who were as "pure and innocent as Joseph" and defended the corroboration requirement as a "parliamentary shield" that had been "cast around innocent men" for "wise and sufficient reasons."[34] New Brunswick Senator George William Fowler added, "We must recognize that human nature is human nature. We must, remembering our youth and recognizing that there are weaknesses in human nature ... enact legislation in accordance with the facts."[35]

The legislators' remarks focused equally upon their negative perception of women. They spoke of "wileful" and "designing" young girls, "seducers," "tempters," and "brazen females" of "vicious habits" who might "entrap" the "foolish" young men of the country.[36] Senator Sir Mackenzie Bowell, the former Conservative prime minister, read out a letter he had "received from a judge of the land" that he felt summed up the situation perfectly: "Women of unchaste character will generally swear to anything."[37] Nova Scotia Senator Wilbur Benjamin Ross claimed that there were "girls on the streets of this city, and on the streets of every other city in Canada, who at sixteen years of age could give pointers in vice to women of sixty, and who know things which the average married woman in Canada does not know, never did know, and will never know." These were "the very girls," he insisted, who were "used simply as decoy-ducks for the purpose of extorting blackmail."[38] Somewhat later, Conservative MP John Diefenbaker, whose career as a Prairie criminal defence lawyer in Prince Albert, Saskatchewan, would have given him a close-up view of sexual assault trials, spelled out his views three years before becoming prime minister. Mistakenly citing Lord Coke instead of Lord Hale, he told the House of Commons that "Lord Coke pointed out a long time ago that this type of charge is often laid through motives of malice, revenge, jealousy and so on. … Trial judges have found necessary [to warn jurors] to protect the innocent from probable blackmailing activities of those who through the ages have invariably chosen this means to secure their revenge for wrongs done to them, imagined or actual."[39] Charges "often laid," "probable blackmailing," "invariably," "through the ages," "imagined" wrongs, "malice," "revenge," "jealousy." It was quite a list.

There is little evidence that early twentieth-century Canadian feminists were resisting the waves of legislation mandating corroboration. Feminist reformers were preoccupied at the time primarily with campaigns for rights related to married women's property, dower, and child custody as well as temperance and suffrage.[40] The National Council of Women of Canada (NCWC) and its local chapters did support the passage of a law against a new crime of "seduction" in 1886. Their quarrel with the legislation was that its protection, confined to women of "previously chaste character," was too limited. They also lobbied to raise the age of women protected, but did not fight the requirement for "corroboration."[41] It is difficult to know whether a feminist attack on corroboration would have had much success, but, in retrospect, it seems that the NCWC lost an opportunity to at least try to resist the tide.

Now that Parliament had cemented its mandatory status, the next question was how to define "corroboration." The dictionary equated the term with "strengthening" or "confirming" or "making more sure or certain."[42] But the legislators wanted something more. The *Criminal Code* was revised to state that no one could be convicted of the charge "upon the evidence of one witness, unless such witness was corroborated in some material particular by evidence implicating the accused."[43] It did not stop there. Canadian judges added all sorts of requirements that produced still more hurdles for the prosecution. And, in *Hubin*, the

Supreme Court of Canada would take the doctrine of corroboration to the steepest level yet.

The Evidence Rejected as Insufficient in Law

Leo Hubin was convicted at the trial. The Manitoba Court of Appeal judges disagreed among themselves over that verdict, and the conviction was ultimately overturned at the Supreme Court of Canada.[44] While the judges differed in their assessments, Hubin was set free in the end because of the absence of corroboration. During the three hearings, the judges evaluated many pieces of evidence.[45]

Dr. Walter Henry Gabriel Gibbs, an English-born physician who practised in Selkirk and served as the provincial coroner, told the trial judge that he had examined Sophie after the assault.[46] He testified that he found evidence of "abrasion," a "ruptured hymen," and a "swollen vagina" that appeared to be "of recent origin" and "must have been caused" by "penetration."[47] None of the judges involved in the trial or appeals qualified this testimony as legal corroboration. Since they offered no reasons for failing to do so, we are left to speculate. It was clearly evidence relating to a "material particular" – the sexual injury at the heart of the "carnal knowledge" – so it must not have sufficed because it failed to "implicate the accused." What was in theory an affirming piece of evidence, a medical finding that a prepubescent girl had been vaginally violated, was useless because the doctor could not state whose penis had caused the abrasive rupture. A similar fate befell Sophie Oleksiuk's torn bloomers. An item of tangible, physical evidence that attested to the violence of the sexual assault did not qualify because the rent undergarment failed to disclose who had ripped it.

Prosecutor Andy Moffat was not deterred. He was impressed with his observant and quick-witted young witness and led her through a series of questions about how she had come to identify Leo Hubin. While still at the side of the road that morning, Sophie had taken a pencil from her pocket and jotted down the licence number of Hubin's car on the envelope she was taking to the post office. The police traced the car to an automobile salesman, George Degagné, who identified the McLaughlin coupe as one he had sold earlier to Hubin. Then Sophie was able to identify Hubin's car at a garage by its appearance, licence number, and the unusual cushion in it – a little round one of "black plush" and "sand colour." The envelope with the licence number written in Sophie's hand and the cushion were both labelled as exhibits at trial. The police testified that they had brought Hubin down to the station and placed him in a lineup with four other men. Without hesitation, Sophie had picked him out as the culprit. Hubin admitted to the police that he owned the car and was driving it on the day the offence was committed.[48]

The trial judge was prepared to accept this identification evidence as legally corroborative. The majority of the Manitoba Court of Appeal did as well. But two of the Manitoba appellate judges dissented, emphasizing that Parliament had expanded the "protection given an accused by Lord Hale's dictum" in 1925. Justice James Émile Pierre Prendergast wrote for himself and Charles Percy Fullerton in dissent.[49] Unlike the other Manitoba Court of Appeal judges, who were all of British or Irish descent, Prendergast was the only francophone on the court.[50] Born in Quebec City in 1858, he took his law degree at Laval and practised in Quebec until he moved to Manitoba in 1882. A leader in Leo Hubin's St. Boniface community, its mayor in 1893 and 1896, Prendergast was also president of the Saint Jean Baptiste Society of Manitoba. He sat as a member of the Legislative Assembly from 1885 to 1896 and led the francophone opposition to the new law abolishing separate schools and mandating English-only instruction in 1890.[51]

Purporting to quote from the *Criminal Code* corroboration provision, Prendergast stated, "the proper question in all such cases would seem to be: is there any material particular in the main witness's testimony, that is corroborated by *independent* evidence implicating the accused?"[52] Prendergast was wrong. The section in the *Criminal Code* contained no reference to "independent" evidence. Indeed, none of the code's definitions for corroboration used the word "independent."[53] Where did these judges come up with such a superimposed heavy barrier to believing witnesses who sought criminal protection from sexual assault? They gave no indication.

The Supreme Court of Canada was enthusiastic about the new "independent" criterion, which its judges unanimously upheld in their decision to quash Hubin's conviction. Chief Justice Francis Alexander Anglin at least was prepared to provide some backing. He cited an English Court of Criminal Appeal judgment, *Rex v. Baskerville*, which had adopted the "independent" rule with respect to corroborating testimony given by a criminal accomplice.[54] But it was by no means a foregone conclusion that *Baskerville* should govern in sexual assault cases. The 1916 English decision originated under the common law, not under the codified criminal law that existed in Canada. There was no necessity for Canadian judges to follow the imperial precedent without considering if and why it was relevant under Canadian statutory law. And the English case concerned accomplice evidence, witnesses not obviously on a par with complainants under carnal knowledge statutes. Yet when the Supreme Court of Canada delivered the final decision on this case, its judges picked up the "independent" rule, simply citing *Baskerville* without further analysis or reflection.

And this is what skewered poor Sophie Oleksiuk's identification in the Hubin case. The problem was that all of the identification emanated from Sophie herself. It was Sophie who gave the police the licence number, identified the car and the cushion, and then picked out Hubin from the lineup. That her leads were borne out by third-party evidence from the car salesman, by the physical existence of the car and the unusual cushion, and by Hubin's admission that he was driving the car that morning, did not pass muster. Manitoba Court of Appeal Justice Prendergast wrote, "Nothing that she said and no document that proceeded from her, however much they may strengthen her version, can be corroboration."[55] Citing *Baskerville*, Supreme Court Chief Justice Anglin agreed that the identification evidence implicated the accused solely by reason of the complainant's statement. It did not impress him that there was a multiplicity of such evidence: "Nor can any multiplication of such facts amount to corroboration," he stated. "They lack the essential quality of independence."[56] Sophie, the core source of the identification evidence, was inherently suspect, and nothing could cure her essential lack of credibility. It was as if the judges had lost sight of the purpose of the corroboration rule, which was simply to strengthen the testimony of the female complainant. They were searching for corroborative evidence to replace the testimony of the complainant, to constitute the sole proof of the crime. If it did not cover all the bases on its own, this was grounds for acquittal.

In vain had one of the earlier appellate judges tried to explain the absurdity of the result in this case, the irrational suggestion that the complainant somehow "made up" the licence number, the description of the car, the description of the pillow. He wrote: "The theory that the complainant seeks to connect the prisoner, a person she did not know and never saw before, with the commission of the act, in order to shield another person, is too barren to have a moment's consideration."[57] If the licence number was a fictitious one, how did the police track it to a man she had never met before, whom she then picked out of an anonymous police lineup? Her familiarity with the cushion was a detail she could never have given if she had not been in the car. It was clear, he wrote, that the story was one "she was powerless to invent."[58]

Finally, there were Leo Hubin's inconsistent statements, the ones he gave to the police after being warned that anything he said would be taken down and could be used against him at trial.[59] The prosecution argued that legal corroboration could be found in these, because Hubin's shifting alibis constituted evidence of guilt that was obviously "independent" of Sophie.[60] The final arbiter, the Supreme Court of Canada, held that the trial judge might well have construed the internally inconsistent alibis as some "acknowledgment of guilt." However, since Judge Stacpoole had stopped his analysis after holding that Sophie's identification evidence sufficed, he had unfortunately neglected to mention that he was drawing a legal inference of corroboration from Hubin's statements.[61] So this could not serve the purpose either. Here was a legal interpretation that finally accepted as "corroboration" one of the multiple items put forward by the Crown prosecutor. Yet in final analysis, it too was spurned.

The judicial gloss on the mandatory corroboration rules was draconian. Introducing an "independent" criterion set the evidentiary burden one step farther than the legislators had already gone. Not only were complainants in sexual assault cases labouring under an unsubstantiated presumption that they were untrustworthy, but everything that stemmed from their evidence was now to be summarily dismissed. It practically necessitated finding a witness who watched the sexual assault take place. In crimes of sexual assault, the judges must have known that separate witnesses would rarely be found.

Jack Isaacs, the lawyer who defended Hubin at all three levels of court, recognized as much. "There is perhaps no other species of evidence known in law which demands so much," he wrote in his appellate brief. Yet he was prepared to stand by the results. "Corroboration has been adopted by the Legislature as a matter of public policy and like all such enactments they must inevitably lead to injustices being done in individual cases. That is the price paid to secure public protection," he noted.[62] In this extraordinary case, the evidence of a young girl, whom everyone seemed to believe, was dismissed. In stark contrast, a trial conviction of a man whose conflicting sworn statements provided uncontroverted evidence of his guilt, was vacated. The "public protection" being safeguarded was for men who might be falsely accused in the future. No one seems to have asked why the "public protection" of victims of sexual assault should be left out of the equation – such a consideration was apparently too inconsequential to count. In the words of Hubin's lawyer, it was a matter of "inevitable injustice."

The Aftermath

In the final result, the Supreme Court set aside Leo Hubin's conviction and directed that the matter should be heard again in a new trial. Hubin had been held in the Manitoba Penitentiary since his trial conviction.[63] He had already served five months by the time the conviction was overturned on 30 May 1927. Crown attorney Moffat attempted a second prosecution, but Hubin's defence counsel, Jack Isaacs, argued that his client could not be tried again for a charge that had already been dismissed. In November 1927, an assize jury agreed, and Hubin walked free.[64] Leo Hubin's subsequent fate, and that of his wife and family, remains unknown.

There are no records chronicling what Sophie Oleksiuk or her family and neighbours thought of the outcome. One can only imagine that they were not pleased. Sophie's mother had accompanied her for the medical examination, had been with her in the police station when she identified Hubin, and was undoubtedly present at the trial.[65] There are archival records of a similar 1927 case in which charges of sexual assault were stayed because of insufficient corroboration. There, the Ukrainian girl's family, from east central Alberta, campaigned to overturn what they saw as a grave injustice, complaining persistently to legal authorities, apparently without success.[66] The Oleksiuks must have felt similarly, aware of how credible Sophie had been on the witness stand, appalled at what the legislators and judges had done to the rules of corroboration.

It was left to the resurgent feminist movement of the 1970s to demand retraction of the mandatory corroboration requirements. The second-wave feminist movement made the reform of sexual assault law one of its main targets. Activists from newly founded rape crisis centres and a burgeoning new generation of feminist lawyers lobbied politicians for an overhaul of the *Criminal Code*. Their strenuous and protracted campaigns convinced federal legislators to delete the corroboration requirements in 1976.[67] When male judges then tried to reintroduce corroboration through a revival of Sir Matthew Hale's common law precautions, the feminist lobby campaign had to swing into action once more. In 1982, Parliament was convinced to again amend the *Criminal Code*, passing an explicit prohibition on all corroboration warnings.[68]

That action should have been enough. Yet the stubborn demand for corroboration remains with us well into the twenty-first century. The police are still reluctant to lay a sexual assault charge without it. Prosecutors are still reluctant to take such cases to trial without it. Judges and jurors are still reluctant to convict without it. The eighteenth-century roots of unsubstantiated anxiety over the truthfulness of women and children who experience sexual assault still reach out their ancient tentacles, making a mockery of present-day ideals of even-handed justice and gender equality.[69]

NOTES

I greatly appreciate the assistance of Desirée Hayward, Pascal-Hugo Plourde, Brian Hubner, Marie-Josée Blais, and Rosemary Morrissette Rozyk. An earlier publication provides a briefer comparative analysis of this case: Constance Backhouse, "The Doctrine of Corroboration in Sexual Assault Trials in Early Twentieth-Century Canada and Australia," *Queen's Law Journal* 26 (2011): 297–338.

1 *Hubin v. The King*, [1927] SCR 442.

2 Although Sophie was young, the trial judge assessed her testamentary capacity and ruled she was qualified to give sworn evidence and was not subject to additional statutory requirements that were mandatory for any child giving unsworn evidence. All references to the evidence come from the trial transcript, Supreme Court of Canada Archives, RG 125, part 2, box 483-1192 (1922–62), vol. 556, file no. 5369, series A, *Hubin v. the King*, 1927, pp. 11–56 (hereafter *Hubin*, SCA). There was little press coverage. In the early twentieth century, prairie newspapers reporting on sexual assault cases "invariably noted that the accused had been acquitted or convicted of 'a most serious charge' but claimed that the details were unfit to print." Lesley Erickson, *Westward Bound: Sex, Violence, the Law, and the Making of a Settler Society* (Vancouver: UBC Press, 2011), 120. There were two reports of the trial decision, neither of which specified the crime involved: "Four Years for Serious Crime: St. Boniface Man Sentenced for Offence against Young Girl," *Winnipeg Tribune*, 8 December 1926, 6; "Hubin to Serve Four Years," *Winnipeg Free Press*, 8 December 1926, 6. Three brief references to the Supreme Court decision gave no further details: "Supreme Court Reserves Judgment in Hubin Case," *Manitoba Free Press*, 4 May 1927, 2; "Supreme Court Gives Manitoban New Trial," *Manitoba Free Press*, 31 May 1927, 17; "Circumstantial Evidence Must Be Corroborated," *Winnipeg Tribune*, 31 May 1927, 13.

3 Born in Brentwood, Essex, England in 1868, Stacpoole had been educated at the elite Merchant Taylors' School. He immigrated to Manitoba in 1886, articled with T.L. Metcalfe in Winnipeg, and practised law with Metcalfe, Sharpe, Elliott and Stacpoole until 1924, when he was appointed to the County Court of the Eastern Judicial District of Manitoba. "Judge Stacpoole Dies Following Long Illness," *Winnipeg Free Press*, 28 December 1948; "Memorable Manitobans: Richard Alexander 'Dick' Stacpoole (1868–1948)," Manitoba Historical Society, www.mhs.mb.ca/docs/people/stacpoole_ra.shtml.

4 Andrew Allison "Andy" Moffat (1895–1964) was born in Blandford, Dorset, England, and came to Manitoba in 1904. During the First World War, he served with the Winnipeg 61st Battalion and survived three years as a prisoner of war. He moved to Winnipeg in 1919, studied law at the Manitoba Law School, was called to the bar in 1923, and practised with the Department of the Attorney General until 1929. He would later become Crown prosecutor for the City of Winnipeg, and deputy attorney general for Manitoba. After a stint with the federal Department of Justice, in 1953 he became a senior partner with the firm of Aikins MacAulay. His obituary described him as a "quiet" man with a "wry humor." *Winnipeg Free Press*, 21 May 1964, n.p.; *Winnipeg Tribune*, 21 May 1964, n.p.

5 Trial transcript, *Hubin*, SCA, 13.

6 John (Jack) Myer Isaacs (1892–1979) was born at Abersychan, Monmouthshire, Wales, and educated at the University of Wales (Cardiff). Of Jewish heritage, he moved to Winnipeg in 1911, the year of anti-Semitic riots in South Wales. He articled with fellow Welshman Edmund L. Howell and was called to the bar in 1916. He opened a solo criminal defence practice in 1916. In 1924, the press described him as an "eloquent" lawyer with a memory for detail. Winnipeg Free Press Newspaper Archives, 8 October 1924, https://newspaperarchive.com/winnipeg-free-press-oct-08–1924-p-1. After Jack's younger brother Max joined the firm in 1926, they practised as Isaacs & Isaacs at the Royal Bank Building on 504 Main Street. A third brother, Manly Isaacs, joined the firm in 1932. Jack moved to London, England, in 1936. "Memorable Manitobans: John Myer Isaacs (1892–1979)," Manitoba Historical Society, http://www.mhs.mb.ca/docs/people/isaacs_jm.shtml; press release, "Ten Queen's Counsel on New Year's Honors List," 27 December 1963, Department of Provincial Secretary, Legislative Building, Winnipeg, p. 3.

7 Trial transcript, *Hubin*, SCA, 11–23.

8 Ruben Bellan, *Winnipeg, First Century: An Economic History* (Winnipeg: Queenston Publishing, 1978) 63–4; Brian M. Evans "Migration into Manitoba c.1885–c.1920," in *Winnipeg, 1874–1974: Progress and Prospects*, ed. Tony J. Kuz (Winnipeg: Manitoba Department of Industry and Commerce, 1974) 25.

9 Bellan, *Winnipeg, First Century*, 144–64. The census recorded the Manitoba population as 59.9 per cent British in 1911 (52.6 per cent in 1931), and the Ukrainian 6.7 per cent in 1911 (10.5 per cent in 1931): W.J. Carlyle "Growth, Ethnic Groups and Socio-Economic Areas of Winnipeg" in Kuz, *Winnipeg*, 33.

10 *Winnipeg Telegram*, 13 May 1901, as quoted in Alan Artibise, *Winnipeg: An Illustrated History* (Toronto: Lorimer, 1977), 46.

11 *Senate Debates*, 2nd Session, 13th Parliament (1919), 782. British Columbia MP Frank Bainard Stacey also expressed concern in the House of Commons in 1918 that "the morals of certain nationalities" were "exceedingly lax." *House of Commons Debates*, 1st Session, 13th Parliament (1918), 2: 1699.

12 Nova Scotia senator William Benjamin Ross explained that fixing an age of consent for sexual intercourse was problematic: "Of course, you cannot fix the age with mathematical certainty. Amongst certain races, particularly the black races and the Italians, the age of fourteen does very safely mark the period of puberty; but I am prepared to find that among a large section of Canadian girls the age of fourteen is perhaps too low." *Senate Debates*, 2nd Session, 13th Parliament (1919), 779.

13 *Senate Debates*, 4th Session, 13th Parliament (1920), 698.

14 *Criminal Code, 1892*, SC 1892, c. 29, s. 269: "Every one is guilty of an indictable offence and liable to imprisonment for life, and to be whipped, who carnally knows any girl under the age of fourteen years, not being his wife, whether he believes her to be of or above that age or not." Section 261 provided: "It is no defence to a charge or indictment for any indecent assault on a young person under the age of fourteen years to prove that he or she consented to the act of indecency." The history of the offence sometimes referred to as "statutory rape" began with an inherited imperial statute, an 1861 British Parliament enactment that made it a crime to have sexual intercourse with a girl younger than twelve. *Offences against the Person Act 1861* (UK), 24 & 25 Vict., c. 100, ss. 50–5. The British age limit was raised to sixteen in 1885. *Criminal Law Amendment Act 1885* (UK), 48 & 49 Vict., c. 69, s. 5. Canada retained the original age limit of twelve in its own 1869 statute, raising it to fourteen in 1890. *An Act Respecting Offences*

against the Person, SC 1869, c. 20, ss. 51–3; *An Act to Amend the Criminal Law*, SC 1890, c. 37, ss. 3, 7, 12.

15 *Criminal Code, 1892*, SC 1892, c. 29, s. 269.

16 The judge's oral decision is contained in the trial transcript, *Hubin*, SCR, 56. Since 1915, the provincial government had set up a unilingual school system, where all school-age immigrants learned English as a matter of course. Artibise, *Winnipeg*, 50–2.

17 Monique Hebert, "Les grandes gardiennes de la langue et de la foi: Une histoire des franco-manitobaines, 1916–1947" (PhD diss., University of Manitoba, 1994). The census recorded the Manitoba population as 6.8 per cent French in 1911 (6.5 per cent in 1931): Kuz, *Winnipeg*, 11, 33, 74.

18 He resided at Suite 8 in the Olafsson Block, a downtown Winnipeg apartment with mostly anglophone tenants on 216 James Avenue at the corner of King Street. The year before his arrest, he was listed as living at 147 Alexander Avenue. *Winnipeg City Directory 1925 and 1926* (Winnipeg: Henderson Directories), 359, 925.

19 "St. Boniface Man Sentenced for Offence against Young Girl," *Winnipeg Evening Tribune*, 8 December 1926, 6. *Winnipeg City Directory 1925* (Winnipeg: Henderson Directories), 925. Statement of Facts, Respondent's Appeal record, *Hubin*, SCR, 7–8.

20 The name had been changed to the Criterion Hotel by the time of its demise. Val Werier, "New Year's Eve and Hotel Dies," *Winnipeg Tribune*, 6 January 1964; Vince Leah, "Closing of the Criterion Hotel Will Sadden Some Sports Fans," *Winnipeg Tribune*, 6 November 1976. Clippings held in "Manitoba Scrap Books," Manitoba Legislative Library, M15, p. 121 and M29, p. 102.

21 Statement of Accused Made on September 24th, 1926, Exhibit No. 3, *Hubin*, SCA, 59.

22 Statement of Accused Made on Sept 24th, 1926, Exhibit No. 4, *Hubin*, SCA, 60.

23 *R. v. Hubin* (1927), 36 Man R 373 (CA) 375, 377; trial judge's oral decision, *Hubin*, SCA, 54.

24 *R. v. Hubin* (1927), 36 Man R 373 (CA) at 385.

25 Sir Matthew Hale, *Historia Placitorum Coronae*, vol. 1 (London: Nutt & Gosling, 1734), 635–6. For discussion of the absence of empirical evidence, see Jocelynne Scutt, "Sexism and Psychology: An Analysis of the 'Scientific Basis' of the Corroboration Rule in Rape," *Hecate* (1979): 35–48. For analysis of Hale's reputation as a misogynist and his role in convicting women accused of witchcraft, see G. Geiss, "Lord Hale, Witches and Rape," *British Journal of Law and Society* 5 (1978): 26.

26 For statistics, see Constance Backhouse, "Nineteenth-Century Canadian Rape Law, 1800–1892," in *Essays in the History of Canadian Law*, vol. 2, ed. David H. Flaherty (Toronto: Osgoode Society, 1983), 221–2, and Constance Backhouse, *Carnal Crimes: Sexual Assault Law in Canada, 1900–1975* (Toronto: Irwin Law, 2008), ch. 10.

27 J.W. Cecil Turner, *Russell on Crime*, 6th ed., vol. 3 (London: Stevens and Sons, 1896), 235.

28 It was not until the 1980s that rape within marriage became a crime. *An Act to amend the Criminal Code in relation to sexual offences and other offences against the person and to amend certain other Acts in relation thereto or in consequence thereof*, SC 1980–81–82–83, c. 125, s. 19.

29 *Halsbury's Laws of England*, vol. 9 (London: Butterworths, 1909), 388; Backhouse, *Carnal Crimes*, 171–2, 380–2. In addition to sexual assault offences, corroboration was also attached to some civil proceedings for affiliation, breach of promise to marry, divorce, and claims against a dead person's estate. Criminal prosecutions for perjury, treason, and personation also required corroboration. Two other types of witnesses were singled out: children of "tender years" who had not been sworn and accomplices. Ernest Cockle, *Cases and Statutes on the Law of Evidence*, 7th ed. (London: Sweet and Maxwell, 1946), 156–7; Backhouse, *Carnal Crimes*, 380.

30 *Criminal Code 1892*, SC 1892, c. 29, s. 684 made corroboration mandatory for all charges under ss. 181–90, which included "seduction of girls under sixteen," "seduction under promise of marriage," "seduction of a ward, servant," "seduction of female passengers on vessels," "unlawfully defiling women," "parent or guardian procuring defilement of girl," "householders permitting defilement of girl on premises," "conspiracy to defile," "carnally knowing idiots," and the "prostitution of Indian women," as well as treason, perjury, procuring feigned marriage, and forgery. In 1920, carnal knowledge of a girl "of previous chaste character under the age of sixteen and above the age of fourteen" was added: *Criminal Code Amendment Act*, SC 1920, c. 43, s. 8. In 1925, the following offences were added to the compulsory corroboration rule: "carnal knowledge of girls under fourteen," "seduction of girls between sixteen and eighteen," "seduction of step-child or foster child," "seduction of female employee," "procuring," "carnal knowledge of girls of previous chaste character between fourteen and sixteen," "attempted carnal knowledge of girls under fourteen," "communicating venereal disease," "bigamy," and the abortion offences. *An Act to Amend the Criminal Code*, SC 1925, c. 38; *Criminal Code*, RSC 1927, c. 36, s. 1002. For more details, see "A

History of Canadian Sexual Assault Legislation, 1900–2000," http://www.constancebackhouse.ca/fileadmin/website/index.htm.

31 *An Act to Amend the Criminal Code*, SC 1925, c. 38; *Criminal Code*, RSC 1927, c. 36, s. 1002.

32 On the lack of debate in 1925, see *House of Commons Debates*, 4th Session, 14th Parliament (1925), 14: 3997–4015. Canada's first elected female parliamentarian, Agnes Macphail (an MP from 1921 to 1940), did not speak either.

33 *House of Commons Debates*, 3rd Session, 8th Parliament (1898), 46: 2894–9.

34 Ibid.

35 *Senate Debates*, 2nd Session, 13th Parliament (1919), 780–1.

36 Backhouse, "Nineteenth-Century Canadian Rape Law," 210, 228–32; *House of Commons Debates*, 3d Series (1880), 254: 1662 and 255: 1083–6; *House of Commons Debates*, 3rd Session, 8th Parliament (1898), 46: 2886–2902; *Senate Debates*, 4th Session, 8th Parliament (1899), 402–13; *House of Commons Debates*, 2nd Session, 13th Parliament (1919), 5: 4634; *Senate Debates*, 2nd Session, 13th Parliament (1919), 775–817; *Senate Debates*, 4th Session, 13th Parliament (1920), 694–727. Constance Backhouse, *Petticoats and Prejudice: Women and Law in Nineteenth-Century Canada* (Toronto: Women's Press, 1991), 72–9.

37 *Senate Debates*, 4th Session, 8th Parliament (1899), 402–13.

38 *Senate Debates*, 2nd Session, 13th Parliament (1919), 779.

39 *House of Commons Debates*, 1st Session, 22nd Parliament (1954), 2: 2050. On Diefenbaker's legal and political career, see Denis Smith, *Rogue Tory: The Life and Legend of John G. Diefenbaker* (Toronto: McClelland & Stewart, 1995).

40 Constance Backhouse, *Petticoats and Prejudice*; Gail Cuthbert Brandt et al., *Canadian Women: A History* (Toronto: Nelson, 2011); Joan Sangster, *One Hundred Years of Struggle: The History of Women and the Vote in Canada* (Vancouver: UBC Press, 2019).

41 Louis Henry Davies, MP for Queen's, Prince Edward Island, objected to the requirement for corroboration as a "monstrous" attempt to "nullify the Bill," adding, "we know that practically, it would be impossible to get this corroborating evidence in ninety-nine cases out of a hundred." His intervention was ineffectual. Davies would be appointed to the Supreme Court of Canada in 1901, and elevated to Chief Justice of Canada in 1918, but died in office in 1924, just a few years before the *Hubin* appeal. Backhouse, *Petticoats and Prejudice*, 69–80.

42 *A New English Dictionary*, vol. 2 (Oxford: Oxford University Press, 1893), 1020.

43 *An Act to Amend the Criminal Code*, SC 1925, c. 38, s. 26; *Criminal Code*, RSC 1927, c. 36, s. 1002. "A History of Canadian Sexual Assault Legislation, 1900–2000," http://www.constancebackhouse.ca/fileadmin/website/index.htm.

44 While Isaacs continued as defence counsel throughout, Manitoba attorney general R.W. Craig K.C. replaced Moffat for the prosecution at the top court.

45 This chapter will not consider the legal reception of Sophie's "recent complaint" evidence, her failure to disclose the sexual assault until she returned home, and her subsequent disclosure to her sister and mother. The Canadian courts struggled with whether such statements were admissible, and generally concluded they could not qualify as legal corroboration. See Backhouse, *Carnal Crimes*, 174–6.

46 Dr. Gibbs (1872–1952) obtained his medical degree from the University of Manitoba in 1908, and served as mayor of Selkirk (1922, 1926–7), coroner, and member of the Selkirk Board of Trade. He ran unsuccessfully federally and provincially for the Liberal Party in 1925, 1927, and 1932. "Ex-Mayor of Selkirk Dies in B.C.," *Winnipeg Free Press*, 1 May 1952, 13, link available on the Manitoba Historical Society website, http://www.mhs.mb.ca/docs/people/gibbs_whg.shtml.

47 Dr. Gibbs also testified that Sophie had not yet started to menstruate. Trial transcript, *Hubin*, SCA, 24–6.

48 Exhibits 2 and 5 and trial transcript, *Hubin*, SCA, 15–17, 30–58.

49 Three Manitoba Court of Appeal judges concluded that there was sufficient corroboration: Chief Justice William Egerton Perdue, Walter Harley Trueman, and Robert Maxwell Dennistoun. James Émile Prendergast and Charles Percy Fullerton dissented.

50 All five judges were Canadian-born. Perdue (1850–1933) was born in Brampton, Ontario, studied law with Sir John A. Macdonald, moved to Winnipeg in 1882, and became a bencher and president of the Law Society of Manitoba. "On Bench since 1903, Successor Not Named," *Winnipeg Tribune*, 10 October 1929. Trueman (1870–1951) was born in Saint John, NB, practised law there until he moved to Winnipeg in 1908, ran as a provincial Liberal candidate, was a Presbyterian and Member of the Order of AF and AM (Masons), and was appointed to the bench in 1923. "W.H. Trueman K.C., Justice of Manitoba," *Winnipeg Tribune*, 15 April 1923. Dennistoun (1864–1952) was born in Peterborough, Ontario, where he practised after his call in 1888. He was a bencher of the Law Society of Upper Canada, a Commander of the Order of the British Empire, a Mason, and a member of the Manitoba Club. He was appointed to the bench in

1918. "Robert Maxwell Dennistoun," Manitoba Historical Society, http://www.mhs.mb.ca/docs/people/dennistoun_rm.shtml. Fullerton (1870–1938) was born in Amherst, NS, practised law in Halifax and Sydney, and moved to Winnipeg in 1906, where he joined Aikins, Robson, Fullerton and Coyne. He was appointed to the bench in 1917. "Charles Percy Fullerton," Manitoba Historical Society, http://www.mhs.mb.ca/docs/people/fullerton_cp.shtml. On Prendergast's francophone heritage, see Lionel Dorge, "James-Émile-Pierre Prendergast," *Le Manitoba, reflects d'un passé* (Saint Boniface: Les éditions du blé, 1976), 144.

51 Dorge, "James-Émile-Pierre Prendergast," 144; "James Emile Pierre Prendergast (1858–1945)," Manitoba Historical Society, http://www.mhs.mb.ca/docs/people/prendergast_jep.shtml.

52 *Rex v. Hubin* (1927), 36 Man R 373 (CA) at 378; emphasis added.

53 *Criminal Code*, RSC 1906, c. 146, ss. 301, 1002; *An Act to Amend the Criminal Code*, SC 1925, c. 38, s. 26; *Criminal Code*, RSC 1927, c. 36, ss. 301, 1002.

54 *Hubin v. The King* (1927), 48 CCC 172 (SCC) at 172–3, citing *Rex v. Baskerville*, [1916] 2 KB 658. Only one judge from the Manitoba Court of Appeal, Walter Harley Trueman, made earlier reference to *Baskerville*. Trueman made no comment on the oddity of the new "independent" criterion and resolved the case on the other corroborating evidence. *Rex v. Hubin* (1927), 36 Man. R. 373 (CA) 381–6.

55 *Rex v. Hubin* (1927), 36 Man R 373 (CA) 378.

56 *Hubin v. The King* (1927), 48 CCC 172 (SCC) 173–4.

57 *Rex v. Hubin* (1927), 36 Man R 373 (CA) 384–5, per Walter Harley Trueman.

58 Ibid.

59 *Hubin*, SCA, 49.

60 At the divided Manitoba Court of Appeal, Prendergast was prepared to dismiss the inconsistencies as minor discrepancies, while his colleague Trueman took the opposite view. "That both statements are false I have no doubt. That one is assuredly false need alone be stated," Trueman wrote. The conclusion that the accused was "lying," he ruled, sufficed for corroboration. *Rex v. Hubin* (1927), 36 Man R 373 (CA) at 379–81, 385–6.

61 *Hubin v. The King* (1927), 48 CCC 172 (SCC) at 174–80.

62 *Hubin*, SCA, 91.

63 *Hubin*, SCA, 57. Judge Stacpoole ordered a four-year term on 7 December 1926.

64 A search for this second prosecution turned up no relevant records: see Provincial Archives of Manitoba, Court of Queen's Bench and County Court Criminal Registers, Schedule A0107, microfilm M1196 (1872–1949); Court of Queen's Bench Criminal Pockets, ATG0007A, microfilm

M1245 (1872–1989). Partial details were found in "Hubin Can Not Be Tried Again," *Winnipeg Tribune*, 16 November 1927, 7, noting that the prosecution apparently laid a "slightly different charge," the jury held that the defence of "autrefois convict or autrefois acquit" applied, and Hubin could not be tried again on "substantially the same charge." It is unclear from the press account what charge was laid, or whether the same charge might have received a different result. Given the Supreme Court recommendation for a new trial, the result seems odd in any event.

65 *Hubin*, SCA, 24, 40, 42.

66 The defence lawyer for the young man accused of carnal knowledge of a girl under fourteen threatened the girl's mother and grandmother with a defamation suit if they continued to sully his client's reputation. Frances Swyripa, "Negotiating Sex and Gender in the Ukrainian Bloc Settlement," in *Telling Tales: Essays in Western Women's History*, ed. Catherine A. Cavanaugh and Randi R. Warne (Vancouver: UBC Press, 2000), 245–6, citing Provincial Archives of Alberta, 72.26/7649, carnal knowledge under fourteen, Bruce (1927). See also 72.26/4696, seduction under promise of marriage (over sixteen and under eighteen), Vegreville (Kaleland) (1922), in which the lawyer consulted by an irate father whose daughter's seducer had his conviction quashed on a technicality twice wrote the attorney general to complain that persistent rumours that there would be no retrial had upset the entire neighbourhood.

67 *The Criminal Law Amendment Act, 1975*, SC 1974–75–76, c. 93 received Royal Assent on 30 March 1976. A half-step had occurred earlier in the *Criminal Code* revisions of 1954, which enacted a new section 134: "Notwithstanding anything in this Act or any other Act of the Parliament of Canada, where an accused is charged with an offence under section 136, 137, subsection (1) or (2) of section 138 or subsection (1) of section 141, the judge shall, if the only evidence that implicates the accused is the evidence, given under oath, of the female person in respect of whom the offence is alleged to have been committed and that evidence is not corroborated in a material particular by evidence that implicates the accused, instruct the jury that it is not safe to find the accused guilty in the absence of such corroboration, but that they are entitled to find the accused guilty if they are satisfied beyond a reasonable doubt that her evidence is true." *Criminal Code*, SC 1953–54, c. 51. A full tracking of the corroboration legislation in the *Criminal Code*, from its beginnings in 1892 to the year 2000 can be found on my website, www.constancebackhouse.ca, under the heading "Law" and organized by offence and by year.

68 In 1982, section 246.4 was enacted to provide: "Where an accused is charged with an offence under section 150 (incest), 157 (gross indecency), 246.1 (sexual assault), 246.2 (sexual assault with a weapon, threats to a third party or causing bodily harm) or 246.3 (aggravated sexual assault), no corroboration is required for a conviction and the judge shall not instruct the jury that it is unsafe to find the accused guilty in the absence of corroboration." *An Act to amend the Criminal Code in relation to sexual offences and other offences against the person and to amend certain other Acts in relation thereto or in consequence thereof*, SC 1980–81–82–83, c. 125, s. 19.

69 Holly Johnson, "Limits of a Criminal Justice Responses: Trends in Police and Court Processing of Sexual Assault in *Sexual Assault in Canada: Law, Legal Practice and Women's Activism*, ed. Elizabeth Sheehy (Ottawa: University of Ottawa Press, 2012), 613–34.

6

The Execution of Tommasina Teolis: Capital Punishment, Gender, and Ethnicity in the First Half of the Twentieth Century

DONALD FYSON

Browsing through popular accounts of hangings or murder trials in Canada, or in Quebec, one is more than likely to come across the tale of Tommasina Teolis.[1] Teolis was a forty-six-year-old Italian woman living in Montreal who was hanged at Bordeaux Jail on 29 March 1935 for having her much older husband, Nicola Sarao, murdered by two young Italian men, Leone Gagliardi and Angelo Donafrio. The apparent motive was insurance fraud. While murder for financial gain was not unknown in cases of spousal homicide, with American and English parallels,[2] what has attracted the voyeuristic attention of popular historians – as it did contemporary journalists – in Teolis's case was that she was decapitated during the hanging. This most violent of ends fixed Teolis's unique place in Quebec and Canadian history, in a manner reminiscent of, but even more explicitly violent, than Edith Thompson's botched execution in England a decade earlier.[3] Indeed, in popular treatments of Teolis's case, the murder and the joint trial that led to the conviction and execution of the three accused are most often simply lead-ins to discussions of the beheading itself, which is then sometimes presented as a trigger for dramatic changes, such as the forced retirement of the official hangman, Arthur Ellis, or the regalvanization of the capital punishment abolitionist movement in Canada.[4]

The Teolis case has also been touched on in the relatively extensive scholarly literature on the history of spousal murder and the death penalty in Canada. However, unlike the Thompson case in England, which often occupies centre stage in such discussions there, Teolis is often barely mentioned, if at all, in the Canadian literature.[5] As well, in contrast to studies of other immigrant women sentenced to death in Canada in the first decades of the twentieth century, such as Angelina Napolitano or Florence Lassandro, existing examinations of the Teolis affair have focused largely on the clear gender biases in the case, paying little or no attention to its ethnic dimensions.[6] Yet Teolis was one of only two women sentenced to death in post-Conquest Quebec who were of neither French nor British (or Irish) descent, and the only one to actually be executed.[7]

Teolis's journey through the justice system and onto the scaffold can nevertheless tell us a great deal about the relationship of both women and immigrants to capital punishment and public discourse in Quebec and Canada in the first half of the twentieth century. This chapter provides a detailed examination of the affair, focusing on the sentence and execution of Teolis as a way of grasping the interplay of gender and ethnicity in the history of capital punishment in Quebec.[8] This includes an analysis of the construction of the execution, and of Teolis herself, in the contemporary press, in later debates, and in popular historiography, in the wake of her decapitation. I also consider her case in comparison with the nine other Quebec women (both francophone and anglophone) sentenced to death between the turn of the twentieth century and the end of executions in Quebec in 1960 (see the appendix at the end of this chapter) and examine differences between Quebec and the rest of Canada with respect to capital punishment of women. Additionally, I address issues such as the representation of criminalized women and ethnic minorities in the press; the gendered arguments used by capital punishment abolition activists in search of commutations; and the voice, persona, and agency of women convicted of murder and sentenced to die.

The study is based on the very ample surviving documentation concerning the case. Most notable are the capital case files of the three hanged and of other Italians and women similarly condemned to death in Canada during the period. These include both the trial transcript and subsequent documentation;[9] similar files assembled by Quebec's Department of the Attorney General;[10] the original coroner's and court proceedings;[11] newspaper accounts drawn from major Montreal newspapers, both English and French, along with a broad selection of other Quebec newspapers and a smaller sampling of the Canadian and international press;[12] and debates and committee reports of the House of Commons. Very largely absent from these mainly official records, are sources providing direct access to Teolis's voice, and thus to what Anette Ballinger had tellingly called the "alternative truth" that accused women might deploy in the face of the "official" truth established by the police and the courts.[13] Teolis was illiterate, meaning that there is nothing similar to the cache of letters Ballinger used in looking at Edith Thompson's case. After she was arrested, Teolis also refused to make a statement to police officers, an act of agency that also silenced her voice for future historians. Finally, as we will see, her counsel decided not to call her to the stand during her trial. Her voice is thus very muted in the official record, although I will refer to it where possible.

The first section of this chapter establishes the base for the discussion: the family background, the murder itself, and a brief factual overview of the judicial proceedings prior to execution. The next two sections consider how gender and ethnicity played out in Teolis's case, and how it compared to other Quebec and Canadian cases. The final section examines press coverage of the beheading itself, Teolis's place in subsequent debates concerning the death penalty in Canada, and her mythicization in subsequent popular historiography.

Background

The Sarao-Teolis Family

Both Sarao and Teolis came from the same village in Italy, Conca della Campania, near Naples, in the province of Caserta. They had married there in 1904, when she was sixteen and he twenty-nine. Like many other Italian immigrants, the family arrived in Montreal in several stages via chain migration linked to sojourn labouring. Teolis's father had first come over in 1905; Nicola Sarao arrived as a labourer in 1907, perhaps following his father-in-law. Tommasina Teolis joined her husband a year later, accompanied on the trip by her mother, Giovannina Genova, and two younger sisters.[14] By the 1930s, the Sarao-Teolis family lived in Montreal's Point St. Charles area, one of the areas of Montreal where Italian immigrants congregated. Sarao worked as a street sweeper for the City of Westmount, a stable and desirable job in Depression-era Montreal. Teolis was a housewife who does not appear to have been working outside the house at the time. In 1934, the family was composed of Sarao (fifty-nine years old), Teolis (forty-six), and their two Montreal-born sons, Carmino (twenty-four) and Antonio (eighteen).[15] Also living with them was Teolis's by-then widowed mother (sixty-nine).

Sarao seems to have been an unremarkable Italian working-class man. He was apparently well-liked by his neighbours and co-workers.[16] How Teolis was perceived by the community is largely unknown. As we will see, her lawyer made no attempt at trial to establish her credibility through character witnesses. The only hint comes in a report by the Montreal police at the time she was arrested: "Mrs Sarao was known amongst the Italian Colony, in Montreal, as having on different occasions, had illicit love affairs with different men, that being about all we could learn about her."[17] This is a point to which we will return.

The Murder and the Judicial Proceedings

During the morning of 29 June 1934, Sarao was found dead near Blue Bonnets racetrack, in northwest Montreal.[18] His head had been bashed in, and his body was arranged across a tramway track, to make it look like an accident. Police quickly identified the body, and detectives visited the Sarao-Teolis house, questioning Antonio and Teolis. Antonio interpreted for his mother, since neither of the detectives spoke Italian and she spoke neither English nor French. Teolis attempted to establish her own version of the story. She told the police that, the previous evening, Sarao had left her waiting in the street and had never come back. Later that night, she had sent her son Carmino to the local police station to report Sarao missing.

After further investigation, the detectives became suspicious and decided to detain Teolis and Carmino. They set out canvassing neighbours, with an Italian police officer acting as interpreter. Community solidarity against officialdom seems not to have come into play, and information from other members of the Italian community led police to arrest Leone Gagliardi, a twenty-nine-year-old labourer who had often been seen at the Sarao-Teolis house.[19] After questioning, Gagliardi signed a confession implicating both Teolis and her mother, Genova, in the murder, along with an acquaintance, another young Italian man, twenty-year-old Angelo Donafrio. A shoeshiner who had, until recently, been a successful student at Montreal's Catholic High School, Donafrio then signed a confession of his own. Later, both Gagliardi and Donafrio would withdraw their confessions, Gagliardi asserting that his had been beaten out of him by detectives, while Donafrio claimed that he had been tricked into signing his.

The police version of events was described in the two confessions, which were central to later judicial proceedings – the trial, the guilty verdict, and the decision not to commute. In this view, Teolis was the mastermind of the murder of her husband, egged on by Genova. Gagliardi was Teolis's somewhat unwilling instrument, who acted only after Teolis browbeat and even threatened to kill him, while Donafrio had simply been recruited by Gagliardi to help out. According to the police, Teolis had been trying to get rid of her husband for at least three years, because she was sexually interested in a younger man. She had convinced Sarao to take out several life insurance policies on himself, worth several thousand dollars, with her as the beneficiary. She first tried to get an unnamed woman to poison Sarao, and when that failed, she turned to Gagliardi. She had previously asked him to write to a self-proclaimed American-Italian magician to hex a parish priest she thought responsible for her family losing government relief. Initially, she asked Gagliardi to procure poison for her to use on her husband. When this failed (since Gagliardi had simply bought a laxative), she insisted he push Sarao under a streetcar. In the end, Teolis and Gagliardi devised a plan involving luring Sarao to a deserted area near the Blue Bonnets racetrack, on promise of a labouring job offered by a wealthy patron. Teolis promised Gagliardi a share of the insurance money, which he in turn promised to share with Donafrio. After several false starts, Gagliardi and Donafrio finally followed through and killed Sarao with a piece of wood (the leg from a baby's bed) and a large rock.

Based largely on the two young men's confessions, and following the finding of a coroner's jury, the two men along with Teolis and Genova were formally accused of murder and conspiracy in early July. A preliminary inquest later in July confirmed the charges, based essentially on the same confessions, on physical evidence and on testimony from police officers, from other officials, and from Teolis's sons, Carmino and Antonio. The four were then remanded to the fall sitting of Montreal's Court of King's Bench and imprisoned in the interim.[20] Teolis and Genova were held in Montreal's women's prison, which the Quebec state subcontracted to a Catholic religious order, the Soeurs du Bon-Pasteur.[21]

The trial in September 1934 involved prominent figures from the Montreal legal community. Teolis and Genova had been represented since the earlier proceedings by Mario Lattoni, the son of a pillar of Montreal's Italian fascist elite and himself a rising community leader, though less overtly fascist than his father. Gagliardi's lawyer was Willie

Proulx, an up-and-coming francophone criminal defence lawyer and future judge. Donafrio's counsel was a very young Teddy Meighen, son of the former Conservative prime minister of Canada; it was his first major case. The prosecution was conducted by Gérald Fauteux, future chief justice of the Supreme Court of Canada. The presiding judge was Louis-Joseph Loranger, scion of a longstanding conservative-nationalist Quebec judicial family, and author, some three decades earlier, of a doctoral thesis on the necessary legal submission of women to their husbands.[22]

Genova's trial had been separated from the others, in part because Fauteux intended to use her as a Crown witness. She would eventually plead guilty to a reduced charge and be sentenced to twenty years in the penitentiary. She died in the Kingston penitentiary for women in 1946.[23] The other three defendants also moved for separate trials, but this was denied by Loranger, who also stipulated that the jurors should be French-speaking. Jury selection was protracted, because the lawyers on both sides challenged many potential jurors, and many admitted having already read about or heard of the case and formed an opinion.[24] The trial lasted five days, and featured damning testimony by, among others, Teolis's sons and mother, as well as appearances on the witness stand by both Gagliardi and Donafrio. Donafrio affirmed that, at the last minute, he had tried to stop Gagliardi from killing Sarao. Loranger's charge to the jury was highly unfavourable to the defendants, and, in the end, the jury took only thirty-five minutes to find all three guilty, with no recommendation for mercy. Loranger sentenced all three to death, with the hangings set for 18 January 1935. Further legal manoeuvring ensued, with, for example, an appeal launched by Proulx for Donafrio, which resulted in a stay of execution for all three until the end of March.

As in all capital cases, the sentences were referred to the federal cabinet in Ottawa for a final decision as to clemency. Despite commutation campaigns on behalf of both Teolis and Donafrio, the highly negative reports of Loranger, leaned on heavily in the capital case memoranda prepared by Michael F. Gallagher, the Department of Justice's long-serving civil servant responsible for commutation requests, led Conservative justice minister Hugh Guthrie to recommend against clemency.[25] With clemency denied, the three were hanged at Montreal in the early hours of 28 March 1935, with Teolis being decapitated in the process.

These are the bare bones of the case. Let us now turn to how they played out in terms of gender and ethnicity.

Gender

Historians who have considered how Teolis was represented in the press and in the courts have generally emphasized how, just as in other analogous cases, her persona was constructed so as to provide none of the qualities of femininity meant to evoke positive responses in male jurors, judges, and officials, such as submissiveness, frailty, sexual restraint, marital faithfulness, or motherliness.[26] While this is largely true, the gendered dimensions of Teolis's case were more complex, both because of its particularities and some variations specific to Quebec. Before turning to a detailed examination, it is helpful to situate Teolis within the broader picture of women and capital punishment in Quebec in the first half of the twentieth century.

Women and Capital Punishment in Quebec

Of about 250 people sentenced to death in Quebec from the adoption of the *Criminal Code* in 1892 to the end of executions in 1960, only ten were women (see appendix).[27] This low female death-row presence (about 4 per cent) was nonetheless exactly in line with the rest of Canada. All the Quebec women condemned to die had, like their male counterparts, been accused of murder; none had been accused of infanticide (unlike elsewhere in Canada). Of the ten Quebec women, five were executed, giving them a commutation rate (50 per cent) that was about the same as for Quebec men (46 per cent) and men elsewhere in Canada (50 per cent). This supposedly "equal" treatment of women set Quebec far apart from the rest of Canada, since of the thirty-six women condemned to die in other provinces, only four were executed (11 per cent – and, even if infanticides are removed, 14 per cent). The higher commutation rate of women in Canada as a whole has often been linked to a more "chivalrous" approach to women sentenced to death in the first half of the twentieth century, based on, among other considerations, patriarchal perceptions of women's place in society.[28] In the case of Quebec, however, despite an arguably even more patriarchal view of women – in Catholic francophone society, at least – this link seems not to have held. Quebec seems instead to have been more in line with what Anette Ballinger has observed in England regarding women who killed other adults.[29]

If we zoom in on the Quebec women, other overall traits emerge. Six of the ten condemned women, and four of the five executed, including

Teolis, had been accused of the murder of their husbands. Seven of the ten, and four of the five executed, were from Quebec's majority French-Canadian population, unlike Teolis. All of the executed had been hanged along with other co-accused; in contrast, less than a quarter of the men hanged in Quebec were executed with accomplices. Finally, all but one of the ten women (Teolis) was tried outside of the province's main city, Montreal, whereas half of men condemned to die were tried in the metropolis. Overall, this meant that the most "typical" Quebec woman condemned to death and then executed was a francophone from outside of Montreal who was accused of participating with a man in the killing of her husband (four of ten condemned to die, three of five executed). Teolis fit this portrait only partially.

Teolis was an outlier in another key respect: unlike many cases of spousal murder by wives discussed in the scholarly literature, both in Canada and elsewhere, there is no indication that she was abused by her husband. As Lizzie Seal points out, while the battered wife killing in self-defence is certainly a central trope in both contemporary and current discussions of women who kill their partners, focusing only on these cases risks obscuring those women who did not fit what was fundamentally a gendered and normative use of violence.[30] Yet, unlike Seal's emphasis on "unusual" murders, the lack of domestic abuse as a trigger in Teolis's case was actually no different from the five other Quebec women sentenced to death for killing their husbands between 1892 and 1960.[31] Though the issue remains unresolved, there was contemporary speculation that Teolis had been having an ongoing affair with Gagliardi, more than fifteen years her junior. Again, in this respect, Teolis's case was similar to most of the other Quebec women convicted of murdering their husbands, most of whom were accused of acting in concert with their lovers.

Teolis, Gender, and the Press

All of these aspects of Teolis's case made for fertile fodder in the press. The "Insurance Murder" or "Sarao Murder," as it was most often known, was widely reported in Montreal newspapers, both English- and French-language, right from the discovery of Sarao's corpse through to the execution and beyond. It was also picked up in more concise form by papers elsewhere in the province. Up until the execution, however, it received only limited coverage elsewhere in Canada and in the United States – understandably, as it was not that unusual a murder.

Press representations of Teolis shifted across the period, and conformed to many, although not all, of the stereotypes seen in similar cases of women accused of killing, helping to kill, or conspiring to kill their husbands. Once her suspected involvement in the murder was known, and up until sentencing, Teolis was almost universally presented in a negative light, in both the English- and French-language press. This was epitomized in *Le Petit Journal*, when it called her "la femme Sarao, cette abominable marâtre" – *marâtre* (stepmother) was an inaccurate term in Teolis's case but one that echoed the characterization of Marie-Anne Houde, the accused in an infamous Quebec child-murder case fifteen years earlier.[32] Even her appearance was criticized, especially her weight. "Fat, dirty, calm and collected" was how the *Montreal Daily Star* described her appearance at the coroner's inquest, while *La Patrie* described her as a "grasse personne aux cheveux noirs."[33] The contrast with representations of the other defendants is instructive. Genova was portrayed as an ignorant old woman, an almost comical character when she spoke, but often seemingly completely uninterested. Donafrio's youth was front and centre: "young Donofrio," a "cherub-faced high school boy," led into crime by an older accomplice. Gagliardi was a dark-faced, balding figure with jutting lips, a stereotypical Italian immigrant, implicitly racialized, and emasculated in his submissiveness towards Teolis.[34] Each had a role in the journalistic morality play. In this cast, Teolis was the classic "bad woman." More specifically, she fit perfectly into one side of what has been termed the "muse or mastermind dichotomy," as a cunning and dominant woman able to make men do her bidding.[35]

The negative press image of Teolis evolved over time, progressively slotting her into a more submissive role. In the early stages of the proceedings, the press gave significant place to Teolis's own voice and actions, which were anything but submissive. Before her arrest, she laid out the initial tale of her husband's disappearance, which she repeated both to the police and to the press.[36] When this cover fell apart and she was arrested, she switched to defying police questioning and, despite being confronted with the statements of her alleged co-conspirators, refused to confess or even to make a statement.[37] When she learned that her mother had apparently confirmed aspects of the story to police, the press depicted her as enraged and claimed that the two women fought violently in the police cells until separated.[38] None of this gave the impression of a woman passively accepting her fate, but the perspective shifted during the trial coverage. When newspapers reported what she said, it was no longer in her own voice, but instead filtered through the testimony of others: the police, Gagliardi, her mother, her sons, the nuns at the prison. Teolis herself was portrayed as essentially reactive, with an emphasis on her uncontrolled emotions, such as crying when her sons testified against her, laughing dismissively at her mother's testimony, or verbally abusing an Italian policeman.[39]

The representation of Teolis's persona in the press evolved in other ways as well, notably by deviating from the transgressive norm of the predatory, sexualized female killer and heartless mother. Initial internal police reports had suggested sexual libertinage, and Gagliardi's confession, widely reproduced, tarred her as sexually unfaithful. Early newspaper coverage of the crime itself followed this line, referring, for example, to the affair as a "love plot."[40] However, the sexualized representation of Teolis was very quickly dropped by most newspapers, in favour of a simpler story of basic monetary greed, in some respects defeminizing Teolis's motivations.[41] Similarly, early press coverage portrayed Teolis as having plotted to kill not only Sarao but also one of her own sons, again for the insurance money; hence perhaps the reference to *la marâtre*. The story of the vengeful mother was soon dropped after no one mentioned such a plot in their testimony. Some newspapers then pivoted to another angle of the theme of the bad mother, reporting that Carmino and Antonio had publicly disowned their mother and grandmother. The *Montreal Daily Star* couched this in particularly evocative terms, which no doubt owed far more to the reporter than to Carmino: "'We had always loved her mother and in our younger days we used to look up to her as being our model of simplicity and love,' said Carmino with anger in his voice. 'After what we heard at the inquest, we cannot but feel that all our love has been in vain. If what was said by the detectives is true, we want to disown her and our grandmother.'"[42]

Teolis's persona in the press changed even more profoundly after she was sentenced to death and while she was confined in the women's prison awaiting commutation or execution. Most newspapers ignored her, focusing instead on the appeal of Donafrio and on another concurrent high-profile murder case involving another Italian defendant, Joseph Alisero (who would also eventually hang, a few weeks after Teolis, Gagliardi, and Donafrio). The reports on Teolis that did come out, most notably in *La Presse*, were clearly largely fabricated by the Catholic nuns and priests who controlled access to her in prison. As had been the case in Quebec since the mid-nineteenth century, the church expected those sentenced to death to willingly play a part in a religious pageant where they turned to the faith, embraced God, and stoically accepted their fate, in return for promised salvation.[43] Teolis was portrayed exactly in these terms: resigned to her fate; asking pardon of God and men alike; spending her time knitting, praying, and counting her rosary; taking communion every day; and, above all, submissive, an attitude highly approved of by the nuns. As the *Montreal Daily Star* reported just a few days before the execution, "At the women's jail it is reported that Mrs. Sarao spends most of her time in prayer, telling her beads," and, on the eve of the execution, *La Presse* described her as being "calme, résignée, récitant des prières." Furthermore, several of the accounts put much emphasis on her "profound ignorance," a portrayal entirely at odds with the image of evil mastermind previously advanced, while also claiming that her stay in prison had led her from ignorance to intelligence. The whole redemption tale was crowned by a tearful tableau of reconciliation with both her sons just before her execution, allowing her to reclaim even her motherhood.[44]

This radical change is scarcely credible, especially since other newspaper reports of her last days provided a different view. According to the *Montreal Daily Herald*, a few days before the execution, "Mrs Sarao sits in sullen stupor. She says little and as the days pass becomes more and more morose and despondent." On the day before the execution, *La Patrie* described her as being "dans un état de surexcitation terrible hier" and unable to accept that her sentence had not been commuted. As for motherhood and family, the *Gazette* reported that she was angry because the execution day fell on her wedding anniversary.[45] All of these reports were diametrically opposed to the redemptive image presented in other newspapers.

That Teolis preserved her agency to the end also seems clear from press reports that she attempted to save Donafrio. A week before the execution, she took the unusual step of asking to see Willie Proulx, Donafrio's lawyer. Accompanied by an interpreter, he visited her at the women's prison. There, according to his affidavit, she declared that she knew she would die and that Donafrio's testimony exculpating himself was accurate, adding that Gagliardi had boasted that he had carried out the murder himself. She explained that she had refrained from testifying to this during the joint trial in order to avoid spoiling the faint hope she had of being exculpated (suggesting that she understood more of the proceedings than the press reported), but that now she didn't want to die without telling her story to the authorities. Whether this statement was of Teolis's own volition, or was the result of pressure from her nun-jailers or her confessors, is hard to know. In the end, her effort made no difference. Justice Minister Guthrie was not swayed, and Donafrio was hanged.[46]

Reporters projected onto Teolis the image they wanted, erasing her actual personality in the process. This was far more pronounced in her case than for her two male co-condemned, whose image underwent no such transformation and whose religious experiences, if any, were largely ignored.[47] The persona of Teolis-as-penitent, in particular, conformed to what the church, and conservative francophone elites more generally, thought was salutary for Quebec society. *La Presse* again provides the clearest, and most disturbing, example of this: reminding readers that not only was the execution date Teolis's wedding anniversary, but also marked exactly nine months since she had first been incarcerated, it then continued, "Cette période a été pour elle une sorte de gestation spirituelle et sa mort sera comme une renaissance, lui procurant la délivrance et le bonheur éternels qu'elle ne cesse de demander à Dieu avec le pardon de ses fautes."[48] The recourse to Christian imagery of conversion, devotion, contrition, and redemption was no different for three of the four other Quebec women executed since the turn of the century (Cordélia Viau, Marie Beaulne and Marie-Louise Cloutier).[49] Only Marguerite Ruest, who, like Teolis, had been portrayed as arrogant and abusive during her trial, did not fit the mould. She was portrayed as remaining defiant to the end, although, even in her case, *La Presse* quoted a witness as saying that she had "fait une mort extrêmement édifiante."[50]

Teolis, Gender, and the Law

Legal officials projected similarly classic gender stereotypes onto Teolis, just as they did in the case of other women accused of murder in Quebec and in Canada more generally.[51] Unsurprisingly, given his past views on the necessary submission of women to their husbands, Loranger was particularly prone to gender bias. He referred condescendingly to Genova as "la vieille" and, in recommending that the jury heed the evidence she provided, evoked the simplicity of her testimony and likened her to a child in the witness box who recounts what they saw without considering that they might incriminate their family.[52] His attitude towards Teolis was particularly damning and was linked directly to the patriarchal views he had expressed in his doctoral dissertation. Like the newspaper account, the judge paid little attention to the rumours of sexual infidelity, concentrating instead on the profit motive.[53] In his charge to the jury, echoing the Crown's case, he essentially accused Teolis of coldly conspiring to kill her husband for a small sum of money. In the face of this, "tout homme de coeur se sent indigné, et se refuse à toute sympathie."[54] His sentencing speech revealed even further his misogynistic attitude towards a married woman who had strayed from the submissive norm, while, at the same time, it rejected any special treatment for women based on their sex. Calling Teolis "the very soul of the conspiracy," he excoriated her:

> Unfaithful and criminal wife, there is no pity for you and it is time that the public should know that women, the same as men, are responsible before the law. It is rare that a woman stands in your place and I trust that you may be a painful example to others in the expiation of your frightful crime. I trust that in the short time left you may take the necessary means to repair, in the eyes of your dead husband, of outraged society and the children you have dishonored, the evil you have done.[55]

The appeal to the principle of equal treatment under the law was far from chivalrous, but was not uncommon in the case of female murderers, often deemed unworthy of compassion.[56] Loranger thus both condemned Teolis for not conforming to expected gender roles and also refused her any leeway because of her gender. None of this boded well for her chances at avoiding execution.

The impact of Loranger's views cannot be underestimated. As noted above, like Teolis, the four other women executed in Quebec from the 1890s to the 1950s were hanged along with at least one male accomplice.[57] In several of those cases, the woman was portrayed as worse than her male accomplice, whom she had led on. Gagliardi's "confession" had put much emphasis on this dynamic, describing how Teolis had harried him, physically abused him, and even threatened to kill him unless he did her bidding, to the extent that he was afraid of her. However, Teolis stood out from the other cases in that she was the only woman executed in Quebec for a murder that no one suggested she had participated in directly and for which the evidence against her was very largely circumstantial. Often, these circumstances would have triggered a commutation, but Loranger, and Department of Justice official Michael F. Gallagher, following his lead, stacked the deck strongly against Teolis. At trial, the only direct evidence of Teolis's implication in planning the murder came from the confessions of Gagliardi and

Donafrio. The Crown had apparently pinned much hope on the testimony of Genova as well, obtained in exchange for a plea deal, but at trial she managed to avoid any statement directly implicating her daughter, revealing a comprehension of the proceedings completely at odds with her portrayal as ignorant and child-like.[58] In theory, the confessions of Gagliardi and Donafrio were supposed to serve as evidence only against themselves, not against their accomplices, so they should not have applied to Teolis. Loranger did point this out to the jury in his charge, but he also expended much effort summing up the circumstantial evidence that grounded the Crown's case against her – and, as we saw above, made his own views about Teolis quite clear. The jury obliged Loranger by finding Teolis guilty. From that point onwards, the commutation process kicked in. At that stage, Loranger was no longer bound by normal rules of evidence. Hence, in his report on the case, he had no problem stating that it had been established at trial that Teolis had long been plotting the death of her husband and urging Gagliardi to do the deed, even though this was based solely on Gagliardi's confession. Gallagher echoed this supposed finding in his memoranda for the minister of justice and went further still: he insisted that not only had Teolis been proven guilty but that she was the "most guilty" of the three. This concept of guilt did not exist in law (unlike the notion of variable responsibility) but could evidently be applied in the arbitrary exercise of the royal prerogative. Gallagher also reported having discussed the case further with Loranger, "who is of opinion that the guilt of the woman, Teolis, is established beyond any possible doubt."[59] With such weight of opinion against her, Teolis's fate was largely sealed.

Abolitionists and Commutation

As was the case in many (but not all) capital conviction cases in Canada, campaigns were launched for commutation of the death sentences, though only for Teolis and Donafrio. The campaign for Donafrio was based very largely on appeals focusing on his youth.[60] As for Teolis, she was the subject of two separate campaigns. One was based largely on appeals to gender, advanced by abolitionists who intervened in many capital cases and drawing on the methods and ideas of the international abolitionist campaign. The other was community-based and more connected to her ethnicity.

The most notable abolitionist appeal in favour of Teolis was taken on by the Montreal-based Canadian Prisoners' Welfare Association and its long-serving secretary, John Kidman. Since its foundation in the late 1910s, the association had regularly written letters and mounted campaigns to have death sentences commuted, including in cases involving condemned women. For example, in the 1920 case of Marie-Anne Houde, the "wicked stepmother," the association mounted a large, and eventually successful, Canada-wide campaign to have her death sentence commuted. In the 1929 case of Marie Beaulne, while the association did not organize a petition campaign, Kidman did write a letter arguing that, on principle, women should not be hanged. When Teolis was convicted, the association thus had a long track-record of intervening in such cases.[61]

In his appeals for commutation on Teolis's behalf, Kidman did refer to her Italian background, but his main argument concerned gender. Kidman's letters deployed the standard abolitionist themes of the period, combining "chivalrous" and patriarchal conceptions of women's subordinate place in society. He also appealed explicitly to the international abolitionist context. Kidman's first attempt to have Teolis's death sentence commuted, a telegram sent to Justice Minister Guthrie a few days before the initial January 1935 execution date, summed up his arguments: "Recent French newspaper story shows reared Italy amid ignorant poor circumstances hard life bore several children. Anglican churching service suggests process childbirth makes woman expose life every time. Press dispatches France Christmas report president reprieved woman who murdered father. Every execution woman England raises storm protests Home Secretary." In March, Kidman sent letters requesting commutation for both Donafrio and Teolis. The Donafrio letter referred to his youth, stating, among other arguments, that the British custom had been to commute death penalties for all youths under twenty-one. In Teolis's case, gender was again front and centre: Kidman recognized her guilt but went on to argue that women's childbearing role entitled them to special consideration, and that although eschewing what he called "feminine executions" might seem discriminatory, "discrimination between the sexes is seen everywhere."[62] All of these were themes that had been raised in earlier campaigns, such as those in favour of Houde and Beaulne.

This gendered take was echoed by others calling for commutation. A long letter from the secretary of the Montreal-based Eleva Science Church opened by describing Teolis as "a beguiled, and helpless stranger, in our midst," thereby grounding the appeal in her ethnicity, but then adopted a resolutely maternalist stance, focusing on her qualities as a mother and woman, and placing the blame for the murder squarely on Gagliardi, who it presented as a sexual predator who had ensnared her. The letter also made direct reference to the recent execution in New York of another Italian woman, Anna Antonio, who had hired two men to kill her husband, ostensibly for insurance money (although, unlike Teolis, Antonio was a battered wife).[63] The maternalist stance and the emphasis on childbearing was echoed in another series of commutation appeals made (erroneously) to Quebec premier (and attorney general) Louis-Alexandre Taschereau by one Mme Antoine Parent of Montreal, who additionally suggested that Teolis was not entirely mentally responsible because of her motherhood.[64] The appeal to differential treatment based on Teolis's gender even made it into the House of Commons: a day before the execution, Conservative MP Thomas L. Church, an abolitionist, asked the justice minister whether there was any hope of commutation for Teolis, "as she is a woman." Guthrie's answer, echoing Loranger and Gallagher, was no.[65]

Overall, the abolitionist campaign to have Teolis's death sentence commuted was relatively muted, especially in comparison to previous campaigns in Canada – not only that for Houde, but also that in favour of Angelina Napolitano in 1911, which reached international proportions.[66] Far more significant for the Teolis case was the petition campaign emanating from Montreal's Italian community.

Ethnicity

Italians and Capital Punishment in Quebec

In Quebec in the first third of the twentieth century, there was a dramatic upsurge in the number of members of ethnic minorities (i.e., non-francophone and non-anglophone) sentenced to death and executed for murder. Between 1900 and 1935, recent European immigrants and their children made up about a third of those condemned to death and those executed in Quebec. This was a huge overrepresentation: ethnic minorities accounted for only about 5 per cent of Quebec's population in 1931. Among those hanged from these "other" ethnic groups, two-thirds were of Italian descent. Italians thus accounted for a little over 20 per cent of executions in Quebec at a time when they constituted just 1 per cent of its population. Their overrepresentation was even more pronounced in Montreal itself: of thirty-five condemned who were executed in Quebec's largest metropolis, sixteen – almost half – were

Italians, though they made up less than 3 per cent of the population of the judicial district. Compared to other groups, Italians condemned to death were less likely to have their sentences commuted: almost two-thirds were executed, compared to a little over half of francophones and about 40 per cent of anglophones and other Europeans.[67] Such figures reflected the prejudices of the time, and the "foreign" origin of condemned Italians was regularly commented on in alarmist tones by the press, especially conservative French Catholic newspapers.[68]

Ethnicity, Language, the Press, and the Law

One might expect the case of Teolis, Gagliardi, and Donafrio to have evoked similar ethnically charged commentary. As noted above, Teolis was the only non-francophone woman ever to be executed in post-Conquest Quebec, and one of only two minority women sentenced to death in the same period (other than those of British or Irish descent), making her case even more noteworthy.[69] And yet, quite surprisingly, and in striking contrast to the coverage of Quebec and Canadian murder cases earlier in the century involving accused of Italian descent, the reporting on the Sarao murder and subsequent trials made relatively little reference to ethnicity. That said, there were certainly some egregious instances of prejudice and stereotyping. In describing Genova at the preliminary inquest, for example, the *Montreal Daily Star* said that she stood silent while the charges were read "but sputtered voluble Italian when the interpreter told her what it was all about." The same newspaper later highlighted what it saw as the absurdity of the translation process during the trial.[70] Drawing on a passing reference in Gagliardi's confession, some newspapers emphasized Teolis's recourse to sorcery, often associated with Italian immigrants.[71] More subtly, throughout the period, the French-language press in particular had great difficulty with the spelling of Italian names. Most references to ethnicity in the Teolis case were only in passing: at most, articles might refer to the victim or the accused as being Italian or speaking in Italian. Many major articles on the case said nothing whatever about the ethnicity of the defendants.

There was also little overt reference to ethnicity in the discourse of judicial officials concerning the case. Loranger, for example, made no direct mention of the ethnicity of the defendants in his charge to the jury or in his report on the case. At most, in commenting on Donafrio's defence, the judge trotted out a quotation in Italian (badly spelled by himself or perhaps by the stenographer): "Si non e vero e bene trovato," which he translated as "Si ce n'est pas vrai, c'est bien trouvé." However, this variant of Giordano Bruno's adage had been used in French literature since the nineteenth century, untranslated, to refer to an ingenious but unproven theory.[72] Loranger's declaration was pounced on by Donafrio's counsel on appeal, but not as a sign of prejudice; instead, the judge was accused of thereby presenting a too-direct rebuttal of defence theories.[73] Gallagher was more explicit on ethnicity, stating right from the beginning of his memorandum that "all three are Italians," but he did not return to the issue.[74]

This downplaying of the ethnicity of Teolis and her fellow accused may reflect the relative normalization of Montreal's Italian community by the mid-1930s, and especially the increasing importance of conservative and even fascist tendencies among its elite, which were encouraged by Italian consular officials. All of this rendered the community more palatable to the province's conservative francophone elites in particular and to Conservative politicians more generally, including at the federal level.[75] Whatever the causes, the result was that, unlike in many other capital cases in Canada in the early twentieth century, Teolis's ethnicity does not seem to have weighed heavily on judicial and executive decisions made regarding her.[76]

This did not mean that Teolis's ethnicity was unimportant in her dealings with the law, particularly when it came to language. The Quebec justice system functioned mainly in French, though sometimes in English, with the language of juries and proceedings largely following the language of the accused. Yet neither Teolis nor her mother spoke or largely understood either French or English, Italian being their only language. This set them apart from their co-accused, Gagliardi and Donafrio, and even from their own family: Teolis's sons spoke both English and French as well as Italian.[77] The two women were thus linguistically marginalized, particularly compared to the men accused alongside them.[78] The heavily gendered dimension of language competence left Teolis entirely at the mercy of her interpreters: initially her sons, until they disowned her; then an Italian police officer; then her lawyer or the court interpreter. Teolis – and Genova – was thus in linguistic isolation during court proceedings, a fact that few observers seemed to fully grasp. In a later declaration (filtered through the nuns), Teolis stated to a journalist that she understood nothing of the procedures during the trial. While this was attributed to her ignorance, it seems far more likely that she was referring to language.[79] On occasion, newspapers reported that the two women appeared uninterested in the proceedings; again, this was far more likely a language issue rather than an actual lack of interest.[80] Indeed, with the exception of the testimony of her sons, the only moments when newspapers reported Teolis's emotional reactions came when proceedings were in Italian, which allowed her to understand, and laugh or get angry.

The language barrier worked to further dampen Teolis's already obscured voice. The only direct quotation from her during the trial that was reported in the press came after the guilty verdict, in response to the judge's traditional invitation to speak before sentence was pronounced: "Mrs. Sarao said, in Italian, 'I am not guilty.'"[81] The brevity, and the language, are symbolic of the mutually incomprehensible relationship between Teolis and the justice system. Language, then, was a further dimension of the combined influence of ethnicity and gender in Teolis's case: since all other women sentenced to death in Quebec since the nineteenth century were either French- or English-speaking, they would have benefited from proceedings in their own language.

Teolis and the Italian Community

Montreal's Italian community was heavily invested in the trials of Teolis, Gagliardi, and Donafrio. Newspaper accounts describe large crowds at the preliminary proceedings and at the trial itself, while Donafrio's appeal was funded by subscriptions from the community.[82] This interest did not mean that the Italian community was necessarily favourable to the three accused. After all, the victim, Sarao, was also Italian and was well-liked by his neighbours and co-workers, and his two sons had very publicly taken a position against their mother. As the *Montreal Daily Star* reported, "considerable feeling has been aroused throughout the city by the crime, and reports are rife of high feeling in the Italian community, where the idea of a compatriot having been slain for his insurance money has caused a furore."[83] This "furore" may help explain why, unlike in many previous cases of Italians sentenced to death in Quebec, Italian consular officials apparently did not intervene in favour of commutation, and the priests of Montreal's Italian parishes supported only the campaign in favour of Donafrio.[84] It is difficult to say more about the resonance of the affair within the city's Italian community. I have been unable to consult significant runs of Montreal Italian newspapers of the time, and the affair does not seem to have entered collective memory, as filtered through collected and published oral histories or local community histories.[85] Reporting in Italian-language newspapers in other cities appears to have been summary, with brief articles in Toronto's *Il Bollettino Italo-Canadese* and New York's *Il Progresso Italo-Americano*, suggesting that it did not become a cause célèbre within the Italian immigrant community.[86]

Furthermore, though Teolis was represented by Mario Lattoni, a leading figure in the community, he served her quite poorly at trial. Teddy Meighen and Willie Proulx, counsel for Gagliardi and Donafrio, respectively, were quite active, but Lattoni did very little during the prosecution's case against Teolis and called no witnesses at all in her defence (a fact that Loranger did not fail to point out to the jury). Nor did he put her on the stand in her own defence, as Meighen and Proulx did for their clients in rebuttal of their confessions. The reasons for this are unclear. At the time, Lattoni was heavily involved in the high-profile murder case of Joseph Alisero. Interestingly, the Italian consul in Montreal, Giuseppe Brigidi, intervened actively in Alisero's case, in contrast to his inaction on that of Teolis and her co-accused.[87] Lattoni was the lawyer for Genova as well as her daughter, which placed him in direct conflict of interest, since Genova testified against Teolis. Whatever the case, by failing to put her on the stand, Lattoni deprived Teolis of her one opportunity to present her own "alternative truth": her story was told only through the testimony of other, often hostile, witnesses. Lattoni's final address to the jury apparently made little impact: in contrast to those of Proulx and Meighen, it was ignored by most newspapers.[88] Finally, after the verdict, Lattoni declined to appeal, purportedly because Teolis had no money for this. Yet, money does not seem to have been a bar in the case of Alisero, which Lattoni carried through (unsuccessfully) to appeal. In the end, support from Montreal's Italian elite, represented by Lattoni, was of very little help to Teolis.

One might suggest that this was because Teolis did not conform to conservative Italian precepts about her role as a wife, and perhaps because her rumoured sexual infidelities made supporting her unpopular in the Italian community. The matter was, however, more complex. Once Teolis had been sentenced to death, her anticipated end did lead to an important collective action on the part of the Italian community: a petition campaign for commutation, initiated by Lattoni, and then taken up by other members of the community.[89] The petition garnered the support of over 600 people in Montreal and in Toronto – a mid-sized campaign compared to other capital case pardon petitions from the same period (Donafrio's petition, for example, listed just under 900 names), but still a significant effort. Like the case itself, the text of the petition intertwined both ethnicity and gender. It affirmed (inaccurately) that Teolis was the first Italian woman in Canada to be sentenced to death and that the petitioners accepted the verdict and sentence but that, "being all Italians, [they] nevertheless feel it repugnant to their racial instinct and feelings that a woman should receive this extreme penalty." In fact, about 20 per cent of the petitioners appear not to have been of Italian origin. Still, this was overwhelmingly a community affair, in contrast to the petition for Donafrio, where Italians made up less than half of the petitioners.

Petition campaigns grounded in minority-group identities were a common feature of commutation efforts at the time, including in several of the cases involving people of Italian descent in Quebec.[90] For example, the 1905 case of Antonio Giacconi, the first Italian sentenced to death in Quebec, led to a large (and ultimately successful) commutation campaign on the part of Montreal's then-nascent Italian community.[91] Overall, of twenty-seven capital convictions of Italians in Quebec between 1900 and 1935, about half led to clemency petitions of one sort or another, of which about half again were organized by the Italian community, often including community leaders. As other scholars have noted, such petitions provided an issue around which group identities could be forged. However, in these other petitions, explicit appeals to ethnicity were rare, likely because ethnicity might be perceived as a negative trait in the condemned. Hence, the Donafrio petition made no reference to his ethnicity, focusing instead on his youth. The explicit reference to Teolis's Italian background thus set her commutation petition apart.

Her petition was also something of an outlier in regard to the place of women. Women had figured very prominently in previous commutation petitions for Quebec women sentenced to death: in the case of Cordélia Viau, for example, about 40 per cent of the petitioners were women, and about 30 per cent in the case of Marie Beaulne.[92] In Teolis's case, women made up only 20 per cent of the signatories overall, and, in Montreal, only about 13 per cent, which is almost the same proportion as in Donafrio's petition. The specific ways in which women, and Italian women in particular, participated in the petition is suggestive of a degree of female activism in the community, which others have noted. In Montreal, most of the signatures of Italian women petitioners were on the same page, suggesting a concerted effort in the context of a club, perhaps. Two-thirds of the Toronto signatories were women, all of them Italian, which hints at activism within the Italian women's community there as well.[93]

One further feature of the petition in favour of Teolis seems to have distinguished it from previous similar petitions emanating from the Italian community: with little direct support from community leaders other than Lattoni himself, most of the petitioners, in Montreal at least, both men and women, appear to have belonged to the popular classes, with only a sprinkling of business owners and professionals.[94] Again, the contrast with Donafrio's petition is striking: the latter garnered far more support from "respectable" members of Montreal society, not only secular leaders of the Italian community, but also two Italian parish priests, quite a few other members of the clergy of various faiths, and the religious teaching staff of a number of Catholic schools. Donafrio, the schoolboy, was a worthy subject of respectable effort in a way Teolis may not have been.

Ultimately, none of these efforts made any difference. Just like for Viau and Beaulne, the petition in support of Teolis was unsuccessful, and she was hanged and decapitated. Donafrio was hanged as well. None of the appeals to gender, youth, or ethnic solidarity saved them from their brutal fate.

Decapitation and Its Aftermath

Press Coverage of the Execution

Press coverage of the execution itself, with an emphasis on the beheading, has been central to most of the later historical accounts of the Teolis case.[95] The incident was covered both nationally and internationally, relayed by several wire services whose stories were reproduced in probably hundreds of newspapers in North America and in Europe. However, the coverage was not uniformly sensationalistic. In Quebec, journalists had been excluded from executions since 1928, explicitly following what had been the practice in England since the beginning of the century.[96] As a result, unlike in the United States, descriptions in newspapers, often based on the statements by sheriffs or other officials, had become both very brief and very formulaic: the prisoner attended mass, was calm, shook the hands of the governor and guards, died rapidly.[97] Of course, both officials and the press initially expected that this would be the case for Teolis's execution as well, and, indeed, very early press reports, including the initial Canadian Press / Associated Press report republished in several out-of-province and international papers, made no mention of her decapitation.[98] This was soon corrected as the news filtered out. Some newspapers – especially in Canada outside of Quebec and in the United States – ran the story under sensationalistic headlines: "Head Torn from Body by Noose" (*Border Cities Star*, Windsor, Ontario, 29 June); "East Woman Decapitated on Gallows" (*Calgary Herald*, 29 June); "Canada Noose Decapitates Woman Killer" (*San Francisco Examiner*, 30 June); "Noose Rips off Woman's Head" (*Austin Statesman*, 29 June); "Executioner of 500 Bungles Job on Woman" (*New York Daily News*, 30 June). In Quebec, headlines put less emphasis on the decapitation, but there were still a few sensationalistic examples: *La Patrie*'s 29 June front-page headline, in huge letters, was "Le câble coupe le cou de la pendue," while the *Sherbrooke Daily Record* (29 June) led the story with "Horror Scenes at Hanging of Woman Slayer." Not all Canadian and American newspapers mentioned the beheading, and, even when they did, many did not include the decapitation in their headlines, simply mentioning it in the article itself.

Beyond the headlines, the content of these news stories was highly problematic. Denied access to the hanging, but thirsty for sensational coverage, several journalists simply made up much of their stories. This was especially true of the United Press (UP) wire story, written by Montreal correspondent James N. Crandall, who invented a whole scene: gallows set up in the snow-covered prison yard; a ceremonial procession across the yard with a lead guard carrying the crown or the mace as a symbol of authority; the rope lengthened accidentally to eighteen feet; the execution watched by prisoners in their cells, including Alisero, who was to be executed a month later and who fainted at the sight; and so on. As the Montreal sheriff pointed out in a private report to the Quebec government, most of this was pure fantasy.[99]

As in American journalistic descriptions of botched executions earlier in the century, most of the newspaper coverage contented itself with characterizing the decapitation as horrible, but essentially a technical failure.[100] When newspapers did seek to apportion blame, it was largely the hangman, Arthur Ellis, who took the brunt for not having properly done his job.[101] As elsewhere, this served to deflect criticism from government officials and, more generally, to avoid any questioning of recourse to hanging as a punishment. Ellis was incensed by the sensationalist press coverage of the affair, sending a letter of protest to Crandall. He also asked Quebec's Department of the Attorney General to intervene on his behalf in what he considered criminal libel on the part of the press (a request that was denied). At the same time, Ellis publicly claimed that the decapitation had been caused by his not being allowed to weigh Teolis in the women's prison before the execution and being given an incorrect weight for her by prison authorities (an assertion also denied by the Montreal sheriff).[102] Contrary to later assertions, Ellis was not terminated immediately, and he hanged a few more people in Quebec, but his contract with the Quebec government was ended later that summer, ostensibly because he had accepted out-of-province contracts. While he later performed at least a few more executions elsewhere in Canada, he died in poverty in Montreal in 1938.[103]

Tellingly, although the decapitation of Teolis did prompt several editorials and letters to the editor, it did not spawn a raft of debate and commentary, even in the Montreal press. A handful of editorials and letters called on governments to rethink the way executions were performed, or called for the abolition of capital punishment, whether for women or across the board.[104] Some commentators likened the hanging of Teolis to an execution in Hitler's Germany: in his widely syndicated column, "Today," American journalist Arthur Brisbane called it a "combination Hitler-Lithuanian execution."[105] But, in general, her violent death was just another passing story, and newspapers quickly moved on to other matters. Within three or four days of the execution, Teolis had dropped almost entirely out of the public eye.

Aftershocks

Teolis's decapitation did have other effects outside of the press. Lattoni, who had witnessed the execution personally, sent a letter to the federal government demanding an inquiry into the hanging, which he described as barbarous. He also made his views known in the press. Hugh Guthrie, the federal justice minister, punted Lattoni's letter on to Quebec, but, grasping the potential political fallout, he also took the unusual step of making an unprompted statement on the case in the Commons. He used this occasion to deny all responsibility, saying that hangings themselves were a provincial responsibility. The Liberal Quebec government, via Premier Taschereau, responded by shutting down any hope of a public inquiry. Privately, the premier ordered a confidential inquiry by the Montreal sheriff, who, as noted above, rejected the sensational press reports and stood by the procedures followed. Taschereau sent the report to Lattoni, on condition that he keep it private, which he did, and the matter rested there.[106]

The Canadian Prisoner's Welfare Association, via John Kidman, also protested, insisting that Teolis's awful end showed that the execution of women must be stopped.[107] In the House of Commons in April 1935, the abolitionist MP Thomas L. Church suggested bringing in a bill prohibiting passing sentence of death on women, but this idea went nowhere.[108] Later that year, the same arguments would be made in the hanging of Elizabeth Ann Tilford in Ontario, also for murdering her husband for insurance money, but again to no ultimate effect.[109]

In the House of Commons, Teolis's decapitation also led to opposition calls for a change in method, from hanging to electrocution or the gas chamber. Bills to this effect were introduced in 1936 and 1937, and the issue was eventually the subject of a parliamentary committee in 1937, which nevertheless voted to retain hanging.[110] The matter rested there until the 1950s, when abolition once again came to the fore. By that time, Teolis had sunk into anonymity.

Teolis's beheading did become, if only briefly, a cause célèbre for capital punishment reformers and abolitionists. But in their discourse, she became a nameless and quite literally headless (and thus faceless) figure, an essentialized victim of a botched hanging. Her treatment was quite different from that of other celebrated Canadian capital punishment cases such as those of Wilbur Coffin or Steven Truscott, or, indeed, analogous cases of women executed in England and the United States, in all of which the names of the executed resonated strongly. Teolis's beheading, as a beheading, was itself regularly brought up in later debates on capital punishment. It was explicitly evoked in Commons debates in 1935, 1936, and 1937. Her fate was discussed several times in the 1937 Commons special committee on capital punishment, including in its final report. The beheading was mentioned in Commons debates in 1950; her case was raised in testimony in 1955 before the Joint Committee on Capital and Corporal Punishment; and, finally, her decapitation was referenced in the 1976 debates on the law that finally abolished capital punishment in Canada. But in every one of these cases, she became an anonymous figure: "the woman decapitated in Montreal some years back," or some variant thereof.[111] The only exceptions were occasional references in Montreal newspapers, such as in coverage of the death of Arthur Ellis in 1938.[112]

The Teolis Myth

Teolis's name and face were eventually restored by popular historians, beginning as early as 1960.[113] But these tended to graft her identity onto accounts that twisted the truth, largely for the sake of sensation. In this sort of work, for example, there are frequent implicit and explicit links to Italian stereotypes, far more than in press coverage and judicial discussion at the time. The case has been given a more sensational name, the "Blue Bonnets murder," a designation it essentially never bore at the time, but that links it with the gambling and vice that often form part of stereotypical depictions of Italian immigrants in North America. Pushing the organized crime trope further, one writer characterized Teolis's co-accused as hitmen whom she hired to kill her husband.[114] Some accounts heavily underscore the link to Italian superstition and sorcery, based on a relatively unimportant portion of Gagliardi's confession that was subsequently misreported in the press.[115] One recent account reprehensibly goes even further: it calls Teolis's marriage to Sarao a product of southern Italy's medieval traditions; refers to the case as a "Sicilian conspiracy"; turns Genova into a black-clad, spaghetti-making Calabrian; and wilfully misspells Teolis's lawyer's name as "Latroni" in order to call him a thief.[116] Even when they avoid such excesses, the accounts uncritically follow the most dramatic contemporary newspaper accounts of the execution. Among other inaccuracies, they overplay the impact of the case on capital punishment administration in Canada, asserting, for example, that it led to the exclusion of journalists from execution scenes, or that it ended Ellis's career as an executioner.[117] All of this misrepresentation and sensationalism is most unhelpful when we truly want to unpack and understand the impact and interplay of factors such as gender and ethnicity in capital punishment in early to mid-twentieth-century Quebec.

Conclusion

The distortion of Tommasina Teolis's story and her persona in popular history accounts mirrored her fate throughout her deadly encounter with the criminal law. Tried, convicted, and executed for murder, Teolis was progressively robbed of her voice, her agency, her personality, and, ultimately, her life by the judicial system, the press, abolitionist politicians, and later historians. Reading between the lines and behind the discourse, it is hard not to see her initially as a strong and determined woman far more than as a victim. As others have pointed out, it is important to not automatically slot women who kill into the category of victim, and to recognize their agency as well.[118] Thus, while one can argue that Teolis was a victim by virtue of being found guilty of killing her husband, sentenced to death, and having her petition for commutation refused, one must also acknowledge her agency in the killing itself. It seems very likely that she was deeply involved in the plan to kill Sarao, even though it is far less certain that she was the mastermind.

Paradoxically, and in different ways, the press and the justice system, while emphasizing Teolis's badness and, thus, her agency, also transformed her into a victim. Along with the reformist-abolitionist movement, they progressively reduced and removed her voice and her agency, relegating her to exactly the passive feminine role that she so clearly refused to fill. The intertwining impact of her gender and ethnicity in this process was evident, but far from straightforward.

Initially cast as a scheming female mastermind, unfaithful wife, and unfit mother, she was fashioned into the classic trope of the "mastermind" husband-killer, a theme emphasized by the judge in her case. At the same time, unlike in many other cases, this gendered representation of Teolis was boiled down to her role as a faithless wife, with relatively little attention paid to accusations of betrayal of motherhood and even less to her supposed sexual impropriety. As well, once she was sentenced, her behaviour was widely reported in conventional Christian terms, which put the emphasis on a woman's necessary submission to God and to her fate. While this was meant to elicit sympathy for Teolis, it also erased her own strong personality. The same held for the abolitionist campaign in favour of her commutation, which emphasized the weakness and vulnerability of her sex.

Superficially, references to Teolis's ethnicity were muted in her treatment by the press and the judicial system, which is surprising, given the contemporary prominence of capital cases involving Italians in Quebec in general and in Montreal in particular. But her Italian background was key nonetheless. First, her linguistic isolation, and the incomprehension it engendered, prevented her from fully engaging in the proceedings. Second, while her case was taken on by a leading lawyer from Montreal's Italian community, he gave no voice to her story at all – possibly for reasons linked to his own community engagement – leaving it to be fashioned by hostile prosecution witnesses. Finally, the relative lack of interest in her case from Montreal's Italian community leaders in general, such as parish priests and consular officials, suggests the limits to ethnic solidarity. At the same time, the lack of success of both her own petition, relying more on popular-class support, and that of her co-accused Donafrio, more classically grounded in "respectable" support, underscores that, in the end, community backing could not outweigh judicial and executive opinion.

Was Teolis executed because she was a woman, and Italian? Given the fate of her co-accused, and the fundamentally arbitrary nature of the commutation process, that would be going too far. But her gender, and her ethnicity, certainly did not help her cause.

APPENDIX

Women Sentenced to Death in Quebec, 1892–1960

Name	Victim	Co-accused	Place of trial	Sentenced	Outcome
Cordélia Viau†	Isidore Poirier, her husband	Sam Parslow,† her lover	Ste-Scholas-tique	December 1898	Hanged 10 March 1899
Marie-Anne Houde	Aurore Gagnon, her ten-year-old stepdaughter	Télésphore Gagnon, her husband (convicted of manslaughter)	Quebec	April 1920	Sentence commuted to life in prison
Emily Sprague	Abraham Gallop, her husband	none	Roberval	June 1926	New trial; acquitted
Doris McDonald	Adélard Bouchard	George C. McDonald,† her husband	Valleyfield	December 1927	Sentence commuted to life in prison
Marie Beaulne†	Zéphyr Viau, her husband	Philibert Lefebvre,† her lover	Hull	June 1929	Hanged 23 August 1929
Béatrice Bernard	Ludger Chapdelaine, her husband	Joseph-Gédéon Bernard, her brother and lover (convicted of manslaughter)	Sherbrooke	January 1934	New trial; acquitted
Tommasina Teolis†	Nicola Sarao, her husband	Leone Gagliardi,† Angelo Donafrio,† Giovannina Genova, her mother (Genova convicted of manslaughter)	Montreal	October 1934	Hanged 29 March 1935

Name	Victim	Co-accused	Place of trial	Sentenced	Outcome
Marie-Louise Cloutier†	Vilmont Brochu, her husband	Achille Grondin,† her lover	St-Joseph-de-Beauce	October 1938	Hanged 23 February 1940
Élise Plante	Irène Dubé, her seventeen-year-old daughter	none	Rimouski	March 1950	New trial; plea bargain; seven years in prison
Marguerite Ruest†	Rita Morel and 22 others (plane bomb)	J.-Albert Guay† and Généreux Ruest,† her brother	Quebec	March 1951	Hanged 9 January 1953

† = executed

NOTES

1 Examples include Frank W. Anderson, *A Dance with Death: Canadian Women on the Gallows, 1754–1954* (Saskatoon: Fifth House Publishers, 1996), 49–54 (along with most of Anderson's other death penalty books); Daniel Proulx, *Juges, policiers et truands: Les dessous de la justice au Québec* (Montreal: Éditions du Méridien, 1999), 23–36; Dale Brawn, *Last Moments: Sentenced to Death in Canada* (Edmonton: Quagmire Press, 2011), 120–1, 267–8; Lorna Poplak, *Drop Dead: A Horrible History of Hanging in Canada* (Toronto: Dundurn, 2017), ch. 9; Jean-Claude Castex, *Crimes et châtiments de Canadiennes*, vol. 2 (Vancouver: P.-O. Éditions, 2017), 41–69; and Éric Veillette, *Répertoire des procès des condamnés à mort du Québec*, vol. 2 (Lanoraie, QC: Éditions de l'Apothéose, 2019), 40–2.

2 For historical cases of American women accused of killing their husbands or other family members for insurance money, see Marlin Shipman, *The Penalty Is Death: U.S. Newspaper Coverage of Women's Executions* (Columbia: University of Missouri Press, 2002), 33–71, 77–80, 135–40; Mark Gado, *Death Row Women: Murder, Justice and the New York Press* (Westport, CT: Praeger, 2007), 41–66; and Gordon M. Bakken and Brenda Farrington, *Women Who Kill Men: California Courts, Gender, and the Law* (Lincoln: University of Nebraska Press, 2009), 62–71. For England, see Judith Knelman, *Twisting in the Wind: The Murderess and the English Press* (Toronto: University of Toronto Press, 1998), 47–52, 57–8, 73–82, 124–5, 127, 218, and Lizzie Seal, *Women, Murder and Femininity: Gender Representations of Women Who Kill* (Basingstoke, UK: Palgrave Macmillan, 2010), 77, 79, 160.

3 In Thompson's case, as well as being placed on the scaffold on a chair as she couldn't walk, rumours also circulated that she was partially eviscerated. On Thompson, see Anette Ballinger, *Dead Woman Walking: Executed Women in England and Wales, 1900–1955* (Aldershot, UK: Ashgate, 2000), 221–57, and Lizzie Seal, *Capital Punishment in Twentieth-Century Britain: Audience, Justice, Memory* (London: Routledge, 2014), 62–5, 123–33.

4 As in Frank W. Anderson, *A Concise History of Capital Punishment in Canada* (Calgary: Frontier Publishers, 1973), 69–73, or Poplak, *Drop Dead.*

5 Discussions of the Teolis case can be found in Sylvie Frigon, *L'homicide conjugal au féminin: d'hier à aujourd'hui* (Montreal: Éditions du Remue-ménage, 2003), 15, 32, 38–9, 156; Joanne Bernier, "'Maricide' au Canada français (1867–1940): Le syndrome de la femme fatale" (master's thesis, University of Ottawa, 1995), 35, 54–5, 108–9, 135; Carolyn Strange, "The Undercurrents of Penal Culture: Punishment of the Body in Mid-Twentieth-Century Canada," *Law and History Review* 19, no. 2 (2001): 352–53; Kimberley White, *Negotiating Responsibility: Law, Murder, and States of Mind* (Vancouver: UBC Press, 2008), 98–9, 105–6; and Ken Leyton-Brown, *The Practice of Execution in Canada* (Vancouver: UBC Press, 2010), 131–2. Apart from Leyton-Brown and White, none devote more than a few sentences to the case. F. Murray Greenwood and Beverley Boissery, *Uncertain Justice: Canadian Women and Capital Punishment, 1754–1953* (Toronto: Osgoode Society for Canadian Legal History and Dundurn, 2000) make no mention of Teolis at all.

6 On Napolitano, see Karen Dubinsky and Franca Iacovetta, "Murder, Womanly Virtue, and Motherhood: The Case of Angelina Napolitano, 1911–1922," *Canadian Historical Review* 72, no. 4 (1991): 505–31; Edward Stoddard, "Conflicting Images: The Murderess and the English Canadian Mind, 1870–1915" (master's thesis, Dalhousie University, 1991), 193–200. On Lassandro, see Lesley Erickson, *Westward Bound: Sex, Violence, the Law, and the Making of a Settler Society* (Vancouver: UBC Press for the Osgoode Society for Canadian Legal History, 2011), 213, 223–7, and Valeria Sestieri Lee, "Italians and the Law in Alberta," *Italian Canadiana* 15 (2001): 47–60.

7 This is based on my ongoing research into capital punishment and executions in Quebec 1760–1960; the other was an Indigenous or Black woman (the sources are unclear) in 1778.

8 On the importance of adopting a multifactorial or intersectional approach to the examination of women who kill, see Seal, *Women, Murder and Femininity*, 14–15.

9 Library and Archives Canada (LAC), RG13. The Teolis-Gagliardi-Donafrio capital case file (TCC) is in volumes 1592–3, and, like most such files, includes both the (lengthy) trial transcript and departmental correspondence and reports concerning commutation and execution. Unreferenced general information on the case in this chapter is also drawn from this source.

10 Bibliothèque et Archives nationales du Québec, Centre d'archives de Québec (BAnQ-Q), E17. On Teolis et al., 1934 #892, 1934 #1860B, 1934 #6319, and 1935 #2721.

11 Bibliothèque et Archives nationales du Québec, Centre d'archives de Montréal (BAnQ-M), TP12,S2,SS26,SSS1 1992-07-005/80 1934 #1073 (coroner's inquest), TP9,S2,SS1,SSS2 2003-06-001/682 #10303 (preliminary hearing and King's Bench trial), and TP9,S2,SS7,SSS1 2002-09-001/1186 1934 #63 (Donafrio's appeal).

12 The main newspapers I consulted were *L'Action Catholique* (Quebec City), *Le Canada* (Montreal), *Le Devoir* (Montreal), *Le Droit* (Hull), *Montreal Daily Herald*, *Montreal Daily Star*, *Montreal Gazette*, *Le Nouvelliste* (Trois-Rivières), *La Patrie* (Montreal), *Le Petit Journal* (Montreal), *La Presse* (Montreal), *Le Quotidien* (Chicoutimi), *Sherbrooke Daily Record*, *Le Soleil* (Quebec City), *Toronto Daily Star*, *Toronto Globe/Globe and Mail*, and *La Tribune* (Sherbrooke). I also conducted full-text searches for the case in the digitized newspapers of Bibliothèque et Archives nationales du Québec, ProQuest Historical Newspapers, Newspapers.com, and British Newspaper Archive. This gave a corpus of about 400 articles directly relating to Teolis.

13 Ballinger, *Dead Woman Walking*, 55 and passim.

14 Genealogical and immigration information is from Ancestry.ca, notably: Boston Passenger Lists, 20 July 1907, SS *Canopic* from Naples (Sarao); New York Passenger Arrival Lists (Ellis Island), 14 May 1908, SS *Brasile*, from Naples (Teolis and Genova); Canada Passenger Lists, 1908–05, SS Brasile (Teolis and Genova); 1911 Census of Canada. On Italian migration to and settlement patterns in Montreal, see Charles M. Bayley, "The Social Structure of Italian and Ukrainian Immigrant Communities in Montreal, 1935–37" (master's thesis, McGill University, 1939); Bruno Ramirez, *Les premiers Italiens de Montréal: L'origine de la petite Italie du Québec* (Montreal: Boréal Express, 1984); Sylvie Taschereau, *Pays et patries: Mariages et lieux d'origine des Italiens de Montréal, 1906–1930* (Montreal: Université de Montréal, 1987); and Claude Painchaud and Richard Poulin, *Les Italiens au Québec* (Hull: Critiques, 1988), 41–80.

15 Obituaries of Carmino and Antonio were published in the *Gazette*, 19 October 1979, 47, and 15 April 1995, 77, respectively.

16 *Montreal Daily Herald*, 30 June 1934, 1; *Gazette*, 30 June 1934, 4.
17 Report by Sergeant-Detective Felix Prysky, 11 October 1934, TCC.
18 Unless otherwise indicated, the narrative here is based on official documentation described in notes 9–11 above.
19 *Gazette*, 3 July 1934, 4.
20 BAnQ-M TP12,S2,SS26,SSS1 1992-07-005/80 1934 #1073 and TP9,S2,SS1,SSS2 2003-06-001/682 #10303; *Gazette*, 26 July 1934, 6.
21 Tamara Myers, "Criminal Women and Bad Girls: Regulation and Punishment in Montreal, 1890–1930" (PhD diss., McGill University, 1996), 207–37.
22 On Lattoni: Filippo Salvatore, *Le fascisme et les Italiens à Montréal* (Toronto: Guernica, 1995), 161–71; Salvatore, "Liborio Lattoni: Da missionario protestante a poeta nella Montreal del primo Novocento," *Italian Canadiana* 13 (1997): 80–106; Claudio Antonelli et al., *I Protagonisti Italiani di Montreal* (Montreal: Basilio Giordano, 1998), 66–9. On Proulx: *La Presse*, 21 and 22 May 1958. On Meighen: T.R. Meighen Family Foundation, http://www.meighen.ca/about1.html. On Fauteux: Sébastien Grammond, "Joseph Honoré Gérald Fauteux," in *The Chief Justices of the Supreme Court of Canada*, 2nd ed., ed. Jean Chevrier et al. (Ottawa: New Federation House, 2019). On Loranger: Pierre-Georges Roy, *Les juges de la province de Québec* (Quebec City: R. Paradis, 1933), 321; Loranger's thesis was *De l'incapacité légale de la femme mariée* (Montreal: Eusèbe Senécal, 1899).
23 *Montreal Daily Star*, 18 October 1934, 3, 13; Ancestry.ca: Ontario, Certificate of Registration of Death, 14 February 1944.
24 *Le Canada*, 2 October 1934, 14, 10; *Gazette*, 2 October 1934, 5 and 2 November 1934, 5.
25 TCC, Gallagher memoranda, 14 January 1935 and 18 March 1935. On the commutation process in Canada and the role of civil servants such as Gallagher, see Carolyn Strange, "Comment: Capital Case Procedure Manual," *Criminal Law Quarterly* 41, no. 2 (1998): 184–97; White, *Negotiating Responsibility*, 17–27; and Strange, *The Death Penalty and Sex Murder in Canadian History* (Toronto: Osgoode Society for Canadian Legal History / University of Toronto Press, 2020), passim.
26 See above, note 5.
27 The quantitative analysis in this section is based on data derived from Lorraine Gadoury and Antonio Lechasseur, *Persons Sentenced to Death in Canada, 1867–1976: An Inventory of Case Files in the Fonds of the Department of Justice* (Ottawa: National Archives of Canada, 1994), supplemented by my ongoing research into capital punishment in Quebec.
28 See, for example, Carolyn Strange, "The Lottery of Death: Capital Punishment, 1867–1976," *Manitoba Law Journal* 23, no. 3 (1996): 607–10;

Greenwood and Boissery, *Uncertain Justice*, 123–5, 138–40; and Erickson, *Westward Bound*, 201–28.

29 Ballinger, *Dead Woman Walking*, 1–2. In this respect, Quebec differed from another heavily Catholic society, Ireland, where, after independence, women sentenced to death were far more likely to be pardoned than men, based largely on chivalrous arguments: Lynsey Black, "'On the Other Hand the Accused Is a Woman …': Women and the Death Penalty in Post-Independence Ireland," *Law and History Review* 36, no. 1 (2018): 139–72.

30 Seal, *Women, Murder and Femininity*, 2–3.

31 Frigon, *L'homicide conjugal au féminin*, 148–9. On Canada, see, among others, Joan Sangster, "The Meanings of Mercy: Wife Assault and Spousal Murder in Post–Second World War Canada," *Canadian Historical Review* 97, no. 4 (2016): 513–45. Kimberley White does make the point that an absence of domestic abuse correlated strongly with the execution of women convicted of killing their husbands, but this does not explain the difference as to such convictions themselves (White, *Negotiating Responsibility*, 104–5).

32 *Le Petit Journal*, 7 October 1934, 19; Peter Gossage, "La marâtre: Marie-Anne Houde and the Myth of the Wicked Stepmother in Quebec," *Canadian Historical Review* 76, no. 4 (1995): 563–97.

33 *Montreal Daily Star*, 3 July 1934, 3; *La Patrie*, 2 October 1934, 2.

34 Examples include *Le Canada*, 26 July 1934, 16, and 5 October 1934, 8 and *Montreal Daily Star*, 5 October 1934, 11 (Genova); *Montreal Daily Herald*, 5 October 1934, 3, and 15 October 1934, 3, and *Le Devoir*, 25 March 1935, 8 (Donafrio); *Montreal Daily Star*, 3 July 1934, 3, and *La Patrie*, 2 October 1934, 1 and 2 (Gagliardi); *Montreal Daily Herald*, 2 October 1934, 3 (Donafrio and Gagliardi).

35 Seal, *Women, Murder and Femininity*, 38–49.

36 *Montreal Daily Star*, 30 June 1934, 3; *Gazette*, 30 June 1934, 4.

37 *La Presse*, 2 July 1934, 4; *Le Canada*, 3 July 1934, 1, 9.

38 *La Presse*, 4 July 1934, 17; *Gazette*, 5 July 1934, 3.

39 *Montreal Daily Herald*, 2 October 1934, 3; *Le Canada* (Montreal), 3 October 1934, 6; *Montreal Daily Star*, 4 October 1934, 3, 15, and 5 October 1934, 11; *Gazette*, 5 October 1934, 4; *La Presse*, 5 October 1934, 27.

40 *Montreal Daily Herald*, 3 July 1934, 1, 3.

41 Only the *Montreal Daily Herald* continued to bring up this theme right until the end: for example, 8 December 1934, 3, and 29 March 1935, 2. On the negative portrayal of women and men killing for profit, see Carolyn Strange and Tina Loo, *True Crime, True North: The Golden Age of Canadian Pulp Magazines* (Vancouver: Raincoast Books, 2004), 61–79.

42 *Montreal Daily Star*, 3 July 1934, 3.

43 Donald Fyson, "The Spectacle of State Violence: Executions in Quebec, 1759–1872," in *Violence, Order, and Unrest: A History of British North America, 1749–1876*, ed. Elizabeth Mancke et al. (Toronto: University of Toronto Press, 2019), 383–407.

44 *Montreal Daily Star*, 8 December 1934, 3, and 26 March 1935, 3, 8; *La Presse*, 12 January 1935, 19 and 22; 6 March 1935, 3; 26 March 1935, 3 and 25; 28 March 1935, 3; and 29 March 1935, 19; *Le Canada*, 29 March 1935, 16.

45 *Montreal Daily Herald*, 23 March 1935, 3; *La Patrie*, 28 March 1935, 3 and 6; *Gazette*, 28 March 1935, 5.

46 *Montreal Daily Herald*, 25 March 1935, 3; *Le Canada*, 25 March 1935, 5; affidavit of Proulx and petition to the Earl of Bessborough, 22 March 1935, TCC.

47 On Donafrio and Gagliardi, see, for example *Le Canada*, 26 March 1935, 7.

48 *La Presse*, 26 March 1935, 3.

49 This observation is based on my reading of the press coverage in their cases, as part of my ongoing research into capital punishment in Quebec, along with the press extracts reproduced in Veillette, *Répertoire des procès des condamnés à mort*. See also the studies of women condemned to death in Quebec and Canada listed above in note 5.

50 *La Presse*, 9 January 1953, 37.

51 See notably Frigon, *L'homicide conjugal au féminin*; Bernier, "'Maricide' au Canada français"; Greenwood and Boissery, *Uncertain Justice*; and White, *Negotiating Responsibility*.

52 TCC, trial transcript, 459, 462.

53 In this respect, I disagree with Kimberley White, who suggests that Teolis's supposed sexual infidelity was important to her judicial treatment: *Negotiating Responsibility*, 98–9.

54 TCC, trial transcript, 477–8. Loranger couched this as presenting the Crown's case, but the comments as to indignation were entirely his.

55 *Montreal Daily Star*, 6 October 1934, 3. Other newspapers presented slight variants on the speech.

56 See, for example, the case of Florence Lassandro, where first-wave feminist Emily Murphy called for her execution on the grounds of equality: Erickson, *Westward Bound*, 225–7; Lee, "Italians and the Law in Alberta," 50.

57 As in Canada more generally: see White, *Negotiating Responsibility*, 104–5.

58 TCC, trial transcript, 368–83; *Le Canada*, 5 October 1934, 16.

59 TCC, Gallagher memoranda, 14 January and 18 March 1935. On the arbitrariness of the commutation process in Canada, see Strange, "The Lottery of Death."

60 On appeals to youth in commutation cases, see Strange, "The Lottery of Death," 610–12.

61 On the petition campaign for Houde: LAC, RG 13, vol. 1507, and White, *Negotiating Responsibility*, 61–3. On Beaulne: LAC, RG 13, vol. 1555; Bernier, "'Maricide' au Canada français," 40, 51, 57–127 passim; Frigon, *L'homicide conjugal au féminin*, 15, 29–30, 32, 38–9; and White, *Negotiating Responsibility*, 106–9. On Kidman and the various prisoners' welfare associations he was involved in, see John Kidman, *The Canadian Prison: The Story of a Tragedy* (Toronto: Ryerson Press, 1947), which nonetheless downplays his role in commutation appeals (15–18); and Ellen Prince, "A History of the John Howard Society of Quebec, 1892–1955" (master's thesis, McGill University, 1956), 21–92.

62 Kidman to Guthrie, 14 January 1935 and 22 and 23 March 1935, TCC.

63 Brahn-Bey to Guthrie, 22 March 1935, TCC. The church had already sent another such letter in January, accompanied by abolitionist pamphlet material: Dumas to Guthrie, 16 January 1935, TCC. On Antonio, see Gado, *Death Row Women*, 41–66.

64 Parent to Taschereau, 16 and 21 January 1935, BAnQ-Q E17 1935 #2721.

65 Dominion of Canada, *Official Report of Debates, House of Commons* (*Commons Debates*), 27 March 1935, 2145.

66 Dubinsky and Iacovetta, "Murder, Womanly Virtue, and Motherhood"; Stoddard, "Conflicting Images," 193–200.

67 This analysis is based on my ongoing research into capital punishment in Quebec. Quebec contrasts with Ontario at roughly the same period, where Carolyn Strange, noting the uptick in immigrant death sentences, nonetheless adds that they were far more likely to be pardoned: "Discretionary Justice: Political Culture and the Death Penalty in New South Wales and Ontario, 1890–1920," in *Qualities of Mercy: Justice, Punishment and Discretion*, ed. Carolyn Strange (Vancouver: UBC Press, 1996), 142–3. It should be noted that, unlike elsewhere in Canada, there were no Indigenous defendants sentenced to death in Quebec in this period, and only one Black defendant (who was hanged).

68 Right from the very first execution of an Italian in Quebec, Francesco Grevola in 1911, Quebec newspapers remarked negatively on their ethnic background: for example, "L'angoissante fin de Grevola … servira d'exemple, espèrent les autorités, à [un] certain clan de la colonie italienne de Montréal trop enclin à jouer du couteau" (*La Presse*, 26 May 1911, 1).

69 Strange also remarks in passing on this absence of immigrant women among the condemned: "Discretionary Justice," 143. On the negative portrayal of Italian women accused of murder elsewhere in Canada, see

Dubinsky and Iacovetta, "Murder, Womanly Virtue, and Motherhood," and Lee, "Italians and the Law."

70 *Montreal Daily Star*, 4 July 1934, 3, and 3 October 1934, 11.

71 *Montreal Daily Star*, 3 July 1934, 3 (reporting inaccurately that this targeted Sarao) and 1 October 1934, 3; *Canada*, 26 July 1934, 16. On recourse to magicians by Italian women who committed murder in Philadelphia, see Joseph W. Laythe, *Engendered Death: Pennsylvania Women Who Kill* (Bethlehem, PA: Lehigh University Press, 2011), 134–44.

72 TCC, trial transcript, 465; Pierre Larousse, *Grand dictionnaire universel du XIXe siècle*, vol. 14 (Paris, 1875), 543. The spelling errors (use of "si" rather than "se," lack of accents on the "è", "bene" rather than "ben") were repeated throughout the official documents in the case and in the press; see, for example, the sources in note 73. In his memorandum for the minister of justice, Gallagher adopted a loose translation of the French version – "If it is not true, it is conveniently imagined" – adding the specifically damning notion of convenience (Gallagher memorandum, 14 January 1935, 21). My thanks to an anonymous reviewer for drawing my attention to these translation issues.

73 TCC, Donafrio factum on appeal, 44; "Avis d'appel," BAnQ-M TP9,S2,SS7,SSS1 2002-09-001/1186 1934 #63, document #10, 4; *Le Canada*, 16 January 1935, 6.

74 TCC, Gallagher memorandum, 14 January 1935.

75 On the rise of fascism among part of Montreal's Italian elite, and the link to conservative Quebec nationalist figures such as Camilien Houde, see Luigi Bruti-Liberati, *Il Canada, l'Italia e il fascismo, 1919–1945* (Rome: Bonacci Editore, 1984); Roberto Perin, "Making Good Fascists and Good Canadians: Consular Propaganda and the Italian Community of Montreal in the 1930s," in *Minorities and Mother Country Imagery*, ed. Gerald Gold (St. John's: Institute of Social and Economic Research, Memorial University of Newfoundland, 1984), 136–58; Martin Robin, *Shades of Right: Nativist and Fascist Politics in Canada, 1920–1940* (Toronto: University of Toronto Press, 1992), 207–32; and Salvatore, *Le fascisme*, 7–50. Lattoni was a case in point: while he later claimed to have been anti-fascist, he certainly frequented fascist circles in the interwar period, headed up an Italian Conservative political club, and called on Italians to back the overtly pro-fascist Houde. On conservative francophone Quebec sympathy for fascism, see Hugues Théorêt, *La presse canadienne-française et l'extrême-droite européenne, 1918–1945* (Quebec: Septentrion, 2018).

76 On the impact of ethnicity in the commutation process, see, in general, Kenneth L. Avio, "The Quality of Mercy: Exercise of the Royal Prerogative

in Canada," *Canadian Public Policy* 13, no. 3 (1987): 366–79, and Kimberley White, *Negotiating Responsibility*, 80–100 (although I disagree with her assessment of the role of ethnicity in Teolis's case).

77 *Le Canada*, 30 June 1934, 16.

78 The trial transcript and newspaper accounts suggest that Gagliardi seems to have spoken Italian and French and understood English, while Donafrio spoke Italian and English at the very least and also understood and read French.

79 *La Presse*, 12 January 1935, 22; *Montreal Daily Star*, 18 January 1935, 3. Although a court-appointed interpreter was present throughout the trial, his job likely did not include interpreting full testimony in English or French to Teolis. The few mentions of him concern interpreting Italian witnesses for the benefit of the judge, jury, and counsel, or interpreting formal statements, such as the verdict, to Teolis.

80 *Montreal Daily Star*, 25 July 1934, 3; *Gazette*, 26 July 1934, 6.

81 *Gazette*, 6 October 1934, 7.

82 *Gazette*, 12 July 1934, 22; *Montreal Daily Herald*, 6 October 1934, 3; *La Presse*, 6 October 1934, 19; *Le Canada*, 16 October 1934, 14.

83 *Montreal Daily Star*, 4 July 1934, 11.

84 Capital case files in LAC, RG13 indicate that Montreal Italian clergy and consular officials participated in commutation efforts in the cases of Antonio Giacconi (1904), Antonio Ferduto (1912), Frank Raffaello (1912), Luigi Romano (1915), Nicola Tomasso (1919), Antonio Sprecarce (1919), Joseph Mauro (1926), Pepitone Gaetano (1928), and Joseph Alisero (1935). One parish priest even petitioned the Prince of Wales, then touring Canada (Vangelisti to the Prince of Wales, 2 September 1919, LAC, RG13, vol. 1502).

85 The only significant surviving run of Montreal's main Italian-language newspaper for the period, the pro-fascist *L'Italia*, is held by LAC, but access has been permanently closed due to condition issues, and there are no plans to digitize the collection. Salvatore, *Le fascisme*, provides an oral history of this exact period, including an interview with Lattoni himself; nowhere is there any hint of the affair. The same is true of other histories of Italians in Montreal that I have consulted.

86 *Il Bollettino Italo-Canadese*, 12 October 1934, 5 (unfortunately, I found no surviving issues covering the execution); *Il Progresso Italo-Americano*, 30 March 1935, 1.

87 Brigidi to Petrucci, 6 April 1935, LAC, RG13, vol. 1592.

88 The most detailed account of Lattoni's address is two short paragraphs in *La Presse*, 6 October 1934, 19. He essentially insisted (correctly) that, without

the evidence of the two confessions, there was little linking Teolis to the crime, but, as we saw, this was a very weak reed to rely on.

89 *Gazette*, 5 March 1935, 15; *Montreal Daily Herald*, 14 March 1935, 3. The petition itself is in TCC.

90 General observations on petition campaigns are based on capital case files in LAC, RG13 I have examined as part of my ongoing research.

91 Bruno Ramirez, "Workers without a Cause: Italian Immigrant Labour in Montreal, 1880–1930," in *Arrangiarsi: The Italian Immigration Experience in Canada*, ed. Roberto Perin and Franc Sturino (Montreal: Guernica, 1989), 126–7; LAC, RG13, vol. 1448. On petitioning by Italian communities more generally in Canada, see John E. Zucchi, *Italians in Toronto: Development of a National Identity, 1875–1935* (Montreal: McGill-Queen's University Press, 1988), 125, 127, 145.

92 For Viau: LAC, RG13, vol. 1436. For Beaulne: LAC, RG13, vol. 1555.

93 Maria Bendinelli Predelli, "Il contributo della donna alla cultura italiana nel Quebec," *Italian Canadiana* 11(1995), 81; Salvatore, *Le facisme*, 34–7; Luigi Pautasso, "La donna italiana durante il periodo fascista in Toronto, 1930–1940," *The Italian Immigrant Woman in North America*, ed. Betty Boyd Caroli et al. (Toronto: Multicultural History of Ontario, 1978), 168–86. Much more work would be needed to elucidate the exact manner in which the petition was put together. One newspaper report referred to the "much-publicized attempt on the part of the Italian colony to have her sentence commuted to life imprisonment" (*Montreal Daily Herald*, 14 March 1935, 3), but I have been unable to find any other mention of the campaign.

94 This is based on a partial analysis of the Montreal signatories to the petition, covering most of the women and a sample of the men, using the city directory of 1934–35.

95 General observations in this section are based on the corpus of newspaper articles described in note 12 above.

96 *La Presse*, 14 March 1928, 23.

97 Leyton-Brown, *The Practice of Execution*, 132; Manuel Truffy, "La couverture journalistique des exécutions au Québec entre 1854 et 1932" (master's thesis, Université du Québec à Montréal, 2018).

98 See, for example, *Montreal Daily Star*, 29 March 1935, 3, 13, and *Winnipeg Evening Tribune*, 29 March 1935, 23.

99 The most elaborate version of the UP story I found was in the *Daily News*, 30 March 1935, 3 and 4. See also *Toronto Daily Star*, 29 March 1935, 29. The sheriff's report, dated 4 April 1935, is in BAnQ-Q E17 1935 #2721.

100 Austin Sarat et al., "Gruesome Spectacles: The Cultural Reception of Botched Executions in America, 1890–1920," *British Journal of American Legal Studies* 1, no. 1 (2012): 14–15.

101 Criticism of Ellis began with the UP story, which, in its more elaborate versions, blamed him for bungling the job. The blame directed at him was amplified over the following days, especially when Lattoni explicitly excoriated him – see, for example, *La Presse*, 30 March 1935, 43, or *Gazette*, 30 March 1935, 5.

102 Ellis to Crandall, 12 April 1935, Ellis to Lanctôt, 16 April 1935, Lanctôt to Ellis, 20 April 1935, all in BAnQ-Q E17 1935 #2721; *Gazette*, 21 July 1938, 9; Joint Committee of the Senate and the House of Commons on Capital and Corporal Punishment and Lotteries, *Minutes of Proceedings and Evidence* (Ottawa: Queen's Printer, 1955), #7, 190–1.

103 Anderson, *A Concise History of Capital Punishment*, 71; BAnQ-Q E17 1935 #3425; *Gazette*, 8 June 1936, 7; 21 July 1938, 9; and 22 July 1938, 1 and 9. Ellis's last execution in Quebec was in mid-June 1935.

104 For example, *La Patrie*, 1 April 1935, 8 (for changing the method of execution); *Vancouver News-Herald*, 30 March 1935, 2 (for abolishing the death penalty for women); and *Ottawa Evening Citizen*, 30 March 1935, 28 (for full abolition).

105 See, for example, *Scranton (PA) Republican*, 1 April 1935, 5. Similar references to the execution being of a sort of "refined barbarism" practised in Hitler's Germany were deployed in England's *Sunday Referee*, quoted, among others, in *Gazette*, 1 April 1935, 4, *La Presse*, 1 April 1935, 19, and *Ottawa Journal*, 1 April 1935 (the latter being included in Teolis's capital case file), and also echoed by a Toronto rabbi in *Toronto Daily Star*, 1 April 1935, 21. Disconcertingly, however, these were in reference to Ellis's formal attire, not his technique.

106 BAnQ-Q E17, 1935 #2721; *Commons Debates*, 1 April 1935, 2279; *Montreal Daily Herald*, 30 March 1935, 1; *Montreal Daily Star*, 1 April 1935, 3; *La Presse*, 1 April 1935, 3; *Gazette*, 1 April 1935, 4; *La Patrie*, 1 April 1935, 3–4, 5.

107 *Montreal Daily Herald*, 29 March 1935, 1. The protest and call for the ban on hanging women was widely publicized in the press and, as noted above, garnered some editorial support.

108 *Commons Debates*, 4 April 1935, 2418.

109 White, *Negotiating Responsibility*, 1–10.

110 For a full account, see Strange, "The Undercurrents of Penal Culture."

111 *Commons Debates*, 4 April 1935, 2418, 2440–1; 13 March 1936, 1078, 1081, 1082; 28 January 1937, 343, 344, 346; 18 April 1950, 1660; 18 May 1976, 13649; House of Commons, *Special Committee on the Criminal Code (Death*

Penalty), Minutes and Proceedings of Evidence (Ottawa: J.O. Patenaude, 1937), 28, 46–7, 49, 53–4, 60, 69; Joint Committee, *Minutes of Proceedings* #7, 190–1 and #18, 573. An early abolitionist history of capital punishment in Canada also anonymized her: Louis Blake Duff, *The County Kerchief* (Toronto: Ryerson Press, 1949), 135.

112 *Gazette*, 21 July 1938, 9; *Devoir*, 21 July 1938, 7; *Le Soleil*, 21 July 1938, 20.

113 Al Palmer, "'Mal'occhio': The Evil Eye that Backfired," *Gazette*, 3 September 1960, 3.

114 Poplak, *Drop Dead*.

115 As in Palmer, "'Mal'occhio.'"

116 Castex, *Crimes et châtiments*.

117 Sébastien Bossé and Chantal Bouchard, *Bordeaux: L'histoire d'une prison* (Boisbriand: Éditions au Carré, 2013), 103–4; Poplak, *Drop Dead*.

118 Anette Ballinger, *Gender, Truth and State Power: Capitalising on Punishment* (London: Routledge, 2016), 4–5, 30–3; Seal, *Women, Murder and Femininity*, 2–3.

7

The *War-Time Elections Act*, Canadian Women's Suffrage, and Constitutional Thought during the First World War

LYNDSAY CAMPBELL

This chapter explores the implications of a discreditable episode in Canadian political and legal history that is seldom fully told in accounts of the First World War period. In the fall of 1917, Robert Laird Borden's Unionists, intent on winning the December election, which was fought over conscription, legislated to prevent women in the West and Ontario who legitimately expected to vote from doing so, in order to undercut support for those Liberals who continued to support Laurier. In this widely unknown story, the women who protested loudest, largely on the Prairies, were voices in the wilderness, tarred with the stain of disloyalty: surely, they were told, the sacrifice of a ballot was a small price to pay to win a war. This episode was also important in the history of Canadian constitutional thought, as the relentless progressivist instrumentalism of the period pushed older constitutional concepts and principles aside and forged new pathways for legal and constitutional interpretation.

By the summer of 1917, Borden's Conservatives were well into the sixth year of their term. Committed to conscription, they confronted the prospect of an election they could lose, partly because of women voters in Ontario and the West. They therefore determined to disfranchise women and others who were likely to vote Liberal while enfranchising women likely to support them. The story is a complicated one.

Borden had promised that his government would not adopt conscription, even while laying its foundations in late 1916.[1] However, by the spring of 1917, voluntary enlistment was no longer proceeding briskly – probably at least in part because recruiting had eased off – and was being outpaced by deaths.[2] On 18 May 1917, recently back from London, Borden introduced conscription through the *Military Service Act, 1917* (*MSA*), which he thought necessary for raising the additional 100,000 men he had committed to the war effort and believed essential to win the war. Quebec's opposition to conscription was well known. Conservatives, the wind of nativism blowing hard at their backs, fretted about opposition from Eastern European immigrants on the Prairies as well.[3]

Liberals had supported an extension of Parliament a year earlier but would not do so again. The venerable Liberal leader, Sir Wilfrid Laurier, insisted that British constitutional tradition denied the state the power to order anyone to kill or die (that was for "Kaiserism") or, indeed, to organize the distribution of labour and employment. Such a departure from principle, he said, required validation through an election.[4] In July 1917, Borden dropped his motion to ask the king for another extension when it did not get the support he sought in the House of Commons. Some Conservatives characterized the refusal to extend Parliament as the fundamental wrong that necessitated and justified reshaping the electorate.[5]

As casualties had grown, so had allegations of governmental misdeeds. The needs of regular Canadians, particularly soldiers and their families, were rumoured to have been subordinated to the profits offered by the unprecedented demands of coordinated wartime manufacturing and its idiosyncratic organization under Sir Sam Hughes, minister of militia until late 1916.[6] Provincial politicians were tarred with scandal, too – over construction projects, liquor law evasion, and other matters. A soldier was paid $1.10 for a day in the trenches and, on discharge, $8 for a suit of clothes and $5 dollars for an overcoat.[7] A soldier's widow received a measly thirty cents per day.[8] By 1917, western Canada had already supplied a larger portion of its military-aged Canadian- and British-born men than had other provinces, although Conservatives ignored these statistics when drafting eligibility for exemptions in the conscription statute.[9] Veterans and military families in the West felt used.

Conservatives confronted the prospect of an election that they were determined to win but in which a vast new body of voters – women in the key battlegrounds of Ontario and the West – seemed likely to vote Liberal. In general, the federal franchise rested on the provincial: the

British North America Act established that unless the federal Parliament provided otherwise, elections to the House of Commons were determined by provincial laws regarding qualifications and disqualifications on sitting, voting and running elections.[10] By 1908, all nine provinces had empowered at least ratepaying, unmarried women to vote municipally.[11] In January 1916, Manitoba Liberals gave women the provincial vote, preserving existing racializing disqualifications, as Ontario and the other western provinces in turn also did.[12] In February, the Conservatives refused to answer the question of whether Manitoba women qualified to vote provincially would be turned away at the federal polls. Two months later, Liberal governments in Saskatchewan and Alberta also gave women the ballot.[13] In October 1916, British Columbia's Conservative government ran a male-only referendum on women's enfranchisement (and prohibition and political corruption) alongside an election. The disgusted electorate turfed the Conservatives, and the incoming Liberals enfranchised women.[14]

By then, Laurier was supporting enfranchisement where women wanted it.[15] In Ontario, the governing Conservatives were suddenly converted: enfranchisement legislation received royal assent in April 1917 and was proclaimed in force on 12 May.[16] By the fall of 1917, women had not yet voted in provincial elections in Manitoba, Ontario, or British Columbia, but they had voted in Saskatchewan and Alberta in June 1917, contributing to the re-election of Liberal governments.[17] Albertans had elected a woman, Louise McKinney, to the legislature. Western women were rallying behind conscription, but there was much support for the Liberals as well. With Quebec lost to Borden's Conservatives, the West was a key election battlefield. With more than a generation of women's mobilization for suffrage finally having borne fruit, provincially enfranchised women's claim to the federal ballot was strong.[18]

Rather than courting outrage by denying women's capacity to reason or bemoaning the likely demise of the family if wives could vote, federal Conservatives turned to the strategic drafting of legislation to undercut women's claims. The *War-time Elections Act* (*WTEA*) and its sibling, the *Military Voters Act, 1917* (*MVA*), were contrived in this context. These were complex statutes aimed at selectively enfranchising and disfranchising Canadians in order to ensure victory for Borden's troubled Conservatives.[19]

Conscription would prove expensive and cumbersome and would not produce the manpower Borden sought. It did, however, prove a robust election platform, as it mobilized divisions among Liberals and brought prominent defectors, including western provincial leaders, to Borden over the summer and early fall of 1917, enabling the founding of the Unionist Party.[20] The *MSA* received royal assent on 29 August, eliciting widespread satisfaction in most of Canada but also uproar and riots, especially in Quebec. Rushed through Parliament in its wake, the *WTEA* and the *MVA* received royal assent in mid-September, and Borden installed his Unionist cabinet on 12 October, with himself at the helm. Preparing for the December election, Unionists contrasted themselves to the remaining Laurier Liberals, as manly men with the fortitude to compel the shirkers to do their duty, especially in Quebec.

These statutes upset the integrity of electoral processes, manipulated the military vote, and disfranchised people who reasonably expected to vote, including provincially enfranchised women, many Indigenous people, and members of ethnic minorities. The regime took aim at western Canada, and Prairie newspapers and parliamentarians bore loudest witness to these injustices. Women's organizations were bitterly divided, between those who felt Unionists must win the election and enact conscription and those who opposed the disfranchising of "all save a few women voters in five provinces of Canada," as a resolution at a Calgary Liberal convention put it.[21] This chapter describes the legal framework and the interwoven federal and provincial politics behind it before considering the constitutional principles at stake, with particular attention to their implications for women's rights. These principles include the law's protection against discrimination against "classes" of people, the idea that voting is a "privilege," and the ideal of a uniform federal franchise.

Histories of Women's Enfranchisement

Parts of this history have been told by biographers of some of the participants and by scholars who have studied the First World War, elections, discrimination, and women's history. Most historians accept the narratives the Conservatives spun in Parliament: that men recognized that women deserved the franchise for their war-time labours, that it would inevitably come anyway, and that the rather natural-sounding, patriarchal first step was to extend the vote to women serving overseas and to male soldiers' close female relatives, on the ground that it was unfair and even undemocratic that men serving overseas were unable to vote, sometimes because they were dead. The women were imagined as deserving proxies for the legitimate voters. This story generally overlooks the fact that most men overseas were already enfranchised, though the voting regime was certainly problematic. Moreover, this narrative makes a statute whose blatant discrimination against people of Eastern European origin is well known sound progressive with respect to women, which it was not.[22] While often acknowledging the Conservatives' deliberate manipulation of the vote in the 1917 election, historians of elections and the franchise in Canada have generally focused on other aspects of this period and have not recognized the disfranchisement of women.[23] The often deliberately complex interconnections among federal and provincial statutory electoral regimes and the politics behind them have seldom been fully explored or understood.

In 1950, Catherine L. Cleverdon expressed scepticism about the genuineness of politicians' rhetoric about enfranchising women in recognition of their devoted wartime service. In her view, Ontario premier Sir William Hearst, for example, in suddenly transforming into an advocate of women's suffrage in early 1917, was reading the wind and possibly complying with Borden's suggestion for garnering votes for Conservatives.[24] Similarly, Carol Lee Bacchi argued in her devastating *Liberation Deferred* (1983) that women's enfranchisement was political, not principled, and that, to win the election, Borden's government enfranchised certain women and disfranchised "aliens" and other potential Liberal voters. Bacchi demonstrated that men (especially Conservatives) were fond of prating about women's devotion and mettle, but what mattered was politics, and it was politically advantageous to appear magnanimous and open minded.[25]

Political biographies reveal key individuals' motivations. Biographers tend to view the *MVA* as creating unfortunate, possibly unintended opportunities for bad behaviour by officials or others, while they condemn the *WTEA* as "a bald, reprehensible gerrymander."[26] Having promised more troops, Borden wrote in his diary, "'Our first duty is to win, at any cost the coming election in order that we may continue to do our part in winning the war and that Canada be not disgraced.'"[27] The most significant fingerprints on the statutory regime belonged to Solicitor General Arthur Meighen and Borden's old friend from Halifax, William Francis O'Connor.[28] In correspondence responding to Borden's question in October 1916 about the prospect of women voting in the five provinces west of Quebec, Meighen said that, in normal times, he would have advised changing the federal legislation to enfranchise women federally where they were enfranchised provincially. However, he anticipated that women of "'alien enemy origin and parentage'"

– known to reside in the West – would be more likely to vote than would women of British origin, and so it would be better to wait until provincial legislation across the country evidenced nation-wide support for female enfranchisement, although this approach would hurt Conservatives in provincial elections in "'Equal Suffrage Provinces.'" Two weeks later, Meighen added an idea, possibly propounded by the political operator Robert Rogers, that if "'the foreign population difficulty'" could be met, it would be excellent to enfranchise women federally wherever they were enfranchised provincially. "'To shift the franchise from the doubtful British or anti-British of the male sex and to extend it at the same time to our patriotic women, would be in my judgment a splendid stroke.'" He "'again'" suggested a subcommittee to take up this subject. Work began.[29]

Volunteers and Conscripts: The *MVA* and the Manipulation of the Military Franchise

The machinations around women's voting were accompanied by a careful manipulation of the military vote, towards the same ends and with implications for the language of rights and privileges, which I discuss below. Historians usually treat the manipulation of the military vote as the result of an unfortunate confluence of poor drafting and opportunistic politicking, but there was more to it. This long war and the shift from voluntary to compulsory service led to conceptual and practical difficulties around the soldier vote. Public commentators on the war often spoke of the "boys" who were "sent," "given," or "sacrificed" by their parents. As "men," though, these same people seemed likely to vote for conscription, unless, perhaps, they themselves had been conscripted.

In April 1915, Canada's twelfth Parliament – by then in its fourth year – enfranchised male British subjects over twenty-one who were serving in the Canadian forces (in or out of Canada) and had resided for at least thirty days in a Canadian electoral district in the six months before signing up. Younger soldiers could not vote.[30] A "volunteer" could vote for the government, the opposition, the independent running in the riding, or someone else whose name the voter supplied. He was to place his ballot in an envelope on the outside of which he specified (in an affidavit) the riding in which he had resided for the requisite thirty days or was a registered voter.[31] The presiding officer would package the ballots and send them to the Clerk of the Crown in Chancery (in Ottawa), who would sort and mail them to the various electoral districts, where they would be recorded, scrutinized, and counted.[32] As historians have noted, submarine warfare threatened this regime, and, in 1917, the *MVA* provided for ballots to be counted in Europe.

In May 1916, BC's Conservatives enacted a readily corruptible regime with little voting oversight to allow male soldiers of any age who were British subjects to vote in their own ridings in elections and referenda.[33] In the election later that year, soldiers leaned more Conservative than the rest of the electorate and more narrowly favoured women's suffrage.[34] Legislating in early 1917, Liberals in Alberta and Saskatchewan set aside two seats for members who represented soldiers, chaplains, nurses, and others serving overseas. Conservative newspapers howled at the marginalization of the soldier vote and protested that naturalized "foreigners," who could vote, were better treated. "Foreigners" noted this Conservative antipathy.[35]

The *MVA* enlarged the wartime franchise among those with military service connections to Canada. The statute enfranchised all British subjects ordinarily resident in Canada, male or female, including minors and "Indians," who were on active service in the Canadian, British, or allied forces. Much more controversially, it also enfranchised all British subjects who had been part of specified British forces in Canada or who had been active in specified Canadian armed forces, even if they had never been ordinarily resident in Canada.[36]

The *MSA* created six classes of conscripted men.[37] Of these, single men in their twenties and early thirties were to report for duty first, in Halifax by 10 December 1917, a week before election day. Military polls were to open around 22 November.[38] For these presumably reluctant military voters, an Order-in-Council permitted extensive departures from the procedural safeguards built into the *MVA*. Military polls could be held anywhere and anytime near Halifax, without the proper appointment or swearing of those presiding over the vote; without the receipt or disposal of the ballots, envelopes, or other election supplies as required in the act; and whether or not the ballot boxes were delivered as set out in the *MVA*.[39] Ensuring the integrity of the conscript vote was evidently not a priority.

As it happened, the call-up date was postponed to 3 January. Military registrars and tribunals were running behind because many conscripts did not report until the last minute, and the government was indecisive about exempting farmers. As well, on 6 December, two ships, one loaded with munitions, collided in the Halifax harbour, the resultant explosion devastating the city.[40] Presumably, conscripts who were not yet in Halifax and could vote as civilians did so in their ridings, but others, not yet on active service, were not yet "military electors."[41]

As in the 1915 statute, and undoubtedly for practical reasons, ballots did not bear the names of candidates, referring only to parties and leaving a space for the voter to name a specific candidate.[42] Some historians have asserted that a political party receiving a vote could designate the riding in which it was to count, once the civilian vote was complete, but this interpretation does not accurately represent the statutory scheme.[43] The statute reflected a recognition that many voters probably could neither specify the candidate they preferred nor name their riding – many were young, and some had never even lived in Canada. The ballot therefore offered the voter the choice of either writing in the candidate's name or voting for the government, the opposition, the "independent candidate," or the "Labour candidate." A certificate accompanying the ballot required the voter to establish eligibility and give the information that would determine the electoral district in which the vote was to count, preferably where the voter had last continuously resided for four months before going into service. Unsure voters could indicate where they had lived, and the district would be identified that way. Otherwise, voters could name some place in Canada where they had lived at some point, and their votes would count there. If all else failed, a voter could simply choose a riding.[44]

Each party's candidates were formally approved by the party leader and duly published in a special issue of the *Canada Gazette*. As in the earlier statute, if a military voter simply picked a party, that party's candidate in the voter's riding would get the vote. If no one in that party was running in that riding, or if the voter named someone who was not a candidate there, the vote would be rejected. Active military electors who were in Canada were subject to these rules; those who had left active service – including women and men under twenty-one – voted at their regular polls, with the deputy returning officer noting in the poll book that they were military voters. European ballot boxes were sent to offices in London, France, or Canada, where they were to be opened at a specified time.[45] At the top of the electoral hierarchy in England and continental Europe were the "Presiding Officers," at least some of whom were political appointees: Garnet Hughes was Sam's son; Charles Smart was a Conservative stalwart, textile entrepreneur, and Hughes protegé; and Frank S. Meighen was apparently Arthur's cousin.[46]

Although under the statute the government could not directly allocate votes, enormous pressure could be applied to voters by the "Deputy Presiding Officer" and the deputy scrutineers and military officers who stood in for them.[47] Laurier Liberal W.T.R. Preston's scathing first-hand account describes emissaries from Canada assessing the likely outcomes in contested ridings and pressuring soldiers to deliver the needed vote. Preston, who was himself jailed during the voting, spoke of Liberal scrutineers being excluded from camps, forged signatures on soldiers' ballot envelopes, fake telegrams to and from soldiers encouraging the recipient to vote Unionist, and soldiers who were "too frank" about their Liberal leanings being sent to the front.[48] Loyal Conservatives were deployed to assist in garnering overseas support and votes in risky ridings, with party managers relaying their needs through Borden's secretary.[49] Suspicious accounts reached the West. One suggested that Liberal-Unionist editors were conspiring to convince the "boys at the front" that a Unionist government was their best hope for improved conditions, even though the "boys" opposed conscription.[50] Ultimately, fourteen ridings across the country went Unionist because of the military vote, although it is difficult to assess to what extent malfeasance produced this result.[51]

Canadian Election Law at the Beginning of the First World War

Even more ambitiously than the *MVA*, the *WTEA* crafted the electorate to win the election for Unionists. It disfranchised classes of voters while purporting to create a single federal franchise that nonetheless rested on the provincial. At the same time, uncertainties around parliamentary intention in electoral legislation from 1898 and 1900 were strategically employed in 1916 and 1917 to keep the franchise male.

In 1885, John A. Macdonald's Conservatives passed the *Electoral Franchise Act*, imposing specific, uniform federal property qualifications and explicitly restricting the franchise to men.[52] The Liberals repealed the act in 1898, causing the federal franchise, outside of the North-West Territories, to revert to dependence on the provincial franchise.[53] In the North-West Territories, a voter had to be a "*bonâ fide* male resident and householder, of adult age, who is not an alien or an Indian" and who had lived in the electoral district for the twelve months before the election.[54] The 1898 statute used conspicuously awkward wording and punctuation to address the federal statute's disabling of provincial disqualifications, language that was preserved, undoubtedly for strategic purposes, in subsequent statutory drafting. Accompanied by the marginal note "Provincial disqualifications not adopted," subsection 6(1) said:

> No person possessed of the qualifications generally required by the provincial law to entitle him to vote at a provincial election, shall be disqualified from voting at a Dominion election merely by reason of any provision of the provincial law disqualifying from [sic] having his name on the list or from voting –
>
> (a) the holder of any office, or
> (b) any person employed in any capacity in the public service of Canada or of the province, or
> (c) any person belonging to or engaged in any profession, calling, employment or occupation, or
> (d) any one belonging to any other class of persons who, although possessed of the qualifications generally required by the provincial law, are by such law declared to be disqualified by reason of their belonging to such class.[55]

The term "class of persons" in paragraph (d) referred to provincial disqualifications based on personal characteristics such as race, ethnicity, or Indigeneity. As well, the *Dominion Elections Act* enacted in 1900 enabled "any British subject" to sit in the House of Commons, subject to disqualifications for people who held remunerative federal offices and certain provincial ones, people with certain contracts with the Crown, and those convicted of corruption-related electoral offences. The act referred to candidates as "persons."[56]

The *Dominion Elections Act* was revised in 1906, to address the 1905 reorganization of the North-West Territories. Part II applied to Saskatchewan, Alberta, and Yukon Territory; Part I applied elsewhere. For Part I provinces, federal voters' lists and qualifications rested on provincial rules, except that provincial disqualifications were deactivated, using the familiar awkward provisions from 1898. In Saskatchewan, Alberta, and Yukon, however, the vote was granted to "every male person ... who, not being an Indian, is a British subject and of the full age of twenty-one years." Part III set out federal voter and candidacy disqualifications for the House of Commons: subject to these various disqualifications and regardless of property ownership, "any British subject" could be a candidate. The word "person" continued to be used for candidates.[57]

The 1906 statute therefore created a puzzle: did it really mean that women were explicitly disfranchised in Alberta, Saskatchewan, and Yukon but could vote elsewhere if provincial legislation so allowed? The efforts of Liberal member of Parliament William Pugsley to characterize the situation as an "anomaly" that could be rectified by enfranchising all Canadian women, or at least those eligible to vote provincially, failed. Conservatives did not want to enfranchise all those potential Liberals, either in February 1916 when Pugsley first raised the question (with two federal seats for Manitoba open and women arguably eligible to vote in by-elections), or in May 1917, when the *WTEA* was being prepared.[58] Borden had been evasive, suggesting that women pursue the provincial franchise and letting them think that they would thereby be enfranchised federally.[59] The *WTEA*, however, preempted provincial rules, harnessing women voters likely to lean Unionist and excising Laurier supporters.[60] Borden even promised, in a letter of September 1917, that, if the Unionists were elected, they would enfranchise all women – just not for this election.[61] Although many women – and men – objected strenuously, it was a price that women who favoured conscription, and suspected the "enemy aliens" among them, were willing to pay.

Militarism and the *WTEA*

The *WTEA* meticulously sliced up the electorate, enfranchising and disfranchising on the basis of gender, race, ethnicity, language, Indigeneity, property and income, and relationship to those serving in the war. Its first two provisions suspended, for the duration of the war and demobilization, Part I of the *DEA*, which applied in the provinces outside of Alberta, Saskatchewan, and Yukon, and extended Part II of the *DEA* nation-wide, restricting the franchise to males over twenty-one who met certain residency requirements, were British subjects, and were not "Indian." The next section made the provincial franchise the basis for the federal, but only for men.[62] To the surprise of Sam Hughes and others who thought women's enfranchisement was important, Meighen, in introducing the bill, nevertheless announced that the bill adopted the provincial franchise in every province.[63]

The next provision of the *WTEA*, which became section 33A of the *DEA*, enfranchised some women across the country, on the basis of their relationship to men who were serving or had served in the war. Women voters had to be British subjects and meet the provincial or

Yukon qualifications for "age, race and residence" required for male voters. Women voters also had to be "the wife, widow, mother, sister or daughter of any person, male or female, living or dead, who is serving or has served without Canada in any of the military forces, or within or without Canada in any of the naval forces, of Canada or of Great Britain in the present war."[64] If the relative was no longer in the service, the woman could not claim enfranchisement unless the relative had either died in service or been properly released from it. The female relatives of a person who joined the navy after the *WTEA* passed but never served outside Canada were not enfranchised.

The *WTEA* next added section 33B to the *DEA*. This provision reproduced – without fixing – the old, poorly drafted provision from Part I that deactivated provincial disqualifications. The provision began, "No person possessed of the qualifications generally required by the provincial law to entitle him to vote at a provincial election shall be disqualified at a Dominion election merely by reason of the provincial law."[65] Women, therefore, could be disqualified by provincial racial barriers under section 33A(1), but "persons" could not be, under section 33B(1). Unionists benefited two ways. First, racialized women could be disqualified by provincial rules, even if their relatives were overseas, which presumably pleased western racists. Second, by any logical interpretation of these two side-by-side provisions, "persons" had to mean men only. The provision could have been reworded over the previous year of careful Conservative drafting, but it conspicuously was not. Further fortifying this argument was section 33B(2), which provided that a "person" disfranchised by provincial income or property qualifications nevertheless gained the federal vote if his son or grandson was serving. Only Quebec and the Maritime provinces, where women could not vote anyway, still had income and property qualifications, so the only "persons" affected by this provision were men.

The *DEA*'s disqualifications were expanded.[66] Conscientious objectors and those waiting for an exemption decision on that ground were disfranchised, as was everyone convicted of violating the conscription statute. Mennonites and Doukhobors, unless they had volunteered for and been placed on active service, were disfranchised, even though both had long been excused from military service. Anyone who voted after 7 October 1917 became ineligible to claim the exemptions from military service available to conscientious objectors, Mennonites, and Doukhobors.

Everyone who was "born in an enemy country" and had become a naturalized British subject after 31 March 1902 was disfranchised. An "enemy country" was one with which "His Majesty is at war." However, a "natural born citizen or subject of France, Italy or Denmark" who had come to Canada before Germany or Austria took over that person's birthplace could escape this exclusion through a sworn statement of the relevant facts. Also disfranchised was every British subject born in a European country whose mother tongue was the language of an enemy country and who had been naturalized since 31 March 1902. If disfranchised on the basis of enemy affiliation, men and their sons were exempt from conscription. All of these disfranchising conditions were lifted if the naturalized British subject, otherwise qualified, was serving or had served outside Canada in the military or within or outside Canada in the Canadian navy or that of Britain or an ally. One could also be relieved from disfranchisement if the commanding officer of a military district certified that one was or had been engaged in active service, had applied but been rejected for medical reasons, or was a grandparent, parent, son, or brother of such a willing person. Also exempted from disfranchisement on these enemy-affiliation grounds were members of Parliament and legislatures, Syrian and Armenian Christians, and female voters entitled to vote because of their male relatives' service.

As a result of the *MVA* and the *WTEA* together, British subjects who had never been ordinarily resident in Canada but had Canadian military affiliations were enfranchised, while Canadian women from the West and Ontario who expected to vote were barred, along with naturalized Canadians, conscientious objectors, and members of pacifist groups. Indigenous and racialized women who were disfranchised provincially were now barred federally as well, even if their closest male relatives were in the trenches.[67]

Unionists justified this regime by explicitly grounding the "right" to vote in military service. Some western Liberals who supported conscription were dismayed to find large numbers of their constituents disfranchised. Unionists urged western women to block their ears to the "rubbish of partisanship" that distracted men and to make the small sacrifice of foregoing the vote a little longer. Laurier's preference, a referendum on conscription, would take too long: Germany would invade, and Canadian children would die as Belgian children had. Loyal women were urged to eschew Laurier, the "Slackers of Quebec," and the "agents of Berlin," and instead to "walk by faith and not by sight" – that is, to spare Unionists from having to publicly justify their discriminatory regime. Unionists urged women voters to remember that "every ballot is a bullet" and that they were on the front lines. Non-voting women were urged to "enlist in the Army Service Corps, seeing to it that the ammunition is got to the polls on December 17th."[68]

Unionist advertising explicitly announced that women were being enfranchised – gaining the "privilege" of voting – so that they would vote for conscription, to bolster the fighting forces and improve the odds of the "boys" coming home alive.[69] Anticipating the objection that women without relatives abroad were also labouring to support the troops, Meighen explained that it was the unparallelled sacrifice of the women who actually faced the death of their close relatives, or had done so, that justified their voting, not just their capacity to represent those abroad (living or dead) or their wartime labours.[70] The objections that Laurier and some western representatives raised to the disfranchisement of naturalized Canadians – that they were loyal to Canada, that they opposed Austro-Hungarian invasions of their homelands – drew aspersions on these immigrants' loyalty and placating assurances that they were also being spared being conscripted to fight their kin, which justified taking their votes away.[71]

The December election was rife with fraud, coercion, and deceit at home and abroad. Rumours that conscription might mean a furlough for loved ones in Europe were quashed after the election.[72] Unionists dangled hints that they would release farmers' sons from the draft.[73] With many pages of the *WTEA* devoted to enumeration and the compilation of new voters lists, and with processes varying across the country, anti-Unionist newspapers reported on confusion and serious partisan improprieties.[74] A Toronto judge was reported to have assessed the impossibility of addressing all the appeals facing him in his courtroom and let 10,000 omitted people onto the voters' lists unless there were actual competent objections.[75] Although women and new Canadians on the Prairies were systematically disfranchised, the Unionist incumbent for North Waterloo was reported to have bragged publicly of his success in having 3,000 or 4,000 German Canadians who had been naturalized in the last ten years restored to the voters' list, while assuring locals that disfranchisement was just for the West.[76] The electoral regime was so complicated and unfair that the *Edmonton Bulletin* ran an advice column called "Have I a Vote?" Liberal newspapers informed readers of the steps to take if denied the vote and warned naturalized Canadians – specifically Americans – to take their naturalization papers to the polls.[77]

When the election was over, Liberals well outnumbered Conservatives in the new parliament, but Unionists outnumbered Laurier Liberals. Conscription and sculpting the electorate had indeed won the election for Borden.[78]

The *WTEA* and Constitutional Theory

In 1913, when constitutional theorist A.H.F. Lefroy contemplated enfranchising women federally, he explicitly avoided such traditional arguments as the injustice of taxation without representation. He doubted the ballot would destroy domestic harmony. He thought the country would benefit if women's proven tendency to promote justice and good causes could flow unhindered through the political system. Enfranchising women was not a matter of recognizing rights but of serving and building the country.[79] Like Lefroy's approach, the enfranchisement debates of 1917 were relentlessly instrumental, but even when constitutional principles were raised, the arguments often betrayed conceptual challenges in invoking such principles where women were concerned. The debates around the *WTEA* invite us to probe certain themes in constitutional theory, including the ideal of a uniform federal franchise, longstanding opposition arguments to "class legislation," and the idea that voting was a "privilege."

A Uniform Federal Franchise

We no longer discuss the uniformity of the federal franchise, but around the turn of the twentieth century we did. As Laurier explained, the fundamental question was whether each legislative body could establish its own franchise (a well-established constitutional tradition) or whether each province should determine its own electorate, with legislative matters distributed between federal and provincial legislatures according to the constitution's division of powers. By 1917 he was arguing that women who held the provincial franchise should also be enfranchised federally. Sometimes he couched this view as a fundamental constitutional principle and sometimes as a workable political solution to a controversial issue. Others framed a uniform federal franchise as an aspect of strengthening and modernizing Canada.[80]

The Conservatives' determination to control which women could vote complicated the arguments around constitutional principles. If the federal franchise were based on the provincial, then women in

Manitoba, British Columbia, and Ontario should, by the end of May 1917, have been entitled to vote, and the *Dominion Election Act*'s exclusion of Saskatchewan, Alberta, and Yukon women should have been treated a remediable "anomaly" – New Brunswicker William Pugsley's word – especially since women could arguably stand for election everywhere, as "British subjects."[81] To keep women from voting, Conservative parliamentarians had to argue that women were not "persons" within the meaning of the *DEA*. Conservatives took this second route, asserting that, moreover, it would be unfair to amend the *DEA* to make women "persons," because then they would be enfranchised in some provinces but not others. However, since the number of parliamentary seats given to a province was based on the census, this approach would simply have broadened the representation of political views in the provinces where women could vote, a situation that the Conservative government surely found more problematic because it favoured Laurier than because it was unfair to provincially disfranchised women, who could, of course, have lobbied their legislatures for the vote.

In two main episodes, Conservatives deflected Liberal efforts to address the emerging urgent problem. In the second, they signalled how they would address it. Early in 1916, two federal seats for Manitoba were empty and awaiting by-elections. Women could vote in Manitoba, and Saskatchewan and Alberta were about to enfranchise women as well. Conservatives deflected Pugsley's effort to get Parliament to clarify that Manitoban women could vote in these by-elections, with the whip, Robert Rogers, even hinting vaguely that Manitoba women might solve the problem themselves by simply voting illegally, as he alleged Saskatchewan women had done in 1912.[82] Manitoba's uncertainties went unaddressed.

Another debate on women's enfranchisement occurred on 16 May 1917, after the Conservatives had postponed it three times. Hints of the future were floated: the selective enfranchisement of women, the disfranchisement of those of "alien enemy birth," and the connection of the franchise to military service. Minister of Justice Charles Doherty asserted that, although Parliament might, for expedience, rely on provincial qualifications, it had "absolute power to determine who shall vote in elections." Laurier agreed about the power but still thought it wiser to leave women's enfranchisement to the provinces. Borden himself claimed that he expected no ill effects from enfranchising women across the country and said they deserved the vote not because of their tremendous devotion to duty but because they deserved a voice in the country's affairs.[83]

Doherty tentatively articulated, as his own interpretation of English law, a proposition that may have been new to Canadian legislators: that women were not "persons" within the meaning of section 10 of the *Dominion Elections Act*.[84] He asserted that the drafters had used "person" to refer to those who had, to that point, been considered potential voters. The drafters used "male person" in Part II with no consciousness of creating a disparity because, to their minds, there was none.

The argument drew unavailing protests from those who pointed out that Ontario had just enfranchised women on the assumption that they would be able to vote federally. Laurier denied that legislators in 1898 could not have contemplated a female franchise. Borden, on the other hand, argued that explicitly excluding women from the vote only in the Part II regions made no sense.[85] Conservatives blocked further debate, and attention turned to conscription.

On 6 September, Meighen introduced the *WTEA*, and the Conservatives slammed it through Parliament in nine days.[86] The idea that a uniform federal franchise was fairer than provincial choice was mobilized to disfranchise women who might vote Liberal, while women's status as "persons" for federal electoral purposes was shaken.

Class Legislation

Another objection to the *WTEA* was that it was "class legislation." I have written elsewhere about the principle in Upper Canadian constitutional thought that legislation should not draw distinctions on the basis of membership in a "class," which covered race, ethnicity, religion, and even membership in a voluntary organization.[87] I have argued that this sense that class legislation was constitutionally impermissible faded in the early twentieth century, as the *British North America Act*, which was silent on individual rights and discrimination, came to dominate the legal imagination. Indeed, in *Quong-Wing v. R.* (1914), the Supreme Court of Canada had waved away this principled impediment to legalized discrimination, upholding Saskatchewan's ban on "Chinese" employing white women. As Justice Louis Henry Davies explained, "there is nothing in the 'British North America Act' which says that such legislation may not be class legislation." The subject matter was provincial, and no federal power was infringed.[88] The dissenting protest of the eldest member of the bench, John Idington, that British thought favoured equality, and that the majority's approach was the type that "begot and maintained slavery," was ignored.[89]

For some critics, calling the *WTEA* "class legislation" amounted to condemning it outright as constitutionally impermissible. One Toronto suffragist called the act "a piece of 'vicious class legislation,' that was 'a far greater menace to us than many legions of foreigners.'"[90] Some parliamentarians also spoke of the disfranchisement of "classes" as self-evidently objectionable.[91]

Often, though, it was the *nature* of the *WTEA*'s classes that unsettled parliamentarians. Edmonton's Frank Oliver and Saskatoon's George McCraney objected to the creation of a "special military class" and the government's decision to link women's franchise to their relationship to soldiers. McCraney applied this logic to the disfranchisement of naturalized men, arguing that Parliament was signalling that any immigrant might one day be put "'in the same position as are the negroes in the southern portion of the United States.'" Meighen responded by pointing out that the western provinces already disfranchised naturalized citizens from Japan and China. When Medicine Hat's William Buchanan objected that all women working in the war – driving trucks and making munitions, for instance – should be enfranchised, Meighen shifted the hypothetical and explained that it was too hard to measure the service of the women knitting and sewing for the Red Cross, and that those facing their menfolk's death were making a sacrifice of a wholly different order. As he said, "'we cannot enfranchise by individuals; we must enfranchise by classes.'"[92] Thus, the *WTEA* probably further weakened the constitutional objection to class legislation.

Rights and Privileges

The third slippery idea related to the *WTEA* concerned the rights and privileges of citizenship. Women's citizenship was provisional, subject to change on marriage – a situation that Borden protested was too complicated to address at the time (after over a year of stalling and drafting minutely detailed disfranchisement provisions).[93] Women's inability to vote was framed differently from men's. Men could be barred because of the public offices they held, for example, or because they belonged to a particular "class of person."[94] Women, however, like minors, were characterized not exactly as disqualified, but as political non-actors – as dependents or non-"persons." There was a sharp disconnect, especially in Conservative rhetoric, between arguments that it was unfair if soldiers could not vote – because they were not in Canada and the logistics were complicated – and arguments about women's disfranchisement.

Debates about soldiers' enfranchisement usually referred to their "rights."[95] For women and naturalized citizens, the term "privilege" was employed as well, and it weakened through this association. The idea that voting was a "privilege" was common, but the word was shifting. Legal scholar Wesley Newcomb Hohfeld's late nineteenth-century use of the term captured its earlier meaning: a privilege was a legal entitlement that one could choose to use or not use and with which no one else could interfere.[96] It was rooted in the constitutional order (recall the privileges of the House of Commons, including freedom of speech in debate) and was a considerably weightier term than it is when we speak today, for instance, of limiting children's video game "privileges."

Introducing the *WTEA* on 6 September 1917, Meighen and other Conservatives framed the problem that the legislation was addressing as the existing system's inability to obtain the votes of soldiers overseas, prisoners of war, the wounded, and those hospitalized for mental health breakdowns, but also the dead. They – even the dead – were the ones whose voting rights and political views were real and substantial, and it was necessary to enfranchise their close female kin, who would hold the same views. As Cleverdon notes, Meighen acknowledged no unfairness to women whatsoever. In the Conservatives' framing, the sole purpose of this election that the Liberals had unfairly required them to call was to further the war effort through conscription. Disfranchising the enemy's (male) kin was argued to be unproblematic because the military brass would not be so inhumane as to send them to fight. The representative logic that justified enfranchising the female relatives of soldiers overseas also conveniently justified not enfranchising the relatives of conscripts, as they were still in Canada.[97] Even if dead, the men overseas were the real voters; women were a troubling, nebulous category, their citizenship conditioned by that of the men to whom they were attached.

In this context, the word "right" tended to be applied to men's entitlement to vote and "privilege" to the entitlements of women and others who were disfranchised. The earlier sense of the meaning of "privilege" had probably been weakening for some time, but the instrumentality of the franchise debates – about service and sacrifice earning women the ballot – obscured the earlier use of the word.[98] In this mucky semantic terrain, and when claimed by a class of not-quite-full persons, a privilege was no longer a serious legal and constitutional entitlement but a reward for the most extreme sacrifice.[99]

Laurier used a mixture of terminology about rights and privileges. An elder statesman steeped in older constitutional thought, he spoke of his own "liberties and ... privileges as a British subject" but also used the term "right to vote" when objecting to the *WTEA*. In May 1917, he used both words in the context of both male and female voters. Pugsley, Borden, and Doherty used the term "rights." R.B. Bennett, turning his menacing sights on naturalized immigrants, observed "the exercise of the franchise is not a right, but a privilege conferred by the State that grants it, and far from being a right, it is a privilege of such importance that too great care cannot be exercised in its grant."[100] The demise of the older use of "privilege" is evident in the assertion of suffragist Laura Marshall Jamieson, in September 1916, that women wanted "no privileges" but only equal rights to property. The word "dower," she said, "smacks of privilege and that is not what women want."[101] Overall, the concept of a privilege as a solid legal entitlement – the sense in which Laurier used it when referring to himself – was slipping. For white men whose allegiances were not in question, the franchise tended to be framed as a "right"; the word "privilege" was becoming the term of choice for those who wanted to bestow or retract it for instrumental reasons.

Conclusion

Narratives about the fundamental changes Canada underwent in the First World War often include the changed role of women – as participants in overseas theatres, as workers in munitions factories and other new employments, and in voting and public life. The Conservatives' meticulously calculated disfranchisement of women, especially in the West, whom they feared would vote Liberal, is often overlooked, even though the *WTEA*'s disfranchisement of other groups is generally acknowledged – if often without disentangling the complex interplay of provincial and federal regimes. Federal legislation also ensured that the close female relatives of conscripts would not thus be enfranchised.

This history of this crisis and the way power was exercised against the vulnerable is important for its own sake, but it also affected constitutional thought. The word "privilege" drifted from the domain of constitutional entitlements towards referring to a reward for good behaviour. The vote became a "right," which (most) men had and women could seek. A uniform federal franchise came to be accepted as a constitutional ideal, even though its purpose was to disfranchise thousands. White women in the West and Ontario were asked to accept the contingency of their citizenship and to make another sacrifice for the war effort, of a ballot they had never used federally but had justly expected. Most accepted the bargain. The thirteenth Parliament did eventually enfranchise most women federally, excluding both men and women who were "Indians" living on reserves, and eliminated provincial influence over the federal franchise.[102] In 1920, the Conservatives overhauled the whole regime and introduced a multitude of now-familiar provisions to ensure the integrity of elections.[103]

The instrumentalism of this period was probably one of the last nails in the coffin for the older constitutional aversion to class legislation. The sense of commitment to a greater purpose was understood to justify injustices large and small, and carving up the electorate on the basis of relationships, occupations, and ethnicity was widely seen as acceptable and necessary. This story of disfranchisement, then, must be understood as an important chapter in the history of constitutional thought in Canada as well as a reminder of the vulnerability of rights in times of crisis.

NOTES

1 See, for example, "No Conscription for Canada Says Premier in House of Commons," *Calgary Herald*, 18 January 1916. See also James H. Gray, *R.B. Bennett: The Calgary Years* (Toronto: University of Toronto Press, 1991), 179–82.

2 Borden heartily denied telling Sam Hughes to ease up on recruiting in March 1917, but Hughes evidently thought he had received that message and said he had not actively recruited after March. See *Official Report of the Debates of the House of Commons of the Dominion of Canada. Seventh Session, Twelfth Parliament, 7–8 George V, 1917* (Ottawa: J. de LaBroquerie Taché, 1918), 3092–4 et seq. (6 July 1917). The various volumes in this series are henceforth referred to as *Debates*.

3 *Military Service Act, 1917* (*MSA*), SC 1917, c 19. See Howard Palmer, *Patterns of Prejudice: A History of Nativism in Alberta* (Toronto: McClelland and Stewart, 1982), 17–60; John Herd Thompson, *The Harvests of War: The Prairie West, 1914–1918* (Toronto: McClelland and Stewart, 1978), 73–93.

4 *Debates*, 18 June 1917, 2392–400. Laurier's additional concerns included twenty vacant seats and the West's entitlement to twenty-two more seats before the next election. Edmonton's Frank Oliver noted the dubious legality and probable conflicts of interest inherent in the number of parliamentarians being paid by government for various military-related tasks (*Debates*, 18 June 1917, 2420–1).

5 See *Debates*, 18 July and 10 September 1917, 3504, 5594–5.

6 On this "saturnalia of grafting," see *Who Shall Rule?* (Ottawa: Central Information Office of the Canadian Liberal Party, 1917), 2. From 1915 through 1917, federal royal commissions investigated contracts for drill sheds, military cloth, submarines, surgical supplies, small arms and munitions (twice), shells, and the munitions industry. See George Fletcher Henderson, *Federal Royal Commissions in Canada, 1867–1966* (Toronto: University of Toronto Press, 1967), 79–81, 83–5.

7 "The Soldiers' Thriteen [sic] Dollars," *Calgary News-Telegram*, 8 December 1917.

8 "Are These Traitors?" *Calgary News-Telegram*, 15 December 1917. For context, see "Minister of Militia Orders New Curtains at $115 per – and Hon. 'Jim' Calder $1000 Carpet," *Calgary News-Telegram*, 8 December 1917. Within weeks of passing the *MSA*, the federal government began revising its support and pension schemes.

9 These figures were given by Frank Oliver, in *Debates*, 10 July 1917, 2302: Nova Scotia: 26%; New Brunswick: 29%; Prince Edward Island: 18%; Quebec: 13%; Ontario: 36%; Manitoba and Saskatchewan together: 45%; Alberta: 55%; and British Columbia: 43%.

10 *British North America Act* (UK), 30 & 31 Vic., c. 3, s. 41.

11 See Sonia Leathes, *Where and How May Canadian Women Vote* (Toronto: Equal Franchise League[?], 1912), and Henrietta Muir Edwards, *Legal Status of Canadian Women …* (Toronto: National Council of Women of Canada, 1908), 51.

12 *An Act to Amend "The Manitoba Election Act,"* SM 1916, c. 36, ss. 1–4. The *Manitoba Election Act*, RSM 1913, c. 59, s. 19, disfranchised, among others, "Indians or persons of Indian blood receiving an annuity or treaty money from the Crown, or who have at any time within three years prior to the said date received such annuity or treaty money."

13 *An Act to Amend the Statute Law*, SS 1916, c. 37, s. 1, amended the *Saskatchewan Election Act*, SS 1908, c. 2, which, by section 11, disfranchised "persons of the Chinese race" and "Indians." The *Equal Suffrage Statutory Law Amendment Act*, SA 1916, c. 5, s. 2 amended the *Alberta Election Act*, SA 1909, c. 3, which, by section 10, disfranchised "Indians."

14 *An Act to Amend the "Provincial Elections Act,"* SBC 1917, c. 23, ss. 3 and 4, amended the *Provincial Elections Act*, RSBC 1911, c. 72, which, by section 7, dictated that no "Chinaman, Japanese, Hindu, or Indian" could vote.

15 See, for example, "Laurier Is Converted to the Cause," *Calgary Herald*, 13 October 1916.

16 Catherine L. Cleverdon, *Woman Suffrage Movement in Canada: The Start of Liberation 1900–20*, 2nd ed. (1950; Toronto: University of Toronto Press, 1974), 41–4; *The Election Law Amendment Act, 1917*, SO 1917, c. 6 (assented to 12 April 1917, in force by order of the lieutenant governor in council, per s. 19), amending the *Ontario Election Act*, RSO 1914, c. 8; Proclamation, 50, no. 19 *Ontario Gazette* (12 May 1917): 577–8. The *Act to Amend the Ontario Voters' Lists Act*, SO 1917, c. 4, and the *Ontario Franchise Act*, SO 1917, c. 5, were also proclaimed 12 May 1917. Ontario women remained ineligible to be candidates.

17 Robert Craig Brown notes that, by 1 July 1917, only Prince Edward Island and Ontario still had Conservative governments: Robert Laird Borden, *A Biography*, vol. 2, *1914–1937* (Toronto: Macmillan, 1980), 99.

18 See Joan Sangster, *One Hundred Years of Struggle: The History of Women and the Vote in Canada* (Vancouver: UBC Press, 2018).

19 *War-time Elections Act*, SC 1917, c. 39 (*WTEA*); *Military Voters Act, 1917*, SC 1917, c. 34 (*MVA*).

20 See Oscar Douglas Skelton, *Life and Letters of Sir Wilfrid Laurier* (New York: Century Co., 1933), 2: 510–50; Roger Graham, *Arthur Meighen*, vol. 1, *The Door of Opportunity* (Toronto: Clarke Irwin, 1960), 170–6 (*Door of Opportunity*).

21 "Alberta Liberals Throw Out a Challenge to Siftonism," *Calgary News-Telegram*, 12 November 1917. See also Sangster, *One Hundred Years of Struggle*, 174–204; Tarah Brookfield, *Our Voices Must Be Heard: Women and the Vote in Ontario* (Vancouver: UBC Press, 2018), 155–72; and Brookfield, "Divided by the Ballot Box: The Montreal Council of Women and the 1917 Election," *Canadian Historical Review* 89 (2008): 473–501.

22 See, for example, "Women Get the Vote, 1916–1919," *Canada: A Country by Consent*, www.canadahistoryproject.ca/1914/1914-08-women-vote.html; Thompson, *Harvests of War*, 109–12. Brock Millman misinterprets the *MVA* and the *WTEA* in several ways and does not note the disfranchisement of women: *Polarity, Patriotism, and Dissent in Great War Canada, 1914–1919* (Toronto: University of Toronto Press, 2016), 171–2. The same can be said of Tim Cook's analysis in *Warlords: Borden, Mackenzie King, and Canada's World Wars* (Toronto: Penguin, 2012), 111. Robert Brown and Ramsay Cook note the selective enfranchisement of women and military voters but do

not acknowledge the effect on the women who were already provincially enfranchised and who expected to vote: *Canada 1896–1921: A Nation Transformed* (Toronto: McClelland and Stewart, 1974), 271.

23 See, for example, J.M. Beck, *Pendulum of Power: Canada's Federal Elections* (Scarborough, ON: Prentice-Hall, 1968), 136–76; W.L. Morton, "The Extension of the Franchise in Canada: A Study in Democratic Nationalism," in *Report of the Annual Meeting of the Canadian Historical Association* (Hamilton, ON, 24–25 May 1943), 79–80; E.A. Heaman, *A Short History of the State in Canada* (Toronto: University of Toronto Press, 2015), 159–60, 160–7; Emily van der Meulen, "Women and the Vote in Canada: A Brief Timeline," in *From Suffragette to Homesteader: Exploring British and Canadian Colonial Histories and Women's Politics through Memoir*, ed. van der Meulen (Halifax: Fernwood Publishing, 2018), 176; Maureen Moynagh and Nancy Forestell, "Unsettling Imperial Ties: Rethinking Suffrage in the Context of Settler Colonialism in Canada," in van der Meulen, *From Suffragette to Homesteader*, 126–41; and Denyse Baillargeon, *To Be Equals in Our Own Country: Women and the Vote in Quebec* (Vancouver: UBC Press, 2019). A commendable popular history is Elections Canada's *History of the Vote in Canada*, 2nd ed. (Ottawa: Office of the Chief Electoral Officer of Canada, 2007).

24 Cleverdon, *The Woman Suffrage Movement*, 42–3.

25 Carol Lee Bacchi, *Liberation Deferred? The Ideas of the English-Canadian Suffragists, 1877–1918* (Toronto: University of Toronto Press, 1983), 137–43. See also Joan Sangster, *One Hundred Years of Struggle: The History of Women and the Vote in Canada* (Vancouver: UBC Press, 2018), 193–9; Veronica Strong-Boag, *The Last Suffragist Standing: The Life and Times of Laura Marshall Jamieson* (Vancouver: UBC Press, 2018), 58–9; Brookfield, *Our Voices Must Be Heard*, 170; Brookfield, "Divided by the Ballot Box."

26 Robert Craig Brown, *Robert Laird Borden, A Biography*, vol. 2, *1914–1937* (Toronto: Macmillan, 1980), 100. See also Beck, *Pendulum of Power*, 139.

27 Graham, *Door of Opportunity*, 147, citing Borden's diary entry for 25 September 1917.

28 Onesiphore Turgeon and J.H. Sinclair believed Meighen had framed the *WTEA*. See *Debates*, 8 and 10 September 1917, 5557, 5567. R. Blake Brown identifies O'Connor as the author of the *WTEA* (and the general returning officer in 1917): "O'Connor, William Francis," *Dictionary of Canadian Biography* (*DCB*), vol. 16, http://www.biographi.ca/en/bio/o_connor_william_francis_16E.html. Desmond Morton attributes the *War Measures Act* to O'Connor, the *WTEA* to Meighen, and the *MVA* to O'Connor and Charles Doherty: Morton, "Polling the Soldier Vote: The Overseas

Campaign in the Canadian General Election of 1917," *Journal of Canadian Studies* 10, no. 4 (1975): 43. Undoubtedly this complex regime was a collective effort.

29 Graham, *Door of Opportunity*, 164–7.

30 *An Act to Enable Canadian Soldiers on Active Military Service during the Present War to Exercise Their Electoral Franchise*, SC 1915, c. 11, s. 1 (*Electoral Franchise Act 1915*). Under the *Militia Act*, RSC 1906, c. 41, s. 10, males over eighteen could serve voluntarily, and younger males could be buglers, trumpeters, and drummers.

31 *Electoral Franchise Act 1915*, ss. 1, 2(5), Schedules A and B.

32 Ibid., ss. 2(7)–(12). The provisions regarding the overseas vote went into force by proclamation of the King in Council in Britain on 5 May 1915. See *Canada Gazette, Part 2*, vol. 48, no. 46, 15 May 1915, 3597–8. Conservative rhetoric, often accepted without examination by later historians, ignored this earlier statute. See, for example, Cook, *Warlords*, 110, who footnotes Desmond Morton, even though Morton actually discusses the 1915 legislation. (See Morton, "Polling the Soldier Vote.") The objections Cook ascribes to Laurier in 1917 were actually raised in 1915.

33 *Military Forces Voting Act*, SBC 1916, c. 41; editorial, *Edmonton Bulletin*, 1 August 1916.

34 Morton, "Polling the Soldier Vote," 41–2.

35 See "Provincial Election on June Seven," *Wainwright Star*, 16 May 1917; "Mr Michener's Splendid Meeting: Disfranchising 35,000 Soldiers the Real Issue," *Red Deer News*, 30 May 1917; "The Sifton Touch," *Alberta Non-Partisan*, 23 November 1917; "The Elections," *Red Deer News*, 13 June 1917; *Soldiers' Representation Act*, SS 1917, c. 4; *An Act to Amend the Saskatchewan Election Act*, SS 1917, c. 5; *Alberta Military Representation Act*, SA 1917, c. 12.

36 *MVA*, s. 1, inserting para. 2(c) and s. 3 into the *Dominion Elections Act*, RSC 1906, c. 6 (*DEA*). See also Morton, "Polling the Soldier Vote," 43. The inclusion of "Indians" (unmentioned in 1915) was an element of the complex regime for Indigenous voters. As outlined below, the federal regime wrapped itself around the various provincial ones, accepting Indigenous disfranchisement in some conditions but rejecting it in others.

37 *MSA*, s. 3(1).

38 See *MVA*, s. 1, adding Part IV, s. 8(1) to the *DEA*.

39 PC 3322, 29 November 1917, *Canada Gazette, Part 2*, vol. 51, extra no. 2, 1 December 1917.

40 See "First Draft Called Out on January 3" and "A Wobbling Government Juggling with the Conscription Act before a Conscript Has Donned the Khaki," both *Calgary News-Telegram*, 8 December 1917.

41 See *MVA*, s. 1, adding Part IV, s. 2(c) to the *DEA*.

42 The problem was not just the temptations offered and logistical problems created by bags of unmarked ballots. The polling of military voters was to begin as soon as the candidates were confirmed, so presumably ballots had to be printed and transported to places like Halifax beforehand.

43 See, for example, Thompson, *Harvests of War*, 142–3.

44 See *MVA*, s. 1, inserting Part IV, ss. 3 and 12(4)–(5), and Forms A and B into the *DEA*.

45 *MVA*, s. 1, inserting Part IV, ss. 10(2) and 12 into the *DEA*; *Canada Gazette, Part 2*, vol. 51, extra, 27 November 1917. See also "Borden Names His Candidates," *Calgary News-Telegram*, 22 November 1917; "Endorsations by Party Leaders," *Calgary News-Telegram*, 26 November 1917.

46 P.C. 3159, 9 November 1917, in *Canada Gazette, Part 2*, vol. 51, extra no. 2, 1 December 1917, 5–6; Tim Cook, "Currie, Sir Arthur William," *DCB*, vol. 16, http://www.biographi.ca/en/bio/currie_arthur_william_16E.html; Desmond Morton, "Smart, Charles Allan," *DCB*, vol. 16, http://www.biographi.ca/en/bio/smart_charles_allan_16E.html; *Debates*, 10 September 1917, 5601–2. All three were in England.

47 *MVA*, ss. 8 and 9.

48 W.T.R. Preston, *My Generation of Politics and Politicians* (Toronto: D.A. Rose Publishing Company, 1927), 364–78. See also "Are Unionists Faking Messages from Soldiers in Old Country?" *Calgary News-Telegram*, 15 December 1917; "R.L. Challenged to Make Perley Cables Public," *Calgary News-Telegram*, 17 December 1917; and "Either Crookedness or Lying," *Calgary News-Telegram*, 5 December 1917.

49 Morton, "Polling the Military Vote," 48.

50 "Voting of Soldiers Overseas Slipping from R.L. Borden," *Calgary News-Telegram*, 6 December 1917.

51 Beck, *Pendulum of Power*, 145–6. Edmonton's Frank Oliver, for example, lost his seat because of the military vote, but the numbers are not self-evidently suspect. Overall, military voters were about 12.5 per cent of the electorate. In most ridings, about one-fifth of registered voters did not vote; also in most ridings, including Oliver's, this gap was larger than the number of military voters. In Calgary East and West, though, which were also vigorously contested, there were actually more military votes than missing registered voters, which may suggest either that Calgarians voted particularly enthusiastically or that military voters' attention was drawn to Calgary. See O.M. Biggar, *Return of the Thirteenth General Election for the House of Commons of Canada: Held on the 17th Day of December, 1917, and*

By-Elections Held during the Years 1916, 1917, 1918 and 1919 (Ottawa: Thomas Mulvey, 1920).

52 *The Electoral Franchise Act*, SC 1885, c. 40, ss. 2 and 3. On the debate about allowing propertied women to vote, see Sangster, *One Hundred Years of Struggle*, 40–2.

53 *Franchise Act, 1898*, SC 1898, c. 14, s. 5(a). See also Morton, "The Extension of the Franchise," 78–9.

54 *The North-West Territories' Representation Act, 1886*, SC 1886 (49 Vic.), c. 24, s. 4.

55 *Franchise Act, 1898*, s. 6(1).

56 *Dominion Elections Act*, SC 1900, c. 12, ss. 3(f), 4–6.

57 *DEA*, ss. 5–11, 31–3, 67–70.

58 See "Commons Defeats Woman Suffrage: Hon. 'Bob' Rogers Cracks Whip, Members Respond," *Globe*, 29 February 1916; *Debates*, 28 February 1916, 1189–206; *Debates*, 16 May 1917, 1485–8, 1489–90. See also Cleverdon, *Woman Suffrage Movement*, 114–17.

59 See, for example, "Premier Borden Replies to an Alberta Woman's Query," *Calgary Herald*, 3 March 1916; "Ontario Women Want Franchise: Premier Refuses," *Edmonton Bulletin*, 16 March 1916; and "From the New Voters to Sir Robert Borden," *Globe*, 13 September 1916.

60 In laying the groundwork for the *WTEA* in mid-1917, Borden's Conservatives took advantage of divisions within the women's movement to gain support for this plan. See "Women's Franchise: Its Manipulation," *Edmonton Bulletin*, 26 November 1917; Bacchi, *Liberation Deferred?*, 140–1; Sangster, *One Hundred Years of Struggle*, 193–9.

61 "Promises Franchise to Canadian Women: Premier Borden, if Re-Elected, Will Also Extend Naturalization to Women Aliens," *New York Times*, 20 September 1917.

62 *WTEA*, s. 1(c), replacing s. 32 of the *DEA*. Provisions also accommodated different provincial regimes regarding residence and domicile.

63 *Debates*, 6 September 1917, 5417–8.

64 *WTEA*, s. 1(d), adding s. 33A to the *DEA*.

65 *WTEA*, s. 1(e), adding s. 33B to the *DEA*.

66 *WTEA*, paras. 2(d) and (e), amending s. 67(1) and adding s..

67 The *Ontario Election Act*, RSO 1914, c. 8, s. 22(1) barred from voting every "unenfranchised Indian of whole or part Indian blood residing or having his domicile among Indians or on an Indian Reserve." The term "unenfranchised" referred to one who had not gone through a legal process that converted a portion of reserve land into the person's

own, privately held land, pursuant to the *Indian Act*, RSC 1906, c. 81. The *Election Law Amendment Act*, 1917, SO 1917, c. 6, together with the *Ontario Franchise Act, 1917*, SO 1917, c. 5, permitted "Indians" in military service to vote provincially, but their female relatives remained disfranchised. The *Act to Confer the Electoral Franchise upon Women*, SC 1918, c. 20, which extended the federal vote to women broadly, based the franchise on provincial qualifications and removed the old language lifting provincial disqualifications, leaving many women disqualified. The *Dominion By-Elections Act, 1919*, SC 1919 (2d sess.), c. 48, s. 2(B) explicitly excluded on-reserve Indians from the finally uniform federal franchise.

68 See *Debates*, 6 and 10 September 1917, 5415–21, 5581. E. Cora Hind, *Why Women Should Support Union Government* (Ottawa: Union Government Publicity Bureau, 1917); "A Mother," *Women of the West We Want You* (Winnipeg: Kingdon Print Co. for Union Government Central Publicity Committee, 1917). See also Graham, *Door of Opportunity*, 168–70.

69 See, for example, "Support Union Government," *Calgary News-Telegram*, 7 December 1917.

70 *Debates*, 6 and 10 September 1917, 5416, 5583–4. Arguments about married women's citizenship being complicated because they might be, or have married, naturalized Canadians whom the Unionists also intended to disfranchise were voiced as well (5578–79, per Borden).

71 See, for example, *Debates*, 6 and 10 September 1917, 5573–4, 5577, 5602–4, 5615–18; "Canada's Duty to Assist in War, Laurier States," *Calgary News-Telegram*, 10 November 1917.

72 "The Editor's Notes," *Calgary News-Telegram*, 21 December 1917.

73 Faced with food shortages and the political risks of conscripting the last young men working on farms and in munitions factories – or, alternatively, conscripting mainly urbanites – Unionists made inconsistent promises associated with an Order-in-Council passed 3 December but not published until 31 December. It let the minister of militia and defence, at his discretion, exempt from military service anyone in agriculture whose exemption application had been refused by a military tribunal and on appeal. See *Canada Gazette, Part 2*, vol. 51, no. 27, 5 January 1918, 2245.

74 See, for example, "No Vote for Stepmothers," *Calgary News-Telegram*, 12 December 1917; "No Disfranchisement for the Men Who Have Sought to Be Exempted," *Calgary News-Telegram*, 20 November 1917; "Here Is a Sample of Tactics Used by Unionists," *Calgary News-Telegram*, 15 December

1917. Correspondence from December 1917 and January 1918 in the papers of Temiskaming district labour candidate Arthur Roebuck alleges Unionist manipulation of the enumeration process and the enthusiastic fanning of anti-Quebec prejudice: see Archives of Ontario, Arthur Wentworth Roebuck fonds, December 1917–21, F45-MU 2458, B294815.

75 "Lax Enumeration Swamps Toronto Appeal Tribunals," *Calgary News-Telegram*, 8 December 1917.

76 See "Kitchener Anti-Conscriptionists Howl Down Sir Robert Borden," *Globe*, 26 November 1917; "The Two-Faced Anti-German Game," *Calgary News-Telegram*, 4 December 1917; "A Most Deplorable Incident," *Calgary News-Telegram*, 28 November 1917.

77 See, for example, "Wholesale Disfranchisement of U.S. Settlers in Western Canada," *Calgary News-Telegram*, 12 December 1917; "The Hand of the Siftons," *Calgary News-Telegram*, 7 December 1917; "Notice to Electors Whose Names Have Been Omitted from the Voters' Lists," *Calgary News-Telegram*, 17 December 1917; "Who May Vote and Who May Not Cast a Ballot," *Calgary News-Telegram*, 12 December 1917.

78 "Liberals Will Predominate in the New Parliament" and "Majority of 48 for the Unionist Gov't," both *Calgary News-Telegram*, 18 December 1917.

79 A.H.F. Lefroy, *Should Canadian Women Have the Parliamentary Vote?* (Toronto: Equal Franchise League, 1913).

80 *Debates*, 16 May and 10 September 1917, 1503–23, 5572 (Laurier), 5594–95 (W.F. Maclean). See also *Who Shall Rule?* (Ottawa: Central Information Office of the Canadian Liberal Party, 1917), 9–10.

81 *Debates*, 16 May 1917, 1482–90. As described above, the list of disqualifications from the 1898 act referred to "persons."

82 "Commons Defeats Woman Suffrage: Hon. 'Bob' Rogers Cracks Whip, Members Respond," *Globe*, 29 February 1916; *Debates*, 28 February 1916, 1189–1206. See also Cleverdon, *Woman Suffrage Movement*, 114–22.

83 *Debates*, 16 May 1917, 1493, 1499–1502, 1506, 1514–15.

84 Ibid., 1492–9. This opinion may have been developed in 1916 by William Francis O'Connor, who advised Doherty and Meighen. See Robert J. Sharpe and Patricia McMahon, *The Origins and Legacy of the Fight for Legal Personhood* (Toronto: University of Toronto Press for the Osgoode Society, 2007), 75–7.

85 *Debates*, 16 May 1917, 1503, 1505, 1508–10.

86 Ibid., 6 September 1917, 5415–17. See also Cleverdon, *Woman Suffrage Movement*, 122–30.

87 Lyndsay Campbell, "Race, Upper Canadian Constitutionalism and 'British Justice,'" *Law and History Review* 33, no. 1 (2015): 41–91.

88 *Quong-Wing v. R.* (1914), 49 SCR 440 at 448. Further, a province could appropriately protect white women, even if doing so might "operate prejudicially to one class or race of people" (449). See also *Cunningham v. Tomey Homma* (1902), [1903] AC 151 (JC PC).

89 *Quong-Wing v. R.* (1914), 49 SCR 440 at 452.

90 Sangster, *One Hundred Years of Struggle*, 196.

91 See, for example, *Debates*, 10 September 1917, 5568 (J.H. Sinclair), 5576 (Laurier).

92 Ibid., 8 and 10 September 1917, 5553 (Oliver), 5561 (McCraney), 5573 (Meighen), 5582 (Buchanan), 5582–5 (Meighen). The debate over Europeans often pivoted on whether they could be treated like Asian Canadians or Indigenous people, whose disfranchisement was seen as self-evidently unproblematic. See, for example, A.K. Maclean, *Debates*, 10 September 1917, 5597.

93 Ibid., 10 September 1917, 5578–9.

94 The qualification here is that, for Meighen, the legal entitlements accompanying naturalization were also provisional for men. He explicitly denied that disfranchising those of "alien enemy birth" or "blood" or who spoke "the language of an alien enemy" amounted to breaking a promise to them: *Debates*, 10 September 1917, 5584.

95 See, for example, "Soldiers Are Refused Their Voting Rights," *Red Deer News*, 4 April 1917.

96 A "right," on the other hand, arose when the law imposed a duty on someone: the second person's "liberty" to do or do not was, through the law, turned into a "duty" with respect to the first person, which gave the first person a legal "right." See Wesley Newcomb Hohfeld, "Some Fundamental Legal Conceptions as Applied in Judicial Reasoning," *Yale Law Journal* 23, no. 1 (1913): 28–44.

97 *Debates*, 6 and 10 September 1917, 5416, 5420, 5577–8, 5584, 5603; Cleverdon, *Woman Suffrage Movement*, 125.

98 On the division in the women's movement between those who insisted on women's equality versus the "progressives" who emphasized the instrumental value of women's political participation, see Sangster, *One Hundred Years of Struggle*, 196–9.

99 See, for example, Meighen, *Debates*, 10 September 1917, 5586. J.W. Edwards, a Tory for Frontenac, referred to the women enfranchised under the *WTEA* as "selected for this honour on this occasion": *Debates*, 10 September 1917, 5571.

100 *Debates*, 16 May, 6 and 10 September 1917, 1477–1508, 1512, 5421, 5574.

101 Strong-Boag, *Last Suffragist Standing*, 58.

102 See *An Act to Confer the Electoral Franchise upon Women*, SC 1918, c. 20, assented to 24 May 1918 (which contained the important proviso, in section 3, that no new voters' lists were to be prepared for any by-election before 1 January 1919, which meant that the *WTEA* and the *MVA* continued to operate for by-elections); and *An Act to Amend the Dominion Elections Act*, SC 1919 (2d sess.), c. 48, s. 2, assented to 7 July 1919. Under section 2D, the 1919 act also provided that women could be candidates, thus cleverly undercutting arguments based on the old wording of the *DEA* that favoured viewing women, as British subjects, as "persons."

103 *Dominion Elections Act*, SC 1920, c. 46, s. 29.

8

Discipline as Deterrence: Labour Relations and the Silencing of Feminist Labour Activists

JOAN SANGSTER AND JULIA SMITH

When flight attendant and union activist Senka Dukovich told a *Globe and Mail* reporter in 1987 that her employer, Wardair, preferred flight attendants to be "squeaky-clean sex objects," she could not imagine the furore her comment would cause. By 1987, some media commentators, certainly feminists, took it for granted that airlines marketed the appearance of their female flight attendants as part of their "service," as much as promoting their food and comfortable seats. Battles had been fought, some won, some lost, in both the United States and Canada over the way flight attendants were portrayed in advertising. Numerous grievances by unionized flight attendants dealt with appearance issues.[1] Dukovich's comment, however, incurred the wrath of her employer. Wardair responded with a personal letter slapping her with a two-week unpaid suspension for maliciously misrepresenting her employer. Even if Dukovich had imagined she might be disciplined, she was also a lawyer who knew that previous arbitrations on the right to criticize one's employer were on her side. Yet this was not the case when her union, the Canadian Union of Public Employees (CUPE), filed a complaint about her suspension with the Canada Labour Relations Board (CLRB). To its surprise, CUPE lost the case in a two-to-one decision.[2]

This chapter asks why the union lost. If Dukovich's CLRB case seemed to contradict precedents, what made it unique? How did the political economy and gendered labour relations of the airline industry, and Wardair in particular, shape this case? What part did Dukovich's feminist politics play in the CLRB judgment? Certainly, the dissenting adjudicator, who wrote an extraordinarily strong rebuke, thought it was critical to Wardair's decision to discipline this employee. Why did Dukovich's statements about Wardair's appearance policies, which today seem common sense, provoke such a virulent response that resonated with two members of the Labour Board? How did this decision shape future cases of employees disciplined for criticizing their employers and efforts of women in the airline industry to secure enhanced dignity in the workplace?

The Players

When she gave the offending interview to the newspapers, Senka Dukovich was a flight attendant (FA) and lawyer who had established herself as an activist and expert on issues regarding women, work, and inequality. Dukovich grew up in Mississauga and attended McGill University before completing a law degree at York University; she was called to the bar in 1975. She began working as a flight attendant while she was in law school, since the flexible work hours could be accommodated to the academic schedule.[3] Originally hired by Air Canada in 1973, Dukovich brought multilingual talents to the job; she spoke English, French, and Serbo-Croatian (she immigrated at age nine with her family, refugees from Yugoslavia). She left Air Canada to work for Wardair, believing the timetable of a smaller, international charter company would be more compatible with her studies. By the time of the grievance, Dukovich had been employed at Wardair for fourteen years, some of those as an in-flight service manager.

While working as a flight attendant, Dukovich was also honing her activist chops and media skills, especially regarding issues of gender inequality. A desire "to travel and be respected" had originally led her to the job; however, she soon saw the lack of respect afforded to many female FAs. During one job interview, a male interviewer asked Dukovich to turn around – clearly, her body was on display – and the original contract she signed with Air Canada stipulated that she had to leave her position when she turned thirty-two or after ten years of service, whichever came first.[4]

Experiences of discrimination and inequality, combined with her legal training, led Dukovich to become involved in her union, the Canadian Air Line Flight Attendants Association (CALFAA, which merged with CUPE in 1986) and its Airline Division Women's Committee (founded by CALFAA in 1982). She served in numerous roles, including president of her local, the local contract chair, chair of the union's negotiating committee, and chair of the Women's Committee. In 1987, she was the third assistant chairperson of her local and an active member of the Women's Committee. As well, she had served as a representative on the employer-employee equity committee.

With a thorough understanding of human rights and labour law, she provided input to union discussions about human rights complaints. One Wardair complaint related to the airline's vision requirements, which FAs felt were related to appearance, not safety. Wardair refused to allow FAs to wear eyeglasses; even those who normally wore contacts had to book off work if, for some reason, they were unable to wear them temporarily. With Dukovich's aid, the union filed a complaint with the Canadian Human Rights Commission (CHRC) and won a positive decision and a financial award for flight attendant Angie Schaepsmeyer.[5] As Dukovich remembers, not only did she experience the same contact lens rule, but she also discovered the company would rather pay her to stay home when she was visibly pregnant in 1975.[6] Most airlines grounded pregnant FAs, claiming safety concerns, but CALFAA argued in court and human rights cases during the 1970s that pregnancy rules were really about appearance: airlines did not think passengers wanted to look at a woman with a pregnant belly. CALFAA lost many of these legal battles, but its persistent arguments contributed to a longer-term win for women: new rights for pregnant workers were added to human rights and labour legislation in 1985.[7]

Dukovich became known outside CALFAA/CUPE circles as a human rights advocate. In 1978, she was a panellist at a public forum on sexual harassment in the workplace. Her comments, reported in newspapers across the country, are worth quoting, given their similarity to the ones she later made, earning her a suspension: "Stewardesses," she argued, "are expected to play up their 'attractive image,' if not outright sexuality, by the airlines that employ them," adding, "No wonder people think hitchhikers and stewardesses are fair game. The airlines have tried to stress our sexuality." Dukovich explained that "the flight attendants' union has helped several female members fight sexual discrimination."[8] Indeed, she had been involved in some of these grievances, often serving as the union's media spokesperson. While her expertise made her a valuable asset to her union, it also made her a target for Wardair, an airline known for its upstart owner, hard-line negotiations with its workers, and hostility to unions.

Dukovich's suspension was not the first time Wardair's testy relations with employees made the news. Labour relations were coloured by the personal history of the airline's founder and "hands-on" owner, Max Ward.[9] A veteran of the Royal Canadian Air Force, Ward established a bush airline in 1952, ferrying supplies and passengers across the north. A decade later, he astutely expanded to international holiday charter flights. Though the company skirted bankruptcy several times, by the mid-1980s it was thriving and looking for new conquests; it even attempted a fare war with the behemoth Air Canada. The year of Dukovich's complaint, Wardair employed 2,664 people and reported sales of $491.1 million and assets of $456.4 million.[10] It prided itself on awards for good customer service that included "roomy seats, fine wines and well-prepared meals served on Royal Doulton china."[11] Ward's successful pathway from bush pilot to entrepreneur epitomized the "self-made man."[12] The National Film Board of Canada even produced a film about him in 1984, fittingly titled *Max Ward*.[13]

While some celebrated Ward's approach, media coverage (even celebratory articles) also mentioned the airlines' "turbulent" labour relations. The airline "pioneered" hated two-tier contracts that gave incoming workers lower pay than veterans, still a point of contention in negotiations in 1987–8. By the time of the Dukovich case, in-flight service managers (ISMs) had become managers par excellence: FAs complained that some ISMs were not trained, experienced flight attendants who knew the job and were there only to find fault. Adding insult to injury, in the early 1980s, Wardair flight attendants were paid less than their counterparts at other major airlines.[14]In keeping with the broader backlash against labour occurring at the time, Wardair played hardball with its workers, especially FAs. When flight attendants staged rotating twenty-four-hour strikes in August 1981, Wardair refused to fly FAs stranded in Europe back to Canada; the company reportedly demanded that competitors do the same and asked the hotel where the workers were staying to evict them.[15] That same year, when Wardair flight attendants staged a thirty-week strike, the company hired 400 non-unionized replacement workers and then fired all of its unionized flight attendants based in Alberta.[16] It threatened to use strikebreakers again in 1984 and 1987. Wardair also targeted union leaders: at one point, most of the Toronto union executive was fired, but they were rehired once a complaint was laid with the CLRB.[17]

It was no exaggeration to say that labour relations at Wardair were historically "bitter."[18] The most recent public conflict prior to, and leading into, Dukovich's case, involved Robert Elder, a FA who was told to remove an earring in his left ear if he wanted to keep his job. The union grieved this as an unwritten rule, not covered in the grooming manual, and one that discriminated against men's personal appearance choices. Veteran arbitrator and labour relations scholar David Beatty upheld the grievance, writing a significant decision that reflected the sense evolving since the 1960s in both the United States and Canada that the employer could not *absolutely* dictate clothing and appearance.[19] Workers had some right to "self-expression," though not if their appearance threatened an employer's business. Beatty found that Elder's earring did not constitute such a threat. Wardair would not accept the decision, and Max Ward's public, homophobic comments linking earrings to gay men and fear of AIDS did not help public relations. Wardair turned to its legal last resort, a judicial review of Beatty's decision. More common in the 1960s and 1970s than later in the century, judicial reviews were the subject of some debate. Legal scholars called for a measure of judicial "restraint" in overseeing arbitral decisions based in administrative law, but, in any case, the courts could ascertain if an arbitrator erred in the law, for example by overstepping their jurisdictional reach.[20] Wardair lost again, despite a dissenting judge who felt compelled to vent about the absurdity of businesses not being able to police earrings and other inappropriate attire.[21]

The press provided detailed coverage of this case and, again, Dukovich was interviewed for the union perspective. In an article published on 28 February 1987, less than one month before the publication of the articles containing the comments for which she would be disciplined, Dukovich spoke about the company's micro-management of female flight attendants' bodies: "They have regulations that dictate to women (flight attendants) the type of earrings they can wear, suitable hairstyles – even the style of bra that should be worn, if you can believe that ... They do have draconian regulations. They're living back in the nineteenth century."[22] By March 1987, then, Wardair appeared to be on a labour relations losing streak, one that received a great deal of public attention and in which Senka Dukovich often played a prominent role.

The Case in Context

The Dukovich case revealed the complicated landscape of labour relations that flight attendants negotiated. The union could file an individual grievance on behalf of an FA if their rights under the collective agreement were infringed; a policy grievance on behalf of the union membership was also an option, if more complicated. The majority of Canadian workers fell under provincial labour law regimes and their labour relations boards, but air travel was federally regulated, so flight attendants dealt with the Canadian Labour Relations Board. Like other labour relations boards, it could draw on international or provincial cases in its reasoning. If an employee experienced discrimination, as it was then defined by federal human rights legislation, they could file a complaint with the Canadian Human Rights Commission, or a collectivity could file a policy complaint relating to systemic discrimination of a particular group.

Dukovich's suspension grew out of her media interviews relating to the decision of the union to file an omnibus complaint with the Canadian Human Rights Commission about systemic discrimination in the airline industry. The prospect of launching a human rights complaint had been discussed for some time in the national CUPE Airline Division Women's Committee. At a November 1986 meeting, members decided to engage in a fact-finding mission to explore an omnibus complaint dealing with systemic discrimination across all airlines. Dukovich took on a leading role in this effort. Since other airlines did not have the "documented specifics" that existed for Wardair, the complaint was eventually narrowed to Wardair.[23] Nevertheless, a ruling against one airline would undoubtedly benefit all FAs working in the industry. Dukovich knew that an individual complainant might be a strategic mistake: another Wardair flight attendant, Luanne Burns, had previously attempted to file an individual complaint but "was told to deal with her own union."[24] According to one human rights journal, the CHRC told Burns that "their policy was not to deal with complaints on dress codes."[25] The omnibus complaint provided a solution: it would address systemic discrimination, of which appearance rules and sexualization were a part. The complaint drafted by Dukovich, with some discussion with CHRC staff, cited contravention of multiple sections of the Human Rights Code, including pursuing a "policy" of discrimination against, and harassment of, women employees. Marshalling statistical evidence, it claimed that the employer discriminated against "visible minorities" in hiring and practised age discrimination against "older" employees, pressuring them into retiring. The press summed up the complaint simply and succinctly: the only FAs hired were "white, fair and female," and feminine appearance was regulated unrelentingly using intimidation and harassment.[26]

Dukovich, acting for the Women's Committee, completed the CHRC intake form, which posited discrimination as a historically "pervasive and policy problem" widespread among the airlines. Prior to submitting the form, she received verbal permission to proceed from her local's union chairperson, Ross Nichol, though he asked for a final copy before it was submitted. She had sent him a copy, which, for logistical reasons, he did not receive before the official submission. During the labour board hearing, Wardair pointed to the submission timeline as evidence that Dukovich was acting solely on her own initiative; disputing that assertion, Nichol confirmed that Dukovich was acting on behalf of the Women's Committee and CUPE.

Knowing the value of media coverage, Dukovich, with Nichol's assent, approached some reporters, who might give the complaint the public visibility the union wanted. Quotes, to which Wardair took exception, also came from the February 1987 interviews following the Elder decision that Dukovich gave to *Toronto Star* and *Globe and Mail* reporters about FA work. *Globe* reporter Robert MacLeod did not deem them "newsworthy" enough to publish at the time; however, the CHRC complaint provided the perfect "hook" for a story. The press zeroed in on the "juiciest" quotes from Dukovich. As well as her "squeaky-clean" remark, they relayed her comments about subtle pressure on older women to leave their positions, fingernail and hair inspections that treated adults like "five-year olds," and rules about shaving underarms and the type of brassieres required. Dukovich charged that Wardair used FAs as "window dressing" to sell seats, making a comparison to other sexist advertising: Wardair "uses women flight attendants like the half-naked woman perched on the sports car in an ad."[27] They are entitled to require women to be well groomed, she stressed, but "they can't regulate underwear, your smile or how much leg you show." Dukovich and Nichol surmised that publicity about the human rights complaint would bring sexist practices to public light. They were right: the story was picked up in papers across the country.

On the heels of articles published in the *Globe and Mail* and *Toronto Star* on 21 March 1987, Wardair's director of cabin services, Peter Bolton, sent a letter reprimanding Dukovich to her home on 3 April. The personal nature of Wardair's reproof was underlined by its disregarding the standard policy of contacting union representatives through the union. Bolton explained that Wardair was "investigating" but took issue with her comments. In her response, Dukovich stressed that her comments were made in her capacity as a union officer and asked that all correspondence go to the union. Wardair clarified that it was not concerned with her right to file a human rights complaint (to do otherwise would have landed them in hot water), but it asked for a meeting with her and union representatives, at which Wardair managers expressed concern with her "defamatory" comments. Dukovich knew the law: in recent decisions, union representatives were given considerable leeway to criticize their employers. She and CUPE made it clear that she was acting in her capacity as a union representative, a point that Wardair conceded.[28]

She and the union were mildly conciliatory. She noted her lack of control over how her words were reported: journalists focused on the most sensational quotes and "edited the hell out of the article." She later testified that her comments were "not presented in the proper perspective" by the reporter.[29] This was far from the contrite apology Wardair sought. The company responded with a two-week suspension for Dukovich, again conveyed through a personal letter to her home. Wardair claimed she should have brought these matters to the company through the bargaining table, but its primary objection was the "untruths" she uttered: she made statements "without foundation" that were "frivolous, vexatious and disparaging," and they had a negative impact on Wardair's business and the morale of its employees.[30] Although Wardair was at pains to assert it was not punishing her for lodging the human rights complaint, many of the elements of her interview that it objected to were intrinsic to the complaint.[31] To union activists, it seemed clear that management was punishing Dukovich for her union activities and her role in the human rights complaint, a view CUPE repeated in the CLRB hearing.

CUPE filed a complaint with the CLRB, citing sections 110, 184, and 187 of the *Canada Labour Code*, which dealt with "unfair" practices in industrial relations. Added to the code in 1972, section 187 has gone through a series of amendments; since 1985 it has referred to something different than unfair practices. The most relevant sections cited by CUPE were 110 and 184: the latter prohibited the employer from "intimidating, threatening or otherwise disciplining" (by suspending, laying off, transferring, changing pay or conditions, and so on) an employee for union activity. These sections were intended to protect employees from employers who used their power to inhibit union activity with various forms of discipline and reprisal.

The hearing took eighteen days, spread over a number of months, from January to August 1988. Some of the records pertaining to the case remain inaccessible, though testimony was covered in the published decision.[32] Before the case could proceed, the employer attempted to have it removed from the CLRB on jurisdictional grounds, stating that it should be a union grievance. The union could have tried either or both avenues for redress, and it did, in fact, later file a grievance relating to the excessive discipline of Dukovich, but it went to the CLRB first. One consideration might have been the absence of a non-discrimination clause in the union's collective agreement with the company, which otherwise might have been the preferable avenue for filing a grievance. CUPE had consistently demanded such a clause in bargaining, but Wardair had always adamantly refused, and it was usually traded off for other gains.

A board of three adjudicators, Chair Brian Keller, Jacques Archambault, and Linda Parsons, heard Wardair's arguments. Keller had worked in employment relations in both the private sector and senior government before starting his arbitration practice around 1988. Archambault, the union nominee, was a member of the professional corporation of industrial relations counsellors and had joined a Montreal law firm in 1984 to head up its labour section. Parsons, a corporate lawyer and the employer nominee, was a relative newcomer, having been called to the bar in 1980. They all concurred with CUPE that the case belonged at the Labour Relations Board.

The board was startled by the increasing number of cases like Dukovich's: for the first fourteen years of its tenure, it had no such cases, but it had heard four in the previous nine months. In a period of employer retrenchment and state efforts to constrain labour's rights, this is not surprising. Indeed, retrenchment was evident in the airline industry. Deregulation was in full swing, and carriers were looking for savings through suppressed wage increases and reductions to the workforce – and they were succeeding.[33] Workers in the private and public sectors were attempting to use the media to publicize their opposition to staffing cuts, efforts to freeze wages, and other regressive measures. Employers fought back.

Despite the historical dearth of cases on point, the CLRB had considerable precedent from other labour jurisdictions to draw from; most of the cases it cited were provincial arbitrations, not CLRB hearings. Until the 1960s, the common law of master and servant (*Edwards v. Levy*, 1860) was still cited by some employers as justification for punishment of workers disciplined for "out of the workplace" behaviour that supposedly damaged their reputation. Employees were disciplined "for insulting and insubordinate behavior as to be incompatible with the continuance of the relationship of employer and employee."[34] As a relic of the past, the master and servant admonition that employees owed employers "fidelity" was less salient by the 1980s, as arbitrations questioned generalized claims on workers' "loyalty," seeking more stringent definitions of the harm supposedly caused to the employer.[35] To fire someone, for instance, employers had to prove that other workers had good reason to refuse to work with the person or, most important, provide concrete evidence that the worker's comments or actions damaged the employer's reputation or obligations and harmed or inhibited its business.[36] Significant decisions had also ascertained that even *illegal* out-of-workplace misconduct by a worker, such as theft – unless directly relevant to job performance – should not result in discharge, since the "employer was not the custodian of the grievor's character."[37]

Discipline for damaging an employer's reputation through the media was becoming more of a contentious issue by the 1980s. Canadian decisions were moving towards rough agreement that union representatives could be extremely critical of their employer, as long as they "acted in good faith" and made the comments in the course of their union duties. Crucially, the comments could not be intentionally "malicious" or "knowingly false or reckless"; this language was imported into Canada from US National Labour Relations Board decisions.[38] If there was increasingly arbitral tolerance for public criticism of employers, there was also a "red line" that union officers could not cross, though arbitrators resisted defining it with "precise guidelines."[39] To recommend "one general response," argued George Adams, arbitrator in the case of a nurse accused of damaging the reputation of a St. Catharines hospital in the press, was too restrictive. Arbitrators' jobs, after all, involved parsing the specificities of each case while also remaining attentive to legal precedent and social context.[40]

The union seemed to have a strong, straightforward case. As a union officer, Dukovich had a right to voice harsh criticisms of her employer, including offering her own subjective point of view. Recent Canadian cases provided backup for this perspective, including a couple of cases that involved Canada Post. Not surprisingly, with a rocky labour relations history, Canada Post was sensitive to workers' public criticisms (and even tried to implement a policy forbidding them to be critical). A vice-president of the Maritime branch of the Canadian Postmasters and Assistants Association was suspended for five days for publicly criticizing proposed changes to rural services that workers believed would lead to job loss. She admitted she was politicizing the issue by urging people to contact their members of Parliament, but the board found for the union.[41] In another Canada Post arbitration in 1988, in which Linda Parsons was an arbitrator, an official of the Letter Carriers Union spoke to a televised session of the Port Coquitlam City Council in British Columbia, attempting to rouse political support against community mailboxes replacing home delivery. In the process, he denigrated the corporation's policy as "constructed on a whim" and perhaps involving "misspent money." The adjudicators admitted that the official "seemed to speak off the top of his head," with some "degree of rhetorical exaggeration and half-truths" but he, too, won his case.[42]

Also revealing is a decision involving a Quebecair strike. A female FA and union officer was dismissed after she told the media that flight attendants no longer felt safe flying because of a strike by ground employees. After FAs also walked off the job, she gave concrete examples of problems on two recent flights, admitting that FAs wanted to inform public opinion "because ... if you only tell it to the employer, they won't do anything." Quebecair claimed that the statements damaged its business, which seems hard to argue with, since no one wants to fly on an airline compromising safety. Yet, the FA's comments were given "a certain immunity" by the adjudicators, and she won back her job. "Recourse to the media" in union disputes, they recognized, was becoming "standard," and union officials have "wider latitude" than other employees in their speech.[43]

Safety was also at issue in the St. Catharines hospital case often cited by other arbitrators. Speaking to the media, a nurse criticized the employer's failure to follow a commissioned report on staffing; she implied that a recent death in the intensive care unit might be attributed to staffing changes and inadequate nursing coverage. The employer filed a complaint against her with the College of Nurses (which was rejected) and disciplined her for untrue statements that "dramatized and sensationalized for [the union's] political gain." The decision encompassed numerous issues, but arbitrator Adams was clear on union officials' latitude for free speech: they should be allowed to express "strong disagreement" in "unflattering terms," and it was inevitable that unions would "politicize" workplace issues, looking for public support. Nor did their comments need to be "timely," made during a strike or over a specific collective bargaining issue, since ongoing union activities, such as "organizing drives, negotiations, grievances," were all part of a naturally adversarial labour-management environment.[44]

Arbitrations also clarified that the "political ideology of the union official" should not elicit discipline or dismissal. A path-breaking ruling involving the Canadian Broadcasting Corporation and the Alliance of Canadian Cinema, Television and Radio Artists bolstered union officials' right to voice their political opinions within union venues without being disciplined for violating the broadcaster's policy on political "neutrality" in reporting. This CLRB ruling came down decisively on the side of unions' rights to engage in political criticism.[45]

While many arbitrations veered towards tolerance of criticism, some upheld employer discipline. Free speech was always more constrained for public servants, who, it was presumed, had *a priori* acquiesced to limitations on expression of their political opinions. In a public sector grievance, an arbitrator warned that workers' "public denunciation of their superiors" is "incompatible with a good relationship and may be interpreted as misconduct." The employee was there to render a "service," and that meant refraining from "attempting to defeat or frustrate what the employer is trying to do, whether the employer is wise or unwise in trying to do it."[46]

Nonetheless, in both the public and private sector, the nature of employees' critique and the context in which it generated publicity were assessed. In another Canada Post dispute, a local union president gave an interview to a New Brunswick radio station in which he confirmed that he had called for the removal of his boss, the Campbellton postmaster. The local argued that services were declining due to the postmaster's "gross negligence" and that his "paternalistic," hostile relationship with workers had reduced morale to an all-time low. Refusing to retract the statement, the union president was suspended for ten days, but the arbitration reduced it to one day, faulting him for not using the collective bargaining process to complain (even though he maintained that the local postmaster stymied all grievances). The right to criticize employers about "terms and conditions of employment" was construed quite broadly, but this did not sanction personal "denunciations" of employers in "unrestrained" language.[47] Attacks on individual managers were, however, somewhat different from Dukovich's criticism of company policies.

The overall tendency, then, was to allow very wide, though not absolute, criticism, with more rigid rules for civil servants. As a recent summary of the right to criticize indicates, union officials can make statements about management that are "vivid and unflattering, rude, discourteous, hurtful, distressing, belligerent, intemperate" or contain "modest exaggerations and half-truths."[48] Vulgarity, profanity, and anger against forepersons and managers were countenanced in the workplace, particularly by union stewards, whom arbitrators said should not be "muzzled into quiet complacency by the threat of discipline by the employer."[49] Of course, decisions about workplace relations were historically gendered: when dealing with men or male-dominated workplaces, the general assumption was that employer-employee interactions could reflect an "ungentlemanly" rough masculinity, including profanity, nastiness, and anger.[50] Perhaps "feminine" jobs like FA were seen differently.

In summary, one could be profane to a manager; claim publicly that the workplace endangered consumers; do something illegal outside the workplace; use exaggeration to rouse public support; and speak about political issues of relevance to the membership. Saying that FAs were portrayed as "squeaky-clean sex objects," however, was out of line.

Wardair's Attack and CUPE's Defence

Wardair's case had multiple attack points. It disputed whether Dukovich spoke for the union; claimed her comments were patently false; and argued that her deliberately "malicious and reckless" remarks hurt Wardair's reputation and incurred harm to the business. The airline astutely selected as its lead lawyer Frederick von Veh, who had decades of experience in employment law and a particular interest in aviation, having represented the Canadian Air Line Pilots Association, done work for the Commission of Inquiry on Aviation Safety, and served as an arbitrator for a contentious case involving an Air Canada pilot demoted after his plane crashed, killing two people.[51] CUPE's lawyer, Michael Church, was newer to the field, having been called to the bar only in 1981; he was employed by Caley Wray, a firm specializing in union-side law, where he continues to practice.

On the first count, the claim that Dukovich acted alone, Wardair failed to make its case. All three adjudicators ultimately agreed that she had acted as a union official. Yet, throughout the hearing, Wardair lawyers continued to insinuate that Dukovich had overstepped her role and was not *really* representing union interests. Proving that she had not been acting as a union official would have rendered her more legally vulnerable. Thus, company lawyers made much of the fact that Nichol had not seen the final version of the human rights complaint before it was submitted, claiming that Dukovich proceeded without proper approval. Despite Nichol's testimony that the union supported the complaint, counsel for the employer insinuated that Dukovich sidestepped procedures to pursue a pet political project.

The company also asserted she did not represent the rank and file. Von Veh pointed out that most members did not know about the complaint until after it was filed, nor, he said, did they care about it; Dukovich was "acting without her co-workers' knowledge and consent" because she had her own "personal agenda." She was not just politically out of control but personally malicious, as she "was acting on her own to get back at inflight supervisors."[52] His charge misrepresented union administrative practices: all complaints, grievances, and so on, were not taken to the entire membership, a fact noted by Adams in the *St Catharines* case when he spoke of the broader "scope of authority" exercised by union officials.[53] Regardless, the strategy to undermine Dukovich's official role was intended to isolate her from the union. It also implied that the Women's Committee, for which she acted, was not really as "official" or important as other union bodies. Comparing Dukovich's case to previous arbitrations, one wonders if she might have been treated differently had she been a union official criticizing job cuts, even with intemperate words.

Even though all the adjudicators ultimately conceded that she was acting as an official, Keller and Parsons simultaneously undermined this defence by implying that her case was not as sound as other ones protecting union officials' speech. They picked out pieces of precedents they liked, ignoring others. They claimed that, unlike the Quebecair case, there was no ongoing strike, and Dukovich's actions were "isolated" from collective bargaining – this despite the fact that other arbitrators had not limited their tolerance for critical comment to strike situations. Moreover, the contention that the human rights complaint was unrelated to bargaining was disputable, as negotiation was ongoing when Dukovich spoke to the media. Adams's *St. Catharines* decision clearly stressed the importance of recognizing "ongoing" adversarial relations, not just strikes, as a context for critical speech.[54]

To prove that Dukovich's claims about appearance regulation were false, Wardair dissected the press commentary in extraordinarily sematic detail. "Squeaky-clean sex objects" was the "subject of considerable testimony," though even the majority concluded that this comment reflected an allowable, though "subjective," point of view.[55] Wardair conceded that strict regulation of appearance was required but argued that it was part of its professional image and superior service.[56]

Managers admitted they "prefer hiring attractive" FAs but added that "personality" was more important. Dukovich had told the reporter about a survey that asked passengers to rank "the attractiveness of flight attendants on a scale of one to five." The company countered that "appearance" was the word used, and Dukovich was pressed to concede the two words were not exactly synonymous.

Wardair's strongest suit was picking apart claims made in the newspaper that lacked exact, quantifiable evidence or instances where Dukovich's quoted words did not match Wardair's words in its *Flight Attendant Manual*. Nearly half of the sixty-page manual pertained to grooming; it was packed with detail extending from what kind of hair barrettes and glasses frames were allowed to the etiquette of "discreet" manners, and to the intricate dos and don'ts of applying "subtle" makeup.[57] Hairstyle was strictly regulated in the manual, but Wardair disputed that women were sent home by in-flight supervisors in the manner Dukovich claimed. Women were not disciplined if supervisors didn't "like" a hairstyle, the company claimed, only if it didn't "fit" the manual rules; in any case, appearance checks were done before boarding, and in-flight supervisors worked on board. The manual did state that legs and underarms must be shaved and fingernails clean, and it specified an approved colour of brassiere (no racy black or red allowed).[58] However, CUPE did not produce witnesses who said their legs were specifically "inspected," and the "colour" of a brassiere, claimed the company, was a different matter than Dukovich's reported words about "company-approved" brassieres.[59]

Wardair also benefited from its own use of unwritten rules around appearance issues. Older employees, Dukovich had said, were pressured to quit. The draft human rights complaint gave examples of "older" women who managers asked, "why don't you quit," after being accused of losing their "enthusiasm and initiative." Others were warned that negative passenger comments on their age and weary attitude counted against them.[60] Union officials who testified supported Dukovich's claim, pointing to an incentive program for early retirement, but the company responded there was no direct evidence of a specific woman being told to quit. Airlines were careful not to leave an overt paper trail of such pressure, as demonstrated in another FA human rights complaint about age discrimination.[61]

Weight restrictions were also part of the unwritten code for FA hiring, but, by the 1980s, airlines were more circumspect than in the past: they avoided shaming "weigh-ins" and written demands that women quit if they were not slender enough. The slippage between the terms "appearance," "beauty," and "demeanour" was also a problem for the union. Dukovich explained to the reporter that demeanour was part of the regulation of "appearance," pointing to an attendant who was fired after the company received a complaint from a passenger that "she did not smile enough." Wardair admitted that they fired her but claimed she was dismissed for this "culminating" incident in a series of problems, an assertion difficult for CUPE to disprove.

In their written report, Keller and Parsons focused not on the overall meaning and context of the comments but rather on precise words. Legs, for instance, were an issue. Dukovich had said that FAs were encouraged to "show some leg," though the manual put this slightly differently, saying that "consideration should be given to the height and leg shape of an employee when deciding skirt length."[62] In the hearing, Wardair managers could not explain why "leg shape" was important, and they conceded that FAs had to enter and leave the plane in "high heels." Nor could they justify why slacks were not allowed, except to assert that the majority of FAs surveyed supported the policy (though a competing union survey showed the opposite). Clearly, FAs were supposed to "show some leg," though this was done through round-about regulations. On the "no slacks" issue, FAs found support in the media from women columnists who thought the rule ridiculous.[63]

To prove that the newspaper interviews had caused morale problems with FAs, Wardair called supervisors who asserted that FAs were "upset" and embarrassed by the article and that one FA had reported "suggestive looks" from passengers the day it was published. An in-flight service manager refused to distribute the *Globe and Mail* with the MacLeod article – a decision that, she claimed, had the approval of other FAs on board. This was second-hand testimony, but it is true that not all FAs were interested in the human rights complaint. Dukovich later reflected on this dynamic of female FAs being hesitant to embrace the agenda of the Women's Committee: not all women considered themselves feminists, and some participated in and enjoyed the constructed image of attractiveness promoted by the airlines.[64] As another FA union leader noted, FAs were originally recruited on the basis of their "caretaker" personalities, which might not translate into vocal opposition to the status quo.[65] The fact that the union periodically built strong feminist, activist campaigns speaks to the power of its own leadership and education and its commitment to making the connection between bad working conditions and sexist policies.

Claims the interviews harmed Wardair's business should have required concrete examples or evidence, if David Beatty's decision in the Elder case was the measure, but it seemed not to be for the majority. All the adjudicators commented on Wardair's extreme sensitivity to image issues: not only did it consider its brand high-quality service, but it was in the process of trying to gain entry into the scheduled carrier routes business. When company lawyers grilled Dukovich on the witness stand, they asked whether the newspaper articles might not result in a "loss of customers." She replied potentially yes, but only if Wardair did not address the concerns of passengers and female FAs. Keller and Parsons's majority ruling, however, spoke of "possible effects" of the newspaper articles on business, making Wardair's concerns "justified." Such vague conjecture was not accepted by Beatty or by arbitrators in other cases when considering negative impact on a business.

Ironically, when Wardair referred to consumer displeasure, it pointed out that women's groups had written to the company threatening to boycott the airline. This was true. Marilyne White, chair of the CUPE Airline Division Women's Committee, wrote an open letter to feminist groups detailing Wardair's sexist policies, justifying the human rights complaint, and urging women to write to Peter Bolton. She also encouraged protests of Dukovich's discipline, which she described as an "effort to intimidate other women from speaking out and supporting the complaint." The Alberta Status of Women Action Committee reproduced the letter, and other feminist publications covered the story.[66] A regional representative on the National Action Committee on the Status of Women (NAC) informed Bolton that she would encourage NAC and other unions to boycott Wardair.[67] One wonders why, if Wardair was worried about losing women's business, it would publicly discipline a feminist activist.

Another irony of Wardair's fear of bad publicity was the immense press coverage of the CLRB hearing, from the initial stories about Dukovich's discipline through to the release of the board's decision in August 1988. In a customer-based industry, airlines' labour relations often made it to the news, but in this instance not all coverage was sympathetic to Wardair. Stories about the case ran in the newspapers that originally aired Dukovich's comments – the *Globe and Mail* and *Toronto Star* – as well as papers in Vancouver, Victoria, Calgary, Regina, Saskatoon, Ottawa, Nanaimo, Red Deer, and Whitehorse. Not everyone appreciated the detailed reporting. In a letter to the editor of the *Toronto Star*, one irritated reader complained that Wardair's record earnings and recent accolades "received very scant attention by the Canadian media," while "the fact that one steward wants to wear a gold earring and one stewardess complained of the company's dress and makeup code ... gets massive coverage."[68]

Reports often zeroed in on salacious details of the arguments. When the union presented a "racy" calendar produced by a group of in-flight service managers and featuring Wardair employees as evidence of the company's hypocrisy about disparaging female flight attendants, the *Globe and Mail* ran the headline "Provocative Calendar Used at CLRB Hearing on Sex Discrimination." The following day, the company's grooming policies garnered the headline "Publicity about Brassiere Policy Humiliating, Labour Hearing Told."[69] Ultimately, media coverage of the CLRB case simply helped draw attention to the problems faced by female flight attendants working at Wardair specifically, and in the airline industry generally.

The company was able to persuade Keller and Parsons that Dukovich's comments were "reckless, untrue and malicious" and made deliberately to mislead: this argument was at the core of the ruling in favour of Wardair. The persuasiveness of the employer's case should be seen within prevailing ideologies of the time. First, even though feminists had initiated discussion of sexual harassment and the discriminatory sexualization of women workers, their arguments had not yet transformed public consciousness or legal thinking. Human rights decisions dealing with dress codes and the sexualization of women in the 1980s, for instance, were scant, and most lagged behind feminist thinking. While requiring female waitresses to be topless was deemed discriminatory by the Ontario Human Rights Commission, most cases were not so blatantly egregious.[70] When Toronto cocktail waitresses protested the requirement that they don a "harem" uniform, they lost their human rights claim and, in a close decision, an appeal of that decision to the courts.[71]

Even a New Brunswick human rights decision cited as a "win" for women was highly ambivalent. Two waitresses were fired for refusing to wear a new "sexually alluring" uniform but won their human rights claim only because the treatment of male waiters was not "comparable." The male adjudicator emphasized that his decision was not a repudiation of all dress codes that "accentuated the sexuality" of employees. Moreover, he was certain *he* could discern "objectively" what was sexually revealing, and the waitresses' costume was not, even though those forced to wear it described it negatively as "hot pants" and a "bunny costume."[72] Fast forward to the early 2000s, and we find human rights commissions that were more sympathetic to women's complaints of sexualization.[73] Recent policy statements from the Ontario Human Rights Commission assert that dress codes that "reinforce stereotypes and sexist notions about how women should look" may contravene the code, as "uniforms may not be based on gender stereotypes."[74] CUPE's claims about sexualization would be heard differently now: as Michael Church put it, Dukovich's case would likely be won in a "heartbeat" today.[75]

Second, despite some important feminist legal achievements in the 1980s, such as pay equity legislation, there was a resurgence of the Right, including anti-feminist, anti-LGBTQ, anti-choice, and anti-immigrant mobilizations. Feminist organizations identified a renewed anti-feminism, including attempts to re-regulate sexuality: women's equality demands had created a "crisis of legitimacy in the traditional family as patriarchy and heterosexuality no longer simply went unquestioned."[76] Men's rights groups complained of reverse discrimination, and the mainstream media asked if feminism had "gone too far," relaying anxieties about the supposed disintegration of the "traditional" gender order.[77] If concepts of "fairness" in workplace punishment were shaped by the general community's sense of values, as Adams claimed, then Wardair was attempting to tap into this anxious current of anti-feminism.[78]

Dissent

Jacques Archambault's dissent was remarkably frank about Wardair's efforts to discredit Dukovich. It also drew more precisely on precedent and assumed a more contextual view of the case. He astutely referred to the publicity of the recent Elder grievance; the loss of this case had weighed heavily on the company, hardening its lines of defence. Moreover, by refusing to have a non-discrimination clause, the company had forced the union to prepare a complaint for the Human Rights Commission. He quoted Dukovich approvingly: "human rights belong to all Canadians."[79] Archambault also articulated what human rights, feminist, and union activists feared was the much larger project of the company: disciplining one activist was a subtle effort to create a "chill" concerning the human rights complaint by discrediting CUPE and Dukovich. Such "discipline" was, as George Adams put it, meant as "deterrence" but also as a community "dramatization" of certain values – that is, the values of the company.[80] The complaint to the CHRC, Archambault pointed out, was "not completely distinct from" the issue that was before the Labour Relations Board, and thus the CLRB's decision risked "encroaching on the jurisdiction" of the CHRC by substituting the board's judgment for that of the commission.[81]

Archambault cited the same precedents as Keller and Parsons but showed how they supported CUPE's case. Dukovich was acting in her capacity as a union representative in the midst of an adversarial collective bargaining situation and, thus, there should be considerable leeway for strong opinions, acute criticism, and even exaggerated statements. In any case, words were easily manipulated by the media for sensational effect. He noted the incessant decontextualized word parsing in the arbitration hearing. Are we not setting a dangerous precedent, he asked, by resorting to "semantics?"[82] He portrayed the views of CUPE and Wardair as both legitimate and starkly oppositional. Arbitrators should not sit in judgment on these "two opposing, clashing philosophies." Dukovich's feminist "philosophy" diverged from the company's views on cultivating its image. In the context of a proposed expansion, and in order to fill seats, it was "selling" an image of FAs as the "pleasing girl next door." A "militant union," CUPE took issue with that image: all of the union witnesses endorsed Dukovich's belief that it made women into "sex objects."[83]

Archambault astutely analyzed the primary discursive tactic of Wardair: portraying Dukovich as an out-of-control, dogmatic feminist, intent on hurting her employer. The language of the company, adopted by the majority report, was a laundry list of code words for "bad feminist." Dukovich was "strident," "militant," "fervent," and eager to "advance her cause with a great sense of purpose" by educating the membership, using "every means to do so" – a classic portrait of a true believer. Perhaps Dukovich's demeanour as a witness reinforced the company's negative assessment of her motives. As Church points out, she was in the unusual situation of being both a witness and a legal expert.[84] As a witness, she was unrepentant; as an expert, she was forthright in her views, even as she was subjected to days of aggressive questioning by the company lawyer. Ironically, she was the exact opposite of the passive, agreeable flight attendant image promoted by the airline industry. Far from being swayed or intimidated when examined by the company lawyer, she was legally knowledgeable and quick on rebuttal. Or, as the majority adjudicators put it more conspiratorially, "she is an intelligent individual and ... at all times aware of what she is doing."[85] If anything, the company lawyer tried to turn Dukovich's education and experience against her.

When the majority rejected the union's argument that Wardair showed anti-union animus, they failed to understand that activists like Dukovich did not separate their feminism and their union activism: they were inextricably linked. They claimed not to dispute her right to advance feminist causes but rather the manner in which she did so. Clearly her "manner" irritated them. Notably, they did not extend the latitude given to other union officials' political ideas to Dukovich's feminism. Other arbitrations made it clear that union representatives had the right to express their opinions and "what they believed to be true"; the politics of feminism did not seem to deserve the same tolerance.[86]

The evidence, Archambault concluded, showed anti-union animus, but he went further, emphasizing Wardair's extraordinary effort to use Dukovich's feminism as a weapon of disparagement. The company, he noted, continually claimed she "acted on a frolic of her own." In forty years, he said,

> I have never witnessed such a systematic, determined and relentless operation, pursued with such intensity, cleverness, talent and eloquence, in an attempt to thoroughly discredit Senka Dukovich not only in the eyes of her constituents, but also in the eyes of the public and the Board. Every means was used to persuade us that Senka Dukovich was dishonest, hypocritical, stubborn, intolerant and uncompromising in every respect.[87]

Wardair even grilled Dukovich on her CV, claiming that she "misled" a potential employer about "her age and her duties at Wardair. No stone was left unturned." This character assassination had a goal: "to try and nip in the bud the initiations of the Women's Committee by impugning the integrity and the personality of a union representative who … boosted a cause that was advanced by the Women's Committee and that Wardair fiercely opposed." If he had written the decision, he concluded, he would have found that Wardair had contravened the *Labour Code* but also would have insisted that the company "cease and desist" the "harassment and intimidation" of Dukovich and the Women's Committee.[88] In the polite land of labour arbitrations, these were strong words.

The Consequences

Even after such an intense employer offensive, the majority's decision still surprised CUPE. Union officials felt that the CLRB had based its decision on matters that the Human Rights Commission should decide.[89] Moreover, the decision seemed to contradict precedent, as one labour law publication immediately noted.[90] The overall tendency in arbitrations was to allow severe criticism of employers rather than encourage companies' discipline of "disloyal" workers. Although the Dukovich case veered away from similar arbitrations and hearings, it did not significantly shift the direction of future decisions. Some arbitrators cited the case in subsequent decisions but did not give it the same gravity as others cases, such as Adams's St. Catharines hospital judgment. When the Wardair decision was cited, it was to uphold discipline against employees whom arbitrators believed had intentionally "misrepresented" or "recklessly disregarded the truth" in public criticisms of their employer.

For example, in 1989, one year after the Dukovich decision, the president of a Brampton transit union was disciplined – albeit with a light one-day suspension – for a critical letter to the mayor and council, copied to the local newspaper. Ostensibly about bad service and low employee morale, the letter also confronted rumours of privatization. When referring to city council, the union leader mistakenly used the word "patronage" instead of "patronizing," which was viewed as incendiary. Because his accusations "willfully distorted the truth" and were "derogatory, unfair, inflammatory," they crossed the "red line" that the Wardair decision supposedly established for union officers. However, the grievor's status as a public servant made this breach of employee "fidelity" especially problematic. The decision also highlighted a problem about fair comment in a time when labour was on the defensive.[91] The union president was urged to use the collective bargaining process rather than the public political arena. Yet, for workers fearing contracting out, privatization, and worsening working conditions, dividing public "political" issues from collective bargaining ones did not make sense.[92]

The Brampton case also cited *Amoco Fabrics Ltd.* (1984) as evidentiary support.[93] Also noted in Dukovich, the *Amoco* case is the most interesting parallel to the *Wardair* one, since it involved a company severely disciplining a feminist labour activist for a public critique about discrimination in the workplace. A textile firm levied a two-week suspension on Jacqueline Saunders after comments she made at an Ontario Federation of Labour women's forum on affirmative action were published a year later in a union newsletter. When first chastised by the company, she was relatively contrite, pointing out that they were reported words, not hers, but also that she believed everything she said to be true. She did not know how her testimony would be reported, and she insisted that she would not intentionally harm the "profitability" of her employer. A complicating factor was that one of the cases of discrimination Saunders cited at the conference involved a woman who reneged on an earlier conversation with her; in the grievance, the woman spoke on behalf of management.

So little seemed to be at stake for the employer in this case. One of Saunders's remarks was simply about pressure and speed up in her department, hardly an earth-shattering critique. The company was not even named in the newsletter, though Amoco claimed that people could figure it out by the union president's local. How a dated, obscure story in a union newsletter could "harm" the business was not explored or proven. The majority decision for the employer was quick to claim that the judgment was not a negative pronouncement on the "valid" cause of affirmative action. Saunders had just gone too far, "beyond hyperbole," using "unfair and false statements." Master and servant thinking was also implied: the employer claimed that her speaking out was an act of "insubordination" that "breached a duty of fidelity." In contrast, the dissenting arbitrator noted how flimsy the case was, and how there was not a "shred" of evidence proving harm to the company.[94]

Jacqueline Saunders's comments seemed small potatoes, but the similarities to the Dukovich case suggest that some arbitrators looked askance at feminist labour activism pursued with any passion. In both cases, the arbitrators rationalized they did not object to feminist goals, only their tactics, which they attacked quite harshly if these tactics moved beyond the bargaining table to a public arena. As the majority summarized their view of Dukovich in the *Wardair* case, "we do not dispute her right to advance [women's issues] ... The issue is the manner in which she chose to advance that cause."[95] The stark difference between the outcomes for feminist activists and other union members disciplined for publicly criticizing their employers is hard to ignore and raises the question, how were feminists supposed to secure change in the workplace without speaking critically and publicly about inequality?

Indeed, human rights advocates believed that Wardair disciplined Dukovich in an effort to discourage future human rights complaints. Kathleen Ruff, publisher of the *Canadian Human Rights Advocate*, argued the following year that the company used Dukovich's suspension to discredit the complaint before it was taken up by the Canadian Human Rights Commission. Dukovich's individual punishment was simultaneously a message to the wider community, an attempt to discredit her ideas and the feminist agenda of the Women's Committee. In response to the treatment of Dukovich, human rights campaigners called for better provisions in the federal law to protect workers against reprisals by employers. As Ruff put it, "if people have a legal right to be free of discrimination ... and a legal right to complain if they are discriminated against, then they should have the right to talk about it without fear of repercussions."[96]

Conclusion

Although Dukovich and CUPE lost the *Wardair* case, whether the discipline achieved what the company hoped for is debatable. The extensive press coverage of the case increased public awareness of the discrimination experienced by female flight attendants. Additionally, though the human rights complaint filed by CUPE stalled, and ultimately was not heard, Wardair was unable to derail the long-term human rights agenda of the union or of Dukovich. On the contrary, the union proceeded with other successful human rights complaints, and the *Wardair* case enhanced Dukovich's work and reputation as a human rights activist. Immediately after the case, she was elected president of her Wardair union local, and, in the ensuing years, she continued to be an outspoken advocate for gender equality in the workplace. She offered input into several cases pertaining to issues in the airline industry, including human rights complaints regarding female flight attendants' right to wear eyeglasses on the job and an important pay equity case that went all the way to the Supreme Court of Canada.[97] Since leaving the airline industry, Dukovich has gone on to a successful legal career. She is a frequent media commentator and event speaker on issues related to gender, work, and the law, and she continues to shape the development of these issues directly in her current role as a lawyer at the Ontario Pay Equity Commission.

Nevertheless, while much has changed for flight attendants in the years since the Dukovich case, troubling continuities persist. In 2018, CUPE filed a complaint with the Canadian Human Rights Commission, this time on behalf of 8,500 flight attendants working at Air Canada. The union alleged that workers were subject to "rampant sexual harassment and discrimination," forced to participate in a "sexualized fashion show" to display new uniforms, and told what kind of undergarments and make up to wear.[98] More generally, the economic context continues to make union activism an uphill struggle. Throughout the 1990s and after, the airline industry periodically pressed for employee concessions to offset airlines' economic woes. Meanwhile, separate contracts for low-cost carriers owned by large airline corporations sanctioned two-tier contracts with lower wages and less secure working conditions for some FAs. Precarious economic conditions can dissuade workers from launching grievances about appearance and working conditions.

The CHRC has not yet issued a decision on the CUPE complaint against Air Canada, but there are some contrasts between the 1987 and 2018 complaints, including the fact that, in 1987, the complaint to the CHRC did not achieve a final outcome. Thinking about appearance codes has also shifted. The recent complaint received widespread media coverage, which included highly critical quotes about Air Canada from union spokespeople, none of whom were disciplined as Dukovich was. This may signal a higher level of tolerance for criticism, at least for feminist issues. The similarities and difference are not lost on Dukovich: "I had a sense of déjà vu when I heard about the recent human rights complaint. It's just like in the 1970s and the systemic complaint I filed as head of the Women's Committee that I was interviewed about and punished for. It's almost identical."[99] The continued efforts of people such as Dukovich and unions like CUPE to challenge human rights violations and management control of appearance have led to important gains for workers, and there is now a far better understanding of gender inequality in the workplace. Yet, as the Air Canada case reminds us, workers' struggle for dignity and respect in the workplace has a long history that continues today.

NOTES

Our thanks to Senka Dukovich and Michael Church for their reflections on this case.

1 Kathleen M. Barry, *Femininity in Flight: A History of Flight Attendants* (Durham, NC: Duke University Press, 2007); N. Jill Newby, *The Sky's The Limit: The Story of the Canadian Air Line Flight Attendants' Association* (Vancouver: Canadian Airline Flight Attendants' Association, 1986); Eileen Boris, "Desirable Dress: Rosies, Sky Girls, and the Politics of Appearance," *International Labor and Working-Class History* 69 (Spring 2006): 123–42; Dorothy Sue Cobble, "'A Spontaneous Loss of Enthusiasm": Workplace Feminism and the Transformation of Women's Service Jobs in the 1970s," *International Labor and Working-Class History* 56 (Fall 1999): 23–44; Joan Sangster and Julia Smith, "Beards and Bloomers: Flight Attendants,

Grievances and Embodied Labour in the Canadian Airline Industry, 1960s–1980s," *Gender Work and Organization* 23 (March 2016): 183–99; Joan Sangster and Julia Smith, "Thigh in the Sky: Canadian Pacific Dresses Its Female Flight Attendants," *Labor: Studies in Working-Class History* 14 (March 2017): 39–64.

2 *CUPE v. Wardair Inc.*, 1988 CarswellNat 889, 76 di 103, 89 CLLC 16,009 (*Wardair* decision).

3 Though flight attendants' "flexible schedule" helped some attend school while remaining employed, it also caused problems. According to Dukovich, some flight attendants were denied unemployment insurance because their schedules led them to be classified as part-time workers. Interview with Senka Dukovich, 29 January 2014.

4 Ibid.

5 *Schaepsmeyer v. Wardair Canada (1975) Ltd.*, 1983 CarswellNat 707, 4 CHRR D/1346 (Can Hum Rts Trib).

6 Email to authors from Dukovich, 26 March 2014.

7 Joan Sangster, "Debating Maternity Rights: Pacific Western Airlines and Flight Attendants' Struggle to 'Fly Pregnant' in the 1970s," in *Work on Trial: Canadian Labour Law Struggles*, ed. Judy Fudge and Eric Tucker (Toronto: Irwin Law for the Osgoode Society for Canadian Legal History, 2010), 283–314.

8 *Toronto Star*, 7 December 1978.

9 Jan Wong, "Bush-Pilot Max Likes to Keep Hands on Wardair's Controls," *Globe and Mail*, 14 March 1988. For Ward's own take on his life, see Max Ward, *The Max Ward Story: A Bush Pilot in the Bureaucratic Jungle* (Toronto: McClelland and Stewart, 1991).

10 Deborah C. Sawyer, "Wardair International Ltd," *Canadian Encyclopedia*, 7 February 2006, https://www.thecanadianencyclopedia.ca/en/article/wardair-international-ltd.

11 Patricia Chisholm, "The End of Ward's Dream: Costs and Competition Close an Era," *Maclean's*, 30 January 1989, 34–5.

12 Ibid.

13 Albert Ohayon, "Max Ward: The NFB Profiles a Canadian Aviation Legend," *NFB Blog*, 4 May 2012, https://blog.nfb.ca/blog/2012/05/04/max-ward-nfb-aviation/.

14 "Airline Counters Union: Wardair Attendants Barred from Flight Home," *Globe and Mail*, 10 August 1981.

15 Ibid.

16 Dick Schuler, "Wardair Prepares for Likely Strike," *Calgary Herald*, 21 February 1984.

17 Interview with Dukovich.

18 Wong, "Bush-Pilot Max."

19 Harold Smith, "Arbitration of Right of Employees to Self-Expression," *Cleveland State Law Review* 162 (1982): 162–80.

20 Paul Weiler, "The Slippery Slope of Judicial Intervention: The Supreme Court and Canadian Labour Relations, 1950–1970," *Osgoode Hall Law Journal* 9 (1971): 1–79. It was also possible for judicial reviews to assess a "lack of natural justice," but this was rare. Mark Thompson, "Judicial Review of Arbitration in Ontario," *Relations industrielles/Industrial Relations* 26 (1971): 471–89; Kenneth P. Swan, "The Supreme Court of Canada, Judicial Review and Labour Arbitration," in *Studies in Labour Law*, ed. Kenneth P. Swan and Katherine E. Swinton (Toronto: Butterworths, 1983), 1–35.

21 *Wardair Canada Inc. v. Canadian Air Line Flight Attendants' Association* (1987), 1988 CanLII 4847 (ON SC), 28 LAC (3d) 142; *Wardair Canada Inc. v. Canadian Air Line Flight Attendants Assn* (Ont. Div. Ct.) (1988), 63 OR (2d) 471, [1988] OJ No. 23. The grievance is covered more extensively in Sangster and Smith, "Beards and Bloomers."

22 Robert MacLeod, "Male Flight Attendant Wins Round Over Right to Wear Earring at Work," *Globe and Mail*, 28 February 1987.

23 Ross Nichol, as quoted in Robert MacLeod, "Discrimination Permeates Airline Industry, Hearing Told," *Globe and Mail*, 5 July 1988.

24 *Wardair* decision, 5.

25 "Women Allege Sexist Dress Code: Canadian Commission Is Slow to Act," *Canadian Human Rights Advocate* 4 (March 1988): 4.

26 "Wardair Stewardesses Used as Sex Object, Complaint Says," *Globe and Mail*, 21 March 1987.

27 Dukovich, as quoted in Alanna Mitchell, "Wardair Employee Defends Remarks," *Toronto Star*, 18 August 1988.

28 *Wardair* decision, 7.

29 Ibid., 8.

30 "Union Files Complaint over Wardair Suspension," *Toronto Star*, 11 May 1988.

31 As quoted in Robert MacLeod, "Wardair Stewardesses Used as Sex Objects, Union Complaint Says," *Globe and Mail*, 21 March 1987.

32 We filed a request for the CLRB case file from Library and Archives Canada, but it was denied. We followed up with a Freedom of Information request but have not received a decision.

33 Leo Panitch and Donald Swartz, *From Consent to Coercion: The Assault on Trade Union Freedoms*, 3rd ed. (Toronto: University of Toronto Press, 2003);

A. Botteri, "Regulation, Deregulation, and Labour Relations in the Airline Industry: A Comparative Study of the US and Canada" (PhD diss., McGill University, 1993).

34 *International Woodworkers, Local 1-85 & MacMillan & Bloedel Ltd.* (1956), 6 LAC 139; *Re Firestone Tire and Rubber Co of Canada Ltd. and United Rubber Workers, Local 635* (1975), 9 LAC (2d) 345.

35 *Re Burns Meat Ltd and Canadian Food and Allied Workers, Local P 139* (1980), 26 LAC 2(d) 379.

36 Donald Brown and David Beatty, *Canadian Labour Arbitration*, 3rd ed. (Toronto: Canada Law Book, 1988), 7–8.

37 *United Automobile Workers, Local 1524 v. General Spring Products Ltd.* (1968), 19 LAC 392.

38 *Cincinnati Suburban Press Inc. (1988)*, 1987–88, CCH, NLRB 19,548.

39 *Wardair* decision, 10.

40 *ONA v. St. Catharines General Hospital* (1982), 2 Can. LRBR 262, [1982] OLRB rep. 441.

41 A. Marie Samson, complainant, and Canada Post Corporation, Arichat, NS, respondent, 29 September 1987. Note this decision also had Archambault and Keller on the board.

42 *Canada Post Corp v. LCUC*, 1988 CarswellNat 988, 75 di 189, 88 CLLC para. 16,064

43 *Fugère v. Quebecair*, 1987 CarswellNat 1039, 72 di 44, 88 CLLC para. 16,035.

44 *ONA v. St. Catharines General Hospital* (1982), 2 Can. LRBR 262, [1982] OLRB rep. 441, 31–2.

45 *Alliance of Canadian Cinema Television and Radio Artists v. Canadian Broadcasting Corporation* (1990), 91 CLLC, para. 16,007 (often referred to as the Goldhawk case). The case finally ended in the Supreme Court: *Canadian Broadcasting Corp. v. Canada (Labour Relations Board)*, [1995] SCR 157, 23142.0

46 T.A.B. Jolliffe, quoted in *Re Chedore and Treasury Board (Post Office Department)*, [1980] CPSRB No. 19, 12. We could not locate the original case, in which Jolliffe made the argument for the employer (the federal government), only the judicial review, which did not overturn the original decision: *Arthur J. Stewart v. Public Service Staff Relations Board*, [1978] FC 133, 1.

47 *Re Chedore and Treasury Board*, [1980] CPSRB No. 19.

48 Michael Lynk, Michael Mac Neil, and Peter Engelmann, *Trade Union Law in Canada* (Toronto: Carswell, 1994), 6.1040, accessed 8 March 2020.

49 *Burns Meats Ltd. and Canadian Food & Allied Workers, Local P139*, [1980] OLAA No. 141, 26 LAC 379.

50 Joan Sangster, "Just Horseplay? Masculinity and Workplace Grievances in Fordist Canada, 1947–70s," *Canadian Journal of Women and the Law* 26 (October 2014): 330–64.

51 "Air Canada Pilot Gets Job Back 5 Years after Crash in Toronto," *Toronto Star*, 19 November 1983. Von Veh graduated from Queen's Faculty of Law in 1967, chaired the Ontario Labour Section of the Canadian Bar Association in 1975, and in the late 1970s served as a Canadian representative at the International Labour Office in Geneva, Switzerland. Von Veh continues to work as a labour lawyer and arbitrator. "Fred von Veh," Mediation.com, http://13.58.18.178/memberprofile/fred--vonveh-v6c1-9c.aspx.

52 "Sex Object Complaint Humiliating Board Told," *Toronto Star*, 12 October 1988.

53 *ONA v. St. Catharines General Hospital*, 1982 CarswellOnt 1019, [1982] OLRB rep. 441, 31.

54 *Wardair* decision, 13.

55 Ibid., 9.

56 Richard Woloshen, "Flying Those Sex-Conscious Skies: Wardair's Dress Codes Are under Fire Again," *Western Report* 3 (9 May 1988): 30–1.

57 *Wardair Flight Attendant Manual*, revised April 1985. The detail was extensive, minute, and designed for a "conventional" look. Hairstyle was policed rigidly. As well, one of the key "don'ts" of behaviour was talking about the job with other FAs while at work. Though the word "gossip" was used, this rule, in fact, prevented discussing job problems and the union.

58 Ibid.

59 Dana Flavelle, "Airline Discriminates against Men, Union Says," *Toronto Star*, 16 August 1988.

60 Draft of amendment to human rights complaint, CUPE papers. "Older" might mean someone with twelve years' service.

61 "Female Flight Attendants Encounter Job Turbulence over Age," *Vancouver Sun*, 17 April 1991.

62 "Wardair Executive Has Problems Explaining Leg Shape Comment," *Globe and Mail*, 29 April 1988.

63 Liane Zimmerman, "You'd Like Max to Know It's Okay for Women to Wear Pants," *Edmonton Journal*, 27 September 1987.

64 Interview with Dukovich.

65 Interview with Pamela Sachs, 24 January 2020.

66 "Working Women Demand Dignity," *Alberta Status of Women Newsletter* (August 1987): 6; "Wardair Women Censored," *Kinesis* (February 1989): 6.

67 Rebecca Coulter to Mr. Bolton, letter copied to CUPE Airline Division, 17 September 1977.
68 Patrick W. Salmon, "Voted Best Airline Wardair Gets Few Pats," *Toronto Star*, 7 April 1987.
69 Robert MacLeod, "Provocative Calendar Used at CLRB Hearing on Sex Discrimination," *Globe and Mail*, 6 April 1988; Robert MacLeod, "Publicity about Brassiere Policy Humiliating, Labour Hearing Told," *Globe and Mail*, 7 April 1988.
70 *Ballentyne v. Molly N' Me Tavern* (1982), 4 CHHR D/1191.
71 *Allan v. Riverside Lodge*, Board of Inquiry, September 1987, BOI 213A.
72 *Doherty and Meehan v. Lodgers International* (1981), 3 CHRR D 628 (NB).
73 *Mottu v. MacLeod and Others*, (2004) BCHRT 67.
74 "OHRC Policy Position on Sexualized and Gender-Specific Dress Codes," Ontario Human Rights Commission, http://www.ohrc.on.ca/en/ohrc-policy-position-sexualized-and-gender-specific-dress-codes.
75 Interview with Michael Church, 21 February 2020.
76 Lorna Weir, Introduction to LAR, University of Ottawa Archives, Canadian Women's Movement Archives (CWMA), Lesbians against the Right, box 44, file 6.
77 Post-feminism newspaper clippings, CWMA, box 27, file 9; Sharon Stone, Case Study of Lesbians against the Right, CWMA, box 44, file 3.
78 George W. Adams, *Grievance Arbitration of Discharge Cases* (Kingston: Queen's University Industrial Relations Centre, 1978), 19.
79 *Wardair* decision, 19.
80 Adams, *Grievance Arbitration*, 26–7.
81 *Wardair* decision, 18.
82 Ibid., 18.
83 Ibid., 15.
84 Interview with Church.
85 *Wardair* decision, 4.
86 *ONA v. St. Catharines General Hospital*, 1982 CarswellOnt 1019, OLRB Rep 441.
87 *Wardair* decision, 21.
88 Ibid.
89 Bob Mitchell, "Labor Board Upholds Flight Attendant's Suspension, *Toronto Star*, 4 January 1989.
90 "Exaggerated Comments by Union Official to Media Not Protected," *Labour Law News* 15 (February 1989): 5. The commentary pointed to the decision in *Canada Post Corp. v. LCUC*, 1988 CarswellNat 988, 75 di 189, (1988) CLLC 16,064, noted above, as a direct contradiction to the Wardair one.

91 A critical question is why unions did not appeal to *Charter* rights to free expression. The answer seems to be that courts had already recognized that the *Charter* had "not made unlawful" aspects of the labour law regime that might impose limits on employee comments. *Re Simon Fraser University and AUCE Loc. 2* (1985), 18 LAC (3d) 361.

92 *Re Brampton (City) and ATU Loc. 1573*, [1989] OLAA No. 74.

93 *Re Amoco Fabrics Ltd. and Amalgamated Clothing and Textile Workers Union, Local 1606*, [1984] OLAA No. 111.

94 Ibid., 8.

95 *Wardair* decision, 14.

96 Lois Sweet, "Rights Act Doesn't Protect Complainants," *Toronto Star*, 4 April 1988. At the time of Dukovich's case, the federal *Human Rights Act* made it a criminal offence to retaliate against someone who had filed a human rights complaint, but critics argued that this it was difficult to enforce, as the police had to investigate and obtain the consent of the attorney general to lay charges. In 1998, the federal government amended the act to provide a non-criminal prohibition, which allows the Canadian Human Rights Commission to investigate cases of retaliation like other complaints.

97 Human Rights Tribunal between Rodney Cremona and Tina Radford and Canadian Human Rights Commission and Wardair Canada, Inc. and Worldways Canada Ltd. (1991); *Canada (Human Rights Commission) v. Canadian Airlines International Ltd.*, [2006] 1 SCR 3, 2006 SCC.

98 Tamar Harris, "Air Canada Flight Attendants Allege Harassment, Discrimination," *Toronto Star*, 29 March 2018, https://www.thestar.com/news/gta/2018/03/29/air-canada-flight-attendants-allege-harassment-discrimination.html.

99 Email from Senka Dukovich to authors, 4 April 2018.

9

Women Not Welcome: *Martinie v. The Italian Society of Port Arthur*

LAURA NIGRO, LORI CHAMBERS, AND MICHEL S. BEAULIEU

On 14 April 1989, Giovannina (Joanne) Ruberto filed a human rights complaint against a fraternal organization, the Italian Mutual Benefit Society of Port Arthur (shortly thereafter and presently the Italian Society of Port Arthur). Although the society had a women's auxiliary, Ruberto believed the men's organization held the only "real" power to get things done.[1] When her application to join the men's group was denied, she asserted that her exclusion was a clear violation of section 1 of the *Ontario Human Rights Code*, which states that every person has the right to equal treatment with respect to services, goods, and facilities without discrimination on the basis of sex in any place "to which the public is customarily admitted."[2] The board of inquiry had to determine whether the society was a "public" facility or service. The society not only claimed private status but also responded that, as a cultural organization based on ethnicity – itself a prohibited ground of discrimination – it was protected under section 17 of the code (section 18 by the time of the hearing).[3]

In June 1995, the human rights tribunal handed down its decision: the society was permitted to discriminate against Ruberto.[4] This hearing had taken place in a context in which legal challenges to male-only organizations were in the news in Canada, the United States, and the United Kingdom.[5] *Martinie* pitted the individual rights of an (Italian) woman against the rights of a collective of (Italian) men who had themselves historically faced discrimination, and it raised the question, can women within cultural groups that face discrimination in the wider society rely upon section 1 of the code to protect themselves from discrimination within their ethnic/religious/cultural communities? Within months of *Martinie*, a similar case, *Gould v. Yukon Order of Pioneers*,[6] was upheld by the Supreme Court of Canada. The latter case has yet to be overturned, *Martinie* remains correct in law, and, to this day, the Italian Society of Port Arthur continues to exclude women.

Martinie is extremely interesting and important. Ruberto challenged a form of discrimination that was so systemic as to appear almost natural and inevitable. Further, the case illustrates the importance of administrative tribunals in the lives of ordinary people of modest means. Yet, little has been written about the hearing.[7] The most extensive existing description of the case is a brief mention in historian John Potestio's memoir, *Becoming Canadian*, and a footnote in his work *The Italians of Thunder Bay*.[8] In both, he briefly discusses his personal involvement with the case as a member of the society and as an advocate for including women. But in neither work does he go into much detail, instead framing the case as emblematic of larger issues in the community and asserting that, as a result, the Italian Ladies Auxiliary Society eventually changed its name to the Italian Ladies Society.[9] This chapter fills a gap in historiography by piecing together the events leading up to the hearing and critiquing the decision itself. The story is told using all extant legal documents as well as personal interviews. Oral history was essential, but the interviews also presented challenges. In particular, the number of those willing to participate was low. In 2008, only Joanne Ruberto and two others agreed to participate, one of whom wished to remain anonymous. Ten years later, five further individuals were willing to speak, and the president of the society, who also happened to have been the president at the time of the *Martinie* hearing, answered questions. The sources for this chapter are predominantly pro-Ruberto. Whatever the limitations occasioned by sources, this history provides a unique window into one Italian-Canadian woman's struggle for equality.

We begin by exploring the gendered shortcomings of Italian-Canadian historiography and mapping the history of Italian mutual benefit societies. The focus then shifts to Ruberto herself and her experiences as a first-generation immigrant and a girl-child. The arguments of Ruberto and the society before the Board of Inquiry are then detailed. The decision itself is critiqued and placed in the wider context of the issue of the inclusion of women in men's organizations in Canada with a particular focus on the decision – and dissent – in *Gould*.

Italian Canadian Historiography and the Italian Society of Port Arthur

The paucity of writing about this case is not surprising. The historiography of Italian Canadians is dominated by male authors who have focused on topics such as religion, immigration, labour, culture, and Italian colonies.[10] Historians such as Donna Gabaccia and Franca Iacovetta have challenged this male-dominated approach and explore women's struggles for social power within their communities. They note that "the least understood aspect of Italian women's diasporic lives is their role as resistors, protesters, and activists."[11] The story of Joanne Ruberto contributes to this emerging historiography.

Her story also contributes to the specific history of Italian-Canadian mutual benefit societies, organizations that were brought to North America by Italians during the first great immigration wave of male sojourners in the early twentieth century and were quickly adapted to meet local circumstances.[12] Italians were looking to escape hardship and to create better lives for themselves, but the policy of the Canadian government was to discourage the permanent settlement of Italians. This attitude was made clear by Minister of the Interior Clifford Sifton, who stated that "no steps are to be taken to assist or encourage Italian immigration to Canada."[13] Male sojourners were met with hostile and racist attitudes from the locals, who were resentful that these "inferior" men were taking "their" jobs.[14] Facing back-breaking labour, long working hours, and inadequate financial compensation, Italian immigrants were forced to look to each other for support, and consequently they established mutual aid or benevolent societies.

While mutual aid societies in Italy intertwined with labour unions, those in North America provided benefits in sickness and death.[15] Some societies also took on a role similar to that of *padroni* by acting as mediators between corporations looking for labourers and individuals seeking work.[16] The earliest of these organizations in Canada – the Società Nazionale – was established in 1875 in Montreal.[17] Its goal was to encourage Italian immigrants to come to Canada and to provide assistance for them.[18] Once immigrants arrived, the concept of *campanilismo* – the sense of loyalty to one's village, town, or region – had them gravitating towards those from the same area in Italy; however, if no such individuals could be found, as was the case outside larger cities, they set aside their regional differences. Such was the case in Port Arthur and Fort William (present-day Thunder Bay).[19]

Due to their relatively small numbers in both cities during the first few decades of the twentieth century, Italians banded together with those outside their original *paesi* (towns). This newfound identity was reflected in the two Little Italies or Italian colonies in Thunder Bay (established in the East End of Fort William, primarily between McIntosh and Christy Streets and the Banning Street area of Port Arthur) and two mutual aid organizations.[20] The Principe di Piemonte in Fort William was established on 24 April 1909 to create a refuge from the "conglomeration of people who exhibited strange and diverse languages and customs."[21] The goal of the organization to promote "Italian customs and culture in all of its endeavours," and it provided various recreational activities.[22] In 1929, the Italian Mutual Benefit Society of Port Arthur was established after a successful turnout of Italians at a picnic in that town.[23] The objective of the founders was to promote Italian culture and provide economic benefits – specifically, "to undertake and transact any class of insurance for which a mutual benefit society may be licensed under the provisions of the Insurance Act."[24]

The nature and objectives of these mutual benefit societies shifted over time. With the eruption of the Second World War, Italians in Canada were deemed enemy aliens. Some were put in internment camps, while others were under heavy surveillance and forced to check in with local police or the Royal Canadian Mounted Police (RCMP). Mutual benefit societies were also targeted.[25] In this context, the Mutual Benefit Society of Port Arthur unanimously adopted a resolution reaffirming its unwavering support for Canada and the British Empire as loyal and law-abiding subjects.[26] In the postwar era, provincial health coverage, the booming capitalist state, and an influx of Italian immigrants – primarily families rather than lone males – meant there was a dwindling reliance on death and sickness benefits as social services and families expanded.[27] While men still wanted to partake in traditional recreational activities to keep their heritage alive, new activities included scholarship programs, providing financial assistance and aid for victims of natural disasters in Italy, and organizing campaigns to raise funds for local retirement homes.[28]

Mutual benefit institutions also altered their legal status to address the changing times. In 1970, the Famee Furlane Mutual Benefit Society in Toronto changed its name to meet the standards, rules, and regulations for a non-profit organization.[29] On 13 October 1970, the Famee Furlane Mutual Benefit Society, a private insurance company, was dissolved, and the Famee Furlane Club of Toronto was born. This change in status allowed the group to avoid taxes and protect its assets. The new goals of the society were those of "a corporation primarily concerned with social, cultural, and recreational activities."[30] Some years later, the Italian Mutual Benefit Society of Port Arthur changed its name to the Italian Society of Port Arthur. The new name reflected new goals: the society "no longer fulfilled its mandate as a mutual benefit society [and] evolved into a fraternal organization."[31] In addition to changing its letters patent in 1989, the society revised its constitution. The new constitution deleted all references to insurance while incorporating new objectives:

A. To unite male persons of Italian descent in and around the City of Thunder Bay for the preservation and strengthening of a fraternal spirit among those of Italian descent.
B. To stimulate and [sic] interest and involvement in community affairs and to promote the Italian culture and heritage.
C. To promote social intercourse between the members and their guests.[32]

It is perhaps not coincidental that these revisions occurred in Port Arthur simultaneously with the challenge presented by Ruberto to the society's membership regulations. Provision of insurance by the fraternity would have placed the society firmly in the realm of providing a service to the public and would thus have precluded their protection under section 17/18 of the *Ontario Human Rights Code.*

The changing demographics of Italian-Canadian communities in the postwar period produced new questions for Italian fraternal organizations.[33] As men and women began to marry non-Italians, the question arose as to who fraternities would consider to be of Italian descent. In Port Arthur, to accommodate male children who had Italian mothers and non-Italian fathers, the society created the title of "associate" members; these were members who could join the society but could not participate in elections or hold executive positions. Male children with Italian fathers and non-Italian mothers, however, were considered full members. In 1958, the society began to allow non-Italian men who married Italian women to become "associate" members. It is noteworthy that this change referred to the new members as men who were "non-Italian but are married to an Italian girl."[34]

For Italian women, three organizations existed. The first two were separate ladies' auxiliaries for each of the fraternal societies: the Principe di Piemonte Ladies' Auxiliary (Fort William) and the Italian Ladies Society of Port Arthur. Each was closely affiliated with the men's societies with the purpose of "assist[ing] the men's club with their activities."[35] The third, the Ladies' Venet Society, was completely autonomous. It was created in the East End of Fort William in 1940, "for the express purpose of uniting women who trace their cultural roots to the Northern regions of Italy."[36] Ruberto was not interested in serving on the auxiliary and was ineligible for the Ladies' Venet Society, as she was of southern Italian descent.

Spearheaded by the efforts of John Potestio, the society did consider the potential inclusion of women in the 1980s.[37] Potestio, who believed that allowing female membership would be an important symbolic gesture, recalls a handful of supportive individuals.[38] The majority of members, however, were staunchly opposed. As he recalled, "the arguments that they were using were absolutely insane. Men would complain going into the club room they would have to watch their language if women were present."[39] Potestio formally presented a resolution to the membership, which was soundly defeated by a vote of 155 to 7.[40] After making "one last emotional plea to the members, Potestio walked out."[41] He sent a letter to the Italian embassy in Ottawa, informing them of the backward opinions and actions in Thunder Bay. There is no doubt that members of the society resented this action.[42] While Potestio's attempt at reform had failed, another opportunity for change would present itself via Joanne Ruberto.

Joanne Ruberto's Struggle for Self-Determination

Ruberto was born on 23 November 1953, in the small rural city of Nicastro (Lamezia Terme), in Calabria, Italy, a city still suffering in the aftermath of the Second World War. Iacovetta summarizes the problems in southern Italy, as revealed by the 1951 Italian census:

> While only 1.5 per cent of northern Italians were found to be living in poverty as defined by government standards, the figure for the south stood at over 25 per cent. Approximately 40 per cent of all southern dwellings lacked sanitary arrangements; over half were without on-site drinking water. Almost 53 per cent of southerners were living in overcrowded conditions ... Rudimentary health services, low levels of education, and high rates of illiteracy filled out the portrait.[43]

Figure 9.1. Joanne's father, Vincenzo Ruberto

Source: Private collection of Joanne Ruberto

Southern Italians often use the term *la miseria* to describe the harsh conditions they faced.[44] While they were "dirt poor," Ruberto considered her family lucky, as her grandmother had a small vegetable farm. It was not enough, however, to sustain their growing family, and the decision was made to seek a new future in Canada. The extended Ruberto family was not alone in this decision: between 1946 and 1971, more than 6.4 million Italians left the country.[45] Even though government-assisted programs were available to immigrants, an overwhelming 90 per cent of Italian immigrants who came to Canada in these years did so through the financial support and sponsorship of their relatives, not the government.[46] Ruberto's family were such people.

Joanne's father, Vincenzo, was the first member of her immediate family to come to Canada, in 1959.[47] He found employment mining in Red Rock, on the north shore of Lake Superior, and working in the bush for Great West Timber Ltd. He rented an apartment in his brother's house on Dalton Avenue in Port Arthur, saved his wages, and, within two years,

Figure 9.2. Joanne, pictured here with her mother and siblings, prior to arriving in Canada

Source: Private collection of Joanne Ruberto

sent for the rest of his family to join him.[48] On 10 November 1961, Vincenzo's family – his wife, Angelina; daughters Caterina (fourteen years old) and Giovannina (Joanne) (eight); and sons Giovanni (six), Francesco (four), and Salvatore (two) – set sail from Naples; ten days later, they arrived at Pier 21 in Halifax. Because Francesco was quarantined on arrival, the family waited eighteen days before being processed.[49] They then caught a train to Montreal, where they stayed to visit extended family. On the snowy evening of 11 December, they arrived in Port Arthur.

Despite the presence of strong and determined women in her life, Ruberto struggled as a child in Port Arthur.[50] She was quick to notice the double standard and restraints placed on her by the patriarchal Italian-Canadian community. She remembers that her brothers were allowed to play wherever they wanted and to participate in extracurricular

Figure 9.3. Joanne as a student at Hammarskjold High School

Source: Private collection of Joanne Ruberto

activities like swimming; she was not. Although her own parents were less strict than some others, she asserts that Italian girls were afforded few liberties. She fought against these restrictions. Most importantly, instead of going to Port Arthur Collegiate Institute, the school for which she was zoned, she attended Hammarskjold High School.[51] This meant she was farther away from prying eyes and the risk that her behaviour would be reported back to her family.

Ruberto was particularly distressed by pressure to get married. Whether it was at church, school, or dances, boys started "sniffing around."[52] Ruberto jokes that her elder sister, Caterina, did not do her "job," because she followed all the rules. Ruberto had to fight with her mother constantly about issues such as dating and going out with her girlfriends. She identified with the typical markers of being Italian, such as speaking the language, and making sausages and wine, but she often found herself rebelling. In doing so, she inadvertently found herself branded as a "bad girl."[53]

When Ruberto was twenty-three years old, just prior to her graduation from Lakehead University, she found out about a one-year position in France as an English teaching assistant. Her family was "up in arms," most hesitant about letting her go:

> When someone does something outside the norm, Southern Italians like to talk. My mother was afraid of *le male lingue* [being bad-mouthed]. But I was picked to go to France and I was proud. It was an accomplishment … My uncle, in trying to talk me out of it, said that people were going to think that I "needed" to go away. Of course, that made me even more determined.[54]

Once in France, Ruberto obtained the freedom for which she had longed. She lived on her own earnings and travelled unaccompanied to see family and friends. On visits, she was shocked to discover that Italy was much more evolved than she had been led to believe. A new feminist movement, rooted in the rejection of the traditional construct of family, a change in gender relations, and the demand for sexual self-determination, had gained ground in southern Italy by the 1970s.[55] Ruberto found it ironic that daughters of Italian immigrants in Canada were held to antiquated standards of morality when women in Italy were experiencing a sexual revolution.[56]

After marrying a non-Italian man in France, Ruberto returned to Thunder Bay and worked as a teacher. She found herself caught between two worlds: "Was I Italian? Was I Canadian? I struggled with that because I didn't feel like I was anything. I was this hybrid thing."[57] When her two daughters were born, Ruberto wanted them to celebrate the best parts of their Italian culture without the gender pressures or limitations she had faced. They learned the Italian language and danced with an Italian dance troupe, Le Stelle Alpine.[58]

Ruberto found herself wanting to get involved in the local Italian community beyond her role as a teacher of Italian. In her opinion, the only organization capable of "getting anything done" was the Italian Mutual Benefit Society of Port Arthur, but she knew that it did not welcome women. Ruberto claims that Sam Federico, then president, encouraged her to join.[59] Federico denies this version of events, maintaining he was encouraging her to join the ladies' auxiliary and that his position always reflected "duly made majority decisions."[60] Believing there was hope, Ruberto had her father procure a membership form, which she filled out as G. Martinie Ruberto. She was rejected and instead invited to join the ladies' auxiliary, but Ruberto "told them to go fuck themselves. I'm not going to be someone you make to go to the kitchen to do all the work and you get all the glory."[61]

For Ruberto, there was no purpose in joining the ladies' society, because, in the eyes of the Mutual Benefit Society, "a woman had really nothing to say. Their word didn't mean anything."[62] Although Ruberto had been expecting to be rebuffed by the men's society, she was still disappointed: "Here I am Italian born ... and really I can't do anything because my Italian-ness means nothing. And what do I pass on to my own children? What rights do my own children have?"[63] She decided to pursue matters further and reached out to John Potestio. They spent months going over the society's constitution and records, in addition to familiarizing themselves with the history of anti-discrimination legislation in Canada.[64]

Martinie v. The Italian Society of Port Arthur

Ruberto's challenge to the society was based in the *Ontario Human Rights Code* (1962), which had its origins in the postwar movement to protect human rights worldwide. After witnessing the atrocities of the Second World War, most particularly the Holocaust, there was a general movement towards the elaboration of human rights around the world. In 1948, the United Nations promulgated the *Universal Declaration of Human Rights*, an international statement in which signatories agreed to uphold a common standard for the protection of basic human rights.[65] Many nations subsequently adopted their own statements of rights. The first explicit articulation of these goals in Canada was the federal *Canadian Bill of Rights* (1960), which upheld the right to equality before the law and freedom of religion, speech, property, association, and the press. These rights were to exist "without discrimination by reason of race, national origin, colour, religion or sex."[66] The *Canadian Human Rights Act* of 1977 further articulated protection from discrimination. However, federal legislation applied only to services, agencies, and organizations under federal control.[67]

Starting with Ontario in 1962, each province adopted its own specific *Human Rights Code* to protect the rights of individuals in contexts under provincial jurisdiction.[68] Ontario's original code explicitly prohibited discrimination based on race, colour, creed, nationality, ancestry, and place of origin, but in 1980 it expanded prohibited grounds to include sex, age, marital status, family status, and handicap. Although provincial codes are not uniform in every aspect, their fundamental function is the same: "to create a climate of understanding and respect for all persons, without discrimination."[69] In Ontario, at the time of the *Martinie* hearing, human rights complaints were adjudicated before boards of inquiry overseen by the Human Rights Commission.[70]

Ruberto asserted she had been discriminated against because of her gender, contrary to the *Ontario Human Rights Code, 1981*.[71] She claimed that the society had violated her right under section 1 to "equal treatment with respect to services, goods and facilities, without discrimination."[72] She argued that the violation of section 1 and the society's decision to discriminate against women reinforced the traditional and stereotypical role of subservient Italian women. Women were good enough to volunteer their time and efforts for the events put on by the society, but they were not valued enough to become members who had a voice in decision-making processes. Section 1 prohibits discrimination in places "to which the public is customarily admitted," but does not prohibit such discrimination in private spaces.[73] But, would the activities of the society be considered services, goods, or facilities? And, if facilities, were they public or private? To answer these questions, the board of inquiry would have to consider previous decisions, which, by 1989, increasingly limited the definition of private space and interpreted services to the public broadly. In Ontario, for example, the courts had held that sports facilities were public spaces and that sporting associations were public services and must provide opportunities for girls.[74] In the United States, the Jaycees and Rotary Clubs – men's clubs explicitly engaged in public service – had been forced to extend their membership to women.[75]

Ruberto anticipated that the society would challenge her assertion that it could be categorized as public and that it provided services to those who were not members. She and Potestio also knew the society would seek protection under section 17 (shortly thereafter, section 18) of the Ontario *Human Rights Code*, which allowed exclusion "where membership or participation in a religious, philanthropic, educational, fraternal or social institution or organization that is primarily engaged in serving the interests of the persons identified by a prohibited ground of discrimination is restricted to persons who are similarly identified."[76] Would Italian men be considered "persons identified by a prohibited ground of discrimination" to the extent that they could exclude Italian women (who also face discrimination)? She filed her complaint on 14 April 1989.

For the next six years, Ruberto recalls "a lot of back and forth" between herself, the lawyers, and the provincial Human Rights Commission.[77] During this time, she remembers being pressured by members of the society to drop her complaint. They even contacted her father with "mean and threatening phone calls, [asking] why are you and your daughter doing this?"[78] When this happened, Ruberto's father became even more supportive of her. His encouragement meant the world to her. When he died in March 1994, her heart was no longer in the fight, but she decided to persevere in his honour.[79]

Martinie v. Italian Society of Port Arthur was finally heard at the Valhalla Inn, Thunder Bay, on 14 June 1995. Loretta Mikus served as adjudicator, or chair of the board of inquiry, and Tony Griffin presented the case for Ruberto. At the time, the Ontario Human Rights Commission had carriage of the case, and Ruberto was technically only a witness. Griffin made it clear they were not interested in monetary damages; instead, they sought a declaration that Ruberto's rights had been violated and acceptance of her membership in the society.[80] The respondents – Sam Federico and the Italian Society of Port Arthur – relied heavily on arguments based in section 18 of the code, which permits discrimination and exclusion for "special interest organizations" on the condition that these groups and organizations serve "only or mostly a particular group of people identified by a ground in the *Code*."[81] Interestingly, however, the basis of their identification was not discussed by either Ruberto or the society; the question of whether Italian men constitute a group "identified by a prohibited ground of discrimination" was therefore not considered. This raises a question not answered by this case: are second-generation white male immigrants subject to discrimination sufficient to secure the protection of section 18?

Because section 18 is an exemption from general rules, it must be read narrowly to prevent discrimination on illegitimate grounds. There are three criteria that any organization must meet in order to claim protection under this section. They must prove that, first, the organization is a religious, philanthropic, educational, fraternal, or social organization; second, it is primarily engaged in serving the interests of the persons identified by the prohibited ground; and, third, its membership is restricted to persons similarly identified.[82] If the society failed to prove that it met any one of these criteria, the benefit of the doubt would favour the complainant, Ruberto.[83]

Figure 9.4. Joanne Ruberto around the time of the hearing

Source: Private collection of Joanne Ruberto

Griffin's argument was twofold: first, the society was engaged primarily in activities that served the interest of the city, not only its members; and second, the society's membership was not limited to Italian men.[84] Griffin argued that the society's actions engaged interests beyond the fraternity, including those of the Italian community at large, through events such as picnics, Christmas banquets, and other festivities.[85] Further, he asserted that protection under section 18 was based on the requirement that membership be restricted to those identified by the organization. The society's objective, as stated by its constitution, is to "unite male persons of Italian descent." The constitution did not, and does not, state that the purpose is also to unite non-Italian men who marry Italian women (or "girls"). Therefore, he argued, the society failed the membership test for inclusion under section 18.

Michael Mauro, the society's legal representative, contested both arguments. He argued that, although the society did provide services to the community at large, its main objective remained meeting the social interests of its members – Italian men. He pointed out that section 18 did not state that the organization had to exclusively serve the interests of its members; rather, the group had to primarily serve the interests of its members.[86] He argued that this section of the code – through the use of the word "fraternal" – was intended specifically for organizations like the Italian Society of Port Arthur, and "if the Commission's interpretation were accepted, s.18 would be rendered meaningless."[87] The objectives of the society were to "unite male persons of Italian descent, stimulate interest in Italian culture and heritage, and promote social interaction between members and their guests."[88] With regard to membership, Mauro countered that it was the society's primary aim to serve male members of Italian descent. While the benefits of social events might extend to those outside the society's membership, this fact was secondary to the goal of creating a fraternal bond among Italian males.[89]

By the end of the day, Mikus ruled in favour of the society.[90] The decision cited the lawyers and Sam Federico, but not Ruberto herself. This silencing of the voice of the complainant is itself disturbing. Mikus found that the majority of the society's time was spent on the interests of the members, even though there was evidence of community participation in the society's activities: "the fact that it *primarily* engages in activities serving the interest of its members persuades me that the Society meets the criteria."[91] With regard to membership, Mikus also agreed that the society was acting within the stipulations of section 18. She opined that, "the associate or partial membership [is] offered to males whose relationship is sufficiently connected to that of the members that they are, in my view, similarly identified."[92] Mikus dismissed Ruberto's complaint.

The decision came as a shock to Ruberto: "I taught Italian school [for twenty-seven years] ... You're telling me that I'm not Italian enough. And I'm the one that is pushing the Italian language so your children have a culture and a language to grow in ... [and] they're telling me that I'm not good enough [and] my girls are second-class [citizens]."[93] She was frustrated with the adjudicator's interpretation of the word "primarily." To her, the society did not primarily serve the interests of its members: "They're lying. All you have to do is look at the Festa [Italiana] to see that."[94] Potestio also noted that the activities of the Italian Society of Port Arthur go "beyond the normal operation of a fraternal society,"[95] and he later asserted that the decision sends the message women are "second-class citizens" – or perhaps mere "girls."[96]

Noticeably silent through this process was the ladies' auxiliary. According to Potestio, this group did not involve itself for two reasons:

> They didn't really think about what the word "auxiliary" meant ... because they had a society of their own, they didn't think it was a big issue ... They played an important role helping the men ... [but] they had no say absolutely in the way the Italian Society ought to be run. The other one I feel almost certain ... is that it probably was pressure from their husbands.[97]

Thus ends the story of Ruberto's challenge. But the issue of membership in fraternal organizations was shortly thereafter revisited by the Supreme Court of Canada.

Martinie Confirmed: Gould v. Yukon Order of Pioneers

The 1996 Supreme Court of Canada decision in *Gould v. Yukon Order of Pioneers* paralleled *Martinie* in many ways.[98] The Yukon Order of Pioneers was established in 1894 as a fraternal order and police group. It limited membership to "men of integrity and good character" who had resided in the Yukon for a minimum of ten years. While its primary focus at the time of the hearing was on "male camaraderie and mutual respect, traditions and secret rites," it also sought to "collect and preserve the literature and incidents of Yukon's history" and provide this history to the public.[99] Madeleine Gould asserted that her exclusion from the order violated section 8 of the *Yukon Human Rights Act* because the collection of history was a service to the public. Further, the history provided by the order, she argued, was distorted by the failure to include the experiences of women. The order responded that historical information was provided to the public – men and women – without discrimination and that the collection of historical materials was not itself a service. Further, it claimed exemption under section 8 as the order promoted the interests of an identifiable group – male pioneers (parallel to section 17/18 of Ontario's *Human Rights Code*).[100] The Yukon Human Rights Commission found for Gould, noting that, although history was not the predominant activity of the Yukon Order, it was not necessary that this be their primary purpose in order to uphold a finding of discrimination. It also held that history would be distorted without female input and that the Yukon Order existed to serve the whole community, despite its references to brotherhood.[101] The Yukon Order appealed.

At the Supreme Court of the Yukon Territory, Wachowich J. overturned the decision of the board, finding that the Yukon Order did not provide goods or services and therefore that discrimination had not occurred under section 8. The collection of information was not a service to the public. The court cited a need to balance the competing interests of gender equality and "the rights of free citizens to form associations with whomever they might wish."[102] This decision was upheld by the Court of Appeal. Hinkson J.A. held that the "starting point is to consider the service that the lodge is providing to the public," and found that this service was the sharing, not the collection, of history. He considered it unnecessary to explore the applicability of section 10.[103] Gould appealed further to the Supreme Court of Canada, where the intervenor, Yukon Status of Women, further added the argument that membership in the Yukon Order was itself "a service offered to the public."[104]

The majority of the Supreme Court of Canada denied Gould's appeal.[105] Iacobucci J. (speaking for Lamer J., Sopinka J., Gonthier J., Cory J., and Major J.) found the service – the history – was provided to the public without discrimination and reference to section 10 was therefore unnecessary.[106] In a much more detailed concurring analysis, LaForest J. noted that "the Act does not prohibit discrimination in all its forms," and he framed the issues in two questions: Was the collection of history a service to the public? And, did the order fall under the protection of section 10?[107] He asserted that the collection of historical material "done by a volunteer and made available to all" did not create a public relationship. Nor did he believe the history of the Yukon would be distorted "by the exclusion of women from its membership."[108] Further, he rejected the argument of the intervenor that membership was itself a service. The spectrum of benefits for the order was small and, "while it may have passed out of fashion to create and preserve fraternal memberships of this kind, it is quite another thing to prohibit the establishment of gender-based organizations."[109] He found that the organization was private, that "what is offered by the Order to its members is an intimate association, an opportunity to socialize in an all-male environment," and that, given this finding, consideration of the section 10 issue was unnecessary.[110]

Importantly, the court split on gender lines, with both L'Heureux-Dubé J. and McLachlin J., separately, in dissent. L'Heureux-Dubé began her decision with the scathing assertion "it is difficult to conceive of a more blatant example of sex-based discrimination."[111] She asserted that the board was within its rights, and correct in law, to find a nexus between the membership and a distorted history being provided to the public, and asserted "this Court should not overturn the Board simply because there is some other reading that this Court prefers."[112] McLachlin explicitly rejected LaForest's argument that membership was not a benefit or service to the public. She found that the Yukon Order had several public functions, including honouring pioneers, and queried, "Can it be right then, that it is denied to one half of the Yukon population, its women?"[113] She rejected the assertion that the Yukon Order was small and private, asserting that it "has arrogated to itself a prominent public profile" that brought it within the purview of the *Human Rights Act*.[114] Further, she rejected LaForest's emphasis on male camaraderie as a justification for privacy: "LaForest places considerable weight on the male camaraderie and fraternal aspects of the order. I would not," she wrote, as, if this suffices for exemption from human rights legislation, any group "could make a convincing argument for the perpetual exclusion of women."[115] Both McLachlin and L'Heureux-Dubé would have upheld the appeal by Gould and restored the original decision of the board. Although *Gould* did not deal with the section 10 issue, this decision upheld the right of a fraternal order to exclude women. This case, and, by default, *Martinie*, has yet to be overturned.

Conclusion

The Italian Society of Port Arthur continues to exclude women. For Ruberto, the society's insistence on being male-only is "a cultural thing. They don't want women coming into their domain and boss[ing] them around … [At the society] they could smoke as much as they want, drink as much as they want, they could play cards as much as they want without anyone telling them what to do."[116] As one member admits, the organization offers men a place of sanctuary: "Who," he asks, "wants to have their wives [at the Italian Hall] when they get to see them all the time?"[117] But the Italian Society of Port Arthur holds significant social power in the Italian-Canadian community. Should this group be able, to quote Justice Beverley McLachlin, to continue its "perpetual exclusion of women"?[118]

In contrast, the Principe di Piemonte of Fort William opened its membership to women in 2018. This decision was spearheaded by then-president Renato Rigato, who saw the injustice his daughters faced. According to his obituary, extending membership in this way was one of the proudest accomplishments of his lifetime.[119] When asked whether the decision in Fort William might sway the Italian Society of Port Arthur, the latter's president, Benny Melchiorre, argued that change remains unnecessary: "I don't see the need for us to be together … They [the Ladies Society] do their thing and we do our thing … In the future, maybe twenty or thirty years down the road it might change … But right now … I don't see a need."[120]

Looking back on the hearing, Ruberto regrets nothing: "I can't keep my mouth shut … I spoke up … You regret more what you don't do than what you have [done]."[121] With recent movements such as Time's Up and #MeToo, Ruberto hopes younger generations in Port Arthur might be more apt to open their doors to female members. If they do not, she foresees both a cultural dilution of the society and a decline in membership.[122]

Martinie and *Gould* effectively deny women a role as equal contributors in their own cultural communities. While collective rights for groups facing discrimination are imperative, as they are "designed to guarantee group survival by protecting [them] from majority interference," the question remains, to what degree can Italian men now be considered a group facing discrimination?[123] Ruberto's story deserves to be remembered: she challenged systemic discrimination, which had been invisible, or at least beyond remediation, to a human rights tribunal. In the failure of the board to find for Ruberto, the *Martinie* case provides a window on intra-community gendered dynamics and the limitations and contradictions of human rights protections, particularly for women within cultural groups. The case is both historically important and currently relevant. It is time for a new challenge similar to *Martinie* and for a decision that would both mirror the dissent in *Gould* at the Supreme Court of Canada and include the voices of women who have too long been silenced.

NOTES

1 Joanne Ruberto interview, Thunder Bay, 11 March 2019. At the time of the hearing, Joanne went by Ruberto Martinie. She is now divorced and refers to herself as Ruberto. We respect this choice throughout.

2 *Ontario Human Rights Code, 1981*, SO 1981, c. 53, s. 1.

3 By the time of Ruberto's hearing, this had changed to *Ontario Human Rights Code*, RSO 1990, s.18, which stated: "Special interest organizations – The

rights under Part 1 to equal treatment with respect to services and facilities, with or without accommodation, are not infringed where membership or participation in a religious, philanthropic, education, fraternal or social institution or organization that is primarily engaged in serving the interests of persons identified by a prohibited ground of discrimination is restricted to persons who are similarly identified." *Ontario Human Rights Code, 1981*, SO 1981, c. 53, s. 17.

4 *Martinie v. The Italian Society of Port Arthur* (1995), 24 CHRR D/169 (Ont. Bd. of Inquiry) (*Martinie*, Ont. Bd. of Inquiry).

5 See *Roberts v. Jaycees* (1984), 104 S Ct. 3244; *Board of Directors of Rotary International v. Rotary Club of Duarte* (1987), 55 LW 4606; *Re Ontario Rural Softball Association and Bannerman* (1978), 21 OR (2d) 395 (HC), affirmed (1979), 26 OR (2d), 134 (CA); *Re Cummings and Ontario Minor Hockey Association* (1978), 21 OR (2d) 389 (HC), affirmed (1979), 26 OR (2d), 7 (CA); *Re Blainey and Ontario Hockey Association* (1986), 26 DLR (4th) 728 (Ont. CA); Ann H. Jameson, "Roberts v. U.S. Jaycees: Discriminatory Membership Policy of a National Organization Held Not Protected by First Amendment Freedom of Association," *Catholic University Law Review* 34 (1984–85): 1055; Michael Burns, "The Exclusion of Women from Influential Men's Clubs: The Inner Sanctum and the Myth of Full Equality," *Harvard Civil Rights and Civil Liberties Law Review* 18 (1983): 321; and Celia Laframboise and Leigh West, "The Case of All-Male Clubs: Freedom to Associate or License to Discriminate," *Canadian Journal of Women and the Law* 2 (1986–88): 335–61. Although the last article focused exclusively on business and professional clubs, not fraternities, the authors' finding that "where these clubs are often described merely as 'social clubs' which provide a relaxed atmosphere for 'boys to be boys,' in fact, they wield enormous influence on the commercial and political lives of the communities in which they are located" (337) is relevant in the context of *Martinie*.

6 *Gould v. Yukon Order of Pioneers*, [1996] 1 SCR 571.

7 *Martinie*, Ont. Bd. of Inquiry.

8 John Potestio, *Becoming Canadian: Memories of an Italian Immigrant* (Thunder Bay: Thunder Bay Historical Museum Society, 2020), 135–7; John Potestio, *The Italians of Thunder Bay* (Thunder Bay: Chair of Italian Studies, Lakehead University, 2005), 19 and 30.

9 Although the name is grammatically incorrect, the women's organization is recognized as the "Italian Ladies Society of Port Arthur." For general information on the *Martinie* hearing, see Bruce Ziff, *Unforeseen Legacies: Reuben Wells Leonard and the Leonard Foundation Trust* (Toronto: University

of Toronto Press, 2000), 230, and Ontario Human Rights Commission, "Balancing Conflicting Rights: Towards an Analytical Framework," https://www3.ohrc.on.ca/sites/default/files/attachments/Balancing_conflicting_rights%3A_Towards_an_analytical_framework.pdf (accessed 8 June 2008), 9.

10 See, for example, Roberto Perin and Franc Sturino, eds., *Arrangiarsi: The Italian Immigrant Experience in Canada* (Montreal: Guernica Editions, 1989); John Potestio and Antonio Pucci, eds., *The Italian Immigrant Experience* (Thunder Bay: Canadian Italian Historical Association, 1988); Walter Temelini, *The Leamington Italian Community: Ethnicity and Identity in Canada* (Kingston and Montreal: McGill-Queen's University Press, 2019); Silvano M. Tomasi and Madeline H. Engel, eds., *The Italian Experience in the United States* (Staten Island, NY: Center for Migration Studies, 1970); John Zucchi, *Italians in Toronto: Development of a National Identity, 1875–1935* (Montreal and Kingston: McGill-Queen's University Press, 1988); and "Italians in Ontario," a special issue of *Polyphony* 7, no. 2 (Fall/Winter 1986).

11 Donna Gabaccia and Franca Iacovetta, "Women, Work, and Protest in the Italian Diaspora: An International Research Agenda," *Labour/Le travail* 42 (Fall 1998): 176. See also Genni Donati Gunn, "Avoiding the Stereotypes," in *Writers in Transition: The Proceedings of the First National Conference of Italian-Canadian Writers*, ed. C. Dino Minni and Anna Foschi Ciampolini (Montreal: Guernica, 1990), 142; Teresa Bosa, "The Italo Canadian Woman in a Changing World," *Canadian Mosaic* (1975): 12–13, 16; Betty Boyd Caroli, Robert F. Harney, and Lydio F. Tomasi, *The Italian Immigrant Woman in North America* (Toronto: Multicultural History Society of Ontario, 1978); Nzula Ciatu, et al., eds., *Curaggia: Writing by Women of Italian Descent* (Toronto: Women's Press, 1998); Mirna Cicioni and Nicole Prunster, eds., *Visions and Revisions: Women in Italian Culture* (Providence, RI: Berg, 1993); Giovanna Del Negro, *Looking through My Mother's Eyes: Life Stories of Nine Italian Immigrant Women in Canada* (Toronto: Guernica, 1997); Rosanna De Rango, "My Elderly Sisters of Italy," *Canadian Woman Studies* 8, no. 2 (1987): 47–9; Karen Dubinsky and Franca Iacovetta, "Murder, Womanly Virtue, and Motherhood: The Case of Angelina Napolitana, 1911–1922," *Canadian Historical Review* 72, no. 4 (1991): 505–31.

12 By 1910, 70 per cent of the immigrants who came to Canada were men. See Vittorio Briani, *Il Lavore Italiano Oltremare* (Rome: Ministero degli Affari Esteri), 247–8, quoted in Clifford J. Jansen, *Italians in a Multicultural Canada* (New York: Mellen Press, 1988), 19. The idea of benevolent groups can be traced back to the early nineteenth century in northern Italy. They originated as a means for those among the middle class, especially artisans, to fight for improved wages, better working conditions, and

the reduction of working hours. See Rudolph J. Vecoli, "Contandini in Chicago: A Critique of *The Uprooted*," *Journal of the American History* 51, no. 3 (December 1964): 412, quoted in Humbert S. Nelli, "Italians in Urban America," in Tomasi and Engel, *The Italian Experience*, 88–9; Daniel Horowitz, *The Italian Labor Movement* (Cambridge, MA: Harvard University Press, 1963), 40; Antonio Pucci, "Community in the Making: A Case Study of a Benevolent Society in Fort William's 'Little Italy'," Thunder Bay Historical Museum Society *Papers and Records* (1978): 16; Joseph LaPalombra, *The Italian Labor Movement: Problems and Prospects* (Ithaca, NY: Cornell University Press, 1957), 3; Nicholas DeMaria Harney, *Eh Paesan! Being Italian in Toronto* (Toronto: Toronto University Press, 1998), 15; and Nelli, "Italians in Urban America," 88.

13 Clifford Sifton, quoted in Robert F. Harney, *Italians in Toronto* (Toronto: Multicultural History Society of Ontario, 1978), 9, and Jansen, *Italians in a Multicultural Canada*, 18.

14 Franca Iacovetta, *Such Hardworking People: Italian Immigrants in Postwar Toronto* (Kingston and Montreal: McGill-Queen's University Press, 1992), 109.

15 This is not to say that mutual benefit societies in Italy were not concerned with financial benefits. See Horowitz, *The Italian Labor Movement*, 12; LaPalombra, *The Italian Labor Movement*, 2; and J.S. McDonald, "Italy's Rural Social Structure and Emigration," *Occidente* 12 (September/October 1956): 443–6, quoted in Nelli, "Italians in Urban America," 89.

16 *Padroni* is the term referring to Italian labour agents who acted as mediators between Italian labourers and companies in North America, South America, and Australia. See Robert F. Harney, "Montreal's King of Italian Labour: A Case Study of Padronism," *Labour/Le travail* 4 (1979): 57–84; Humbert S. Nelli, "The Italian Padrone System in the United States," *Labor History* 2 (Spring 1964): 153–67; Robert F. Harney, "The Padrone and the Immigrant," *Canadian Review of American Studies* 5 (Fall 1974): 101–18; and Luciano J. Iorizzo, *Italian Immigration and the Impact of the Padrone System* (New York: Arno Press, 1980).

17 The Italian Club of Tampa (L'Unione Italiana) was a forerunner of more than 1,400 mutual aid societies that flourished in Italian neighbourhoods throughout the United States. See Anthony P. Pizzo, "The Italian Heritage in Tampa," in *Little Italies in North America*, ed. Robert F. Harney and J. Vincenza Scarpaci (Toronto: Multicultural History Society of Ontario, 1981), 137.

18 In 1902, it was renamed the Italian Immigration Aid Society for Canada. See A.V. Spada, *The Italians in Canada* (Ottawa: Riviera Printers and Publishers, 1969), 96–7, and Nicoletta Serio, "Canada as a Target of Trade and Emigration in Post-Unification Italian Writing," in Perin and Sturino, *Arrangiarsi*, 110.

19 On 1 January 1970, the twin cities of Port Arthur and Fort William merged to form the city of Thunder Bay.

20 Antonio Pucci, "The Italian Community in Fort William's East End in the Early Twentieth Century" (master's thesis, Lakehead University, 1977), xvi. There were, and are, also regional groups in the Lakehead, such as the Gran Sasso Club, the Venet Society, and the Alpini Group, but they are smaller and less influential. See Potestio, *The Italians of Thunder Bay*, 28. For the East End, see Roy Piovesana, *Italians of Fort William's East End, 1907–1969* (Thunder Bay: Institute of Italian Studies, Lakehead University, 2011).

21 Pucci, "The Italian Community in Fort William's East End," 207.

22 *Constitutions, By-Laws and Rules of Order Società Italiana di Benevolenza Principe di Piemonte of Fort William*, May 2005, article I, Name and Objective, 7. Games such as bocce, tresette, briscola, and scopa were provided: Edward C. Banfield, *The Moral Basis of a Backward Society* (Glencoe, IL: Free Press, 1958), 66.

23 John Potestio, *The History of the Italian Mutual Benefit Society, 1929–1984* (Thunder Bay: Italian Mutual Benefit Society of Port Arthur, 1985), 6.

24 Ibid., 15.

25 The trustees of the Order Sons of Italy of Ontario were arrested by the RCMP on suspicion of being fascists, and mortuary and benefit funds were frozen: Gabriele Pietro Scardellato, *Within Our Temple: A History of the Order Sons of Italy of Ontario* (Toronto: Order Sons of Italy of Canada, 1995), 19.

26 Antonio Pucci, "Thunder Bay's Two Little Italies, 1880s–1940s," *Polyphony: The Bulletin of the Multicultural History of Ontario* 9, no. 2 (1987): 58.

27 The Trieste Lodge of Hamilton is an early example. In 1961, a majority of members voted to remove sick benefits. The mortuary fund remained for a few more years, but it too was eventually phased out in 1968. In 1994, the Mutual Benefit Society of the Order Sons of Italy of Ontario was fully dissolved: Scardellato, *Within Our Temple*, 90–1.

28 At the local level, the Italian Mutual Benefit Society, with the help of C.W. Cox, mayor of Port Arthur, raised $2,571 by March 1953. Luciano Iorizzo, "The Italians of Oswego," in Harney and Scarpaci, *Little Italies in North America*, 175, and Potestio, *History of the Italian Mutual Benefit Society*, 63.

29 Gianni Grohavez, *The First Half Century / Il Primo Mezzo secolo, 1932–1982: Famee Furlane* (Toronto: Town Press, 1982), 105.

30 They had acquired land on which to build a facility: ibid., 105.

31 *Martinie*, Ont. Bd. of Inquiry, 2.

32 *Constitution of the Italian Society of Port Arthur*, 1992, amended 2006, article I – Name.

33 Women and children made up half of the annual Italian volume to Canada by the mid-1950s. By the decade's end, more than 81,000 women had come, making up just over 30 per cent of the total volume of Italian immigrants during this decade: Iacovetta, *Such Hardworking People*, 78.

34 *Constitution of the Italian Society of Port Arthur*, article I – Name.

35 *Thunder Bay Mosaic: Ethnic Community Profiles* (Thunder Bay: Thunder Bay Multicultural Association, 1983), 37. In April, the society holds its annual spring tea, with proceeds donated to the Canadian Cancer Society and the Northern Cancer Research Foundation. They also help with the Festa Italiana in August.

36 The group still focuses on "celebrating the customs, traditions, and festivals of their homeland in addition to fundraising for multiple local charities": Rev. Dan Lapolla, *Diocese of Thunder Bay Newsletter*, Spring 2018, 9.

37 There were some organizations, including branches within the Order Sons of Italy of Ontario, that decided to open up their membership to women; however, this practice was uncommon: Francesco Saverio Nitti, *Scritti Sulla Questione Meredionale*, vol. 4 (Bari: Editori Laterzza, 1909), 328, quoted in Pucci, "The Italian Community in Fort William's East End," 209.

38 Participant B interview, Thunder Bay, 6 July 2008; Potestio, *Becoming Canadian*, 134–7.

39 John Potestio interview, Thunder Bay, 9 July 2019. This is similar to arguments made in cases in the United States in which both the Jaycees and Rotary International depicted themselves as social clubs in which men could "relax": *Roberts v. Jaycees* (1984), 104 S Ct. 3244; *Board of Directors of Rotary International v. Rotary Club of Duarte* (1987), 55 LW 4606; Jameson, "Roberts v. U.S. Jaycees"; Burns, "The Exclusion of Women."

40 John Potestio interview, Thunder Bay, 9 July 2019. Potestio did not remember the exact date of this vote, and the society refused to share the records.

41 Sam Federico interview, Thunder Bay, 31 July 2008.

42 An unknown individual took Potestio's picture down from the wall of presidents, leaving it on the ground. Potestio likened this act to something he witnessed when travelling to the Soviet Union in 1974 and the removal of evidence of Trotsky's role in the revolution: Potestio interview, Thunder Bay, 9 July 2019.

43 Iacovetta, *Such Hardworking People*, 8.

44 John Potestio, *In Search of a Better Life: Emigration to Thunder Bay from a Small Town in Calabria* (Thunder Bay: Thunder Bay Historical Museum Society, 2000), 22–31.

45 Giuseppe M. Lucrezio and Luigi Favero, "Un Quarto di Secolo di

Emigrazione Italiana," *Studi Emigrazione* 9, nos. 25/26 (March/June 1972): 8. By 1951, 85,000 Italian immigrants had settled in Ontario and 152,245 in Canada. By 1961, the Italian population in Ontario rose to 275,000 and in Canada to 450,351. See Alberto Di Giovanni, "Preface," in *The Luminous Mosaic: Italian Cultural Organizations in Ontario*, ed. Julius Molinaro and Maddalena Kuitunen (Welland, ON: Éditions Soleil, 1993), 2; Jansen, *Italians in a Multicultural Canada*, 30; and John Zucchi, "Cultural Constructs or Organic Evolution? Italian Immigration Settlements in Ontario," in Molinaro and Kuitunen, *The Luminous Mosaic*, 30.

46 Bruno Ramirez, *The Italians in Canada* (Ottawa: Canadian Historical Association, 1989), 8.

47 Ibid.

48 Chain migration was a popular method for Italians to establish themselves permanently overseas. The majority sent for only one or two relatives at a time. The process influenced Italian immigrants to come to certain cities and towns where their family and fellow *paesani* were already established. See Franc Sturino, "Contours of Post-War Italian Immigration to Toronto," *Polyphony* (Summer 1984): 127–30; Franc Sturino, *Forging the Chain: A Case Study of Italian Migration to North America, 1880–1930* (Toronto: Multicultural History Society of Ontario, 1990); and Sturino, "Italian Emigration: Reconsidering the Links in Chain Migration," in Perin and Sturino, *Arrangiarsii*, 63–90.

49 Ruberto's father wanted the family to continue their journey without the child, and collect him later, but her mother refused: Joanne Ruberto interview, Thunder Bay, 11 March 2019.

50 Ruberto describes her grandmother, Caterina Ruberto (née Paola), as a self-sacrificing woman who would "take food from her own mouth and give it to us [the grandchildren]." In ill health, she was advised not to go to Canada, but asserted that "even if she just got off the plane and saw her kids and then died, it would be worth it." The family was reunited, and Caterina lived to the age of eighty-four: ibid.

51 Ruberto recalls her father being more liberal than most Italian fathers at the time: ibid.

52 Just as there were expectations placed upon young women, there were those for young men as well. When it came to dating (courtship), boys were encouraged to date Italian or Italian-Canadian girls who embodied the virtues of chastity, obedience, and domesticity – traits that *inglesi* (Canadian or non-Italian) women were not believed to possess. See Potestio, *In Search of a Better Life*, 117.

53 Ruberto interview, 11 March 2019.

54 Ruberto interview, Thunder Bay, 5 August 2019.
55 See Elena Zambelli, Arianna Mainardi, and Andrea Hajek, "Sexuality and Power in Contemporary Italy: Subjectivities between Gender Norms, Agency and Social Transformation," *Modern Italy* 23, no. 2 (2018): 129–38, and Judith Adler Hellman, "Italian Feminism: Women's Movements in the Red Belt of Italy," *Canadian Woman Studies* 8, no. 2 (1987): 88–92.
56 Ruberto interview, March 2019.
57 Ruberto interview, Thunder Bay, 21 July 2019.
58 Ruberto interview, Thunder Bay, 15 July 2008.
59 Ibid.
60 Sam Federico interview, Thunder Bay, 31 July 2008.
61 Ruberto interview, Thunder Bay, 2 February 2019.
62 Ruberto interview, 15 July 2008. The ladies' society does award two bursaries of one hundred dollars each to one male and female student with the highest first-year marks in postsecondary education – the students must be children of members in good standing. As for members of the ladies' society, the benefits available are rather limited, most related to costs of a banquet. See *Constitution of the Italian Ladies Society of Port Arthur*, 11 September 2000, 3, 4.
63 The rights to which Ruberto was referring included discounts for hall rentals and the cost of meals and death benefits to help cover funerary costs. See Ruberto, 15 July 2008.
64 The first such explicit legislation in Ontario was the 1944 *Racial Discrimination Act*, intended to address the problem of the unwillingness of shopkeepers and other service providers to serve non-white members of the public by displaying "Whites Only" signs. But this was insufficient, and in 1954 discrimination was prohibited in the "accommodation, services or facilities available in any place to which the public is customarily admitted." See *Fair Accommodation Practices Act*, 1954, SO 1954, c. 28.
65 Robert J. Sharpe and Katherine E. Swinton, *The Charter of Rights and Freedoms* (Toronto: Irwin Law, 1998), 13, and Ontario Human Rights Commission, *Human Rights Policy in Ontario* (Toronto: Government of Ontario, 1999), 8.
66 Ontario Human Rights Commission, *Guide to the Human Rights Code* (Toronto: Government of Ontario, 1999), 7.
67 *Canadian Human Rights Act*, SC 1976–77, c. 33, s. 1.
68 Sharpe and Swinton, *The Charter of Rights and Freedoms*, 14.
69 Ontario Human Rights Commission, *Guide to the Human Rights Code*, 8. It is perhaps not surprising that Ruberto did not receive an expansive interpretation of her rights as a woman. Ruth Frager and Carmela Patrias have amply illustrated the hesitation with which human rights activists viewed questions of sex discrimination. See Ruth A. Frager and Carmela

Patrias, "Human Rights Activists and the Question of Sex Discrimination in Post War Ontario," *Canadian Historical Review* 93, no. 4 (2012): 583–610.

70 The Human Rights Commission was responsible for the administration and enforcement of the *Human Rights Code* in Ontario, and, at the time of this hearing, it was the role of boards of inquiry to make the final decisions in cases. See Ontario Human Rights Commission, *Guide to the Human Rights Code*, 6; *Human Rights Code*, RSO 1990, c. H.19, s. 29. Now, cases are heard by the Ontario Human Rights Tribunal, and tribunals are not under the supervision of the commission, which has an educational function: see https://www.ohrc.on.ca/en/human-rights-system. Further, individuals have carriage of their own cases, and the commission has a legal department dedicated to helping individuals to file claims.

71 *Ontario Human Rights Code, 1981*, SO 1981, c. 53. From the time Ruberto filed to the date of the hearing, the Ontario *Human Rights Code* underwent a revision.

72 Ibid., s. 1.

73 Judith Keene, *Human Rights in Ontario* (Toronto: Carswell, 1983), 12–13. Ruberto also asserted that the society had violated her rights under section 8 of the code, in which it is stated "No person shall infringe or do, directly or indirectly, anything that infringes a right under this Part." This argument was not considered by the tribunal so is not further developed here.

74 *Re Blainey and Ontario Hockey* Association (1986), 26 DLR (4th) 728 (Ont. CA).

75 *Roberts v. Jaycees* (1984), 104 S Ct 3244; *Board of Directors of Rotary International v. Rotary Club of Duarte* (1987), 55 LW 4606; Jameson, "Roberts v. U.S. Jaycees"; and Burns, "The Exclusion of Women." Despite these contemporary decisions, Ruberto does not remember using any case precedents. The hearing summary states only the cases used by the commission for its decision and those cited in the respondent's argument.

76 *Human Rights Code, 1981*, SO 1981, c. 53, s. 17. By the time of Ruberto's hearing, this had changed to *Human Rights Code*, RSO 1990, c. H.19, s. 18.

77 It is worth noting that such delays are not uncommon in human rights hearings.

78 Ruberto interview, 2 February 2019.

79 Ruberto interview, 5 August 2019.

80 *Martinie*, Ont Bd of Inquiry, 1.

81 Ontario Human Rights Commission, *Guide to the Human Rights Code*, 71; Ziff, *Unforeseen Legacies*, 142.

82 Ontario Human Rights Commission, 8. Defences and Exceptions, 17 September 2015, Ontario Human Rights Commission, http://www.ohrc.on.ca/en/policy-preventing-discrimination-based-creed/8-defences-and-exceptions.

83 *Martinie*, Ont Bd of Inquiry, 5.

84 The term "primarily" in this case has been interpreted as "for the most part," as opposed to "solely." Ontario Human Rights Commission, "Balancing Conflicting Rights," 10.

85 *Martinie*, Ont Bd of Inquiry, 5.

86 To reinforce its argument, the respondent relied on the cases of *Sehdev v. Bayview Glen Junior Schools Ltd.* (1998), 9 CHRR d/4881 (Ont Bd of Inquiry), and, more importantly, *Gould v. Yukon Order of Pioneers* (1989), 14 CHRR d/176 (SC YK). *Sehdev* upheld the school's strict uniform policy, which precluded the admission of a young Sikh student who wore a turban. *Gould* upheld the denial of membership to a woman in a fraternal organization deemed to be private. This decision was later upheld by the Supreme Court of Canada and will be further discussed in this section.

87 *Martinie*, Ont. Bd. of Inquiry, 7.

88 *Constitution of the Italian Society of Port Arthur* 1992 (as amended in 2006), article II.

89 *Martinie*, Ont. Bd. of Inquiry, 7.

90 The Human Rights Commission relied on their own set of cases involving discrimination in addition to the *Gould* hearing. These included the following: *Zurich Insurance Company v. Ontario Human Rights Commission* (1992), 16 CHRR d/255 (SCC); *Margaret Caldwell v. St. Thomas Aquinas High School* (1984), 6 CHRR d/2643 (SCC); *Tomen and Smith v. Ontario Teachers Federation and Ontario Public Schools Teachers Federation* (unreported); and *Gregory v. Donauschwaben Park Waldheim Inc.* 13 CHRR d/505 (Ont. Bd. of Inquiry).

91 *Martinie*, Ont. Bd. of Inquiry, 20 (emphasis in original).

92 Ibid.

93 Ruberto interview, 11 March 2019.

94 Ibid. The Festa Italiana is held every year, drawing thousands of people from all different ethnic backgrounds over the August long weekend, with raffles, food, fireworks, and entertainment.

95 John Potestio, "The Italian Cultural Presence in Thunder Bay," in Molinaro and Kuitunen, *The Luminous Mosaic*, 223.

96 John Potestio interview, Thunder Bay, 9 July 2019.

97 Ibid. See also Potestio, *Becoming Canadian*, 136–7.

98 *Gould v. Yukon Order of Pioneers*, [1996] 1 SCR 571.

99 Ibid., para. 22. Clearly this organization was a white men's group although this was not stated explicitly in the membership rules.

100 Ibid. It is noteworthy that, while section 18 in Ontario requires that the identifiable group be one that faces discrimination, this is not explicit in section 8 of the Yukon act.

101 Ibid., paras 24–6.
102 *Gould v. Yukon Order of Pioneers* (1991), 14 CHRR D/176, 87 DLR (4th) 618 at 671, as cited in *Gould v. Yukon Order of Pioneers*, [1996] 1 SCR 571, para. 31.
103 *Gould v. Yukon Order of Pioneers* (1993), 18 CHRR D/347, 100 DLR (4th) 596 at 606; *Gould v. Yukon Order of Pioneers*, [1996] 1 SCR 571, para. 38.
104 *Gould v. Yukon Order of Pioneers*, [1996] 1 SCR 571, para. 20.
105 Much of the decision focused on the standard of correctness for the review of human rights decisions. It is not discussed in detail here, as it is not relevant to *Martinie*.
106 *Gould v. Yukon Order of Pioneers*, [1996] 1 SCR 571 1, paras 4–16.
107 Ibid., paras 41 and 44.
108 Ibid., paras 70 and 77.
109 Ibid., para. 81.
110 Ibid., paras 86 and 87.
111 Ibid., para. 98.
112 Ibid., paras 117 and 118.
113 Ibid., paras 169 and 171.
114 Ibid., para. 173.
115 Ibid., para. 174.
116 Ruberto interview, 15 July 2008.
117 Participant A interview, Thunder Bay, 5 June 2008.
118 *Gould v. Yukon Order of Pioneers*, [1996] 1 SCR 571 at para 174.
119 Obituary, Renato Rigato, *Thunder Bay Chronicle Journal*, 27 July 2019.
120 Benny Melchiorre interview, Thunder Bay, 12 July 2019.
121 Ruberto interview, 11 March 2019.
122 Ibid.
123 Joseph Eliot Maguet, "Collective Rights, Cultural Autonomy and the Canadian State," *MacGill Law Journal* 32 (1986): 184.

10

Internal and External Advocacy for Legal Reform: The Genesis of the 1986 Ontario *Family Law Act*, 1967–1986

TAYLOR D. STARR

No doctrine exists that the value of a contribution towards the family home, farm, or business by way of management, physical labour, cooking, housekeeping, or childcare is sufficient to give a spouse making such contribution – and these are almost invariably wives – any share in the business, farm, home or property.

– Law Reform Commission of Canada, *Family Property* (1975)

This committee intends to monitor application of the new law which is only an inadequate first step in recognizing women's contribution to the economic partnership in marriage. We shall continue to pressure for further vitally needed progressive amendments to this bill in Ontario.

– Press Release, 50/50 or Fight, 16 March 1978

In the wake of feminist pressures elicited by the Supreme Court of Canada's decision in *Murdoch v. Murdoch* (1973), the Law Reform Commission of Canada gave the stark assessment of matrimonial property law quoted above.[1] The *Murdoch* decision, which denied Irene Murdoch a proprietary interest in the family ranch to which she had contributed over the course of her marriage of twenty-five years, shocked Canadians. According to Mysty Clapton, women's groups across the country adopted Irene Murdoch's narrative as the basis for the matrimonial property law reform movement. Yet, Mary Jane Mossman has argued that the use of this case as the focal point for the matrimonial property law movement underrepresented most women's reality, because such law reform was beneficial only to those who could assert a claim to substantial property at marriage breakdown – a minority of cases in Canada.[2] Regardless, following *Murdoch*, there was an outcry for legislative reform from many women's groups in Canada. Lori Chambers has asserted that, since *Murdoch* was about rural/farm women, feminists could have used the case to advance understandings of the wider negative stereotypes about women's labour beyond domesticity. However, the reforms of the 1970s and 1980s were not ready to address the "artificiality of the public/private divide that pervades property law and social thinking."[3]

This chapter builds on existing scholarship by focusing on the forces at work in achieving family law reform in late twentieth-century Ontario. It does so by examining both external and internal advocacy – that is, respectively, the efforts of advocacy groups who were outside the legal profession, and the roles of female lawyers and judges, who were internal to that profession. In making this distinction, I recognize that internal and external advocacy were not mutually exclusive. Individual lawyers such as Linda Silver Dranoff exemplified the ways in which internal and external advocacy reflected a hybrid movement. The relationship between legal and political institutions also broadens the definition of internal advocacy to include governmental organizations and commissions.

At this time, the women's movement led to a large influx of women into androcentric spaces, which shaped the kinds of changes women sought with respect to the laws governing their lives inside and outside the legal profession. In Ontario, both internal and external feminist advocacy was necessary to advance family law reform. Both types of advocacy helped shape public opinion and, by doing so, establish a climate receptive to reform. The *Murdoch* case made many Canadians aware of how existing laws worked in opposition to women's needs upon marriage breakdown; the uproar in response to that decision facilitated internal and external organizing efforts – by individual lawyers, women's commissions, and broad coalitions, alongside the wider feminist movement. Together, they paved the way for changes to existing laws. This confluence of internal and external efforts reinforces the argument that the feminist movement was not only "hybrid" and ideologically diverse, but also that multiple layers of activism were operating at the same time.[4]

In addition, this chapter analyses how the law reform process was tied to broader social and cultural forces and illustrates how this process struggled to eradicate patriarchal mores to which legal institutions continued to subscribe. To demonstrate the continuity of family law and the patriarchal concepts that underpinned it, I begin with a brief discussion of the history of married women's property law from the nineteenth century and then examine family law in the latter half of the twentieth century. After providing this context, I explore the years following 1967, when the Ontario Law Reform Commission (OLRC) commenced an investigation into how laws dealing with family matters should be amended to respond to changing economic and social conditions. This section discusses influences on the OLRC as well as feminist advocacy, including the Royal Commission on the Status of Women (1970) and the political and social climate in Quebec.[5] This section culminates with the passage of the *Family Law Reform Act* (*FLRA*) of 1975 and the *FLRA, 1978*.[6]

The next section analyses the fight for reform from 1978 to 1982. It explores the judicial fallout from the *FLRA, 1978* through the lens of *Leatherdale v. Leatherdale* (1982), in which the Supreme Court of Canada caused an uproar by awarding the wife only one-quarter of the assets held in her husband's name.[7] This case, and feminist advocacy on the issues pertinent to it, provides a fruitful basis for a discussion of the inadequacy of the *FLRA, 1978*. In this section, I juxtapose the perspectives of two women internal to the Canadian justice system: Justice Bertha Wilson, who was, at the time, on the Ontario Court of Appeal, and Linda Silver Dranoff, a Toronto lawyer and activist who represented Barbara Leatherdale. I examine Wilson's decision in the important case of *Pettkus v. Becker* (1978), which influenced understandings of the rights of common law couples on dissolution of the relationship in ways that contrasted vividly with the continued denial of wives' right to property vested in their husbands' name.[8]

The final section traces the political and media responses to the need for "50/50" legislation after 1982, and how the Supreme Court's decision in *Leatherdale* provided a catalyst for reform of the *FLRA, 1978*, which, as *Leatherdale* proved, left too much to judicial discretion. It highlights the work of individuals and the Justice Committee for Family Law Reform in clearing the final hurdle in the process to secure more equitable legislation.

The historical methodology adopted here is not limited to examining pivotal moments in the Canadian courts, such as the *Murdoch* and *Leatherdale* decisions. I draw on archival material from the era, including newspaper articles, correspondence, advertisements, pamphlets, commission reports, Hansard transcripts, petitions, judicial biographies, oral history interviews, and memoirs. Combining and comparing multiple sources demonstrates how women fought to reform the law, culminating in the *Family Law Act*. By investigating historical sources beyond legislation and case law, we can gain more profound knowledge of how women's advocacy was able to produce a larger understanding of needs-based lawmaking.

Janet Hough suggests that feminist approaches to law reform illustrate the philosophical and political development of mainstream feminism. In addition, law reform efforts have revealed how the fundamental premises of liberal philosophy have served to absorb, contain, and neutralize feminist politics.[9] Since internal and external advocacy involved attempts to employ, adjust, and ultimately move beyond the liberal ideal of equality, it is important to understand how feminism became constricted, even neutralized, when it entered the law reform arena during this time.[10]

The Ontario *Family Law Act* was influenced by two significant and interrelated factors. First, the reforms reflected the external feminist discourse of late twentieth-century Canada, which drew on the language expounded in reports from the Royal Commission on the Status of Women and the Ontario Law Reform Commission. At the same time, the internal process involved lawyers in advocacy groups that were prepared to hold the provincial government accountable for the implementation of such recommendations – Linda Silver Dranoff, the Ontario Status of Women Council, the Ontario Committee on the Status of Women, the Justice Committee for Family Law Reform – as well as judgments rendered in the voice of a covert and pragmatic feminist, Justice Bertha Wilson, on the Ontario Court of Appeal.[11] Second, the new law reflected the efforts of women inside the legal profession in Ontario who pushed against the headwind of resistance to challenging ideas on matrimonial property law that were ingrained within institutional patriarchy in the legal profession as a whole. Despite the fact that women were entering the legal profession in unprecedented numbers in this period, family law reform proved a difficult fight, requiring both internal and external advocacy.

Historical Antecedents and Context

In the 1870s and 1880s, legislative reforms – reflected in various provincial Married Women's Property Acts – provided that, with respect to the acquisition, holding, and disposition of property, married women would have the same rights as single women.[12] Prior to these acts, single women had not been subject to any extensive disabilities in relation to property: disabilities were incurred upon marriage. The new laws removed the idea that marriage meant assignment of the wife's property to the husband, and they granted married women access to separate property with loss of neither title nor interest. Yet, despite such changes, laws continued to reflect enduring patriarchal entrenchment. Thus, although law reform granted the gradual extension of property rights to some women, they were still denied proprietary interest in family assets despite their domestic contributions.

Historiography on nineteenth-century matrimonial property law reform explains how the patriarchal state worked in opposition to women's efforts to secure equal rights.[13] Before reform, legal thinking that stressed "chivalry" wrote women out of the narrative under the framework of coverture and explicit patriarchy.[14] Even with reform, according to Lori Chambers, amendments to nineteenth-century matrimonial property law in Ontario did not consider the social inequalities that limited women's access to property.[15] Problems in the legislation were characteristic of the nineteenth-century belief that a wife's labour, while central to family maintenance and happiness, was part of the marital duties that a wife owed to her husband, and was therefore undeserving of economic remuneration. Chambers has further argued that law reform was not in itself a remedy to the economic inferiority of married women in the nineteenth century.[16] Her observation that the history of married women's property law relates only to those who are able to earn and to own is of particular importance when exploring how the Ontario *Family Law Act* of 1986 came into being. Economic and social structures of inequality facing women in both the nineteenth and twentieth centuries proved resilient barriers to women's full enjoyment of the fruits of legal reform.

Family property law did not change substantively between the reforms of the nineteenth century and the 1960s. Towards the end of that decade, women all over the country were participating in the hearings for the Royal Commission on the Status of Women (RCSW). In Quebec, some questioned the ability of the report of the RCSW to capture the Québécois identity, yet the commission's demands for equality were widely accepted throughout the province.[17] Following the Quiet Revolution, Quebeckers were discarding Catholicism as a measure of identity, and Quebec women were fighting to shed their traditional image as submissive, house-bound mothers of large families.[18] Joan Sangster points out that the RCSW commissioners were a homogeneous group of white, well-educated, middle-class professional women, although they did represent "urban, rural, regional and linguistic constituencies" – to a large extent, in response to concerns about accommodating the views of women from Quebec.[19] It is clear that the call for law reform specific to women and family law was a result of insight from the perspective of the political and legal elite at the time. Within the legal profession, feminist lawyers attempted to demonstrate to all Canadian women how the law worked to oppress them within family structures and to limit their recourse upon marriage breakdown.[20]

Mossman notes that law reform commissions in common law jurisdictions have been described as "filling the vacuum between the retreat of the creative judiciary, and the unresponsiveness of the legislative bodies."[21] She has questioned the RCSW's underlying assumption about how the law would have improved the status of women, and identifies how the proposed "removal" of old-fashioned ideas intensified the growing faith in the legal system to answer complex questions about social reform. According to the Royal Commission report, legislative changes would have reflected and reinforced the concept that law was an important tool to cause meaningful societal changes.[22]

The limitations of property law reforms of the nineteenth century and the recommendations of the RCSW contributed to the Ontario Law Reform Commission's investigation of the laws dealing with family matters and to subsequent external advocacy about the impact of such laws on women. Two main women's groups sought changes in existing laws at the time. The Ontario Committee on the Status of Women (OCSW) was a grassroots feminist volunteer group established in 1970. Its purpose was to seek implementation in the Ontario legislature of the recommendations of the Royal Commission on the Status of Women that were provincially related. The Ontario Committee is sometimes confused with the Ontario Status of Women Council (OSWC; sometimes called the Ontario Council on the Status of

Women), an organization appointed by the government of Ontario. The OSWC was established in response to the recommendation in the *Report of the Royal Commission on the Status of Women* (1970) that each province and the federal government set up advisory councils, which would have direct input in their respective governments' policymaking. Both the OSWC and the OCSW advocated for change in family law. The groups are examples of how internal (Ontario Council) and external (Ontario Committee) advocacy worked to create meaningful change with respect to legal reform following the RCSW and the *Murdoch* decision.

The strengths and weaknesses of the RCSW were replicated in the work of the Ontario Committee on the Status of Women.[23] Lorna Marsden and Beth Atcheson reported that "the OCSW chose an operating structure that allowed it to move relatively quickly but did not make it a priority to seek out and include women of different political-ethno-socio-economic backgrounds. We allied when the opportunity arose, but we did not seek to become a representative organization."[24] The RCSW and Ontario Committee examined legal problems on the basis of gender and were conscious of the idea that racialized women might approach the legal system differently. Yet, the Ontario Committee was focused on the recommendations from the RCSW, which spoke in terms of "all women" and "all Canadians."[25] On the other hand, the Ontario Council had members who were representative of Indigenous and Black communities.

Simultaneously, outside these specifically legal organizations, feminism grew organizationally stronger after 1970; as Sangster points out, it was not an ideologically homogeneous movement.[26] The years following 1970 saw a long-term transformation, responding to forces that had been fermenting below the surface in Canadian society. Women's collective consciousness regarding their place in society transformed, to a large extent through their sense of discontent with existing laws.[27] The changes that unfolded in the 1960s and 1970s were attributable in part to the new demographic of women who worked outside the home.[28] In family law reform advocacy, a demographic of educated, socially aware feminists emerged in the latter half of the twentieth century. Among them were women lawyers, who created a new avenue for the pursuit of social transformation. In the 1967–86 period, the numerical surge of women internal to the legal profession contributed to widespread recognition for change.[29] Internal advocacy for family law reform was a privileged space.

The Ontario Law Reform Commission and Family Property Law: Context and Influences (1967–1978)

The Ontario Law Reform Commission investigation, which began in 1967, sought to shift the ways in which law reform was practised across the country. It looked, in particular, to the example of Quebec. According to Jim Phillips and Philip Girard, a widespread trend of the post-war period was the rise in no-fault divorce throughout the developed world.[30] With the formal reduction of patriarchal and paternal authority, marriage became understood as a union of equals. In Canada, this change was most evident in Quebec, which Girard and Phillips characterize as a "looser Scandinavian-inspired community of autonomous individuals," with its reforms of the 1960s and 1970s.[31] According to Constance Backhouse, during these years, rapid change in traditional gender roles was central to the transformation of Quebec.

In 1970, the Fédération des femmes du Québec (FFQ) published a forty-six-page guide to the discussion of matrimonial regimes in the *Report of the Royal Commission on the Status of Women* and distributed thousands of copies across the province. Monique Bégin was an important influence in this campaign, and she demonstrated how to lobby for the implementation of the report's recommendations. Backhouse asserts that the FFQ was a tough network of women who brought pressure to bear on their powerful husbands in government to respond to feminist demands.[32] Powerful women in Quebec were using their social position to illuminate the importance of changes in matrimonial property law to meet the demands of the feminist movement. Women such as Claire L'Heureux-Dubé, Claire Casgrain, Réjane Laberge-Colas, Alice Desjardins, Albanie Morin, Monique Bégin, and Jeanne Sauvé were all influenced by the social momentum of something much larger than their individual work.[33] For example, while L'Heureux-Dubé's was a judge on the Quebec Superior Court, she was also situated at the front of a feminist restructuring of society, which corresponded with the wider impacts of the Quiet Revolution and the growing influence of women in the legal profession.[34]

In this context, the volume on family property law (Part IV) of the 1974 OLRC *Report on Family Law* took particular interest in the equal division of property that had already been implemented in Quebec:

> In 1968 the Civil Code Revision Office in Quebec published its *Report on Matrimonial Regimes.* A new basic law of matrimonial property, *An*

> *Act respecting matrimonial regimes,* based on the Report's recommendation, came into force on July 1, 1970. The new regime of "partnership of acquests" was essentially designed to provide for separation of property during marriage and equal division of property acquired after marriage upon death, divorce, or change of matrimonial property regime.
>
> In reviewing the present law in the context of the changed society in which we live, and encouraged by the work being done in other jurisdictions, both at home and abroad, we have not only made proposals for reform of Ontario's matrimonial property law, but have made proposals for a radical departure from existing principles. Nothing less will suffice.[35]

The reference to a "radical departure from existing principles" highlights the extent to which law reformers in Ontario were willing to go at this time and anticipates some of the larger changes to matrimonial property law that dated from the nineteenth century.[36] In its investigations, the ORLC was influenced by Quebec's social, cultural, and legal reform. Indeed, in its 1974 report, the commission asserted that Quebec's marital property law reform "combines the best features of the systems of separation of property and community property without attracting the disadvantages of either ... thereby allowing a degree of equality that is unattainable under present Ontario law."[37] As the OLRC's recommendations eventually became recognized and implemented on a national scale, Quebec reforms in this area influenced not only its neighbouring province but also the country as a whole.[38] The recommendations of the OLRC report contributed to the understanding that women were entitled to equal division of assets upon marriage breakdown.

When the OLRC considered family property law, it observed that the reforms of the nineteenth century embodied an ideal of *formal* equality. Women were granted the same rights as men to control and dispose of the property in which they had a legal or equitable interest.[39] Those reforms did not challenge the substantive inequality of most husbands and wives, nor were they intended to do so. In contrast, the OLRC acknowledged that the economic contribution of the wife was crucial to the acquisition of wealth held in the other's name, and it concluded that the separate property regime perpetuated unfairness against many women and undermined the modern view that marriage meant equal partnership. Influenced by Quebec reforms, Part IV of the *Report on Family Law* made significant and transformative recommendations in relation to a new matrimonial property regime. This regime would be designed to implement a model of distributive justice that would minimize substantive economic disparities between husbands and wives.[40]

A lack of distributive justice and a failure to recognize "the economic contribution of the wife" were exemplified in the Supreme Court of Canada's decision in the *Murdoch* case (1973) to reject Irene Murdoch's claim to a proprietary interest in the family ranch, despite her contributions to it over a long marriage. The decision produced outrage from women all over Canada and unquestionably contributed to law reform that sought to resolve the predicament of women in a position similar to that of Irene Murdoch.[41] Canadian women identified with her and were conscious of how easily they could find themselves in the same predicament.[42] Justice Bora Laskin famously dissented in *Murdoch*. In his arguments, he referred to the concept of constructive trust based on unjust enrichment. ("Constructive trust" is an equitable remedy imposed by the court to benefit a party who has been wrongfully deprived of a legal property right because of unjust enrichment. "Unjust enrichment" is a cause of action when a person receives an endowment at the other person's expense, without good legal reason.) Laskin stated that constructive trust could be applied in a matrimonial context to award Irene Murdoch a share of property acquired during marriage. This dissent was viewed as positive and potentially powerful by women, including feminist lawyers.[43]

After the *Murdoch* decision, the Ontario Committee on the Status of Women announced that it would hold its first public forum on property rights on 19 February 1974. Lorna Marsden and Beth Atcheson recount how the OCSW, from 1971 to 1985, undertook work on women's rights, with family law reform as one of its top concerns. The OCSW was part of the surge of groups seeking fundamental changes in the law, public policy, and institutions.[44] Shortly after the OCSW's public meeting, the first Ontario family law bill (Bill 117) was introduced in the provincial legislature, in June 1974. This bill drew on recommendations in the OLRC *Report on Family Law* for an equalization scheme.[45] With the passage of this bill, the *Family Law Reform Act, 1975* (formally called *An Act to reform certain Laws upon Marital or Family Relationships*) came into effect.[46] It was a direct response to *Murdoch*, and can be considered an interim measure to show governmental concern while more comprehensive solutions were developed. In his statement to the Ontario legislature on 12 May 1975, Attorney General John Clement remarked that

> the family is vital to individual and social development but much of the existing family law is based upon a social and economic environment which no longer exists. It is patronizing toward women, and it contradicts the fact that wives are individuals first, not satellites of their husbands. While the courts in Ontario have gone a considerable distance toward attaining equitable results in specific cases, the legislation which forms the basis for much of our family law must itself be revised in order to reflect our present social and economic environment.[47]

Clement proclaimed the importance of the new act in paving the way for change: "We are deeply involved in the examination and review of family property law including the law related to the matrimonial home and to support obligations. I expect to bring forward in the near future some proposals for legislative change in those areas. We acknowledge the need for reform, and this Act is tangible evidence of our commitment."[48]

Women in the province became more actively engaged in learning about legislative change in this area, and the Ontario Committee organized a meeting to inform them of the new developments. A public meeting on family property law held on 29 October 1974 at the Ontario Institute for Studies in Education had five hundred delegates in attendance.[49] The OCSW undertook a survey of its members to gauge their views on competing proposals and agendas, since women were divided on the fundamental issue of whether property was to be shared throughout a marriage or only when it broke down.[50]

Linda Silver Dranoff, a Toronto lawyer, was vital in shaping the ways in which the recommendations of the OLRC became public knowledge.[51] Dranoff's advocacy could be considered similar to the work done by Monique Bégin in Quebec. According to Dranoff, during the 1970s, family law reform was forced onto the public agenda to meet women's concerns. The Royal Commission on the Status of Women recognized marriage as an equal partnership; so, too, did the Ontario Law Reform Commission's *Report on Family Law* and the subsequent summary pamphlet compiled by the Ontario Committee on the Status of Women (prepared by Rosalie Abella, Linda Silver Dranoff, Mary Eberts, and Jane Maddaugh).[52] Within Ontario, the OCSW began to publicly push for legal reform and to provide women with access to legal information about their rights upon marriage breakdown. The provincial attorney general's office distributed 50,000 copies of the summary pamphlet to educate the public and promote change (see appendix A).[53] However, recommendations for reform were not a panacea.

Women's efforts seemed successful when Ontario became the first common law province to try to achieve equity for women in family law, through the *Family Law Reform Act, 1978* (formally titled *An Act to reform the Law respecting Property Rights and Support obligations between Married Persons and in other Family Relationships*), enacted on 31 March 1978.[54] The *FLRA, 1978* was a step forward over the previous act, as it divided marital property into defined family and non-family assets. Spouses were given more rights to family assets, though the sharing of non-family assets was limited. The new law applied retroactively to all existing marriages. The *FLRA, 1978* was not without shortcomings. In particular, it redefined marriage as an economic partnership and demanded equal division of property acquired during marriage, with the implicit expectation that women should achieve economic self-sufficiency at marriage breakdown.[55]

While its stated purpose – that is, recognizing that the marriage relationship assumes that both parties contribute, and therefore that both are entitled to equal family assets – was unprecedented, the legislation, in practice, was a compromise, and was open to interpretation. Some courts interpreted its provisions as to the limited sharing of property as requiring a wife to become self-sufficient once the marriage broke down. However, any property she received could have been insufficient, depending on each individual case and overall family wealth. Moreover, under this legislation, if a woman received any property, she did not deserve support.[56] The reforms under the *FLRA, 1978* meant that women were "running hard to stand still," and the male-dominated bench worked to hinder their progress by offering narrow interpretations of the law.[57]

Linda Silver Dranoff, Bertha Wilson, and Legal Battles with Systemic Patriarchy (1978–1982)

The Ontario *Family Law Reform Act, 1978* provided for an equal division of "family assets." The legislation defined "family assets" as property (used for shelter, transportation, recreation, and household purposes, among others) owned by one or both spouses and ordinarily used or enjoyed by them or their children while they resided together.[58] The act applied only when a marriage had broken down and a court application for property division had been made. This section addresses the shortcoming of the 1978 act and how feminist advocacy pushed for additional family law reform that would allow for absolutely equal division of all assets at marriage breakdown. The central focus of advocacy during this period dealt with redefining a wife's access to non-family assets.

The legislative debates on the bill that became the *FLRA, 1978* illustrate some of the concerns about the proposed legislation. Some members of provincial Parliament (MPPs) expressed worries that courts were likely to disregard the *FLRA* and be governed by the federal *Divorce Act*.[59] When some of his colleagues asked for the *FLRA* to be amended to recognize that women were deserving of non-family assets at marriage breakdown, Liberal MPP Albert Roy chided them for not having enough "faith in the courts" to interpret spousal support based on circumstances.[60] Many male MPPs thought that there was no need to share property because courts could award spousal support: they failed to recognize that such a monetary award might not be paid and that enforcement measures were often unsatisfactory. New Democratic MPP Melvin Swart noted that, for a long time, the courts had made decisions that favoured men:

> I ... am concerned about the court system, which I think over the years has shown some partiality to the male. I think that is disappearing. I hope it's disappearing. But I am not sure that legislation should be changed to take into account that partiality if any is there. It seems to me that it's the job of the Attorney General to see that there is no such partiality, and it seems that is where the change be made. I wear a button which says, "50–50." I support that fully, and it seems to me that the clause which we have here is a 50–50 clause.[61]

The clause might, as Swart remarked, have been 50–50, and the law itself fair and equitable, but lawyers discovered problems when the law was applied. Both internal and external women's groups realized that the law would not work in every woman's best interest. Internally, Justice Bertha Wilson applied principles such as constructive trust in precedent-setting ways to ensure greater equity. Externally, Linda Silver Dranoff tapped into the eruption of feminist activism to foster a new perspective on the importance of law reform for women.[62]

According to Bertha Wilson's biographer, Ellen Anderson, Wilson was concerned with how the division of family property would be integrated with spousal support upon marriage breakdown.[63] Wilson wanted women to have both property entitlement *and* spousal support, and for women to know exactly what they were entitled to. She believed that "the new laws reflected a profound shift in social consensus and accordingly, that the courts had a duty to enforce this duly authorized legislation."[64] *Pettkus v. Becker* (1978) made new law on the issue of division of property between unmarried couples if property was held by only one of the common law spouses.[65] The decision was unanimous, but it was Justice Wilson who provided the interpretation of constructive trust principles central to the decision.

In 1960, Lothar Pettkus, drawing on his savings, purchased land for a beekeeping business. Following the purchase, his common law partner, Rosa Becker, paid their living expenses for five years. Becker also contributed substantially to the business over the course of their relationship, and when the relationship ended in 1974, she commenced court action seeking entitlement to half the land and a share in the business. The trial judge awarded Becker forty beehives plus earnings from those hives. Because the trial judge dismissed her claim to a half interest in the land and business, she appealed to the Ontario Court of Appeal. Writing for the court, Wilson overruled the trial judge and ruled that Becker receive one-half interest in the lands owned by Pettkus. The ruling was not well received by Pettkus, and he appealed to the Supreme Court of Canada, where a six-member majority agreed with Wilson and ruled in Becker's favour.[66] While Pettkus managed to avoid paying what was due under the judgment, and Becker received nothing, the case is nonetheless significant because it redefined how the courts thought about constructive trust principles for common law couples.[672]

Wilson was, of course, aware of Laskin's dissent in *Murdoch*, and she also knew that the *FLRA, 1978* did not explicitly state that common law couples share assets equally.[68] So, if the case were to be appealed to the Supreme Court, she understood that there was a high probability that it would establish constructive trust in the common law.[69] In 1978, Wilson's judgment did not receive much publicity. The public reaction came two years later, with Brian Dickson's Supreme Court judgment. At that point, even the *Globe and Mail* concluded that "Miss Becker has won her case. She has received her fair due."[70] Sadly, Becker later committed suicide, and her note blamed the justice system for forcing her into it.[71] Despite her bitterness, her legal victory arguably went beyond what the *FLRA, 1978* mandated for married couples at this time.

Backhouse notes that Wilson's personality was such that she was able to nudge some of the most influential judges on the Supreme Court of Canada to begin rethinking judicial perspectives on gender equality, and, although her feminism was covert, many activists still viewed it as a step forward in Canadian family law.[72] By 1980, motivated by the reality that the *FLRA* applied only to married spouses, Wilson redefined jurisprudence.[73] The question for her was whether a wife's (or common law partner's) effort in contributing to the acquisition of family assets could be satisfied through an unequal division of family assets or "whether it could be compensated with access to non-family assets ... even when she had made no direct financial contribution to the acquisition of those assets."[74]

Unmarried women in Ontario were pleased with the outcome in *Pettkus v. Becker*, which demonstrated a judicial inclination to come to the aid of women in common law relationships, using the evolving equitable doctrine of the constructive trust to confer property rights at the end of a relationship. It seemed as if the courts were more willing to accept arguments on constructive trust when the couple was not married, because it would mean that judges did not have to make any alterations to expectations of the domestic duty of a wife. Despite years of "women's liberation," the interpretation of the *FLRA* for married women was still dependent on older societal norms. This anachronism was illustrated in the case of *Leatherdale v. Leatherdale*: the main difference between Rosa Becker and Barbara Leatherdale was that the latter was confined by her status as a married woman, as the common law had yet to recognize that married women's domestic work made any kind of economic contribution.[75]

Linda Silver Dranoff acknowledged that the *FLRA, 1978* was an improvement over the previous legal situation. However, once she began to represent clients under the new law, she witnessed how difficult it was to make it work for women in the face of judicial discretion.[76] In the case of Barbara Leatherdale, the long tradition of chivalry and patriarchy combined to undermine the fairness goal of the new legislation.[77]

After nineteen years of marriage, Barbara Leatherdale and her husband, Douglas, separated in 1978. Barbara was the household manager throughout the course of their marriage. She worked in a bank for nine and a half years and in the home for the other nine and a half years as caregiver to their children.[78] Barbara hired Dranoff, who was confident that she would be able to benefit from the new *FLRA*. Douglas was an employee of Bell Canada and owned Bell Canada shares and registered retirement savings plan (RRSP) pension assets. He opposed Barbara's claim to any share of the pension assets and the shares. The question, in this case, then, was the interpretation of "non-family assets."

Dranoff's recollection of the initial decision on 31 January 1980 confirmed her hope about the changes in the new law:

> Justice John J. Holland presided over the trial and ordered that the Bell Canada shares and the RRSPs – in fact, *all* of the couple's assets – be shared equally. He was very clear that this was fair since there had been real teamwork and a true pooling of finances and efforts during the marriage. The husband's assets were worth $50,000, and the wife's were worth $10,000; Justice Holland ordered the husband to pay $20,000 to the wife as an equalization payment. My hope was vindicated – the new law would be good for women. The judge ruled that investments and pensions, although defined in the FLRA as non-family assets, were, in fact, the product of the joint effort of the spouses and, therefore, according to section 4 (5), had to be shared.[79]

That decision, however, would not hold. The first barrier was that, at the Ontario Court of Appeal, Justice Lacouricère took the position that the application had not been made under the correct section of the *FLRA*, and, therefore, that the trial judge could not give the relief requested.[80] Dranoff was not successful in persuading Lacouricère that he had interpreted the *FLRA* too narrowly. On 14 November 1980, the Court of Appeal reversed the trial decision and directed that "the wife was not entitled to any part of the value of the Bell shares or the RRSPs or to receive any payment towards her legal costs."[81] Barbara Leatherdale's domestic work and contribution to the marriage, home, and family did not count. The Court of Appeal's strict interpretation of the *FLRA* meant that non-family assets could not be divided equally unless the wife had made a direct financial contribution to their acquisition.[82]

Toronto Star columnist Michele Landsberg expressed her discontent with this ruling, describing the decision as "strange and ominous."[83] She asked, "Wasn't the whole point of family law reform that a wife's work, in and out of the home, should weigh as heavily on the scales of justice as her husband's? Does it seem fair and right to anyone else that a couple's savings should go entirely to the husband?"[84] It was in this context that

Figure 10.1. Linda Silver Dranoff and Shirley E. Greenberg at the Supreme Court of Canada for the hearing of *Leatherdale v. Leatherdale* (1982)

Dranoff appealed to the Supreme Court of Canada. Present on the panel for the appeal were Justices Bora Laskin, Roland Ritchie, Brian Dickson, Jean Beetz, Willard Estey, William McIntyre, and Julien Chouinard. Initially, Dranoff was ecstatic when Laskin took the lead in questioning:

> Here was a judge who had experience with the issues raised in the *Leatherdale* case. He had been on the panels that had heard … three cases dealing with farm assets. He had written the dissenting judgment in the *Murdoch* case, stating that he would have ruled that Irene Murdoch was entitled to a property interest in the farm based on the common law of constructive trust, considering her extraordinary contribution of work money, and money's worth … He was on the majority panel that gave Rosa Becker a one-half interest in the bee-keeping business owned in the name of her common-law partner based on the law of constructive trust arising from her work, which set a new precedent in the law of property sharing between common-law partners.[85]

Yet, in *Leatherdale*, the Supreme Court touched upon but did not fully determine the issue of the relationship between section 8 of the *FLRA, 1978* and the common law constructive trust doctrine. Barbara Leatherdale had sought a division of non-family assets either under section 8 of the *FLRA* or on the basis of the doctrine of constructive trust. By a margin of 6–1, the court ruled in her favour in part, but it did not consider what, for Dranoff, was the key question of constructive trusts. Laskin, writing for the majority, declined to decide whether the trust doctrines had survived the enactment of the new *FLRA*. As he stated, "the disposition made here on the basis of specific statutory provisions of the only assets that were in issue leaves no room to consider the application of constructive or resulting trusts. Whether these institutions survive the FLRA in other circumstances need not be considered here."[86] In his *Murdoch* dissent, he had been concerned with the protection of rights in relation to constructive trust principles and matrimonial property sharing. Advocates of family property law reform criticized Laskin's judgment in *Leatherdale* as inconsistent with his opinion in *Murdoch*, but, in many ways, the inconsistency in his line of reasoning in the two cases had to do with the unevenness of family law itself as it attempted to sort out the enormous complexities of family property.[87] Laskin's decision galvanized women to advocate for further reform.

Despite the criticism levelled at the decision, the Supreme Court of Canada had found a spousal interest in property not acknowledged by the Ontario Court of Appeal: the majority allowed Barbara Leatherdale a share of non-family assets, which had been denied to her by the Appeal Court. In his dissent, Estey J. noted that he would have provided more, based on the statute's definition of contribution to family assets. Although the majority found that the work in the home by itself would not amount to a sufficient contribution, Estey could see no valid reason why household management should not, in the appropriate circumstances, qualify as such a contribution. The Supreme Court allowed Barbara Leatherdale's appeal in part, finding that she had contributed within the meaning of section 8 as a wage-earner during nine of the nineteen years of marriage, and it awarded her $10,000 – half of the trial court's assessment. The majority held that her domestic duties did not constitute a contribution to the acquisition of the Bell Canada shares.[88]

Dranoff's representation of Barbara Leatherdale is further evidence of women "running hard to stand still." *Leatherdale* was the first case to ask the Supreme Court of Canada to interpret the *FLRA, 1978*. Dranoff was initially confident that Laskin's line of reasoning exemplified in *Murdoch* would work in favour of her client's interests, and her disappointment with the decision was shared by women all over Ontario. Women who had worked tirelessly to reform the law were astounded when Barbara Leatherdale did not receive what they thought the *FLRA, 1978* had promised. That law specified equal division of family assets and discretionary treatment of non-family assets. Law reform advocates believed, with respect to the latter, that courts would be guided by the vision of marriage as a partnership of equals, but, in the end, courts applied a narrow interpretation. That reading was based in judicial insistence on a direct financial contribution to non-family assets – in *Leatherdale*, neither the Ontario Court of Appeal nor the majority of the Supreme Court of Canada was willing to consider indirect contributions to non-family assets.

Justice Estey's dissent on *Leatherdale* questioned why a city wife should not be rewarded similarly to Becker for her contribution.[89] Dranoff had asked the court "to take the larger view and not be blinded by the nature of the asset, or the kind of contribution made, but to interpret the FLRA broadly with a view to its intention to recognize the mutuality of the marriage."[90] To interpret the *FLRA* narrowly rendered it inadequate to its purpose of meaningful family property law reform. The changing family dynamic in the 1980s confronted systemic patriarchy and the old belief that wives owed unpaid domestic services to their husbands. In the view of the Supreme Court of Canada, and the Ontario Court of Appeal before it, Barbara Leatherdale would have had to prove a financial contribution to the property itself, rather than to the marriage, if she were to achieve remuneration for non-family assets under section 8 of the act.[91] Dranoff was frustrated by this aspect of the decision, and it ignited in her a determination to embark on a new course of action to amend the law. She was conscious, however, that, for any change in the law to be possible, the solution would have to already be in the public and political consciousness.[92]

Partial Victories for Women Do Not Equal Justice (1982–1986)

Immediately following the Supreme Court decision in *Leatherdale*, Dranoff began to lobby for changes to the *FLRA*, placing the blame for that judgment not so much on the courts themselves as on the legislation that allowed too much judicial discretion:

> The result is unacceptable. The law must be changed. There must be no doubt that a husband and wife are entitled to share equally all assets

> accumulated during the marriage. The OLRC had recommended this in 1974, and they were right. It was unfair that Barbara Leatherdale got only 25 percent of the pension and investment assets. The decision did not acknowledge a woman's role in the marriage as a homemaker and child-care provider. The Court admitted how difficult it was to interpret the FLRA.[93]

Media outlets immediately took interest in the decision. The *Globe and Mail* published an article the day after the Supreme Court's ruling that quoted Dranoff, who stated that "it's a partial victory, but I wouldn't say it's a good decision for women."[94] Louise Dulude, a lawyer with the National Action Committee on the Status of Women, criticized the decision as "an absolute disaster" for housewives who do not have economic independence in the public sphere.[95] The *Kingston Whig-Standard* noted that the court had failed to consider the weight of a wife's sacrifices when she leaves paid employment to support her husband in his breadwinner role.[96] The decision "gives little or no weight to the idea that a husband's business success might be psychologically linked to the support he obtains, and the confidence he gains, from a happy home life."[97] Laura Sabia assessed the issue in her column in the *Toronto Sun*, where she depicted the bill as "half-assed – better than what we had, but weak and full of loopholes. It left far too much discretion to the judiciary."[98] Laskin, "the famous dissenter" on the *Murdoch* case, would not find his decision in *Leatherdale* granted the same approval by feminists. Instead, they quoted and extensively endorsed Estey's dissent.[99]

It was becoming apparent, too, to legal professionals in other provinces that Ontario's *FLRA* was inadequate. Donald MacDougall, law professor at the University of British Columbia and editor of the *Canadian Journal of Family Law*, described the *FLRA* as "conservative by North American standards and [observed] that much more protection is guaranteed for married women in the three Prairie provinces and particularly in Quebec and British Columbia, where practically everything is divided equally."[100]

Leatherdale was discussed in the Ontario legislature eight days after the Supreme Court's decision was released. Attorney General Roy McMurtry began to consider changes to the *FLRA* in response to the widespread upsurge of frustration and concern.[101] On 21 December 1982, he formally announced a review of the *FLRA*. At the same time, he asserted that the law had been a success, as the sharing of property had significantly improved. He cited cases such as *Silverstein*, *Bregman*, and

Weir, where the "homemaker spouse" received a substantial property award.[102] He also mentioned that, in the *Leatherdale* case, the wife had received half of the family assets, in addition to a considerable portion of the non-family assets.[103] Nonetheless, McMurtry acknowledged that the law needed to be improved: "Now that we have had almost five years' experience with our Family Law Reform Act … it is time to pause and consider whether there may be some improvements indicated by the passage of time and the wisdom of hindsight."[104]

While McMurtry's announcement was a positive sign, Dranoff's experience in the *Leatherdale* case convinced her that collective action was required to ensure that appropriate changes were made to the law. She joined a number of prominent men and women, including Doris Anderson, Florence Bird, Stephen Lewis, and Laura Sabia, to launch an "a non-partisan group," the Justice Committee for Family Law Reform (JCFLR), in 1983, to further encourage reform.[105] The members agreed that equal sharing of a family's assets needed to be accomplished through legislative reform.

The JCFLR used the media to advance its campaign, capitalizing on the credibility and influential positions of its members to secure publicity. Bird, for example, was extremely reputable, known for her work as a journalist, senator, and chair of the 1970 Royal Commission on the Status of Women. Tapping into the power of its members, both women and men, the JCFLR was able to direct considerable attention to the importance of family law reform, including organizing press conferences when legal decisions were unfair to women.[106] Its most critical work was the distribution of a petition titled "Petition for Fairness in Our Family Property Laws" (reproduced in appendix B). The petition emphasized the failure of the law to recognize domestic work as an economic contribution and drew attention to the need for further reform to address the fact that the *FLRA* "is not interpreted consistently by our courts, so the outcome of individual cases is not predictable." Ultimately, the JCFLR obtained 2,300 signatures.[107]

On 19 April 1984, Dranoff took advantage of the opportunity provided by the presence of Attorney General McMurtry at a meeting of the Women's Law Association of Ontario to ask him when the law would be amended:

> Mr. Attorney General, when will you bring in family law reform providing for equal sharing of all assets accumulated during marriage between husband and wife, not just family assets like the house, car, recreational property, but now also savings, investments, pensions, and business

assets? When will you recognize the contribution to the financial worth of the family of women who manage the home and raise the children?[108]

The next month, Dranoff wrote to McMurtry on behalf of the JCFLR, enclosed the committee's petition, and took the opportunity to include recommendations about spousal support, enforcement of support obligations, and the matrimonial home.[109] McMurtry and Dranoff's correspondence and a one-on-one meeting advanced the prospects for reform legislation.[110] She was able to utilize her relationship with the attorney general to effectively establish a group of internal advocates as part of the JCFLR after the *Leatherdale* decision.[111]

All this effort contributed to the Ontario *Family Law Act* (*FLA*) of 1986. Yet it is clear, based on the Hansard debates and reports in the media, that the act would not have passed in its present form if the Conservatives had remained in power. Indeed, Conservative premier Frank Miller was the only provincial party leader who would not support a commitment to equal division of all assets accumulated during marriage.[112] Although political setbacks occurred between 1984 and 1985, by the time David Peterson, a Liberal, became premier in 1985, family law reform was at the top of his government's agenda. The Ontario *Family Law Act* contained everything Dranoff had worked for, including a recognition of marriage as an equal partnership:

(7) The purpose of this section is to recognize that child care, household management and financial provision are the joint responsibilities of the spouses and that inherent in the marital relationship there is equal contribution, whether financial or otherwise, by the spouse to the assumption of these responsibilities, entitling each spouse to the equalization of the net family properties, subject only to the equitable considerations set out in subsection (6).[113]

Recalling the enactment of the new law, Dranoff opined that "the crusade for family law reform was won."[114]

Despite this victory – achieved, in large part, through the efforts of women in a unique moment in Canadian legal history – the new act did not represent a simple narrative of progress. Internal and external advocacy had paved the way for the *FLA*, but the law did not address all problems inherent in family property law. The limitations of reform were noted in a 1991 interview with Lil Sherizen. She was one of the earliest Jewish women lawyers, called to the bar in Ontario in 1931, and a lot of her legal work focused on poor women and their family law issues. Sherizen was one of many female lawyers who did not necessarily think that the particular reforms associated with the *FLA* were to be celebrated:

> I felt very badly when this family unit, the joint family ownership, you know, husband and wife now... now have a family home, and they are each entitled, no matter whose name the property is in, if you live together, you are each entitled. Now, I don't think that is quite right, because in the smaller type of [cases], where there [are] very poor people and they have a family home, ... [the wife] is met with the theory that she has to sell the home, or she has to give her husband half, or he can control her, he can walk in there with a gun and scare the life out of her every day ... [When] the home is now worth a million dollars, [there are remedies], but what do you do with the poor little woman who has nothing?[115]

The *FLA* was a step forward from the *FLRA* in that it provided some women with the right to share family assets gained throughout the marriage. However, not all families had sufficient resources to separate and divide property and still be in good financial standing. Some couples had no property at all, and such problems continue today, where, for example, the issue of how to "share" a rented apartment pursuant to the *FLA* is still problematic.

Conclusion

This chapter has investigated how different groups and individuals, both internal and external to the legal and political systems, advocated for family law reform in the province of Ontario. Feminist activism was integrated into reform in both covert and overt ways, as various groups and individual women, including eventual Supreme Court of Canada justice Bertha Wilson and lawyer-activist Linda Silver Dranoff, confronted patriarchy in family law systems. Yet, despite some successes, feminist advocacy still amounted to "running hard to stand still." Even in the context of late twentieth-century Canada, reformers were still seeking to dispel patriarchal myths about chivalry that worked against women's equality, and they were still encountering obstacles in the pursuit of changes in family law.

Women's collective organization and powers of political persuasion together with public interest cleared the final hurdle towards 50/50 legislation in the Ontario *Family Law Act* of 1986. My examination of the genesis of this act provides a nuanced understanding of the dynamics of law reform. Family law reform, specifically in late twentieth-century Ontario, was dependent on women working both inside and outside the legal profession. Internal advocacy, a position from which women had been barred historically until 1897, was vital, but so too was the influence of external advocacy, including of grassroots organizations, some of which were inspired by changes in Quebec in the 1960s. The decades-long process of family property law reform in Ontario provides an excellent lens for assessing the historical significance of both internal and external advocacy.

As this chapter has demonstrated, change was incremental between 1967, when the Ontario Law Reform Commission began its investigations, and 1986, when the *Family Law Act* was passed. During that time, both legislation and jurisprudence implied that women's domestic contributions were undeserving of fair compensation at dissolution of marriage or a common law relationship. These understandings were ingrained in laws, and in how judges interpreted those laws when they were challenged. In attempting to make strides forward, advocacy groups and individuals found themselves limited by the premises of liberal philosophy, which had served to contain and neutralize feminist politics.[116] Both internal and external advocacy were required to change such thinking. While the activists behind the *Family Law Act* considered the new law a victory, law reform, even the 1986 act, did not remove all remnants of dated legal traditions and patriarchy, nor did it provide poor women with many options at marriage breakdown – it largely addressed the needs of middle-class women in late twentieth-century Ontario. This chapter has treated the *Family Law Act* as an endpoint because, after 1986, the law remained stable, with few amendments. That does not mean, however, that internal and external advocacy for family law reform is over.

APPENDIX A

Ontario Law Reform Commission Report (1974) Pamphlet Distributed by Attorney General

SUMMARY OF RECOMMENDATIONS OF
THE ONTARIO LAW REFORM COMMISSION
REPORT ON FAMILY PROPERTY LAW

Distributed By:

Ontario THE MINISTRY OF THE ATTORNEY GENERAL

SUMMARY OF RECOMMENDATIONS OF
THE ONTARIO LAW REFORM COMMISSION
REPORT ON FAMILY PROPERTY LAW

This pamphlet is reprinted with the kind permission of the Ontario Committee on the Status of Women, an independent volunteer organization, for whom it was prepared by lawyers Rosalie Abella, Linda S. Dranoff, Mary Eberts and Jane Maddaugh.

••••••••••••••••••••••••

Copies of the Ontario Law Reform Commission Report on Family Law may be obtained from the Queen's Printer, Queen's Park, Toronto.

APPENDIX B

Justice Committee for Family Law Reform, "Petition for Fairness in Our Family Property Laws," 25 April 1983

Ontario's Family Law Reform Act needs to be changed so that all property acquired after marriage, except gifts and inheritances, shall be shared equally by husband and wife. The Ontario Law Reform Commission in 1974 recommended a deferred community of property regime and we ask the Government at this time to review and reconsider the Commission's proposal. The artificial distinction between "family" and "non-family" assets should be abandoned, since not all families chose to put their life savings into a home or cottage; many chose savings accounts, bonds, stocks, RRSPs, pensions, etc. Equal sharing of after-acquired property is equitable and advances the legislative intention in the current preamble which acknowledges marriage as a partnership. We need unequivocal statutory guidelines to make the outcome in family law matters more predictable and straightforward.

For Fairness in Our Family Property Laws

We are concerned that Ontario's Family Law Reform Act does not treat women fairly nor recognize the contribution a woman makes to the economic partnership of marriage. The law limits sharing to "family assets" (only the house, car, cottage, furnishings) and unfairly excludes investments, savings, pensions, and business unless the wife made specific financial contribution, as a wage earner, or the husband is very wealthy. The law does not show that society values the full-time home maker or the homemaking efforts of the wage-earning wife. The law does not assure the widowed their fair share of assets accumulated during marriage. The Family Law Reform Act is not interpreted consistently by our courts, so the outcome of individual cases is not predictable. As a result, there is too much costly litigation.

We support fairness in our family property laws:

1. A husband and wife should share all assets accumulated during the marriage.
2. A deferred (until after marriage breakdown) community property system as recommended by the OLRC in 1974 should be instituted.
3. A husband and wife should be required to share equally the value of their private pension plans and savings.
4. On the death of a spouse, the survivor should get at least what he or she would have received from a property division or marriage breakdown.
5. The matrimonial home should be jointly owned during the marriage, not just on termination of the marriage.

Signed by 2300 individuals from "all walks of life"

NOTES

1 Law Reform Commission of Canada, *Family Property*, Working Paper 8 (Ottawa: Information Canada, 1975), 10; Mysty S. Clapton, "*Murdoch v. Murdoch*: The Organizing Narrative of Matrimonial Property Law Reform," *Canadian Journal of Women in the Law* 20 (2008): 206.

2 Clapton, "*Murdoch v. Murdoch*"; Mary Jane Mossman, *Families and the Law in Canada* (Toronto: Emond Montgomery, 2004), n16.

3 Lori Chambers, "Women's Work, Relationship Breakdown and the Division of Farm Property," *Canadian Journal of Law and Society* 25 (spring 2010): 93.

4 Joan Sangster, *Demanding Equality: One Hundred Years of Canadian Feminism* (Vancouver: UBC Press, 2021), 4–5, 8.

5 Constance Backhouse, *Claire L'Heureux-Dubé: A Life* (Toronto: University of Toronto Press for the Osgoode Society, 2017), 205.

6 Philip Girard and Jim Phillips, "Rethinking the Nation in National Legal History: A Canadian Perspective," *Law and History Review* 29 (May 2011): 621.

7 *Leatherdale v. Leatherdale*, [1982] 2 SCR 743.

8 *Pettkus v. Becker*, [1978] 20 OR 105 (Ont. CA).

9 Janet Hough, "Mistaking Liberalism for Feminism: Spousal Support in Canada," *Journal of Canadian Studies* 29 (1994): 147.
10 Ibid., 161.
11 Wilson did not label herself a feminist. See Ellen Anderson, *Judging Bertha Wilson: Law as Large as Life* (Toronto: University of Toronto Press for the Osgoode Society, 2001), xiv. However, scholars have argued that her judicial decisions and underlying goals were important components of the feminist agenda and emerging feminist consciousness. See Constance Backhouse, "Justice Bertha Wilson and the Politics of Feminism," *Supreme Court Law Review* 41 (2008): 34; Colleen Sheppard, "Feminist Pragmatism in the Work of Justice Bertha Wilson," *Supreme Court Law Review* 41 (2008): 84; and Clare McGlynn, "Book Review of Ellen Anderson, *Judging Bertha Wilson*," *Feminist Studies* 11 (2003): 307.
12 Ontario Law Reform Commission, *Report on Family Law, Part IV: Family Property Law* (Ontario Ministry of the Attorney General, 1974) (OLRC, *Report*), 2.
13 Feminist legal historians writing after *Murdoch* began to pay attention to the ways in which matrimonial property law reform of the nineteenth century has affected women's relationship with the laws that compelled their subservience within family structures. See Lori Chambers, *Married Women and Property Law in Victorian Ontario* (Toronto: University of Toronto Press for the Osgoode Society, 1994); Bettina Bradbury, *Wife to Widow: Lives, Laws, and Politics in Nineteenth-Century Montreal* (Vancouver: UBC Press, 2011); Constance Backhouse, "Married Women's Property Law in Nineteenth-Century Canada," *Law and History Review* 6 (1988): 211–57.
14 Backhouse, "Married Women's Property Law," 213.
15 Chambers, *Married Women and Property Law*, 183.
16 Ibid. "Companionate patriarchy" existed when women entered the institution of marriage. Bradbury, *Wife to Widow.* Constance Backhouse asserts that statutes of nineteenth-century English-speaking Canada after Confederation represented significant reforms, offering women more rights than those held by their sisters in the early part of the century. Backhouse, "Married Women's Property Law."
17 Backhouse, *Claire L'Heureux Dubé*, 205.
18 Ibid.
19 Joan Sangster, *Transforming Labour: Women and Work in Postwar Canada* (Toronto: University of Toronto Press, 2010), 238.
20 Chambers, *Married Women and Property Law*, 13.
21 Mary Jane Mossman, "'Running Hard to Stand Still': The Paradox of Family Law Reform," *Dalhousie Law Journal* 17 (1994): 18. M. Kirby,

"Change and Decay or Change and Renewal" in *Reform the Law: Essays on the Renewal of the Australian Legal System*, ed. M. Kirby (Toronto: Oxford University Press, 1983), 12. See also Toni Williams, "Re-Forming 'Women's' Truth: A Critique of the Report of the Royal Commission on the Status of Women in Canada," *Ottawa Law Review* 22, no. (1990): 725–59.

22 Mary Jane Mossman, "Families and Family Law," in *Women and the Canadian State / Les femmes et l'état canadien*, ed. Caroline Andrew and Sanda Rodgers (Montreal and Kingston: McGill-Queen's University Press, 1996), 106.

23 Beth Atcheson and Lorna Marsden, *White Gloves Off: The Work of the Ontario Committee on the Status of Women* (Toronto: Second Story Press for the Feminist History Society, 2018), 3.

24 Ibid.

25 Ibid.

26 Joan Sangster, *Transforming Labour*, 270.

27 Ibid.

28 Ibid., 238.

29 Linda Silver Dranoff, "Women as Lawyers in Toronto," *Osgoode Hall Law Journal* 10, no. 1 (1972): 178.

30 Girard and Phillips, "Rethinking the Nation," 621.

31 Ibid.

32 Backhouse, *Claire L'Heureux-Dubé*, 229.

33 Ibid.

34 Ibid.

35 OLRC, *Report*, xii.

36 Chambers, *Married Women and Property Law*, 4.

37 OLRC, *Report*, 52.

38 Ibid.

39 Ibid., 53.

40 Ibid.

41 Vanessa Gruben, Angela Cameron, and Angela Chaisson, "'The Courts Have Turned Women into Slaves for the Men of this World': Irene Murdoch's Quest for Justice," in *Property on Trial: Canadian Cases in Context*, ed. Eric Tucker, James Muir, and Bruce Ziff (Toronto: Irwin Law for the Osgoode Society for Canadian Legal History, 2012), 160.

42 Ibid.

43 Carol Rogerson, "From Murdoch to Leatherdale: The Uneven Course of Bora Laskin's Family Law Decisions," *University of Toronto Law Journal* 35 (Autumn 1985): 481.

44 Atcheson and Marsden, *White Gloves Off*, 1.

45 Ibid., 160.
46 *Family Law Reform Act, 1975*, SO 1975, c. 41.
47 *Ontario Legislative Assembly Debates* (Hansard), 29th Parliament, 5th Session, 12 May 1975, n.p., https://www.ola.org/en/legislative-business/house-documents/parliament-29/session-5/1975-05-12/hansard-1.
48 Ibid.
49 Atcheson and Marsden, *White Gloves Off*, 160.
50 Ibid., 162.
51 One of the ways Dranoff worked to disseminate knowledge was a twelve-page special report for *Chatelaine* in September 1983, explaining family law across Canada. Dranoff also routinely answered questions from ordinary women in her regular *Chatelaine* column from 1979 to 2004, popularizing a wider knowledge of the law.
52 Rosalie Abella, Linda S. Dranoff, Mary Eberts, and Jane Maddaugh, *Summary of Recommendations of the Ontario Law Reform Commission Report on Family Property Law* (Toronto: Ministry of the Attorney General, 1974).
53 Linda Silver Dranoff, *Fairly Equal: Lawyering the Feminist Revolution* (Toronto: Second Story Press, 2017), 145.
54 *Family Law Reform Act, 1978*, SO 1978, c. 2; Dranoff, *Fairly Equal*, 149.
55 Anderson, *Judging Bertha Wilson*, 101.
56 *Family Law Reform Act, 1978*, SO 1978, c. 2.
57 Mary Jane Mossman, "'Running Hard to Stand Still,'" 10.
58 *Family Law Reform Act, 1978*, SO 1978, c. 2, s. 3(b).
59 Hansard, 31st Parliament, 2nd Session, 16 March 1978; *Divorce Act*, SC 1967–68, c. 24.
60 Hansard, 31st Parliament, 2nd Session, 16 March 1978.
61 Ibid.
62 Backhouse, "Justice Bertha Wilson," 36.
63 Anderson, *Judging Bertha Wilson*, 100.
64 Ibid., 101.
65 Ibid.
66 *Pettkus v. Becker*, [1980] 2 SCR 834.
67 Pettkus married another woman in 1976, who also fought in the courts for a declaration of a half-interest in the properties. In a 1982 hearing, he insisted he had given all of his assets to his new wife and owned nothing. See Peter Bowal, "Becker v. Pettkus: Limits of the Law" (unpublished paper, University of Calgary, January 2009).
68 Anderson, *Judging Bertha Wilson*, 103; *Becker v. Pettkus*, [1978] OJ No. 3398, 87 DLR (3d) 101 (Ont. CA).
69 Anderson, *Judging Bertha Wilson*.

70 "Fair Shares," *Globe and Mail*, 27 December 1980.
71 "Woman's Suicide Ends Fight for Rights," *Globe and Mail*, 12 November 1986.
72 Backhouse, "Justice Bertha Wilson," 46. Mary Jane Mossman, "Bertha Wilson: 'Silences' in a Woman's Life Story," in *Justice Bertha Wilson: One Woman's Difference*, ed. Kim Brooks (Vancouver: UBC Press, 2009), 298.
73 Anderson, *Judging Bertha Wilson*, 105.
74 Ibid., 106.
75 Before *Leatherdale*, the Supreme Court of Canada had dealt only with cases involving claims to property arising from their direct contributions: *Murdoch v. Murdoch*, [1973/1975] 1 SCR 423; *Rathwell v. Rathwell*, [1978] 2 SCR 436; *Pettkus v. Becker*, [1980] 2 SCR 834.
76 Dranoff, *Fairly Equal*, 148.
77 Anderson, *Judging Bertha Wilson*, 106.
78 Dranoff, *Fairly Equal*, 148.
79 Ibid., 149.
80 Ibid.
81 Ibid., 150.
82 Anderson, *Judging Bertha Wilson*.
83 Michelle Landsberg, "Will Family Law Reform Let Us Down?" *Toronto Star*, 9 March 1981.
84 Ibid.
85 Dranoff, *Fairly Equal*, 156.
86 *Leatherdale v. Leatherdale*, [1982] 2 SCR 743 at 760, per Laskin CJ.
87 Rogerson, "From Murdoch to Leatherdale," 541.
88 *Leatherdale v. Leatherdale*, [1982] 2 SCR 743 at para. 141.
89 Dranoff, *Fairly Equal*, 156.
90 Ibid.
91 *Leatherdale v. Leatherdale*, [1982] 2 SCR 743 at 745.
92 Dranoff, *Fairly Equal*, 156.
93 Dranoff, Statement Outside the Court to the Media, 6 December 1982; Dranoff, *Fairly Equal*, 159.
94 "Ruling on Wife's Shares Hinges on Her Wages," *Globe and Mail*, 7 December 1982.
95 Dranoff, *Fairly Equal*, 162.
96 "Women Are Still Denied Justice in Marriage Property Rulings," *Kingston Whig-Standard*, 8 December 1982, cited in ibid.
97 "Dividing the Spoils," *Globe and Mail*, 8 December 1982.
98 Dranoff, *Fairly Equal*, 162.
99 Ibid.

100 Victor Paddy, "Equal Work Doesn't Pay," *Maclean's*, 20 December 1982.
101 Ibid.
102 Attorney General Roy McMurtry, Hansard, 32nd Parliament 2nd Session, 21 December 1982. *Silverstein v. Silverstein*, [1978] OJ No 3415; *Bregman v. Bregman*, 1978 CanLII 2189 (Ont. SC); *Weir v. Weir*, 1978 CanLII 1620 (Ont. SC).
103 McMurtry, Hansard, 21 December 1982.
104 Ibid.
105 Dranoff, *Fairly Equal*, 165. The founders consisted of Doris Anderson, Thomas Bastedo, Florence Bird, Harry Brown, June Callwood, Catherine Charlton, Shirley Greenberg, Lynn King, Stephen Lewis, Kay Macpherson, Clifford Nelson, Laura Sabia, Harriet Sachs, and Geraldine Weldman.
106 Ibid., 167.
107 Justice Committee for Family Law Reform, "Petition for Fairness in Our Family Property Laws," 25 April 1983.
108 Dranoff, *Fairly Equal*, 167.
109 Ibid., 178.
110 Ibid. McMurtry met Dranoff on 1 October 1984.
111 Ibid.
112 Jackie Smith, "Miller Silent on Women's Equal Pay Question," *Toronto Star*, 16 April 1985.
113 *Family Law Act*, SO 1986, c. 4, s. 7.
114 Dranoff, *Fairly Equal*, 197.
115 Christine J.N. Kates, "Interview with Mrs. Lil Sherizen Charon," Archives of Ontario, Osgoode Society Oral History Archive, 16 May 1991, 34–5.
116 Hough, "Mistaking Liberalism for Feminism," 161.

Index

PUBLICATIONS OF THE OSGOODE SOCIETY FOR CANADIAN LEGAL HISTORY

2023 Lori Chambers and Joan Sangster, eds., *Essays in the History of Canadian Law Volume XII: New Perspectives on Gender and the Law*
Ian Kyer, *The Ontario Bond Scandal of 1924 Re-examined*
Jonathan Swainger, *The Notorious Georges: Crime and Community in British Columbia's Northern Interior, 1909–25*

2022 Jim Phillips, Philip Girard, and R. Blake Brown, *A History of Law in Canada Volume II: Law for the New Dominion, 1867–1914*
J. Barry Wright, Susan Binnie, and Eric Tucker, eds., *Canadian State Trials Volume V: World War, Cold War and Challenges to Sovereignty, 1939–1990*
Constance Backhouse, *Reckoning with Racism: Police, Judges and the RDS Case*

2021 Daniel Rück, *The Laws and the Land: The Settler Colonial Invasion of Kahnawà:ke in Nineteenth-Century Canada*
Lyndsay Campbell, *Truth and Privilege: Libel Law in Massachusetts and Nova Scotia, 1820–1840*
Martine Valois, Ian Greene, Craig Forcese, and Peter McCormick, eds. *The Federal Court of Appeal and the Federal Court: Fifty Years of History*
Colin Campbell and Robert Raizenne, *A History of Canadian Income Tax Volume I: The Income War Tax Act 1917–1948*

2020 Heidi Bohaker, *Doodem and Council Fire: Anishinaabe Governance through Alliance*
Carolyn Strange, *The Death Penalty and Sex Murder in Canadian History*

2019 Harry Arthurs, *Connecting the Dots: The Life of an Academic Lawyer*
Eric Reiter, *Wounded Feelings: Litigating Emotions in Quebec, 1870–1950*

2018 Philip Girard, Jim Phillips, and Blake Brown, *A History of Law in Canada Volume 1: Beginnings to 1866*
Suzanne Chiodo, *The Class Actions Controversy: The Origins and Development of the Ontario Class Proceedings Act*

2017 Constance Backhouse, *Claire L'Heureux-Dube: A Life*
Dennis G. Molinaro, *An Exceptional Law: Section 98 and the Emergency State, 1919–1936*

2016 Lori Chambers, *A Legal History of Adoption in Ontario, 1921–2015*
Bradley Miller, *Boarderline Crime: Fugitive Criminals and the Challenge of the Boarder, 1819–1914*
James Muir, *Law, Debt, and Merchant Power: The Civil Courts of Eighteenth-Century Halifax*

2015 Barry Wright, Eric Tucker, and Susan Binnie, eds., *Canadian State Trails Volume IV: Security, Dissent and the Limits of Toleration in War and Peace, 1914–1939*

David Fraser, *"Honorary Protestants": The Jewish School Question in Montreal, 1867–1997*

C. Ian Kyer, *A Thirty Years War: The Failed Public /Private Partnership That Spurred the Creation of The Toronto Transit Commission, 1891–1921*

2014 Christopher Moore, *The Court of Appeal for Ontario: Defining the Right of Appeal, 1792–2013*

Dominique Clément, *Equality Deferred: Sex Discrimination and British Columbia's Human Rights State, 1953–84*

Paul Craven, *Petty Justice: Low Law and the Sessions System in Charlotte County, New Brunswick, 1785–1867*

Thomas Telfer, *Ruin and Redemption: The Struggle for a Canadian Bankruptcy Law, 1867–1919*

2013 Roy McMurtry, *Memoirs & Reflections*

Charlotte Gray, *The Massey Murder: A Maid, Her Master and the Trial That Shocked a Nation*

C. Ian Kyer, *Lawyers, Families, and Businesses: The Shaping of a Bay Street Law Firm, Faskens 1863–1963*

G. Blaine Baker and Donald Fyson, eds., *Essays in the History of Canadian Law Volume 11: Quebec and the Canadas*

2012 R. Blake Brown, *Arming and Disarming: A History of Gun Control in Canada*

Eric Tucker, James Muir, and Bruce Ziff, eds., *Property on Trial: Canadian Cases in Context*

Shelley A.M. Gavigan, *Hunger, Horses, and Government Men: Criminal Law on the Aboriginal Plains, 1870–1905*

Barrington Walker, ed., *The African-Canadian Legal Odyssey: Historical Essays*

2011 Robert J. Sharpe, *The Lazier Murder: Prince Edward County, 1884*

Philip Girard, *Lawyers and Legal Culture in British North America: Beamish Murdoch of Halifax*

John McLaren, *Dewigged, Bothered and Bewildered: British Colonial Judges on Trial*

Lesley Erickson, *Westward Bound: Sex, Violence, the Law, and the Making of a Settler Society*

2010 Judy Fudge and Eric Tucker, eds., *Work on Trial: Canadian Labour Law Struggles*

Christopher Moore, *The British Columbia Court of Appeal: The First Hundred Years*

Frederick Vaughan, *Viscount Haldane: The Wicked Step-father of the Canadian Constitution*

Barrington Walker, *Race on Trial: Black Defendants in Ontario's Criminal Courts, 1850–1950*

2009 William Kaplan, *Canadian Maverick: The Life and Times of Ivan C. Rand*
R. Blake Brown, *A Trying Question: The Jury in Nineteenth-Century Canada*
Barry Wright and Susan Binnie, eds., *Canadian State Trials Volume 3: Political Trials and Security Measures, 1840–1914*
Robert J. Sharpe, *The Last Day, the Last Hour: The Currie Libel Trial*

2008 Constance Backhouse, *Carnal Crimes: Sexual Assault Law in Canada, 1900–1975*
Jim Phillips, R. Roy McMurtry, and John Saywell, eds., *Essays in the History of Canadian Law. Volume 10: A Tribute to Peter N. Oliver*
Gregory Taylor, *The Law of the Land: Canada's Receptions of the Torrens System*
Hamar Foster, Benjamin Berger, and A.R. Buck, eds., *The Grand Experiment: Law and Legal Culture in British Settler Societies*

2007 Robert Sharpe and Patricia McMahon, *The Persons Case: The Origins and Legacy of the Fight for Legal Personhood*
Lori Chambers, *Misconceptions: Unmarried Motherhood and the Ontario Children of Unmarried Parents Act, 1921–1969*
Jonathan Swainger, ed., *The Alberta Supreme Court at 100: History and Authority*
Martin Friedland, *My Life in Crime and Other Academic Adventures*

2006 Donald Fyson, *Magistrates, Police and People: Everyday Criminal Justice in Quebec and Lower Canada, 1764–1837*
Dale Brawn, *The Court of Queen's Bench of Manitoba 1870–1950: A Biographical History*
R.C.B. Risk, *A History of Canadian Legal Thought: Collected Essays*, edited and introduced by G. Blaine Baker and Jim Phillips

2005 Philip Girard, *Bora Laskin: Bringing Law to Life*
Christopher English, ed., *Essays in the History of Canadian Law Volume 9: Two Islands, Newfoundland and Prince Edward Island*
Fred Kaufman, *Searching for Justice: An Autobiography*

2004 John D. Honsberger, *Osgoode Hall: An Illustrated History*
Frederick Vaughan, *Aggressive in Pursuit: The Life of Justice Emmett Hall*
Constance Backhouse and Nancy Backhouse, *The Heiress versus the Establishment: Mrs. Campbell's Campaign for Legal Justice*
Philip Girard, Jim Phillips, and Barry Cahill, eds., *The Supreme Court of Nova Scotia, 1754–2004: From Imperial Bastion to Provincial Oracle*

2003 Robert Sharpe and Kent Roach, *Brian Dickson: A Judge's Journey*
George Finlayson, *John J. Robinette: Peerless Mentor*
Peter Oliver, *The Conventional Man: The Diaries of Ontario Chief Justice Robert A. Harrison, 1856–1878*

Jerry Bannister, *The Rule of the Admirals: Law, Custom and Naval Government in Newfoundland, 1699–1832*

2002 John T. Saywell, *The Law Makers: Judicial Power and the Shaping of Canadian Federalism*

David Murray, *Colonial Justice: Justice, Morality, and Crime in the Niagara District, 1791–1849*

F. Murray Greenwood and Barry Wright, eds., *Canadian State Trials Volume 2: Rebellion and Invasion in the Canadas, 1837–38*

Patrick Brode, *Courted and Abandoned: Seduction in Canadian Law*

2001 Ellen Anderson, *Judging Bertha Wilson: Law as Large as Life*

Judy Fudge and Eric Tucker, *Labour before the Law: Collective Action in Canada, 1900–1948*

Laurel Sefton MacDowell, *Renegade Lawyer: The Life of J.L. Cohen*

2000 Barry Cahill, *"The Thousandth Man": A Biography of James McGregor Stewart*

A.B. McKillop, *The Spinster and the Prophet: Florence Deeks, H.G. Wells, and the Mystery of the Purloined Past*

Beverley Boissery and F. Murray Greenwood, *Uncertain Justice: Canadian Women and Capital Punishment*

Bruce Ziff, *Unforeseen Legacies: Reuben Wells Leonard and the Leonard Foundation Trust*

1999 Constance Backhouse, *Colour-Coded: A Legal History of Racism in Canada, 1900–1950*

G. Blaine Baker and Jim Phillips, eds., *Essays in the History of Canadian Law Volume 8: In Honour of R.C.B. Risk*

Richard W. Pound, *Chief Justice W.R. Jackett: By the Law of the Land*

David Vanek, *Fulfilment: Memoirs of a Criminal Court Judge*

1998 Sidney Harring, *White Man's Law: Native People in Nineteenth-Century Canadian Jurisprudence*

Peter Oliver, *"Terror to Evil-Doers": Prisons and Punishments in Nineteenth-Century Ontario*

1997 James W. St. G. Walker, *"Race," Rights and the Law in the Supreme Court of Canada: Historical Case Studies*

Lori Chambers, *Married Women and Property Law in Victorian Ontario*

Patrick Brode, *Casual Slaughters and Accidental Judgments: Canadian War Crimes and Prosecutions, 1944–1948*

Ian Bushnell, *The Federal Court of Canada: A History, 1875–1992*

1996 Carol Wilton, ed., *Essays in the History of Canadian Law Volume 7: Inside the Law – Canadian Law Firms in Historical Perspective*

William Kaplan, *Bad Judgment: The Case of Mr. Justice Leo A. Landreville*

Murray Greenwood and Barry Wright, eds., *Canadian State Trials Volume 1: Law, Politics and Security Measures, 1608–1837*

1995 David Williams, *Just Lawyers: Seven Portraits*
Hamar Foster and John McLaren, eds., *Essays in the History of Canadian Law Volume 6: British Columbia and the Yukon*
W.H. Morrow, ed., *Northern Justice: The Memoirs of Mr. Justice William G. Morrow*
Beverley Boissery, *A Deep Sense of Wrong: The Treason, Trials, and Transportation to New South Wales of Lower Canadian Rebels after the 1838 Rebellion*

1994 Patrick Boyer, *A Passion for Justice: The Legacy of James Chalmers McRuer*
Charles Pullen, *The Life and Times of Arthur Maloney: The Last of the Tribunes*
Jim Phillips, Tina Loo, and Susan Lewthwaite, eds., *Essays in the History of Canadian Law Volume 5: Crime and Criminal Justice*
Brian Young, *The Politics of Codification: The Lower Canadian Civil Code of 1866*

1993 Greg Marquis, *Policing Canada's Century: A History of the Canadian Association of Chiefs of Police*
Murray Greenwood, *Legacies of Fear: Law and Politics in Quebec in the Era of the French Revolution*

1992 Brendan O'Brien, *Speedy Justice: The Tragic Last Voyage of His Majesty's Vessel* Speedy
Robert Fraser, ed., *Provincial Justice: Upper Canadian Legal Portraits from the Dictionary of Canadian Biography*

1991 Constance Backhouse, *Petticoats and Prejudice: Women and Law in Nineteenth-Century Canada*

1990 Philip Girard and Jim Phillips, eds., *Essays in the History of Canadian Law Volume 3: Nova Scotia*
Carol Wilton, ed., *Essays in the History of Canadian Law Volume 4: Beyond the Law – Lawyers and Business in Canada 1830–1930*

1989 Desmond Brown, *The Genesis of the Canadian Criminal Code of 1892*
Patrick Brode, *The Odyssey of John Anderson*

1988 Robert Sharpe, *The Last Day, the Last Hour: The Currie Libel Trial*
John D. Arnup, *Middleton: The Beloved Judge*

1987 C. Ian Kyer and Jerome Bickenbach, *The Fiercest Debate: Cecil A. Wright, the Benchers and Legal Education in Ontario, 1923–1957*

1986 Paul Romney, *Mr. Attorney: The Attorney General for Ontario in Court, Cabinet and Legislature, 1791–1899*
Martin Friedland, *The Case of Valentine Shortis: A True Story of Crime and Politics in Canada*

1985 James Snell and Frederick Vaughan, *The Supreme Court of Canada: History of the Institution*

1984 Patrick Brode, *Sir John Beverley Robinson: Bone and Sinew of the Compact*

David Williams, *Duff: A Life in the Law*

1983 David H. Flaherty, ed., *Essays in the History of Canadian Law Volume 2*

1982 Marion MacRae and Anthony Adamson, *Cornerstones of Order: Courthouses and Town Halls of Ontario, 1784–1914*

1981 David H. Flaherty, ed., *Essays in the History of Canadian Law Volume 1*